# THE EFFECTIVE DEPOSITION

# THE EFFECTIVE DEPOSITION

## TECHNIQUES AND STRATEGIES THAT WORK

### REVISED THIRD EDITION

**DAVID M. MALONE**
Trial Run, Inc.
Washington, D.C.

**PETER T. HOFFMAN**
Professor of Law
University of Houston School of Law
Houston, Texas

**ANTHONY J. BOCCHINO**
Jack E. Feinberg Professor of Litigation
James Beasley School of Law
Temple University
Philadelphia, Pennsylvania

**NATIONAL INSTITUTE FOR TRIAL ADVOCACY**

Malone, David M., Peter T. Hoffman, and Anthony J. Bocchino, *The Effective Deposition: Techniques and Strategies That Work,* Revised 3d ed. (NITA, 2007).

ISBN 978-1-60156-047-6

FBA 1047

Library of Congress Cataloging in Publication Data available

10 09          10 9

To


The Memory of
Robert F. Hanley,
My Teacher and Friend
— D.M.M.


Sarah and Alice
— P.T.H.


Lynn, Jennica, and Mike
—A.J.B.

The cases and incidents described in this text are drawn from the authors' imaginations, based upon experience. The names are not intended to refer to any living persons or actual companies, except that we have occasionally used the names of teaching colleagues to heighten their interest in reading our work. Many of the names selected for the fictitious characters are Lithuanian, to show respect and support for the successful Lithuanian freedom movement.

# CONTENTS

# FOREWORD TO THE THIRD EDITION

The first deposition courses taught by the National Institute for Trial Advocacy some twenty-three years ago focused on the mechanics of questioning opposing witnesses to obtain new information and the procedures by which that information could be used to control witnesses at trial and present admissions and other evidence. These goals of teaching deposition skills remain important, but, as the path of litigation leads more and more toward non-trial resolutions (arbitrations, mediations, negotiated settlements, dismissals and limitations by motion), depositions are used as much or more in those contexts as they are in trials.

Some researchers say that more than ninety percent of cases filed, both federal and state, are resolved in some way before the jury or judge is called upon to make a decision. Attorneys must still conduct discovery depositions to learn the evidence they will have to meet in the litigation—they just may have to meet that evidence earlier in a *Daubert* hearing, in responding to a summary judgment motion, or in defending a settlement position before a mediator. This shift has occurred slowly over the past fifty years, but it has clearly been accelerated by the pressure on civil courts because of the drug-case loaded dockets of the criminal courts. Until that quagmire is resolved, by decriminalization or summary treatment of minor drug offenses (like "drug court" where defendants can quickly challenge "drug tickets" for minor, personal violations), access to our court system by civil litigants will continue to be expensive and time-consuming for all involved. It is amusing in a way to reflect on the fact that our judicial system was itself created as an "alternative dispute resolution" system, so that trial-by-combat, trial-by-ordeal, or trial-by-oath could be abandoned as uncivilized. Our current system of ADR is an attempt to avoid the modern trial-by-ordeal faced today by litigants in every toxic tort, product liability, or antitrust case.

This book cannot correct this distortion, but at the least we can recognize the shift away from actual trials and deal with the utility of discovery by deposition in the most modern context. Where appropriate, therefore, we specifically cover using depositions to respond to expert challenges, meet motions to dismiss or for summary judgment, and provide information for use in mediations. The information on which "alternate resolutions" are based still needs to be discovered, unless the resolution is an accounting one achieved merely by splitting the baby. We have tried to remind attorneys that, although there is less and less chance everyday that matters will actually wind up in trial, there is still a great chance that the best result—trial or non-trial—will be obtained by taking better depositions, defending depositions more effectively, and thereby increasing the storehouse of knowledge on which you advise your client of the best strategies.

From our teaching and lecturing across the country, the authors have found that the level of deposition practice—that is, the skill with which attorneys execute this most important discovery tool—varies enormously, and that variation does not correlate with age or experience as much as it does with the degree to which the takers and defenders have thought through their proper roles and the most effective way to achieve their goals. We hope that this book will be of practical use to all attorneys who want to obtain the best results for their clients by mastering the facts and anticipating their opponents' proof.

—D.M.M, P.T.H, A.J.B

# PART ONE

# THE LAW

## CHAPTER ONE

## THE MECHANICS OF TAKING AND DEFENDING DEPOSITIONS

*Mechanics will kill you.*—Trial Attorney Warren S. Radler

Few hard and fast rules control the conduct of depositions; yet you must carefully observe the few that do exist so that the product of the deposition—the transcript—is valid and useful months or years later when the witness or his memory is perhaps long gone.

The mechanics of taking and defending depositions are quite simple, but to avoid mistakes you must be thoroughly familiar with the applicable rules. Small or inadvertent mistakes can cost money and time, and prevent the use of valuable deposition testimony on behalf of your client. To avoid such mistakes, you should carefully read and study the rules and statutes applicable to discovery in your jurisdiction.

The Federal Rules of Civil Procedure applicable to depositions and discovery have been amended several times through the years. While the Federal Rules or some variation of them have been adopted by the vast majority of the states, a number of states have chosen to incorporate only some of the recent Federal Rules amendments while ignoring or rejecting others. Many states have also deviated from the Federal Rules by developing their own unique discovery rules that may be in substitution for one or more of the Federal Rules or merely supplement what is contained in the Federal Rules. To further complicate matters, a substantial number of state and federal courts have adopted local rules supplementing or modifying the rules concerning discovery. Because of the many variations between jurisdictions in the rules governing depositions, you must carefully check the rules in your own jurisdiction. This book will discuss how to take and defend depositions under the Federal Rules of Civil Procedure, but some of the more common state variations on these rules will also be discussed.

## 1.1 WHOSE DEPOSITION MAY BE TAKEN?

You may take the deposition of any person, including witnesses who are not parties to the action.[1] While some other discovery devices such as interrogatories are limited to parties alone, depositions may be taken of anyone who you believe may have knowledge of relevant information. In addition to the parties to the action, depositions may be taken of agents and employees of the parties, former parties, non-party witnesses, and, in special circumstances, the attorneys of the parties.[2] Although this is normally not done, a party expecting to be unavailable for trial and wanting her testimony presented through a deposition may even take her own deposition. In addition, it is not unusual for a party to take the deposition of its own expert witness for the purposes of preserving trial testimony. Corporations can be deposed through their officers, directors, and managing agents, and organizations generally may be deposed through their designees. Note, however, that you must seek leave of court to take the deposition of a person confined in prison.[3]

## 1.2 RULE 30(B)(6) DEPOSITIONS

Many times, employees or agents of corporations, partnerships, governmental agencies, or associations such as labor unions have valuable information relevant to some issue in a case, but you may not know the identity of the particular person in the organization with that information. Or, more than one person has the necessary information, with each knowing something pertinent. While a series of depositions can be taken until all persons with pertinent information have been identified and deposed, the Federal Rules of Civil Procedure provide an easier and more efficient method.

Pursuant to Rule 30(b)(6), the deposition of a corporation, partnership, association, or governmental agency may be noticed. In the notice of deposition, the taking attorney designates the matters on which examination is requested without naming a particular person to be de-

---

1. Fed.R.Civ.P. 30(a)(1).
2. Generally, a deposition of opposing counsel is only permitted when the party seeking to take the deposition has shown there are no other reasonable means to obtain the information, the information is relevant and not privileged, and it is crucial to the case. *See, e.g., Shelton v. American Motors Corp.,*805 F.2d 1323, 1327 (8th Cir. 1986). *See also* Fed.R.Civ.P. 26(b)(3) (provides for discovery of trial preparation material (or its equivalent) that the other party is unable to procure without undue hardship).
3. Fed.R.Civ.P. 30(a)(2).

posed. The organization must then prepare and produce one or more witnesses who are knowledgeable about the matters designated in the notice of deposition so that the witnesses can give complete, knowledgeable, and binding answers. This duty exists even if there is no one currently with or employed by the organization who has knowledge or memory about the particular matter. A witness still must be prepared to testify about the topic to the extent the information is reasonably available from documents, past employees, or other sources. If the witness produced is not knowledgeable about the designated matters, the organization may be required to prepare and produce another witness and may also be subject to Rule 37(d) sanctions. In other words, the organization must make reasonable efforts to find and present the requested information through the witness or witnesses of its choosing.

## 1.3 TIMING

26(d)

Under Rule 26(d), no discovery, including depositions, is permitted in most cases until after the parties have conferred to plan discovery pursuant to Rule 26(f). The purpose and timing of the conference are discussed in § 4.1. Certain cases—the very unusual or the very routine, which would not benefit from having the parties confer—are exempt from this prohibition.[4] The prohibition on discovery until after the parties have conferred can be modified by an order within the case or by agreement of the parties. The prohibition on early discovery can also be disregarded if the notice of deposition contains a certification, with supporting facts, that the witness is expected to leave the United States and be unavailable for examination in this country unless deposed before the parties have conferred.[5] However, a deposition taken before the parties have conferred because the witness is leaving the United States cannot be used against a party who shows that it was unable through the exercise of diligence to obtain counsel to represent it at the deposition.[6] By the same token, depositions can only be used against parties who had notice of their taking.[7]

Must have notice.

---

4. Fed.R.Civ.P. 26(a)(1)(E) and (f).
5. Fed.R.Civ.P. 30(a)(2)(C).
6. Fed.R.Civ.P. 32(a)(3).
7. Fed.R.Civ.P. 32(a).

## 1.4 PRIORITY

The concept of priority—that the party first noticing the taking of deposition has a right to complete the taking of that deposition before the opponent may take a deposition—has been abolished under the Federal Rules of Civil Procedure. Now, no such priority exists in discovery and either party may notice a deposition even though a previously noticed deposition has not been completed.

## 1.5 SCHEDULING OF THE DEPOSITION

As a matter of convenience and courtesy, most depositions are scheduled by agreement among the parties. By cooperating, you can avoid conflicts in both the lawyer's and the witnesses' schedules, and you can avoid the expense of motions to reschedule the time for the deposition. Several courts, by local rules, require that, before noticing a deposition, the parties must attempt to arrive at a mutually agreeable date, and further that no deposition can be scheduled when the party noticing the deposition is on notice of the unavailability of opposing counsel. Absent agreement, the date set in the notice of deposition will control unless a witness or a party objects and moves for a protective order rescheduling the deposition.[8]

A party may object to the deposition date or time.[9] A non-party may also timely move to quash a subpoena if it "fails to allow reasonable time for compliance."[10] The motion is brought in the court issuing the subpoena (which must of course be a court that has personal jurisdiction of the intended deponent, since non-parties are not automatically subject to the jurisdiction of the forum court).

## 1.6 GIVING NOTICE OF THE DEPOSITION

Rule 30(b)(1) requires that the party intending to take the deposition must give written notice of the deposition to all other parties to the ac-

---

8. Fed.R.Civ.P. 26(c)(2). *See* Chapter Twelve, Protective Orders and Applications to the Court.
9. *Ibid.* Rule 32(a) states that a deposition may not be used against a party who, having received less than eleven days' notice of the deposition, has promptly filed a motion for a protective order under Fed.R.Civ.P. 26(c)(2) and the motion is pending at the time the deposition is held. Fed.R.Civ.P. 32(a).
10. Fed.R.Civ.P. 45(c)(3)(A)(i). *See also* Fed.R.Civ.P. 45(c)(1) (providing for the award of costs and other relief for imposing undue burden and expense on a subpoenaed witness).

tion. The notice must state the following: the time and place for taking the deposition; the name and address of each person to be examined if known or, if not known, a general description sufficient to identify the witness or the particular class to which the witness belongs. Further, if a subpoena *duces tecum* is to be served on the witness, the notice must include or attach a list of the materials in the subpoena that are to be produced at the deposition. The notice of deposition may list more than one witness to be examined. Finally, Rule 30(b)(2) requires that the notice state the method by which the testimony is to be recorded: stenographic, videotape, or audiotape.

The notice requirements for Rule 30(b)(6) depositions (where a corporation, partnership, association, or governmental agency is required to designate a witness or witnesses to testify about specified topics) are the same as for other depositions, with two differences: the notice must designate with reasonable particularity the matters on which examination is requested, and no witness need be identified by the notice-giver. Except for 30(b)(6) depositions, no rule requires that the notice designate the subject matter of the deposition.

An example of a notice of deposition and of a 30(b)(6) notice of deposition are contained in Appendix A.

### 1.6.1 Time requirements for giving notice.

Rule 30(b)(1) does not require a specific number of days notice of a deposition. Indeed, all that is required is "reasonable notice." Rule 32(a) suggests that eleven days is prima facie "reasonable notice."[11] However, the Advisory Committee Note adds that this provision "is not intended to signify that eleven days' notice is the minimum advance notice for all depositions or that greater than ten days should necessarily be deemed sufficient in all situations." In short, sufficient notice depends on the circumstances of each case, but you should always check local court rules to see if they provide for a minimum number of days for notice.

Upon motion, the trial court may enlarge or shorten the notice time required[12] and may, as part of a protective order or scheduling order under Rule 16(b), impose a specific notice requirement on the par-

---

11. Fed.R.Civ.P. 32(a) states that a deposition shall not be used against a party who received less than eleven days' notice of the deposition and who promptly moved for a protective order under Fed.R.Civ.P. 26(c)(2), if the motion was still pending at the time designated for the deposition.
12. Fed.R.Civ.P. 30(b)(3).

ties.[13] Because of the strong policy encouraging agreement on dates, there should be little occasion for formal motions practice concerning the adequacy of notice.

### 1.6.2 Service of the notice of deposition.

The party taking the deposition must serve the notice of deposition on every party to the action.[14] The notice should be served on a party's attorney or on the party himself if he is proceeding *pro se.* Service may be made either by personal service on the attorney or party, or by first-class mail addressed to the attorney's or party's last-known address. Personal service is accomplished by: delivering a copy to the attorney or party; leaving a copy at the attorney's or party's office with a clerk or other person in charge; leaving it in a conspicuous place in the office; or, if the office is closed or there is no office, leaving it at the attorney's or party's residence with someone of suitable age and discretion who is living there.[15]

## 1.7 GEOGRAPHIC LOCATION OF THE DEPOSITION

A deposition may be taken at any location on which the parties and the witness agree. If no agreement can be reached, as discussed below, the geographic location depends to a large extent on whether the witness is a party or non-party.

### 1.7.1 Parties.

Absent other controlling rules, the deposition of a party may be scheduled for any location, subject to the court's power under Rule 26(c)(2) to grant a protective order designating a different place. The burden to apply for relief is on the person wishing to change the location from that given in the notice of deposition, but the courts appear to have developed some general rules governing where depositions can be taken. In addition, several federal courts have adopted local court rules governing the place of taking of depositions.

---

13. Fed.R.Civ.P. 26(c)(2) and 26(f).
14. Fed.R.Civ.P. 30(b)(1).
15. Fed.R.Civ.P. 5.

### 1.7.2 Plaintiffs.

A defendant may take the deposition of a plaintiff in the geographic area where the plaintiff resides, has a place of business, is employed, or filed the lawsuit. The courts have found many exceptions to this rule and look at the realities of the situation, such as relative financial burdens on any of the parties.

### 1.7.3 Defendants.

A plaintiff usually must depose a defendant in the geographic area of the defendant's residence, place of business, or employment. Again, courts usually do not enforce this general rule when to do so would result in an injustice or undue financial hardship.

### 1.7.4 Corporations.

Corporate officers, directors, or managing agents may usually be deposed at the principal place of business for the corporation, as well as where they live. Depositions of mere employees or agents are treated the same as the deposition of any non-party witness: their depositions must occur within 100 miles of the place where the witness resides, is employed, or regularly transacts business in person.

### 1.7.5 Non-parties.

The place of deposition for a non-party is governed principally by Rule 45(c)(3)(A)(ii) concerning subpoenas. That rule states that the target of a deposition subpoena may be required to attend only within 100 miles of the place where the person resides, is employed, or regularly transacts business. (The subpoena would issue from whatever federal district court exercised jurisdiction over that location.)

A party may always agree with a witness for the witness's deposition to be taken at some place other than where the witness can be subpoenaed. Many times, it may well be more efficient to agree to pay the witness's expenses for coming to another location than for the parties' attorneys to journey to the witness. But where no such agreement is possible, Rule 45 dictates the location of the deposition.

## 1.8 NUMBER OF DEPOSITIONS

The Federal Rules of Civil Procedure impose two separate and distinct limitations on the number of depositions the parties may take in a case. First, Rule 30(a)(2)(A) limits plaintiffs, defendants, and third-party defendants to ten depositions per side unless the parties have stipulated in writing to a different number or the court has given leave for a greater number. Note that the restriction is on the number of depositions per side, not per party. Therefore, a single plaintiff would be entitled to ten depositions and three co-defendants would have ten depositions to share among them. The discovery planning conference is usually the place where the parties discuss different limitations among themselves, since Rule 29 allows the parties to stipulate to different numbers of depositions if they can do so within the court's schedule for discovery. If the parties cannot reach a stipulation, the discovery conference with the court under Rule 16(f) may provide an opportunity to alter the number of depositions.[16]

Rule 30(a)(2)(B) establishes the second limitation and states, in effect, that a person can only be deposed once absent a stipulation or court order. (However, a person who has acted as a designee to provide testimony in a Rule 30(b)(6) deposition may be deposed in a "named deponent" deposition without violating this provision.)

## 1.9 LENGTH OF DEPOSITIONS

Rule 30(d)(2) imposes a seven hour, one–day time limitation on the length of depositions.[17] Note that, under this limitation, the seven hours must occur on one day rather than extending over two or more days. The court may, by order, impose a different limitation on a specific witness or on all the depositions in a case. The parties may also alter the time limits by written stipulation. (A statement of the stipulation included in the deposition record would be sufficient to satisfy this requirement of a "writing.") Only actual deposition time is counted and not the time necessary for reasonable breaks and lunch.[18] In a 30(b)(6) deposition,[19] each designated witness's testimony is counted as a separate deposition for purposes of calculating time (although it is reasonable to wonder whether this is consistent with the Advisory

---

16. *See* § 4.1.
17. Fed.R.Civ.P. 30(d)(2).
18. Advisory Committee Note to Rule 30.
19. *See* § 1.2.

Committee's opinion that a Rule 30(b)(6) deposition counts as one deposition, despite the designation of multiple witnesses).

Additional time may be allowed by the court if needed for fairness or if the deposition is impeded or delayed for any reason. Parties considering extending the time for a deposition—and courts asked to order an extension—might consider a variety of factors. The Advisory Committee Note suggests some of the situations in which additional time might be permitted:

- if the witness needs an interpreter, that may prolong the examination. If the examination will cover events occurring over a long period of time, that may justify additional time;

- in cases in which the witness will be questioned about numerous or lengthy documents, it is often desirable for the interrogating party to send copies of the documents to the witness sufficiently in advance of the deposition so that the witness can become familiar with them. Should the witness nevertheless not read the documents in advance, thereby prolonging the deposition, a court could consider that a reason for extending the deposition;

- if the examination reveals that documents have been requested but not produced, that may justify further examination once production has occurred;

- in multi-party cases, the need for each party to examine the witness may warrant additional time, although duplicative questioning should be avoided and parties with similar interests should strive to designate one lawyer to question about areas of common interest;

- similarly, should the lawyer for the witness want to examine the witness, that may require additional time;

- finally, with regard to expert witnesses, there may more often be a need for additional time—even after the submission of the report required by Rule 26(a)(2)—for full exploration of the theories upon which the witness relies.

## 1.10 COMPELLING THE WITNESS'S ATTENDANCE

The procedure for compelling a witness to attend his deposition depends on whether the witness is a party; an officer, a managing agent, or director of a party; or a non-party.

### 1.10.1 Parties.

Any party may require an individual party to appear at a deposition merely by serving a notice of deposition on the party-deponent and the other parties. Any party may also require an officer, director, or managing agent of a party to attend its deposition by serving a notice of deposition,[20] but the notice must name or adequately describe the witness and state that the witness is an officer, director, or managing agent.[21]

### 1.10.2 Non-parties.

Absent an agreement to appear voluntarily, non-party witnesses may be required to attend their depositions only if subpoenaed.[22] The subpoena, in addition to requiring the witness to appear, may also command the witness to produce designated documents and other evidence.[23]

### ISSUANCE OF SUBPOENA

Any attorney may sign and issue a subpoena if the subpoena is for an action pending in a court in which the attorney is authorized to practice, even if the deposition will take place in another district.[24] In other words, if the case was filed in the Northern District of Texas, a Northern District of Texas attorney may sign a subpoena directed to a deponent who is within the Northern District of Texas or within 100 miles of the court. If, in that same case, a deponent is located in the District of New Jersey, the Texas attorney may still sign the subpoena, which issues from the New Jersey district court, the court having personal jurisdiction over the deponent, because the Texas attorney is authorized to practice in the forum court in Texas. A subpoena from the Texas court could not "reach" the New Jersey deponent. Clerks of any U.S. district court have blank subpoenas available. While clerks of district courts may issue signed, blank subpoenas, there is no reason to resort to this more difficult procedure when attorneys themselves may

---

20. Fed.R.Civ.P. 37(d).
21. *El Salto, S.A. v. PSG Co.*, 444 F.2d 477 (9th Cir. 1971).
22. Fed.R.Civ.P. 30(a)(1).
23. Fed.R.Civ.P. 45(a)(1).
24. Fed.R.Civ.P. 45(a)(2) and (3).

sign and issue subpoenas. The attorney taking the deposition should fill in on the subpoena the name of the district in which the deposition is to be taken, as stated in the notice of deposition, as well as the other requested information, and sign the subpoena to complete issuance.

An example of a subpoena and of a subpoena *duces tecum* are contained in Appendix A.

*Subp: only personal service*

## SERVICE OF THE SUBPOENA

Anyone eighteen years or older and not a party to the action may serve the subpoena, but the server must take reasonable steps to avoid imposing undue burden or expense on the witness. Unlike the service of the notice of deposition or even the summons commencing the action, subpoenas cannot be served by mail; only personal service is acceptable. The server must deliver the subpoena to the witness and concurrently tender one day's witness fees and mileage allowance (unless the subpoena is issued on behalf of the United States or one of its officers or agencies). The witness fee in effect at the time of this writing is $40.00 per day and the time period includes the time necessary for going to and from the place of the deposition.[25] If the witness travels by common carrier, then the most economical rate reasonably available must be paid as long as the method used was reasonable and the shortest practical route was followed.[26] If the witness travels by private car, the General Services Administration mileage rates (currently at $0.48 per mile) should be used.[27] The clerks of the U.S. district courts usually have information about current rates.

When serving a corporation or organization with a subpoena, for instance for a Rule 30(b)(6) deposition, the server should leave the subpoena with an officer or a managing or general agent to ensure that the corporation receives actual notice.

Following service, the party responsible should file a proof of service with the clerk of the district court, but in practice this is not often done unless a witness has failed to appear for his deposition and contempt proceedings are being brought. The proof of service should state the name of the person served, the date, and the manner of service, and be signed by the person who made the service.

## GEOGRAPHIC LIMITATIONS ON SERVICE

A deposition subpoena may only be served within: the district of the court from which the subpoena has issued; 100 miles of the place

---

25. 28 U.S.C. § 1821(b).
26. 28 U.S.C. § 1821(c)(1).
27. 28 U.S.C. § 1821(c)(2).

of the deposition; or the state where the deposition is to occur if the state has a statute or court rule authorizing such service. The court may also authorize extended service of the subpoena if a federal statute so permits.[28]

## 1.11 REQUIRING DOCUMENTS TO BE BROUGHT TO THE DEPOSITION

Generally, you will want to have documents or other tangible evidence produced prior to a deposition so that you can be completely familiar with the material before having to question about it. Rule 34 (for parties) and Rule 45 (for non-parties) establish the procedure for requiring the production of tangible evidence. The mechanics of these rules, as applied to the production of evidence outside a deposition, are beyond the scope of this discussion, but sometimes, because time is short or production will occur some geographic distance away, you will want to schedule the production as part of the deposition.

### 1.11.1 Parties.

You can arrange the production of documents and other tangible evidence by a party-witness at a deposition by agreement of the parties or by serving a request to produce pursuant to Rule 34. While some confusion exists about the issue, Rule 30(b)(5)[29] suggests that a request to produce is the exclusive means of requiring the production of evidence by a party at a deposition. The request to produce must be served on every party to the action and is usually served with the notice of deposition.

### 1.11.2 Non-party witnesses.

You may require a non-party deposition witness to produce documents and other tangible evidence at a deposition by using a subpoena *duces tecum* provided for by Rule 45. While a subpoena *duces tecum* can be issued and served entirely separate from the taking of a deposition, the subpoena commanding the witness to appear at a deposition may also command the witness to bring and produce documents and other tangible items of evidence for inspection.

---

28. Fed.R.Civ.P. 45(b)(2).
29. "The notice to a party deponent may be accompanied by a request made in compliance with Rule 34 for the production of documents and tangible things at the taking of the deposition. The procedure of Rule 34 shall apply to the request."

The procedure for issuing a subpoena *duces tecum* is the same as that given above for the issuance of a subpoena *ad testificandum* but the notice of deposition will be different. When a subpoena *duces tecum* has been served on a witness, you must attach to, or include in, the notice a designation of the materials to be produced as set forth in the subpoena.[30] The easiest and most convenient method of doing this is to refer to the subpoena *duces tecum* in the notice of deposition and attach a copy of the subpoena to the notice, which is then served on the other parties to the action.

## 1.12 SCOPE OF DISCOVERY DURING THE DEPOSITION

The scope of what can be discovered through a deposition is very broad: "Parties may obtain discovery regarding any matter, not privileged, that is relevant to the claim or defense of any party, including the existence, description, nature, custody, condition, and location of any books, documents, or other tangible things and the identify and location of persons having knowledge of any discoverable matter. * * * Relevant information need not be admissible at the trial if the discovery appears reasonably calculated to lead to the discovery of admissible evidence."[31]

The Federal Rules do not define relevance, but the term is defined in Federal Rule of Evidence 401, which states that "'Relevant evidence' means evidence having any tendency to make the existence of any fact that is of consequence to the determination of the action more probable or less probable than it would be without the evidence." Defining the exact scope of what is relevant requires examining the pleadings in the case to determine the specific claims and defenses alleged there and asking whether the information being sought relates in some way to the court's resolution of the issues raised by these claims and defenses (including matters affecting the credibility of potential witnesses). The particular fact being sought through discovery does not itself have to be alleged in the pleadings, but the fact must have some relationship to the claims and defenses that were raised. In considering what is

---

30. Fed.R.Civ.P. 30(b)(1).
31. Fed.R.Civ.P. 26(b)(1). While the scope of discovery—relevance to a party's claim or defense—is broad, it is actually a curtailment of what was previously permitted. The Federal Rules, up to the adoption of the 2000 amendments, defined the scope of discovery as relevance to the "subject matter involved in the pending action." Under the current version of Rule 26(b)(1) the court may still permit discovery under the previous standard, but only upon a showing of good cause. The 2000 amendment was designed to curtail expensive and broad-ranging discovery inquiries, but there has been little actual effect on what the courts are permitting.

relevant, it is also necessary to look at the substantive law concerning the claim or defense being alleged.

The information being sought does not always directly relate to a party's claim or defense. For example, evidence relating to impeachment of a likely witness, or information about similar happenings, or-ganizational arrangements, or the filing system of a party should all be discoverable under this standard. Determining what is relevant requires looking at the particular circumstances of each case.[32]

There should be very few instances when a party needs discovery of information that is not relevant to a party's claim or defense. When this does occur the court has the power, upon a showing of good cause, to expand the scope of discovery to "any matter relevant to the subject matter involved in the action."[33] The exact dividing line between evidence that is relevant to a claim or defense and that which is relevant to the subject matter of the action is hazy at best.

Even though the information being sought is relevant to the claim or defense of a party, the court may nevertheless limit discovery be-cause 1) it is unreasonably cumulative or duplicative or is obtainable from some other source that is more convenient, less burdensome, or less expensive; 2) the party seeking the discovery has had ample op-portunity through other discovery in the action to obtain the informa-tion sought; or 3) the burden or expense of the proposed discovery outweighs its likely benefit, taking into account the needs of the case, the amount in controversy, the parties' resources, the importance of the issue at stake in the litigation, and the importance of the proposed discovery in resolving the issues.[34] In short, the court may impose lim-its on discovery if what is being proposed is unreasonable.

## 1.13 THE DEPOSITION ITSELF

### 1.13.1 Before whom may the deposition be taken?

Depositions conducted in the United States, its territories, and its insular possessions may be taken before any person authorized to ad-minister oaths either by the laws of the United States or of the place in which the action is pending or before a person appointed by the court in which the action is pending.[35] In practice, the deposition is

---

32. Advisory Committee Note to Rule 26.
33. Fed.R.Civ.P. 26(b)(1).
34. Fed.R.Civ.P. 26(b)(2).
35. Fed.R.Civ.P. 28(a).

taken before a court reporter who is also a notary public. Although the rules permit the deposition officer and the person recording the testimony to be two different persons, economy and efficiency usually dictate that one person serve both functions. The parties may stipulate to having the deposition taken before a non-notary or someone who, for instance, is an employee of one of the lawyers.[36] In other words, if the reporter does not show up for a deposition, the parties could agree that a secretary in the office could take the deposition in shorthand. Special rules, contained in Rule 28(b), govern the taking of depositions in foreign countries.

### 1.13.2 Recording of the deposition.

Under Rule 30(b)(2), the party noticing the deposition may choose the method of recording the testimony: sound, sound-and-visual, or stenographic (*i.e.,* audiotape, videotape, and stenographic). The party taking the deposition shall state the method of recording in the notice of deposition and shall bear the expense of the recording. A party may also arrange for a non-stenographic deposition to be transcribed. Any other party, at its own expense and after giving notice to the witness and other parties, may designate another method of recording in addition to the method given in the notice of deposition.[37] While the party noticing the deposition is free to choose any method of recording the deposition, Rule 32(c) requires the presentation of deposition testimony in videotape or audiotape format, where available and when requested by any party, unless the use is solely for impeachment. That is, if a party takes a non-stenographic deposition, that party must be prepared to present that deposition in non-stenographic form.

The recording is usually done by the deposition officer, who is a notary public, but the rules permit it to be done by someone acting under the officer's direction and in the officer's presence.[38] Of course, as noted above, the parties can stipulate otherwise.

### 1.13.3 Conduct of the deposition.

The rules governing the conduct of depositions are relatively few. Under Rule 30(b)(4), the deposition officer shall begin the deposition with a statement on the record that gives 1) the officer's name and business address, 2) the date, time, and place of the deposition, 3) the name of the witness, and 4) an identification of all persons present.

---

36. Fed.R.Civ.P. 28(a) and 29.
37. Fed.R.Civ.P. 30(b)(3).
38. *Ibid.*

The deposition officer shall also swear the witness on the record. At the end of the deposition, the officer shall state on the record that the deposition is complete and shall also recite any stipulations between counsel concerning the custody of the transcript or recording and exhibits as well as any other matters which have been agreed upon. Videotape and audiotape depositions have some further requirements that are discussed in Chapter Eighteen.

Examination and cross-examination may proceed as permitted at trial as provided by the Federal Rules of Evidence.[39] Under Rule 30(c), other witnesses cannot be excluded from the deposition room without first obtaining a protective order under Rule 26(c)(5). All objections made at the deposition to the qualifications of the officer taking the deposition, the manner of taking it, the evidence presented, the conduct of the deposition, or any other objection to any aspect of the proceedings are to be noted by the officer on the deposition record,[40] but the deposition shall proceed with the testimony being taken subject to the objections.[41]

Rule 30(d)(1) requires that any objection to evidence made during the deposition be stated concisely and in a non-argumentative and non-suggestive manner. Thus, for example, the classic objection, "You can answer, if you know," is made explicitly impermissible. Further, you can instruct a witness not to answer a question only when necessary to preserve a privilege, to enforce a previous court order limiting examination ("counsel may ask the witness about liability but not damages"), or to seek an order limiting or terminating the deposition.

Any documents or other exhibits produced during the deposition are to be marked for identification and annexed to the deposition if any party requests it. Copies may be substituted for the originals if requested so long as copies are provided and the parties have an opportunity to compare the copies with the originals. The copies will thereafter serve as the originals. The court has the power to require the originals to be attached if there is reason for doing so.[42] Note that in modern practice, documents may be exchanged and stored electronically and electronic versions of documents can and often are used during the course of the deposition. Of course, under Federal Rule of Evidence 102, photographic, xerographic, or electronic duplicates

---

39. *See* Fed.R.Evid. 6. The Federal Rules of Evidence apply with the exception of Rules 103 (rulings on evidence) and 615 (exclusion of witnesses). Fed.R.Civ.P. 30(c).
40. Fed.R.Civ.P. 30(c).
41. *Ibid.*
42. Fed.R.Civ.P. 30(f)(1).

("duplicate originals") are as admissible as the actual original item for nearly all purposes.

For reasons of economy, one or more of the parties may choose not to attend the deposition, but instead to serve written questions in a sealed envelope to the party taking the deposition. The party taking the deposition is required to transmit the questions to the officer conducting the deposition, who shall propound the questions to the witness and record the answers verbatim.[43] As a tactical matter, such an approach is ordinarily used only when the witness is willing to cooperate with the party submitting the questions so the answers may be prepared in advance.

A related procedure is to take the entire deposition by written questions. The procedures are set forth in Rule 31 and are usually used when the witness is distant but is willing to cooperate, or the matters upon which examination is to occur are routine, such as authenticating a document.

The parties may also agree, by a stipulation in writing or by a court order, that the deposition be taken by telephone or, under Rule 30(b)(7), other remote electronic means such as satellite television.[44] However, you should generally make use of a telephone deposition only when you do not think it necessary to observe the witness's demeanor and the cost of attending the deposition is relatively high.

### 1.13.4 Stipulations.

The Federal Rules of Civil Procedure permit the parties to stipulate in writing that a deposition may be taken before any person, at any time or place, in any manner, and when so taken may be used like any other deposition.[45] As a practical matter, the parties, if on working terms, will stipulate to most issues that arise concerning deposition problems, rather than petition the court for some form of relief or protective order. In general, it is recommended that lengthy and complex stipulations be avoided (*e.g.,* those concerning the objections which must or may be made) because of the possibility of confusion or ambiguity. The parties could instead recognize that the deposition is taken under the Federal Rules of Civil Procedure and take up stipulations on an *ad hoc* basis.

---

43. Fed.R.Civ.P. 30(c).
44. Fed.R.Civ.P. 30(b)(7).
45. Fed.R.Civ.P. 29.

### 1.13.5 Post-deposition requirements.

Following the conclusion of the deposition, the deposition officer and the parties have several further obligations:

1. Under Rule 30(e), review, correction, and signature must be requested by the witness or a party before completion of the deposition, or else they are waived. Once the request is made and the transcript is available, the witness has thirty days to review the deposition. Many states provide that the witness automatically has the opportunity for review, correction, and signature unless the parties and the witness waive that opportunity (which was the old approach under the Federal Rules of Civil Procedure). It is recommended that no party waive the opportunity to read and correct; the witness should know what binds him, and the parties should know what they have to meet at trial.

2. The witness then has thirty days to make any changes in the form and substance of the deposition and to provide a statement of any reasons for the changes.[46] Such changes are not limited by the rule to errors in transcription made by the reporter; if the witness misheard the question, for example, she may change her answer (although, of course, the original answer remains in the original transcript, for whatever use is appropriately made of it at trial). Indeed, if the questioning attorney misspoke, but the witness answered the intended (not the spoken) question, the witness may change the question, and that would actually make the transcript more accurate than any other change.

3. Under the Federal Rules, the witness is only required to sign a statement containing any corrections to the transcript and the reasons for the changes. If no corrections are made, the witness is not required to sign anything. Many states require the witness to sign the transcript regardless of any corrections unless the parties have waived signing or the witness is ill, cannot be found, or refuses to sign. In these states, if the deposition is not signed within thirty days of being given to the witness, the deposition officer shall sign it and include a statement of the reasons for the failure to sign. If the witness gives a reason for refusing to sign, this must be stated as well.

4. The deposition officer shall certify that the witness was duly sworn by the officer and that the deposition is a true record of the witness's testimony.[47] Under Rule 30(e), the certificate should also state whether a witness or one of the parties requested the witness to review

---

46. *Ibid. See* §15.1.
47. Fed.R.Civ.P. 30(f)(1).

the deposition and shall attach any changes made by the witness to the questions or answers.

5. Unless otherwise ordered by the court, the deposition officer is to place the deposition in an envelope or package, seal the envelope or package, endorse the title of the action on it, mark it with "Deposition of [give name of witness]," and promptly send it to the attorney who arranged for the transcript or recording, normally the deposing attorney. The attorney is then required to safely store the deposition and protect it from loss, destruction, tampering, or deterioration.[48]

6. Under Rule 30(f)(2) the officer shall retain a copy of the recording of a videotape or audiotape deposition or the notes of a stenographic deposition.

7. The party taking the deposition is to give prompt notice to all other parties of the filing of the deposition.[49] What this requirement means, however, is unclear since there is no longer a requirement of filing, but only of delivery to the attorney who arranged for the transcript or recording. It may be that the Advisory Committee simply overlooked amending Rule 30(f)(3) to require the party taking the deposition to give notice of the receipt of the deposition, but the Advisory Committee Note does not discuss this section of the rule.

8. The officer is to furnish copies of the deposition to any party requesting one upon payment of a reasonable charge therefor.[50]

---

48. *Ibid.*
49. Fed.R.Civ.P. 30(f)(3).
50. Fed.R.Civ.P. 30(f)(2).

# PART TWO

## TAKING DEPOSITIONS

### CHAPTER TWO
### PURPOSES OF TAKING DEPOSITIONS

*Ignorance never settles a question.*—Disraeli

Each side in a typical case has a number of discovery devices available: interrogatories, document subpoenas, requests for admission, requests for production, orders for physical and mental examination, informal (non-judicial) investigations, and, of course, depositions. Depositions are the most effective of these for learning what a witness or party has to say about the facts of the case and the theories and approaches an opponent is entertaining. The opportunities provided by depositions—to follow up, to probe, and to challenge—and their ability to be used with any witness, not just parties, account for their effectiveness and popularity.[1]

Depositions can be taken for many, often overlapping, purposes. Broadly speaking, the three primary reasons to take depositions are: first, to gather information; second, to perpetuate testimony; and third, to facilitate settlement. While these purposes are not mutually exclusive, knowing the reasons or objectives for taking the deposition allows you to organize and phrase your questions in a way that maximizes your effectiveness.

## 2.1 GATHERING INFORMATION

The most common reason for taking a deposition is for gathering information. Depositions allow inquiry regarding what is going on in the case, what are the facts, how the events occurred, what the other side knows, what information supports your version of events, what the weaknesses are in your own case, where the flaws exist in the opponent's case, what other witnesses might have useful information,

---

1. *See* Chapter Three for a discussion of the advantages and disadvantages of depositions.

and so on. In addition to gathering facts, the deposition provides information about the demeanor and likely effectiveness of witnesses at trial or some other case-dispositive proceeding. In short, the deposition is being taken for the purpose of discovery. Several different reasons exist for gathering information in a case, as is discussed below.

### 2.1.1 Finding out what you don't know.

One of the most important reasons for taking a deposition is to learn new information about the case. Typically, what your client and any friendly witnesses have to say about what happened will be known through informal fact gathering, but there will still be many blank spots in the facts of the case. Like a nineteenth century explorer deciding on a route by looking at a map of Africa and seeing the many vacant areas on the map, the deposing counsel seeks to fill in the gaps in the facts left by clients and friendly witnesses. Often the only ones who can fill in those blank spots are witnesses who won't cooperate or the opposing party who, of course, cannot be interviewed without permission of that client's attorney. Where was the plaintiff going before the collision with your client's car? What happened at the meeting where your client claims the defendants fixed prices? And so on. With the African explorer the only way of filling in the blank areas is to go and look. With litigation, a good way to fill in those blanks (together with discovery of documents) is to take the depositions of witnesses to find out what they have to say about the facts of the case.

### 2.1.2 Confirming what you think you know.

A second purpose for taking depositions is to confirm what is believed to be already known. Often, based on documents and information from clients and friendly witnesses, the facts of the case are believed to be known. The version of the facts from clients, friendly witnesses, and their documents is not necessarily replicated by opposing parties, their friendly witnesses, and their documents. If the opposing parties and witnesses agree with your witnesses, then greater confidence is warranted that this will be an undisputed area at trial. Perhaps a stipulation can even be reached with the other side about these points. On the other hand, if the witnesses disagree, this will be known before trial when there is still an opportunity to marshal the proof in favor of your version of events, or to adjust case theories and themes to the new or different view of the facts. The worst possible scenario is to discover only at trial, when little can be done to meet the situation, that what was thought to be undisputed is actually hotly contested. Effective depositions avoid this problem.

### 2.1.3 Testing out legal and factual theories.

One objective of the discovery process is to test out whether the necessary facts exist to support a particular legal theory. At the discovery stage of a case each side will not only be trying to figure out what happened, but also will be attempting to develop a legal and factual theory for presenting the case to the court in the most persuasive light. Because the factual story is often incomplete at this stage, a party may be considering several different factual and legal theories. Only after discovery is complete can the attorney determine which version of the facts is most likely to be accepted as true and, in turn, what legal theory or theories can be supported by those facts.

Every legal theory depends on the existence of certain key facts as well as a host of supporting ones. The information-gathering aspect of discovery seeks to elicit facts which support a favorable legal theory or theories. If a particular legal theory is not supported by the facts, it may be necessary to abandon that theory and pursue another theory. Let's take a typical car accident personal injury case where the plaintiff claims that a collision, and the plaintiff's resulting injuries, were caused by the defendant's driving at an unsafe rate of speed and failing to keep a proper lookout. The plaintiff's factual theory is that the defendant was speeding and not paying attention to the road just prior to the accident.

During discovery, each side will not only seek admissions that support its own legal and factual theories, but will also try to find weaknesses and flaws in the opponent's theory. The plaintiff will try to gain whatever evidence it can of the defendant's speeding and failing to pay attention to the road, as well as gain admissions to weaken the defendant's defenses to the plaintiff's case. The defendant will do the exact opposite. For instance, the plaintiff may find out that the defendant was not looking at the traffic in front of her at the time of the accident and had not looked at it for the last half-block before the collision, but might also find out that the defendant was driving at the legal speed limit. From this information, the plaintiff has an admission that supports one legal and factual theory (failing to keep a proper lookout) but is not able to support another (proceeding at an unsafe rate of speed). Based on this information, the plaintiff may choose to abandon the unsafe rate of speed theory and proceed only on the failing to keep a proper lookout theory. Similarly, the plaintiff will have learned which questions will be successful during cross-examination at trial in supporting a chosen legal and factual theory and which will not.

Not only will a party test out the possible legal and factual theories to be presented at trial, but it will also look for support for bringing or defending a case-dispositive motion, such as for summary judgment. For example, in a breach of contract action the defendant may take the plaintiff's deposition seeking an admission that the plaintiff had failed to exercise a right of first refusal in a timely manner. Similarly, the plaintiff may take the defendant's deposition in hopes of getting an admission that the right of first refusal was in fact exercised properly. If the plaintiff is successful in getting this admission and the defendant cannot offer any contradictory evidence on this point, the admission can be used to support the defendant's request for summary judgment.

It may turn out, after discovery is completed, that certain key facts do not exist to support any of the plaintiff's potential theories or to weaken the defendant's theories. If that is the case, and no alternative theory remains viable, the plaintiff may have to dismiss the action or settle on the best terms available.

### 2.1.4 Preparing for trial.

The use of depositions to test legal and factual theories at the same time provides the predicate for trial testimony. One of the cardinal rules of almost all cross-examination is never to ask a question to which you do not know the answer. Depositions are where those answers are found. Answers during the deposition that were favorable to your legal and factual theory provide safe areas of inquiry on cross-examination at trial. If the witness changes his answer at trial from what was given in the deposition, then the deposition is available for impeachment. On the other hand, if the answer to a deposition question was unfavorable, then that question should not be asked at trial.

Another rule of cross-examination is to ask only questions that ask for facts and that do not contain characterizations or subjective terms. For instance, most trial lawyers would not ask a question on cross-examination of the opposing party such as, "Just before the accident, you were going very fast?" (unless it can be followed up with questions showing how fast the opponent was going). The witness can honestly answer such a question with a "No" if he believes he was going fast, but not "very" fast, or does not believe he was going fast even though he was traveling well over the speed limit. But depositions are safe places to ask such questions. If the witness agrees with the characterization during the deposition then that characterization can be the subject of trial questioning. Even if the witness does not agree with the characterization during the deposition, the facts supporting the characterization can be elicited to support jury argument at the conclusion of the trial. Thus at deposition the question, "Why don't you think you were going too fast?" can be asked, a response received, and inquiry can be had of the bases for the witness's characterization. Those bases may turn out to be illogical, otherwise subject to attack, or patently incredible, and a trial cross-examination can be fashioned to demonstrate just that.

In short, depositions are the time to try out possible story lines that could be created on both direct and cross-examination. Successful story lines become part of the trial theory of the case. Unsuccessful story lines will dropped from the trial case theory, but may in fact provide insight as to what the opponent's trial theory will likely prove to be. For this reason, many trial lawyers prepare their cross-examinations from the depositions in the case, and most of them at least start their preparation with the depositions, and then move to other sources for their questions. At a minimum, deposition testimony will serve as a means to lock in the testimony of witnesses, so that deposition testimony that is inconsistent with trial testimony can be admitted as impeachment by prior inconsistent statement pursuant to Federal Rule of Evidence 613, and as substantive evidence pursuant to Rule 801(d)(1)(A).

*PIS*

## 2.2 PRESERVING TESTIMONY

In addition to gathering information, you can use a deposition to preserve testimony. The reasons to preserve testimony will be discussed in full below, but at the outset note that while the goals of information gathering and preserving testimony overlap to some extent, they may also conflict. For example, the purpose of deposing the witnesses for the opposing side is to prepare to attack their expected testimony at trial, not to preserve what is likely to be harmful testimony. Nonetheless, taking the deposition of a harmful witness will have the effect of preserving that testimony, both good and bad, if the witness should later prove to be unavailable for trial. One of the more unpleasant experiences a trial lawyer may have is to have taken a thorough and complete deposition of an opponent's witness, only to have that deposition used at trial as the means of presenting the testimony of an unavailable witness pursuant to Federal Rule of Evidence 804(b)(1). Although that danger exists, a party is always better off having complete information regarding the possible testimony of a witness, so that it can be anticipated and attacked, than not knowing it at all.

### 2.2.1 Locking in testimony.

Let's face it: not all witnesses are as fully respectful of the truth as we might wish. In fact, some are out-and-out liars while others, to be charitable, merely have memory problems. Depositions provide control over witnesses who deviate from their prior deposition testimony by providing a means of punishing them at trial through impeachment or by encouraging truthful recollection by using the deposition to refresh their memories. Depositions freeze the witness's story so that the witness can deviate from it only at her peril.

### 2.2.2 Substitute for live testimony.

If a witness becomes "unavailable" for any reason—death, illness, being beyond the subpoena power of the court, forgetfulness, or by claiming a privilege—the Federal Rules of Civil Procedure[2] as well as Federal Rules of Evidence[3] permit the use the witness's deposition testimony as a substitute for live testimony. Depositions become critically important when a witness is elderly, is in danger of disappearing prior to the trial, lives a great distance from the court, or for any other reason is not likely to be able to testify at trial. In addition, the deposition testimony of opposing parties, as well as the depositions of witnesses as to statements attributable to opposing parties, are admissible as substantive evidence when offered as party admissions,[4] for impeachment by a prior inconsistent statement,[5] or, in more limited circumstances as a prior consistent statement.[6] While often not as persuasive (or interesting) as live testimony, deposition testimony, especially when presented by videotape, can be an effective substitute and be utilized, not only to provide testimony, but also as admissible designations that can be used during opening statements and closing arguments.

### 2.2.3 Basis for temporary injunctive relief and motions.

Litigants frequently use depositions to support applications for preliminary injunctions as well as case-dispositive motions, such as motions for summary judgment. Used in this way, depositions substitute for affidavits or declarations, which are not easily attainable from adverse parties, witnesses associated with the adverse party, or hostile witnesses.

---

2.   Fed.R.Civ.P. 32(a)(3).
3.   Fed.R.Evid. 804(b)(1).
4.   Fed.R.Evid. 801(d)(2)(A–E); Fed.R.Civ.P. 32(a)(2).
5.   Fed.R.Evid. 801(d)(1)(A); Fed.R.Civ.P. 32(a)(1).
6.   Fed.R.Evid. 801(d)(1)(B).

## 2.3 FACILITATING SETTLEMENT

Depositions facilitate settlement in four ways: permitting evaluation of the witness and attorney, opening lines of communication, presenting information to the opposing side, and punishing the witness.

### 2.3.1 Evaluating the witness and attorney.

Face-to-face confrontation in a deposition permits each side to evaluate the witness being deposed and make judgments about the credibility of the witness and how the judge or jury will perceive the testimony. When the witness comes across as especially believable or unbelievable, it affects the settlement value of the case. In addition, each side will also make judgments about the abilities of opposing counsel that will influence the amount at which a case will settle.

### 2.3.2 Opening lines of communication.

The deposition setting provides an opportunity for counsel to talk with each other. A deposition may be the first time the two sides have had the opportunity to talk seriously other than over the telephone. At depositions of the principals in the case, if serious settlement discussions do occur, the availability of the parties will sometimes facilitate a quick settlement.

### 2.3.3 Presenting information to the opposing side.

The deposition can also be a time to provide favorable information about your case to the other side with the hopes of bringing about a favorable settlement. A competent deposition taker will often ferret out the same information by careful and thorough questioning, but not all deposition takers are competent. Witnesses in a deposition are usually instructed to answer only what the questions ask for and never to volunteer, but sometimes there is information, not otherwise discovered, that the opposing party needs to know to reach a appropriate conclusion of the case. This is especially true where the likely resolution of the case, as in most cases, is a negotiated settlement.[7]

---

7. Several methods of providing favorable information to the other side are discussed in §§ 13.5 and 14.11.

### 2.3.4 Punishing the witness.

While not an ethically permissible basis for taking a deposition, a potential result of rigorous cross-examination during a deposition is that a party or key witness finds the whole experience so distasteful and unpleasant that settlement occurs on favorable terms for the other side. The witness or party may simply say that she is not going to go through the same experience again at trial and she may persuade or instruct counsel to settle. By the same token, a deposition may end up consuming so much of a party's or witness's time that the further demands of preparation for trial and the trial itself may not be an acceptable cost. Again, punishing the witness is not ethically permitted as the purpose for taking a deposition,[8] but it is frequently a by-product of a deposition taken for other, legitimate reasons. In any event, a punishing deposition will nearly always communicate to an opposing party with decision-making authority on settlement and settlement amount the weaknesses of their position in the lawsuit. When confronted with the stark reality of negative facts, accumulated in a persuasive manner, parties often become more amenable to a faster resolution of the case.

As will be discussed later in this text, the objectives of a deposition will determine, to a large extent, the questioning approach for a witness. Questioning for obtaining admissions is different in form, tone, and structure than questioning pursued solely to obtain information known to the witness. When multiple objectives exist, the questioning may be different in different sections of the deposition, or it may be necessary to determine which objectives are more important and then adopt a questioning approach consistent with that determination. Obviously, then, a clear understanding of the purpose for which deposition testimony is sought is a necessary prerequisite to deposition planning.

---

8. Fed.R.Civ.P. 11.

# CHAPTER THREE

## ADVANTAGES AND DISADVANTAGES OF DEPOSITIONS

*Pickaxe, shovel, spade, crowbar, hoe and barrow, Better not invade, Yankees have the marrow.* — Samuel Woodworth

Depositions are the most powerful discovery device available to a litigator, but certainly not the only one. Just as a shovel is sometimes preferable to a hoe, other types of discovery may be better suited than a deposition for acquiring the necessary information in a particular situation. Depositions are excellent for obtaining some types of information and less effective for other types. Before deciding to take a deposition, a decision must be made as to whether the deposition of a particular witness is the best discovery device, considering the case, the type of witness, and the type of information being sought. That decision proceeds from an understanding of the advantages and disadvantages of depositions.

## 3.1 ADVANTAGES

There are many advantages to using depositions as a discovery device.

### 3.1.1 Unfiltered information.

Depositions provide the unfiltered story of the opposing party's (or witness's) story in the deponent's own words, without editorial input from opposing counsel. Since an opposing party may not be contacted without opposing counsel's permission,[1] information as to what is in her mind is available only through depositions, interrogatories, and requests for production and for admission. With interrogatories, opposing counsel usually obtains the necessary information from the client

---

1.  *See* ABA Model Rules of Professional Conduct Rule 4.2.

and edits the answers to provide the least amount of usable information that is still responsive to the question. The information provided by the opposing party to her attorney and what is actually put down on the paper in response to the interrogatory often have scant resemblance to each other·

On the other hand, the witness himself answers at a deposition. The opposing counsel may influence the answer by careful preparation of the witness and by advice during the deposition, but to a large extent the witness's own answers, minimally edited by opposing counsel, are obtained.

### 3.1.2 Opinions, mental impressions, and subjective information.

Because the witness answers your questions directly and the answers are not filtered through opposing counsel, and because such information, although not necessarily admissible, can lead to admissible evidence, deposition questions can elicit the witness's opinions, mental impressions, and subjective information. Contrast this with interrogatories, the other major discovery device, where the answer is edited by a lawyer and follow-up questions (through a second set of interrogatories) are cumbersome at best. For example, consider a typical interrogatory and the answer that might be given:

> Interrogatory No. 22: Please describe how the accident occurred.
>
> Answer: The defendant's automobile collided with the plaintiff's automobile.

Nor will it help to rephrase the interrogatory to state:

> Interrogatory No. 22: Please describe in detail how the accident occurred.
>
> Answer: The defendant's automobile collided very hard with the plaintiff's automobile.

Such interrogatories will almost always draw less than useful responses. Opposing counsel will often edit any response to provide as little useful information as possible. Now compare this with a deposition:

> Q.  Tell me how the accident occurred.
> A.  Well, the other car hit me.

> Q. Okay, let's back up. Where were you when you first saw the plaintiff's car?
>
> A. I was east of the intersection of Kirby and Mattis.
>
> Q. How far east?
>
> A. About fifty feet.
>
> Q. What lane were you in?
>
> A. The curb lane.
>
> Q. How fast were you going?
>
> A. About fifteen miles per hour.
>
> Q. Why were you going so slow?
>
> A. The light looked like it was about to change.

And so on.

Depositions are the only useful discovery device for obtaining spontaneous interpretive information such as how an incident occurred, the details of a conversation, or the recollection of an eyewitness. Such matters as mental impressions, emotional reactions, or anything to do with thought processes are best obtained through depositions, which provide the opportunity and tools to probe the witness's knowledge and memory.

### 3.1.3 Ability to follow up.

When an answer to an interrogatory is evasive or does not provide the requested information, the only available options are accepting the response given, bringing a motion to compel, or drafting and sending a new interrogatory better crafted to obtain the information needed—an option that is severely limited because of the limitation in most jurisdictions on the number of interrogatories.[2] Even worse, all the questions must be composed in advance. If the answers raise facts of interest, but are incomplete, the only real way of following up is with additional interrogatories, and answers to those interrogatories are at least thirty days away (not counting any extensions of time you have agreed to or the court has granted).

Depositions, on the other hand, allow immediate follow-up questions until the area of inquiry is exhausted. For instance, evasive or non-responsive answers can be quickly attacked forcing the witness to answer:

---

2. *See* Fed.R.Civ.P. 33(a) limiting the number of interrogatories to twenty-five.

Q. Where were you when this conversation was going on?

A. Do you mean at the beginning or end?

Q. Let's take both. Where were you at the beginning?

A. I was over by the door.

Q. Where were you at the end?

A. I was still by the door.

Q. Did you ever move away from the door during the conversation?

A. No.

Q. Who started the conversation?

A. It just started.

Q. Well, who said the first word?

A. I did.

The ability to follow up is also important when a line of questions suggests new leads. Perhaps something about the way the witness answered or looked indicates there is more than the answer alone suggests. For instance, if a witness pauses unusually long or starts the answer in a hesitating way, this often encourages follow-up questions. Sometimes the phrasing of the answer will suggest a lead:

Q. Did she say anything about the contract?

A. Not at that time.

Q. Was something said about the contract at another time?

Interrogatories rarely provide such hints and, when they do, follow-up, for the reasons noted above, is difficult.

The ability to follow up on a witness's answers also allows the examiner to attack or attempt to weaken harmful answers or to structure questions in a manner designed to elicit admissions for use at trial or in a motion for summary judgment.

Q. You weren't paying attention to the car in front of you when you were approaching the light?

A. That's not true. I certainly was paying attention.

Q. Let's see. You told me a moment ago that you had seen a boy by the side of the road, correct?

A. Yes.

Q. You also told me that you were worried the boy was going to run out into the street, right?

A. Yes.

Q. So you were keeping your eyes on the boy to make sure he didn't run out in front of your car, true?

A. I guess so.

Q. When you were watching the boy you weren't watching the car in front of you, right?

A. Right.

Q. You told me that you noticed the car in front of you only a few moments before you ran into it?

A. Yes.

Q. And the reason you did not notice the car in front of you until just a few moments before you ran into it is because you were watching the boy?

A. OK.

Q. You weren't paying attention to the car in front of you because you were paying attention to the boy?

A. I guess so.

Q. Actually sir, it's a fact, and not a guess, that your concern for the boy caused you not to pay attention to the car in front of you.

In short, depositions provide flexibility allowing adjustment to whatever the answers might be and to pursuit of new lines of questioning as necessary.

### 3.1.4 Spontaneous answers.

Depositions provide a witness's unrehearsed response without allowing a long period of time to reflect on the answer. Contrast this again with interrogatories, where a party and the party's attorney will have a minimum of thirty days to think about how to phrase the answer in its least damaging form. Of course, witnesses can rehearse answers to expected questions in a deposition, but the ability to attack a subject from several different angles means the witness will eventually have to answer spontaneously.

### 3.1.5 Fast moving.

Depositions can be scheduled and taken upon "reasonable notice" to the other side.[3] By contrast, interrogatories, the next most commonly used discovery device, need not be answered until a minimum of thirty days after service.[4] When information is needed quickly, depositions are the discovery method to use.

Speed is particularly important when a record of a witness's story is necessary while memories are fresh and have not started to fade. For example, in a personal injury case the recollection of a non-party witness is almost always most accurate when close in time to the event, as opposed to shortly before trial, several months or years later. Similarly, when witnesses are likely to become unavailable, depositions preserve their stories for later use at trial or in some form of alternative dispute resolution.

The fast-moving nature of depositions also becomes important when discovery deadlines are close at hand. The ability to schedule a deposition quickly provides information about and from a witness in time to incorporate that information in the case theory. Of course, informal investigation is available at all times, even prior to filing an action, but when quick action is needed, there is nothing faster than a deposition.

### 3.1.6 Face-to-face confrontation.

Depositions are the only discovery device that allows counsel to meet the opposing party face-to-face. The same is true regarding those witnesses who refuse to respond to more informal fact investigation such as interviews by counsel or by investigators. Face-to-face confrontation has several advantages. First, it forces the witness to tell his story while under oath and while facing the opposing party or at least the party's attorney. A party theoretically is also under oath when answering interrogatories, but, in reality, the oath is frequently glossed over at the time of signing. Thus, while the answers are formally attributable to the witness, impeachment at trial with interrogatory responses is often unsatisfactory and unpersuasive, as the witness muddies the water

---

3. Rule 30(b)(1) provides only for reasonable notice. What is reasonable will vary from jurisdiction to jurisdiction and from case to case, *see* § 1.6.1, but is usually less than the thirty days provided for answering interrogatories. Under Rule 26(d) a party cannot seek discovery from any source until after the planning conference required by Rule 26(f), unless authorized by stipulation or court order, where special circumstances exist. *See* §§ 1.3 and 4.1.

4. Fed.R.Civ.P. 33(a).

with claims that she did not quite understand the lawyer's language in the interrogatories and answers, that she was not precisely certain of the purpose or significance of the interrogatories, and that she thought the oath merely meant that she had seen and read them, not that she agreed with every word. Although this is a clear abrogation of her obligations, and those of her counsel, the jury is likely to side with the lay witness, at least to the extent that they will not give much weight to the attempted impeachment. (Where her counsel crafts the interrogatory answers to avoid disclosure, he is intentionally frustrating discovery. He may also be perpetrating a fraud on the court, since such answers are being submitted as the witness's answers, while in fact they are not.) In comparison, the circumstances of the administration of the oath and the formal questioning at a deposition often will impress on a witness the importance of truthfulness and carry weight if they are to read to a jury.

Second, face-to-face confrontation allows evaluation of the impression the witness will likely make at trial. Does the witness appear shifty and disingenuous or honest and forthright? Will a jury sympathize with the witness or reject the witness because of his arrogance? These questions and more regarding the credibility of witnesses can be answered, at least preliminarily, by putting the witness through the rigors of a deposition.

Third, depositions allow development of a personal relationship with the witness. While usually not successful with a party, a non-party witness may be "seduced" by charm to recount the story in an advantageous way, or she may be intimidated by a stern manner into backing off from harmful testimony. A stern manner during a deposition may cause a witness to be more cautious at trial, even under more gentle questioning.

Fourth, depositions allow evaluation of the abilities and behavior of opposing counsel. The attorney may be passive or aggressive, prepared or unprepared, articulate or bumbling, and so on. After the deposition, a better gauge of what is faced at trial is available.

Fifth, depositions allow deposing counsel to demonstrate trial prowess by incisive and penetrating examination, command of the deposition room, likeable personality and, of course, photogenic good looks. The evaluation of counsel is a two-way street and an assessment will be made by opposing counsel as to deposing counsel's likely impact on a judge or jury.

Finally, depositions provide an opportunity to discuss settlement when the opposing attorney and client are together. Many cases are

*Non-party - can any get depos & docs*

settled following a deposition because it is the first time the attorneys have met face to face and had the chance to evaluate the effectiveness of key witnesses.

### 3.1.7 Information from uncooperative witnesses.

Outside of court or a deposition, nothing requires a witness to answer a lawyer's or an investigator's questions. In fact, a witness can refuse to say anything to either side. When a witness does refuse to cooperate, the only discovery device available to get that person's story is a deposition. Finally, only depositions and subpoenas for the production of books, documents, and things can be used with non-party witnesses;[5] all of the other discovery devices—interrogatories, requests for admission, notices to produce—can be used only against a party.

### 3.1.8 Generate fewer objections.

Depositions can be contentious, with the attorneys arguing with each other and seeking the judge's assistance to referee their disputes. Nonetheless, compared to interrogatories, depositions generate fewer objections, and when objections are made they do not stop the deposition. The simple fact is that answering interrogatories is one of the most frustrating, boring, and irritating tasks a lawyer is called upon to perform. As a result, it is often much easier to object to an interrogatory than to answer it, if only because of the annoyance factor of the interrogatory. An objection avoids the need to answer to the extent the interrogatory is objectionable.[6] The attorney posing the interrogatory must then bring a motion to compel to obtain a ruling on the objection. But the motion to compel comes with the risk that, if the judge finds the objection to be valid, the party bringing the motion may be assessed the objecting party's reasonable expenses in responding to the motion.[7]

On the other hand, it is comparatively easy to sit and listen to your witness answer questions. Boredom may be a factor, but rarely does there arise the intense desire to engage in the sophistry that is generated by interrogatories. Even if defending counsel objects at deposition, the objections do not excuse the witness from answering. As a result, depositions usually generate far fewer objections and yield far more information than any other type of discovery.

---

5.  Fed.R.Civ.P. 45.
6.  Fed.R.Civ.P. 33(b)(1).
7.  Fed.R.Civ.P. 33(b)(5) and 37(a)(4).

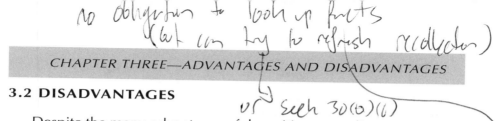

*No obligation to look up facts*
*(but can try to refresh recollection)*

## 3.2 DISADVANTAGES

*or Seen 30(b)(6)*

Despite the many advantages of depositions as a discovery device, several drawbacks must also be considered.

### 3.2.1 Failures of memory or lack of knowledge.

Sometimes witnesses cannot remember or never knew the facts about which you are asking. For instance, you ask the president of the Widget Corporation how many widgets were sold in 2004, and the truthful answer may be, "I don't recall." While frustrating, there is not much that can be done other than to try to refresh the witness's memory in some way. There is no right to ask the witness to look up the information, although often a polite request to do so can achieve positive results. Even more frustrating is to ask the witness the same question and have the witness respond that she doesn't know the answer, but some other witness does.

Quite simply, if a witness honestly does not know the answer to a question or cannot remember the answer and nothing refreshes the witness's memory, there is nothing that can be done. Furthermore, when asking for information that is numerical in nature, such as financial data, "I don't remember" is frequently the best and most likely truthful answer.

To a certain extent, these problems can be avoided by advance preparation. The documents containing the necessary information or those which can be used to refresh memory may be the subject of a request to produce or subpoena in advance of the deposition. Another alternative is to schedule a Rule 30(b)(6) deposition, requiring the corporation or other organization to designate a witness who must be reasonably prepared to testify about particular, identified matters.[8]

Often the best approach is not to take a deposition at all, but to send interrogatories requesting the desired information (assuming the information is being sought from an opposing party). Interrogatories search both the files and the memory of a party, and the collective memory of an institutional party, by requiring the party to take all reasonable steps to provide the requested information. "I don't remember" will not suffice if the party can find the information with some reasonable amount of work. Files must be checked, records examined, and other employees asked to provide the necessary information. A deposition cannot do this (unless it is a 30(b)(6) deposition). (However, where a search of the files is the reasonable way to find the information, the burden to

---

8. *See* § 1.2.

conduct such a search may be shifted, on request to the court, to the inquiring party where the burden would be the same for either.[9]

### 3.2.2 Experience with cross-examination.

All but experienced witnesses are anxious about cross-examination. They may become flustered, confused, or nervous. Obviously, this may cause the jury not to believe them. But all of us improve with practice and that is what a deposition allows a witness to do—improve with practice—by putting her through some semblance of cross-examination during a deposition. When trial comes, the witness will know better what to expect from cross-examination, will be better prepared, and will be more effective in response to questions and the attorney's demeanor already experienced during the deposition.

### 3.2.3 Helps to prepare opponent's case.

All attorneys, at one time or another, have had the experience of taking a deposition of a witness and watching the defending attorney scribble down every answer the witness gives. The reason for this may be thoroughness or just compulsive note taking, a skill often learned in law school, but often the attorney has not previously interviewed the witness or interviewed the witness with the completeness of the deposition. The answers to deposition questions, in such a circumstance, are as new to the defending attorney as to deposing counsel, and as such the process of learning information and preparing for trial is available to opposing counsel at the same time.

Even when opposing counsel is a more conscientious opponent who has prepared the witness, it is the scheduling of the deposition that forced that preparation, of the witness and counsel, by causing careful review of the known facts of the case. Absent the deposition, this work may not have been done, or at least it might not have been done at such a beneficial juncture in the litigation.

### 3.2.4 Expense.

Depositions cost money. The time of the court reporter and the preparation of transcripts are costs in the litigation. In addition, the time consumed in preparing and taking the deposition must be accounted for, either against the contingent fee or as billable hours. Inter-

---

9. Fed.R.Civ.P. 33(d).

rogatories and informal investigation also take time, but out-of-pocket expenses are usually less.

Depositions become even more expensive when travel is involved. Non-party witnesses and defendants must normally be deposed close to their residence or place of business or employment. Plaintiffs are usually deposed where the litigation is pending or at their residence or place of business or employment.[10] When litigation is national in scope, the travel costs can be prohibitively high. Interrogatories, subpoenas, and requests for admission, on the other hand, can be sent electronically or by mail.

### 3.2.5 Reveal theories.

Deposition questions often reveal the legal and factual theories of the questioning attorney's case. For instance, if the defendant's questions in a breach of contract case concern the plaintiff's efforts at exercising an option under the contract, the plaintiff's attorney will be able to guess that this will be one of the defenses raised, and he will prepare the plaintiff's case accordingly. Perhaps revelation of theories is not a concern, because everyone involved knows from the pleadings and the facts of the case what will be raised, but if there is a desire to try to conceal a theory until trial, depositions may be contra-indicated as case theory will more likely be transparent.

### 3.2.6 Cannot obtain legal theories.

If the plaintiff's attorney asks the defendant in a deposition if she is claiming the plaintiff was contributorily negligent, the defendant's attorney should object that the question calls for a legal opinion. Although the witness should still answer, subject to the objection, the defendant's attorney will be right. In contrast, while interrogatories cannot ask purely legal questions, they can properly ask for a party's contentions ("Are you contending that the plaintiff failed to mitigate its damages? If so, please state all facts on which you base this contention.").[11] As a consequence, interrogatories may be a slightly superior means for obtaining some additional information about the opponent's legal analysis.

*Contention Rogs vs. Depo Questions*

---

10. *See* § 1.7.
11. Fed.R.Civ.P. 33(c).

# CHAPTER FOUR

# PLANNING AND SCHEDULING DEPOSITIONS

*The best laid schemes o' mice and men Gang aft a gley…*
— Robert Burns

Effective discovery requires planning and coordination. In particular, depositions can be combined with other methods of discovery and with each other in order to achieve the maximum discovery as efficiently as possible. Carefully planned discovery is essential to conducting successful litigation and requires thought about what information is needed to prepare a case for trial or settlement and how best to obtain that information.

## 4.1 THE DISCOVERY PLAN

Discovery in the U.S. district courts is not left entirely to the control of the parties. Instead, in most cases the parties are required to confer about, among other things, the discovery to occur in the case and to submit the results of these discussions to the court in the form of a proposed discovery plan. This proposed discovery plan then serves as the basis for a scheduling order that includes provisions concerning the discovery in the case as well as other matters.[1]

Let's start with the proposed discovery plan. Under Rule 26(f) the parties are required to confer, except in a narrow class of excepted cases or when the court orders otherwise, to draft a proposed discovery plan giving the parties' views and proposals concerning:

> 1. what changes should be made in the timing, form, or requirements under the mandatory disclosures portion of the rules,[2] including a statement as to when the mandatory disclosures were or will be made;

---

1. Fed.R.Civ.P. 16(b), 26(f).
2. *See* § 4.2.1.

2. the subjects on which discovery may be needed, when discovery should be completed, and whether the parties should conduct discovery in phases or be limited to particular issues;

3. what changes should be made to the limitations on discovery imposed by the Federal Rules or local rules and whether additional limitations should be imposed; and

4. whether the courts should enter any protective orders[3] or other orders affecting scheduling and discovery.[4]

Finally, in the planning conference, the parties must also discuss the "nature and basis of their claims and defenses and the possibilities for a prompt settlement or resolution of the case,"[5] and how to proceed with the mandatory disclosures under Rule 26(a)(1). The parties may also discuss other matters to be included in the scheduling order even though not listed in Rule 26(f). The parties need not agree on each of the topics discussed, but the proposed discovery plan should clearly set forth each side's position.

Unless shortened by local rule because of an expedited schedule or because the case falls within the narrow category of exempted cases, the planning conference should be held as soon as practicable, but not later than twenty-one days before a scheduling conference is held or a scheduling order is due. The parties' attorneys are jointly responsible for submitting the proposed discovery plan, in writing, to the court within fourteen days of the planning conference. The court may by local court rule shorten the time for submitting the proposed discovery plan or excuse the parties from submitting a written report and permit them to report orally.[6] Form 35 in the Appendix to the Federal Rules of Civil Procedure is an example of the type of report expected to result from the planning conference.[7]

The court will use the proposed discovery plan in issuing a scheduling order under Rule 16(b) unless the case is of a type exempted under the local rules. The scheduling order will set time limits for joining other parties and amending the pleadings, filing motions, and completing discovery. In addition, the scheduling order may modify the times for the mandatory disclosures and supplementing discovery; modify the limits on the extent of discovery; set the dates for any conferences before trial, the final pretrial conference, and the trial date; and make

3. Fed.R.Civ.P. 26(c).
4. Fed.R.Civ.P. 16(b) and (c).
5. Fed.R.Civ.P. 26(f).
6. Fed.R.Civ.P. 26(b).
7. A copy of Form 35 is contained in Appendix A.

any other appropriate orders. The court is to issue the scheduling order as soon as practicable but not later than ninety days after the defendant appears or 120 days after the complaint has been served on a defendant.

Depending on the type of case and the results of the planning conference, some scheduling orders contain detailed timetables and directions for conducting discovery, while others do no more than set a cut-off date for when discovery must be completed. Many of the suggestions made in the following pages concerning the sequence and scheduling of discovery may be reflected in the scheduling order or may be left to the parties to develop as the litigation progresses.

The requirement of a planning conference in Rule 26(f) provides you with the opportunity to thoughtfully explore the discovery strategy to be followed in a case. Before the conference the attorneys must think through in great detail what discovery they need in the case. Even in jurisdictions that do not follow some version of Rule 26(f), it is still useful to consider what discovery is necessary and how it should be conducted. Some of the issues to be considered are:

- how many depositions are needed;
- what witnesses should be deposed;
- in what order the witnesses should be deposed;
- a limit on the length of the depositions;
- any special rules necessary for the taking of the depositions, such as excluding other witnesses from the deposition room;
- whether time limits and content of the mandatory disclosures should be modified;
- the use of other discovery devices, such as interrogatories, before depositions are taken;
- waiver of the limitation on the number of interrogatories;
- any special orders needed for the taking of discovery, such as a protective order concerning trade secrets;
- whether discovery should proceed in phases, either by witnesses or topics, to avoid duplicative discovery and to set the stage for any summary judgment motions;
- whether counsel should confer regularly to review and make suggestions for modifying the scheduling order.

The above is a suggested list of topics that attorneys should think about before the planning conference. A particular case may have a longer or shorter list of concerns. Sometimes you may conclude that, even though a topic may be appropriate for inclusion in the scheduling order, a desire for flexibility in conducting discovery or worries about revealing litigation strategy may prevent proposing it as part of the discovery plan. This, however, in no way lessens the need to think about the topic. Effective planning requires that attorneys consider these issues at some point during the course of the case; Rule 26(f) merely requires that it happen early in the litigation.

## 4.2 COORDINATING DEPOSITIONS WITH OTHER DISCOVERY

Coordinating a deposition schedule with other discovery requires several steps. The first of these is deciding what information is needed to pursue claims or defense. Second, attorneys must determine from what sources they can get this information. Third, they need to decide on the best method of obtaining the information. Finally, they need to decide on the order for getting the information.

Let's take as an example a case where the plaintiff is claiming lost profits as a result of a defendant's failure to purchase the number of signs required under a purchase agreement. In representing the defendant, based on information from the client, the attorney knows that the plaintiff is a small manufacturer of electronic signs. The contract was for the sale of a large quantity of a particular type of electronic sign manufactured by the plaintiff. The plaintiff purchases most of the component parts of the signs from various vendors and assembles them into the finished product. The plaintiff's main contribution to the product is the assembly. The plaintiff is a small corporation with a president, a purchasing agent, a bookkeeper/accountant, and a plant foreman.

At this point, one key defense is to attack the plaintiff's calculation of lost profits, and to prepare for this the attorney intends to take whatever depositions are necessary. What information do you need before taking depositions? A short, incomplete list includes:

- a list of the vendors of the parts used in assembling the signs.
- the prices and terms for the purchase of the parts;
- any calculations by the plaintiff of costs and profits for the manufacturing of the signs;

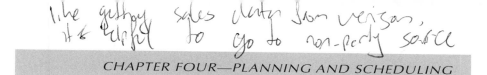
*like getting sales center from verizon, it is useful to go to non-party source*

- any accounting records concerning manufacturing expenses;

- the name of the employee who decided what parts to purchase.

With thought, you could add many more items to this list, but these few illustrate the point.

Once the information needed has been identified, the next step is to identify the possible sources of this information. In the example given, all of the information being sought is likely to be available from the plaintiff, but some information, such as the prices and terms for the purchase of the parts, should also be available from the different vendors who provided the parts. The defendant's attorney, of course, is not limited to seeking information from just one source if more than one is available. But in choosing a source, such factors as cost, ease of obtaining the information, and the credibility of the source are likely to control.

The third and fourth steps are determining how to go about getting the information and in what order. The best answer to these questions is to look at the different discovery devices available for use.

### 4.2.1 Mandatory disclosures.

Absent a stipulation, a court order, or a case falling within the narrow class of excepted cases, parties litigating in the U.S. district courts must disclose, without awaiting a formal discovery request, certain basic information about the case. Specifically, each party shall provide to all other parties in the case:

> 1. the name and, if known, the address and telephone number of each individual likely to have discoverable information that the disclosing party may use to support its claims or defenses, unless solely for impeachment, identifying the subjects of the information;
>
> *W*
>
> 2. a copy, or a description by category and location, of all documents, data compilations, and tangible things that are in the possession, custody, or control of the party and that the disclosing party may use to support its claims or defenses, unless solely for impeachment;
>
> *Docs*
>
> 3. for inspection and copying, a computation of any category of damages claimed by the disclosing party, making available for inspection and copying all non-privileged material upon which the computation is based, including materials bearing
>
> *Dmgs*

*Mandatory Disclosure – Set forth support for your affirmative case*

on the nature and extent of any claimed injuries; and

4. for inspection and copying, any insurance agreement that may be available to satisfy all or part of any judgment which may be entered in the action or to indemnify or reimburse for payments made to satisfy the judgment.[8]

The disclosures are to be made in writing at or within fourteen days after the planning conference, unless a party objects to making disclosures because not appropriate for the case, or the parties stipulate or the court orders a different time.[9] While the mandatory disclosures assist with the discovery process, there is no requirement to identify witnesses or documents having or containing information harmful to the disclosing party's position; all that is required is the disclosure of witnesses and documents upon which the disclosing party intends to rely. Therefore, while perhaps accelerating discovery, the mandatory disclosures do not relieve you of the fundamental burden of developing your own proof.

### 4.2.2 Interrogatories.

Imagine the deposition of the plaintiff's purchasing agent and what could happen:

COUNSEL FOR DEFENDANT:

Q.  Now sir, please tell me the name of all vendors from whom the plaintiff purchases parts for use in manufacturing the electronic signs which are the subject of this action.

A.  Well, let's see. We purchase most of the circuit boards from Zenith, but several of the more specialized ones come from JVC. The sign casings come from a small firm in town, Acucom, and we get some parts from jobbers.

Q.  Any other vendors?

A.  Oh, sure. We use over thirty vendors, but I know I can't remember them all right now.

Q.  Do you have a list of the various vendors?

A.  Yes, back at the office.

Q.  Counsel, I suggest that you provide me with the list and

---

8.  Fed.R.Civ.P. 26(a)(1).
9.  *See* Fed.R.Civ.P. 26(a).

we finish as much as we can today and then continue the deposition tomorrow after I have a chance to review the list.

COUNSEL FOR PLAINTIFF:

Give me a request in writing and I will take it under advisement. Quite frankly, I see no need to continue this deposition and cause further inconvenience and expense for my client. As you know, depositions are limited to seven hours on one day. If you wanted a list of our vendors you knew how to get it without waiting until the middle of this deposition. I will tell you now that I will resist any efforts to resume this deposition at a later time.

The defendant's lawyer could have avoided all of these problems if before the deposition he had sent the plaintiff a set of interrogatories asking for the names of all vendors supplying parts for the signs.[10] Of course, the interrogatories could also ask for any other information that would be helpful in conducting the deposition, such as a description of the parts, the purchase price, quantities, and so on.

Interrogatories are one of the most useful deposition preparation tools when used for certain limited purposes because, through them, an attorney can obtain information in advance. In factually complex cases, the first wave of discovery routinely consists of interrogatories sent soon after the litigation commences, with the answers to be used, in part, to help prepare for the later depositions. The advantages of using interrogatories in preparing for depositions are several:

Interrogatories can be used to identify factual data and information that a witness is not likely to recall at deposition. As illustrated above, if a witness cannot remember the correct answer to a question, there is little the lawyer taking the deposition can do except attempt to refresh the witness's memory. If, however, you have obtained such information by sending interrogatories before the deposition, you can question the witness without concern about memory failures. When a deposition witness may be questioned about objective information in the hands of the opposing party, such as data, calculations, lists, or other information that the witness will not likely recall easily, the deposing attorney can obtain this information through interrogatories before the deposition.

---

10. If the information was called for by a previous discovery request, but was not provided, the Advisory Committee Notes to Rule 30(d)(2) states "that may justify further examination once production has occurred."

Interrogatories can help identify potential deposition witnesses and documents. Interrogatories frequently ask about all witnesses who have knowledge of the facts—who attended an event or meeting, participated in a transaction, and so on. Similarly, interrogatories often ask a party to identify all documents referring to a particular event or resulting from a transaction. The purpose of these types of interrogatories is, among other things, to identify potential deposition witnesses and documents that the opponent will be asked to produce. While the attorney can and should ask these same questions at the depositions of key witnesses as a method of confirming the accuracy of the interrogatory answers, these witnesses many times do not have comprehensive knowledge of other witnesses and documents. For instance, the plaintiff's president in our example may know others who attended the meetings that she attended concerning parts orders, but she may not know who attended other meetings when she was not present. Similarly, the defendant in a personal injury case may be unaware of those witnesses to the accident who were later located by his lawyer or a private investigator. The advantage of interrogatories over depositions in identifying witnesses and documents is that the opposing party cannot rely solely on his or her current memory of facts. Instead, the party answering the interrogatory must make reasonable inquiry of all of its employees and agents and conduct a reasonable search of all records.[11]

Interrogatories can identify who in a company or organization has knowledge about a topic. Imagine again the deposition of the plaintiff's purchasing agent in the breach of contract case. One of the facts the attorney representing the defendant wishes to know is the name of the person who decided what parts were to be purchased for manufacturing the signs. An obvious method of obtaining this information is to ask about it during the purchasing agent's deposition. The response might be something like, "I am not sure, but I think it was our president." When the president's deposition is taken, her answer is, "No, it wasn't me. I'm pretty sure it was an outside designer." And so goes the game at increasing expense and inconvenience. Sending a simple interrogatory before the first deposition asking who made the decision about what parts to purchase would avoid this difficulty and greatly facilitate later discovery.

Of course, you can use a Rule 30(b)(6) deposition[12] to accomplish the same objective by asking the plaintiff to designate, for the deposi-

---

11. *Miller v. Doctor's General Hospital*, 76 F.R.D. 136 (D.Okla. 1977); 8 C. Wright & A. Miller, *Civil Procedure* § 2177, n.22 (West 1994).
12. Fed.R.Civ.P. 30(b)(6). *See* § 1.2.

tion, a person who is or will be prepared to testify about who decided on what parts to purchase. Conducting a deposition for this purpose alone would be more expensive than posing an interrogatory on the same subject. Rule 30(b)(6) depositions work best when a list of specifications is attached so that a whole body of information can be obtained. When, however, the corporation or organization having the desired information is a non-party, a Rule 30(b)(6) or "named-deponent" deposition is the only discovery method available.

Interrogatories can be used to narrow the issues. Rule 33(c) states "[a]n interrogatory otherwise proper is not necessarily objectionable merely because an answer to the interrogatory involves an opinion or contention that relates to fact or the application of law to fact…." In other words, interrogatories may ask about an opponent's legal contentions in the case,[13] Being able to ask about an opponent's legal contentions in a case can be very helpful in narrowing the issues. For example, in a negligence action it would be proper to ask in an interrogatory for the plaintiff to identify the acts and omissions claimed to constitute the defendant's negligence. In the breach of contract case described above, the defendant may ask in an interrogatory whether, for example, the plaintiff is claiming consequential damages as a result of the alleged breach. The answer to such an interrogatory would help narrow the issues in dispute by informing the defendant of what it will need to defend against. Because a party often will not be certain about what is being contended until after the facts have been fully explored, the court may order that contention interrogatories need not be answered until after discovery on the issue has been completed or until a pretrial conference or other later date.[14]

While interrogatories are generally useful in preparing for depositions, drawbacks do exist:

- interrogatories may only be directed to a party and cannot be used with a non-party;[15]

- interrogatories do not work well when asking about opinions, mental impressions and subjective information;[16]

- answers are filtered through and drafted by lawyers;

- interrogatories draw more objections than other types of discovery;

---

13. Interrogatories calling for pure law, divorced from the facts of the case, are still improper. Advisory Committee Note to 1970 Amendment to Rule 33.
14. Fed.R.Civ.P. 33(c).
15. Fed.R.Civ.P. 33(a).
16. *See* § 3.1.2.

- answers are difficult to follow up;
- evasive answers are difficult to control;
- interrogatories need not be answered for thirty days;[17]
- interrogatories are limited to twenty-five unless modified by court order or stipulation;[18]
- require careful drafting.[19]

Interrogatories may alert an opponent to the areas on which there will be questioning in a later deposition. As a result, at the later deposition, the witness will be better prepared. Interrogatories submitted pursuant to Rule 33(c) asking about a party's opinions and contentions are particularly troublesome because of their tendency to inform opponents of possible lines of defense to be taken at later depositions.

Using interrogatories may also cause delay in taking depositions, thereby allowing the opponent to gain the initiative. Under the Federal Rules of Civil Procedure, interrogatories cannot be sent until after the planning conference required by Rule 26(f) unless by stipulation or leave of court.[20] Courts often grant extensions of time for answering interrogatories, particularly early in an action, thereby further delaying the discovery process. If one side delays taking depositions until interrogatories have been answered, the other side will often gain a valuable psychological momentum by proceeding with its own depositions. Where speed and initiative are important, an attorney may well forgo interrogatories until a later stage of the litigation and commence taking depositions at the earliest possible moment.

In addition, absent special considerations many courts permit only one set of interrogatories to an opponent. As a result, a party may want to defer asking any interrogatories until after all or a majority of the depositions have been taken so that the interrogatories can be used to tie up any loose ends.

Like all else in litigation, no absolute rules apply to coordinating depositions with interrogatories. An attorney must consider and decide each situation individually to decide whether any information is needed before taking depositions. If so, the next question will be whether interrogatories are the best method of obtaining that information.

---

17. Fed.R.Civ.P. 33(b)(3).
18. Fed.R.Civ.P. 26(b)(2), 33(a).
19. *See generally* § 3.1.
20. Fed.R.Civ.P. 26(d) and 33(a).

### 4.2.3 Document requests.

Lawyers frequently use depositions to question witnesses about documents. When documents are in the hands of an uncooperative non-party, taking a deposition in conjunction with a subpoena *duces tecum* was once the only method of forcing pretrial production of the documents. Now, under Rule 45(a), documents may be subpoenaed from a non-party without a deposition. For a party, the Federal Rules of Civil Procedure seem to suggest that the only permissible method of obtaining documents is by a request to produce,[21] but as a practical matter many party-witnesses respond to a subpoena *duces tecum* without objection. The advantage of using a subpoena *duces tecum* is the shorter response time provided under Rule 45 than under Rule 34.

When it can be done without unduly delaying the taking of the deposition, an attorney should obtain documents in advance rather than having them produced at the deposition. Advance production allows time to study the documents, check with other sources about information contained in the documents, and more carefully formulate questions for the deposition. Producing documents at the deposition causes delays while attorneys study the documents and creates the risk that the questioner may not recognize a potential area of questioning until after the deposition has concluded. Since an opponent has thirty days in which to respond to a notice to produce, document production has to occur at an early stage of the litigation if it is not to delay depositions.

But it is often difficult to get an opposing party to produce documents within the thirty days provided by Rule 34. Instead, they may resist by asking the court for extensions of time or by merely failing to respond until compelled to do so by the judge in the case. It is usually better to proceed with depositions rather than wait for weeks and months to obtain the documents requested, reserving a right to resume the deposition if later-obtained documents create a legitimate need.

When taking the deposition of a non-party witness, it never hurts to call the witness and ask them to produce documents voluntarily in advance of the deposition. If the attorney explains that this will help shorten the deposition, such a tactic is often successful. Of course, parties and represented witnesses must be contacted through their counsel.

---

21. Fed.R.Civ.P. 30(b)(5).

RFA ← authentication → but ship maybe letter

### 4.2.4 Requests for admission.

Requests for admission, if successful, may help to eliminate the need to prove essential facts and may reduce discovery costs by rendering unnecessary those depositions that otherwise would be needed to establish the disputed fact. Requests for admission are particularly useful to authenticate documents in the hands of non-parties who would otherwise have to be deposed to obtain the necessary proof. For instance, in a personal injury case copies of the medical records may be available but, in order to authenticate them, the attorney must either depose the hospital records custodian or call her as a witness at trial. If the opposing party is first requested to admit the record's authenticity, you may be able to avoid the need for the deposition or, if it takes place, to impose its cost on the party.[22]

The drawback of requests for admission is that they are time consuming. The opposing party has thirty days in which to respond, and courts readily grant extensions of time if the requests are made early in the litigation.

Before expending the time to draft requests for admission, it makes sense to call the opposing counsel to see if a stipulation to the same topics is agreeable. A telephone call is often better received than a discovery request and more likely to achieve what you are seeking.

As a practical matter, requests for admission are not really a discovery device at all, but more like a formalized request for a stipulation. A party who will not agree to stipulate to a fact is also unlikely to answer a request for admission. This is particularly true because there is usually no penalty for unreasonably denying a request for admission. Very few courts actually require an opposing party who has denied a request for admission to pay the reasonable expenses incurred in proving the truth of the fact contained in the request.[23]

### 4.2.5 Self help.

While not a discovery device provided for by the Federal Rules of Civil Procedure, self help is often the best way of obtaining information. Conducting an informal investigation of the facts by calling up potential witnesses and asking them to explain what happened, by requesting an individual or company to voluntarily reveal documents, by taking her own photographs, and so forth, an attorney or paralegal

---

22. Fed.R.Civ.P. 37(c).
23. Fed.R.Civ.P. 37(c)(2).

can often find out what is needed without the expense of hiring a court reporter or incurring witness fees.

There are drawbacks to such an approach. Any information obtained is usually not under oath. (You can always ask for a sworn statement; whether you will be successful in getting one is another matter.) The information cannot be used in court if the witness becomes unavailable, and impeaching the witness who later changes her version of the facts is usually more difficult than with a deposition.

Besides being typically cheaper than formal discovery, the greatest advantage of self help is that the attorney will not normally be required to share the results of her investigation with the opponent.[24] Contrast this with taking a deposition where the opposing attorney gets to listen to every question and answer and even ask questions of his own, all at the expense of the attorney noticing the deposition.

Formal discovery and self help are not the only ways to find the information necessary for preparing the case. Negotiations with opposing counsel, mediation efforts, pretrial conferences, talking with experts, opponent's pleadings, and responses to motions for summary judgment and other types of motions are all ways of finding out information concerning your case.

## 4.3 COORDINATING DEPOSITIONS WITH EACH OTHER

Once the order in which discovery is to proceed has been decided, it is still necessary to decide on the order of the depositions. Deciding on the order of depositions depends on the facts of the particular case. However, we can at least identify the factors to be considered when making this decision.

Is it necessary to obtain evidence from one witness before deposing another witness? Often litigation is similar to building a house: you must lay the foundation before you can erect the walls. Similarly, in litigation an attorney may need to obtain evidence from one witness as a prerequisite to questioning another witness. For instance, the defendant in a personal injury case who is challenging the extent and permanency of the plaintiff's injuries will probably want to depose the plaintiff about the injuries before deposing the plaintiff's medical expert about the prognosis for the plaintiff's recovery. Likewise, in the breach-of-contract action described earlier, the defendant would gen-

---

24. There are limited circumstances when an opposing party may have access to an attorney's "work product," but they occur very rarely. *See* Fed.R.Civ.P. 26(b)(3).

erally want to find out from the purchasing agent what parts were necessary to manufacture the signs before questioning the bookkeeper/accountant about the manufacturing cost.

Should key or minor witnesses be deposed first? Sometimes the attorney and the client will be unfamiliar with the facts giving rise to the dispute, the structure of the industry, or the general background to the lawsuit. For instance, in the breach-of-contract action neither the lawyer nor the defendant may know much about the sign market or the plaintiff's opportunities to mitigate damages. When background information is needed, often facts from minor witnesses should be obtained before proceeding to interrogate key witnesses.

When background information is not necessary or is already available, the general rule is to depose key witnesses before minor ones. The reason for this general rule is that deposing the key witnesses first affords less time for them to prepare to testify. Also, as a matter of human nature, if the key witnesses have an opportunity to review the deposition testimony of minor witnesses or to familiarize themselves with what the minor witnesses are going to say, the key witnesses are more likely to adapt their own stories to those of the minor witnesses. Minor witnesses, because they usually have less at stake, are less likely to take the time and expend the effort to conform their stories to the expected stories of the key witnesses. Where, however, a case has more than one key witness with similar knowledge, it may be wise to leave the deposition of one of them until close to the end of discovery. In that way, after completing discovery of the other witnesses, if there are some unanswered questions, there is still a key actor who can be questioned.

When should expert witnesses be deposed? In most cases, expert witnesses must provide a report of their opinions and the reasons for them as well as any exhibits that support the opinions or summarize them. The report must also contain the expert's qualifications, compensation, and previous experience testifying. An expert may not be offered for deposition, and an attorney should not want to depose an expert, until they provide this report.[25] The report will provide important assistance in preparing for the expert's deposition. Even with those experts who need not provide a report or in those jurisdictions where it is not required, it makes sense to wait until the end of discovery so that the expert will have fully developed the opinions to be given at trial and until there is a chance fully to understand the facts in the case.

---

25. Fed.R.Civ.P. 26(b)(4)(A).

## 4.4 SCHEDULING THE DEPOSITION

Should depositions be scheduled early or late in the discovery process? Again, this depends on the facts of the case. Early scheduling of depositions permits a lawyer to freeze the witnesses' stories before memories fade more than they already have; put pressure on the opponent by requiring them to go on the defensive; and question witnesses, particularly parties, when they are likely to be less prepared; discover gaps in the case while there is still time to rectify them; and develop evidence early in the litigation that may allow a summary judgment or a quick settlement of the case.

On the other hand, if the opponent's key witnesses are likely to disappear or otherwise become unavailable for trial, the deposition may only serve to preserve harmful testimony that will benefit the opponent. Early depositions may also force your opponent to be better prepared for trial than if depositions had been scheduled at a time when it was too late to correct any defects in the opponent's case that were revealed by the deposition. Finally, the deposition of the plaintiff's medical expert in a personal injury case often is delayed until as late in the litigation as possible to take advantage of any improvement in the plaintiff's injuries.

Rule 30(a)(2)(A) limits the number of depositions, absent a stipulation, court order, or local rule to the contrary, to ten per side. Caution dictates that counsel not use up all ten early in the discovery process in the event she discovers additional important witnesses later in the case. She should hold at least one or two in reserve.

## 4.5 DURATION AND INTERVALS

The obvious answer to the question of how long a deposition should last is "as long as necessary," within the seven hour, one day constraints of Rule 30(d)(2). Of course, the hour and day limits of Rule 30(d)(2) may be increased or decreased by stipulation or court order. Depositions have no magic length; some last for only a few minutes, while others, with the appropriate stipulation or court order, last days or weeks. But, depositions are an expensive form of discovery and the longer they last the greater the burden on the clients. When, however, the testimony is complex or presents surprises, it sometimes makes sense to slow down the process by stipulating or seeking a court order extending the deposition. When a deposition continues overnight or on to a later date, there is an additional opportunity to analyze what the witness has said. Counsel should be aware that, the longer the break, the more likely it is that the witness will also have time to reflect on the previous testimony and to correct any errors or misstatements.

The interval between depositions is often as much a function of the lawyers' and witnesses' schedules as it is of strategic planning. Where questioning counsel has the freedom to control the schedule, the time between depositions should be sufficiently long to permit review of the prior deposition testimony and to prepare for the next deposition, but no longer. The longer the break, the more complete and thorough the opponent's preparation of the next witness will likely be. Not only will the opposing counsel have briefed the witness about what has occurred in prior depositions, but the witness may even have read the prior deposition transcripts. Short intervals—even taking several depositions on the same day—are more likely to result in unrehearsed testimony and pressure the opposing attorney. Thus, there is no hard-and-fast answer—merely considerations to be evaluated.

In those jurisdictions without deposition time limits, a problem that occurs time and again is lack of agreement about the length of the deposition. Typically, the notice for the deposition will recite, "To appear at 9:30 a.m. on the 24th day of June, 2004, for the purpose of providing deposition testimony in the above-captioned matter." Then, at 4:30 or 5:00 p.m. on that day, after a long day of questioning, the deposing attorney says, "Well, let's recess for today, and we will continue tomorrow morning," and the defending attorney says, "No, you noticed this deposition for today, and it will be concluded today. We've had a full workday, so your time with this witness is over."

Unless the length of the deposition is subject to Rule 30(d)(2) or some other limitation, no rule clearly governs here and no magic language can avoid all disputes. Certainly, the deposing attorney should have been more explicit about duration at the outset, because it may result in an incomplete deposition. A simple recommendation may help: counsel, be specific in the notice—don't try to hide the ball. State in the notice: "To appear at 9:30 a.m. on the 24th day of June, 1994; this deposition may take more than one day," or "to continue from day to day." If the defending attorney then wants to try to obtain a protective order before the deposition because she believes this duration to be oppressive, burdensome, or harassing, she is on notice and has the opportunity to object.

## CHAPTER FIVE

## PREPARING TO TAKE THE DEPOSITION

*Speak without emphasizing your words. Leave other people to discover what it is that you have said; and as their minds are slow, you can make your escape in time.* — Schopenhauer

The attitude and approach taken during the deposition is governed by its intended purpose. If the primary purpose is to discover new information, then reviewing things already known, confirming preconceptions, or displaying knowledge of the facts is contrary to the purpose for taking the deposition and wastes valuable opportunities to gain knowledge of yet unknown harmful and helpful evidence.

### 5.1 YOUR FRAME OF MIND

Consider the following two approaches to questioning a witness in a product liability case:

Q. Mr. Mikionis, isn't it true that you should have used harder wood for the header in the garage that held the torsion spring assembly?

A. No.

Q. Don't you agree that the wood was just not hard enough, or dense enough, to hold that spring assembly, given the short screws that were used?

A. No.

Q. With the wallboard installed over the wood header, the screws just didn't have enough penetration into the wood to safely hold that spring assembly, did they?

A. I don't agree.

Q. Well, why don't you tell me why you don't agree?

A. The primary cause of the failure of this spring assembly system was the use by the installer of an impact wrench to drive the screws into the header, through the wallboard. That wrench drove the screws past snug and stripped the wood, so that there was really no way that they could be relied upon to hold anything, much less a powerful spring assembly like this one.

Compare that "cross-examination" style of questioning (ending with the frustrated "open" question) with this style:

Q. Mr. Mikionis, you have studied the causes of the failure of the garage door spring assembly, right?

A. Yes, that's right.

Q. Tell me, what caused the failure?

A. The primary cause of the failure of this spring assembly system was... .

Q. What other causes of the failure did you find?

A. A secondary cause was... .

In the first example, the attorney had the mind-set that he knew the causes and merely wanted the deponent to confirm that he was correct. In the second, while the attorney may have believed that he knew the causes, his goal was not to demonstrate what he knew, but to find out what the witness knew. Obviously, open questions are more appropriate for that purpose, but the distinction to be made here is not just in the form of the question, but also in the attitude of the deposing attorney evidenced by the tone and argumentative nature of the examination. Perhaps because of their superior (read "longer") education, many attorneys have come to believe they are omniscient: there are no causes, there are no effects, there are no logical arguments that have not already been discovered, considered, and categorized. That kind of thinking can be fatal on cross-examination; it is equally harmful in taking depositions.

In a deposition, every witness is an "expert" with a superior information base to the questioning lawyer—in some area, however small—because they actually know more about that area (their health, their job, their state of mind, etc.) than anyone else involved in the litigation. They may actually be "experts" under the rules of evidence, hired by the opposing side to provide opinion testimony based upon education and analysis and carbon dating; or they may be "experts" because they know more about their business affairs or pain and suffering or fraudulent intent than anyone else; or they may be "experts" because they know better than anyone else what they saw at the intersection when the cars collided. With that thought in mind, the mind-set should be to take advantage of that expertise. This mind-set is that of an interested student, with the witness being the teacher. This changes the attorney's relationship to an actual expert witness: from adversary, to be bested, to student, to be taught. The same change can occur with fact witnesses, where attorney interest and an open style of questioning encourages the witness to satisfy her desire to be understood and believed.

## 5.2 CREATING THE DEPOSITION OUTLINE

Most attorneys conduct depositions using an outline of topics from which to ask questions. The outline serves as a detailed guide to the areas of inquiry during the deposition and a method of checking before concluding the deposition that all important areas have been covered with nothing forgotten. The deposition outline is a necessary and important tool for conducting depositions, but preparing such an outline requires careful thought.

No perfect method or formula exists for creating the deposition outline. Most lawyers use more than one method and will change the combination of methods to fit the type of case for which they are creating the outline. The objective of all the techniques is to identify every useful topic for inquiry. The best way to accomplish this will vary depending on the party represented, which party controls most of the important information in the case, the size and complexity of the case, the role of the witness in the sequence of events, and myriad other considerations. Below we list and discuss some steps to follow in every case regardless of all other factors.

## 5.3 RESEARCHING THE LAW

To state the obvious, factual inquiry will always center on the facts needed to be proved or disproved at trial. And, in turn, those necessary facts are governed by the legal elements of each claim and defense. Therefore, the first step in preparing the deposition outline is to research every legal issue in the case thoroughly. Only then, with a fix on the law, can the facts needed to establish claims or defenses be anticipated.

Many lawyers will have done the necessary legal research as part of drafting the pleadings, but a surprising number wait until just before trial to determine what each party must prove. It is usually too late by that point to generate the evidence needed to establish a party's case or to refute the opponent's claims or defenses. Finding out what must be proved or disproved while there is still an opportunity to generate those facts through discovery is the much better approach.

Legal research will help to identify the nature and quality of the facts necessary to make a claim or defense. That research will also suggest areas of factual inquiry. If, in upholding a claim of a certain sort, the appellate courts look to certain kinds of facts, it will be important to determine whether those sorts of facts are available in the case at bar. Further, the research regarding a particular claim and defense will reveal additional claims that have been made with similar sorts of facts. For example, in a claim of professional malpractice, the claim can be based on tort or contract principles. When researching the tort law in the area, the cases will usually reveal that a contract claim is available as well. An additional claim having been identified, not only can pleadings be amended, but new areas of factual inquiry are suggested.

Discovery and preparation for trial require flexibility. It is inappropriate to lock down on one legal theory at an early point in the case (unless after careful research there is only one available). Keep as many options available as possible and identify all potentially applicable legal theories. Once discovery is completed, each legal theory can be reviewed and evaluated to determine whether it has any viability. Abandoning a theory late in the case is not a problem, but adding theories can be difficult. The lesson is to keep an open mind and remain flexible by pursuing all potential legal theories until it is clear that one or more have no merit.

## 5.4 IDENTIFYING ALL AVAILABLE FACTS

Once all potentially applicable legal theories have been identified, the next step is to take inventory of all the facts currently available. Sources include clients and friendly witnesses, documentary and other real evidence, expert witnesses, information in government records, interrogatory answers, and others, depending on the particular facts of the case. Information gathering usually continues up to the day of trial, but the ideal is to gather as much information before conducting discovery as is possible. This means carefully interviewing the client, talking with every witness who is willing to do so, visiting the scene of the accident, consulting with experts, reviewing every relevant document, finding out as much as possible about the opposing party and the witnesses who will be supporting the opposition's case, and so on.

By learning as much as possible before discovery depositions, the ability to formulate fruitful lines of questions or even to challenge any lies or discrepancies in the witness's answers is enhanced. But, more importantly, information that suggests new legal or factual theories or leads to explore will be available while the witness is still available for pretrial sworn testimony. Nearly every lawyer has had the unpleasant experience of having their own client reveal some key fact on the eve of trial that changes the entire strategy of the case. If only a particular fact had been known earlier in the case, discovery could have been conducted regarding related facts and it would have been possible to develop new evidence supporting or refuting the particular fact. Careful advance factual investigation will help reduce these situations to a minimum.

While it is impossible to construct an exhaustive list of all the sources and types of information that should be checked before proceeding with a deposition, it is possible to name some of the more important of them:

**Your Client**—Clients usually know the most about their own cases. After all, what happened to or was done by the client is the reason for the lawsuit. Clients know how contracts were negotiated, how accidents occurred, or whatever else is the basis for the action. They often know who will be the best witnesses for their side and the witnesses who likely will be testifying for the other side. In many, if not most, cases the client will be your most important source of information.

**The Deponent Witness**—It makes sense to find out everything possible about the witnesses being deposed. What is their involvement in the case, what are they likely to know, what is their relationship to the parties and other witnesses, what are their personalities, and so forth. "Googling" or doing an Internet search of the witness will sometimes produce useful information, particularly if the witness is of some prominence. Where the witness has testified or given deposition testimony in previous actions, the prior testimony should be reviewed and the attorneys in those cases should be asked about what information or insights they have regarding the witness. If the witness has written any articles or books, these should be read. If a witness has given speeches that relate to the subject of the action, something that sometimes happens with company executives in securities litigation, these also should be reviewed. There are also organizations, such as American Trial Lawyers Association, that collect information about witnesses in recurring types of litigation. If the witness is one of the opponent's experts, there are many additional sources that should be consulted and that will be discussed in Chapter Nineteen, Expert Depositions.

**Experts**—When the lawsuit involves matters requiring expert testimony, consulting experts can help counsel develop an understanding of the technical aspects of the case, and can identify the facts that are necessary to be developed for expert opinions.

**Documents**—It is essential that all documents are reviewed and their importance to the case understood, particularly those documents that relate to the witnesses being deposed. The categories of documents that relate to the witness include those written, received, or read by the witness; documents the witness might be aware of; documents referring to the witness or the witness's actions; as well as any documents that refer in some way to topics about which the witness will be asked to give evidence. Documents provided by your client are a good starting place. In addition, relevant documents are often times available from friendly witnesses. And of course, documents will have been provided by the opponent in Rule 26 mandatory disclosures, as well as in response to Rule 33 interrogatories and formal document production requests pursuant to Rule 34. In addition, a subpoena *duces tecum* can be utilized to require witnesses to bring documents with them to the deposition.

**Friendly Witnesses**—Every unrepresented witness who is willing to talk informally about the case should be interviewed. Even witnesses expected to be hostile should be contacted to confirm those expectations. Potentially hostile witnesses may in fact consent to an interview, the result of which might be one less deposition, or at least a deposition with a sharper focus.

**Pleadings**—The pleadings in the case are always a potential source of facts or at least inquiry regarding facts that support allegations made in them. Every claim and/or defense must, of course, be explored factually with each witness who has potential information that supports those pleadings.

**Previous Discovery or Testimony**—What the opposing party has said in response to interrogatories or what witnesses have said in previous depositions as well as other discovery in the case should be reviewed. There may be pleadings or testimony in related litigation, even in related criminal proceedings, that may be a source of information.

**Visit the Scene**—In a personal injury case, a visit to the scene of the accident provides a better understanding of a witness's descriptions and explanations, and may suggest the use of some sort of il-lustrative aid during the taking of deposition testimony. In a products liability case, for example, a visit to the factory where the product in question was manufactured can be helpful. It makes sense to become personally familiar with the places relevant to the case and the witness who will be deposed.

## 5.5 CONSTRUCTING YOUR THEORY OF THE CASE

After completing the legal and factual research, the next step is to construct potential case theories. Case theory operates on three levels: legal, factual, and persuasive. The legal theory is defined simply as a reason in the law why a verdict in favor of a party will be upheld as le-gally sufficient on appeal. The factual theory is an explanation of what really happened in the case and why. Persuasive theory, sometimes called a theme, provides an organizational construct of the case that comes from a common and well-known view of why things happen. Persuasive theory is rooted in literature, lessons from parents. teachers or religious leaders, or even from popular culture.

The theory of the case, then, is the application of the law to the facts of the case persuasively organized so as to justify a verdict in your party's favor. While simple to define, it is much more difficult to create.

We have already discussed the construction of legal theory. From that legal theory obvious areas of inquiry are demanded and suggest-ed. With that in hand, the construction of case theory moves next to a factual theory of what happened and why. A successful factual theory explains as many of the facts as possible in a way favorable to your cli-ent; in other words, it is a story of what occurred. A successful factual theory need not contain every available fact, but focuses on those facts which are of significance to the legal theory being advanced. There are many ways to assist in constructing a potential factual theory. It is important, however, to keep in mind that at the deposition stage of liti-gation there should be multiple factual theories of the case, or alterna-tive ways of explaining the facts that result in a favorable outcome. The purpose of the depositions in a case is to decide which of the available theories is most plausible and most likely to be persuasive to a jury or any other fact finder.

There are many ways to construct a factual theory. It begins, of course, with the view of the facts obtained from clients, witness in-terviews, and available other discovery. The goal of a case theory is to

*Timelines are quite helpful.*

develop an effective and persuasive story of the case. We will speak more about storytelling later, but the goal for deposition planning is to develop alternate story lines that explain what happened and why in the facts running up to the lawsuit. A good starting place in developing alternate story lines in almost any case is a time line.

### 5.5.1 Time lines.

By placing the events that underlie a lawsuit, including facts from witnesses and facts from documents or other exhibits, on a time line, explanations of what really happened and why may be suggested. The sequence of events oftentimes explains motives and the causes and effects of actions. Just as important, a time line can identify gaps in the evidence that need to be filled in to create an effective case theory. In addition, incongruities will be suggested. A sequence of events as obtained from clients and witnesses, when presented graphically, may not make sense. That is, the story as told by one witness may be inconsistent with other witnesses and/or with other evidence such as documents, photographs of a scene, or explanations provided by a consulting expert witness. The time line may also suggest necessary areas of inquiry of deponent witnesses that fill in the gaps in the evidence.

### 5.5.2 Relationship charts.

A relationship chart is a visual representation of the interactions and potential interactions among the parties, other important actors in the case, and institutions. It is a particularly helpful device in cases where the case theory seeks to explain the motives of the parties for important actions, or inactions. The creation of the chart begins by identifying all the parties and ancillary actors in the case. When in doubt, include a witness or actor in the chart. An actor with an apparently minor role may turn out, because of his or her relationship with a party or institution, to possess case-turning information. Once the actors and institutions are listed, their relationship to each other should be identified by a line, connecting one to the other. Each line is then labeled with significant interactive facts. The completed chart can suggest possible explanations of what happened, and more importantly why, which is the essence of factual theory. From that insight other relationships can be identified and areas of inquiry are suggested for deposition practice.

### 5.5.3 Brainstorming.

Brainstorming is a process of encouraging people to engage in un-restricted thinking about the facts involved in a particular event. This method works best in a group, with one person acting as a leader. An effective brainstorming session has the following rules:

1. there are no bad ideas;
2. self-censoring is inappropriate;
3. do not critique others' ideas;
4. do not comment on others' ideas;
5. the rules of evidence are irrelevant;
6. only facts and not conclusions can be stated;
7. all facts must be recorded; and
8. the session is time-limited.

Using these rules, the leader asks the group to state the good facts and the bad facts that are known in the case. Once they have been listed, the group votes on the three-to-five best and worst facts. Once the voting is over, a critical look at the best and worst facts will suggest appropriate story lines that underlie factual theories for and against each party. The goal, then, of deposition practice will be to confirm the good facts of the case (those supporting favorable story lines) and discredit and/or explain away the bad facts (those supporting unfavor-able story lines), with the end goal being a unified explanation of what really happened and why.

### 5.5.4 Focus groups.

In modern litigation the focus group is a fact of life. Although most commonly used when the litigation of a case is complete and the matter is being readied for disposition by trial and otherwise, pre-deposition focus groups are becoming much more common. This is so partly because the cost of these proceedings when performed by professionals is much more reasonable than as short as five years ago. In addition, lawyers can learn to conduct focus groups themselves, with the only cost being the compensation of the member of the focus group. Although a full description of focus group techniques is beyond the scope of this book, the various approaches have some common goals:

1. identify areas of factual inquiry;

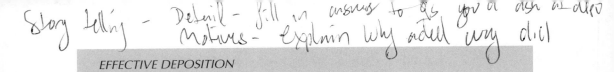

2. alert the lawyers to facts a jury likely will consider as important;

3. identify facts that jurors will expect to exist in light of other facts in the case;

4. identify witnesses a jury would like to hear from; and

5. identify psychological hot issues.

From the recorded results of focus groups, potential story lines are developed, not only those based in the facts as known at the time of the session, but those that can be developed through further discovery.

Finally, with regard to the devices for developing case theories for deposition practice, it should be noted that none of these devices is exclusive of the other, and in a proper case all of the devices can be utilized in order to develop the alternate story lines that will support the factual theory.

The story lines should comprehend all of the characteristics of good storytelling.[1] A good story must:

1. Account for or explain all of the known or undeniable facts. Common sense tells us that a story which contradicts the known facts will be unbelievable to a judge or jury. We will not accept an explanation premised on the world being flat; similarly, no jury will accept a story which conflicts with other facts they accept as being true.

2. Be supported by the details. Judges and juries are persuaded not only by the major facts in the case, but also by all of the supporting details. For instance, the credibility of a witness is enhanced if the witness can recount not just that a key meeting was held, but also where it was held, who was there, when it occurred, what words were used, and so forth. Detail, of course, is not necessary regarding every fact, as that would be overwhelming and perhaps obscure the important facts; detail on important and contested key facts, however, enhances the believability of the story.

3. Explain why people acted in the way they did. Why was the defendant driving too fast just before the accident? Why didn't the plaintiff order substitute parts as soon as it learned the defendant was not going to deliver as promised? Why would the defendants want to fix prices?

DETAIL

MOTIVE

---

1. Steven Lubet, *Modern Trial Advocacy*, Chapter One (NITA 2004).

A good story must have the actors behaving consistently with motivations that a fact finder can understand or else provide a good explanation for why they did not behave in that way.

4. Be consistent with common sense and be plausible. A story may be logical and even true, but if it does not square with the way we believe the world operates, our reaction will be one of skepticism. A story must make sense if it is to be believable.

5. Appeal to our sense of justice and fairness. A good factual theory will not only satisfy the applicable legal theory and therefore entitle you to the verdict you are asking for, but it should also make the listener want you to win, regardless of the law, because it is the fair and just outcome.

The factual theories of the case change during the course of the litigation as new facts—both helpful and harmful—come to light. Some theories are discarded as unsupported by the facts, and other theories can take their place. The factual theory is not a static product created at the beginning of the case and remaining unchanged until trial. In fact, as trial approaches the final factual theory with supporting story lines will be continually revised in response to new information to make it as persuasive as possible.

"Revision" here does not mean that the witnesses are encouraged to change their testimony; it means that different facts are emphasized or combined or downplayed, spending more or less time and more or fewer questions on them. For instance, an effective story requires that it be told by credible witnesses, be supported by admissible and persuasive evidence, and be organized in a logical and understandable manner. During the discovery stage information gathered and witnesses deposed should be evaluated in light of these concerns. As to a witness's answer in a deposition, the following inquiries are appropriate: "Will this evidence be admissible; will this person make a good witness; is this answer consistent with the documents?"

Since this is the discovery stage, all of the facts are obviously not yet known. Therefore, it will be necessary not only to continually revise the story as new facts come to light, but it may also be necessary to have several different stories, each incorporating different possible event scenarios. Factual theories will be discarded, expanded, and refined. Because different factual scenarios may have different legal consequences, legal theory must also be re-examined in light of the factual changes. By the time of trial only one story and one main legal theory should remain—the one that will be presented to the judge, jury, or other fact finder. However, do not be too hasty in getting to that point. Keep an open mind about what happened, and explore all possible scenarios before discarding any of them.

An important warning: the factual theory is not a product of a lawyer's imagination, but must be a truthful and honest presentation of the available evidence. Obviously, lawyers must never manufacture evidence nor urge perjurious facts. Putting aside criminal charges and ethical violations, a theory unsupported by actual facts is destined to fail. What we are talking about in constructing a factual theory is the amalgamation of the facts into a persuasive whole that presents a logical and compelling story of what really happened and why.

## 5.6 IDENTIFYING THE OPPONENT'S FACTUAL AND LEGAL THEORIES

A trial is not just about proving a party's claim or defense, but also attacking or answering the opponent's position. However, you cannot attack something unless you know what it is. Much of the opponent's theory can be gleaned from what was said in settlement negotiations with opposing counsel, the opponent's pleadings, and what has been said by opposing parties and witnesses pre-litigation. The assessment of the opponent's theory will become sharper as the case progresses, particularly when considering the questions asked by opposing counsel in depositions, the information sought through interrogatories, and the documents and other discovery that is requested. The same attention and diligence to researching the opposing party's possible legal and factual theories should be given as has been described regarding your client's positions. Once an understanding of potential legal theories, pro and con, is developed, questions for each deposition must be developed.

## 5.7 GENERATING QUESTIONS

Topics can be generated each for deposition outline in a number of ways. As previously mentioned, most good attorneys do not rely on one particular method for thinking of topics, but will use a combination of approaches. The following is a discussion of some of those approaches.

## 5.7.1 Brainstorming.

Of all of the methods of preparing for a deposition, brainstorming, as described above regarding developing potential case theories, is the best way to identify areas where you need new information. In the large case, assemble the whole litigation team for a day; in the small case, impose on a partner for an hour of her time. If no partner or other lawyer is available, consider using a secretary or spouse. In desperation, brainstorm with yourself. In any event, establish the same ground rules described above, highlighting that there will be no judgmental responses to suggestions for questions, and that no question is too basic or too stupid to suggest.

After describing the case briefly, begin with a three-minute description of the witness or witnesses and their roles in the case. Then open the floor to questions: what do people want to know from this witness that will help them understand the entire case better? Someone in the room, or several someones, should be responsible for taking down all of the questions proposed, without editorializing or omitting.

A second aspect of brainstorming is to bring a healthy curiosity to the process. If there was a telephone conversation, what are we curious about concerning that conversation? Perhaps when it was held, the parties to the conversation, what was said, whether records were made, and so on. Or for an automobile accident, where were each of the drivers going, when did they see each other, how fast were they going, and so forth. Effective brainstorming depends on being curious about the world and particularly about what happened in the case being considered.

The key to successful brainstorming is to get everyone involved and talking. A silly question may provoke an insightful one; an irrelevant remark may lead people to recognize that the bounds of relevance for that witness should be redefined. Anyone who has participated in a brainstorming session in any context has seen the impressive synergies that arise as several minds come at a problem or topic from different perspectives.

If the process hits a slow spot, try to revive the energy by raising a new topic and posing particular questions: "Okay, let's try this: we want to show that the manufacturer knew the product was unsafe in cold weather. How do we show that state of mind?" A white board, on which the main topics are displayed as they arise, helps to recall those topics. Some members of the group will dwell on particular topics while the group moves on, and often the first group will interrupt later with a series of useful questions. Any structure that promotes the free flow of ideas is useful. Books are available on brainstorming, and the procedures are completely applicable to the process of deriving deposition questions (as well as on choosing counts to include in a complaint, or ways to attack an expert on cross-examination, or the choice of graphics for trial).

### 5.7.2 Relating the factual theory to the legal theory.

A good factual theory is not enough if it does not also establish the elements of a legal claim or defense. A factual theory is not constructed for entertainment value, but to win a case. Therefore, to be successful, the facts of the story must make out a claim or defense. This process is appropriate when preparing the deposition outline.

Once the legal and factual theories are developed to the extent possible, the next step is to identify those facts that are missing from the factual theory. In developing the story, consider the following basic questions as a way to improve the deposition outline.

- What happened?
- Who did what?
- Who said what?
- How did it happen?
- Where did it happen?
- Who was involved?
- Who witnessed it?
- Why did it happen?
- What documents would record what happened?
- Who normally would be told about it happening?
- Who can verify it happening?
- What documents can verify it happening?
- What inferences or conclusions can you draw from it happening?
- What facts are missing from the story?
- What are the different ways this story could have occurred? What are all the possible plot variations that could occur in this story?
- If a particular fact is true, what other facts must also be true? If a particular fact is true, what would a normal or reasonable person have done in this situation?

ash abt key facts, but also correlative facts

- If this fact is true, what results or consequences should have been noticed?
- What evidence do you need to prove the elements of the claim? What do you need to refute the opponent's story?

To illustrate how you can use just one of these techniques to generate topics for the deposition outline, assume a breach of contract case. The plaintiff claims that the defendant's sales manager assured the plaintiff's president during a telephone conversation that the plaintiff would replace a missing shipment of expensive computer parts without cost even though there was no legal obligation on the part of the defendant to do so. The plaintiff is now suing because the plaintiff claims the defendant is refusing to live up to its promise. In preparing for the plaintiff president's deposition, the defendant's attorney might want to think about what else would likely have happened if the defendant had promised to replace the parts. Would the president have told anyone about this good news; would a phone log record have been prepared; would the plaintiff's purchasing or parts departments have been notified of the replacement parts; would the plaintiff have sent a confirming letter of the telephone conversation, and so forth. All of these may be useful areas on which to question the witness and should be included in the deposition outline.

One way for you to keep track of what facts are available and what facts you need is to make a proof chart. Such a chart is nothing more than a large piece of paper with the elements of the claims and defenses listed along one side. In its simplest form, the proof chart has only four columns across the top: Supporting Facts, Supporting Facts to Be Discovered, Opposing Facts, and Opposing Facts to Be Discovered. By thinking carefully about the facts already known and what additional facts are needed to prove or disprove each element, the four columns are filled in. The chart is updated as new information is received. Facts contained in the To Be Discovered columns are moved to the Facts columns as discovery progresses. A sample proof chart for the above example follows:

|  | Supporting Facts | Supporting Facts to Be Discovered | Opposing Facts | Opposing Facts to Be Discovered |
|---|---|---|---|---|
| Representation |  |  |  |  |
| Reliance in Good Faith |  |  |  |  |
| Action Based on Representation |  |  |  |  |

The only magical thing about the chart is that it helps to focus on what information is needed to prove the case or disprove the opponent's case. The chart helps organize this thinking and also is a method of recording the ideas generated.

By having columns for the opponent's case, the proof chart also requires consideration and evaluation of what the opposing party will be proving and what evidence is needed to meet that proof. The information in the columns labeled Supporting Facts to Be Discovered and Opposing Facts to Be Discovered serves as the basis for the deposition outline. The chart (which normally will have many more rows and columns) will typically be kept on a computer to ease the movement of facts from column to column and the addition or deletion of facts based on the discovery process. This chart was formerly kept on a large piece of butcher paper taped to the wall where it was available for ready reference. Even the authors of this book, dinosaurs all, have evolved to the electronic form and the ease and convenience it presents. In reality, however, the form does not matter; the concentrated thinking about the evolution of the facts as they relate to proof requirements does.

### 5.7.3 Reviewing the pleadings.

If the deponent is a party, or closely identified with a party, the party's pleadings may raise numerous questions. The questions that ask, "What is your evidence for the allegation in Complaint Paragraph 4?" are not usually profitable. The answers often result in quibbling about what constitutes evidence, or whether this deposition is the appropriate time for a disclosure of exhibits, and so on and so forth.

A better question is to ask, "Do you believe that this allegation or response about control of the other car is accurate?" (or, even better, "Do you believe that the driver of the other car was not paying sufficient attention to controlling his car?"), and then to ask, "Why?" Therefore, when you prepare to take a deposition, review the pleadings, highlight or clip those portions that might provoke discussion, and incorporate them into the deposition outline.

### 5.7.4 Documents.

Reviewing the documents in the case will usually suggest topics for inclusion in the deposition outline. Just as important, the outline should note the need to explore of the content of the documents themselves during witness examination. Questioning techniques regarding documents will be discussed in Chapter Nine, but when constructing the deposition outline, the information sought regarding those documents should be considered and included.

Do not, however, view the use of the documents at the deposition as a goal in and of itself. Documents generate questions: what do phrases or discussions in the documents mean, why was the document written, who wrote the document, what happened to a document, who has seen a document, or what effect did a document have on events. Nothing is gained by asking, "Doesn't this document say that the loan was discussed at the meeting?" because the authenticated document establishes its own content as well as the redundant deposition testimony would.

Chapter Nine, Using Documents, discusses how some attorneys pile up the "relevant" documents at the start of the deposition and end the deposition when they have shown each document to the witness and authenticated it in some way. Because authentication can be accomplished in many other, much less expensive ways (for example, by asking in the request for production for "documents prepared in the normal course of business which relate to...," thereby obtaining not only the documents but an admission that they are authentic business documents of the company) this practice wastes deposition time. In preparing to take a deposition, focus should be on themes, theories, and occurrences, regardless of whether they are recorded in some document. The documents should be useful; they should not be controlling.

### 5.7.5 Reviewing depositions.

*[handwritten: Don't waste depos on authentication]*

Prior depositions in a case are also sources for preparation. First, reviewing the depositions of witnesses who have already been deposed may help generate topics for the deposition outline. Not only will a witness's answers suggest questions, but the types of questions asked by your opponent will also suggest areas for further exploration. Next, your opponent's questions will strongly suggest the legal and factual theories being pursued, providing insight and ideas on how to counter those theories. Finally, spending some time periodically reviewing your own deposition transcripts improves questioning in remaining depositions in that case and in depositions in other cases.

*[handwritten: Prior Depos (ugh, long.)]*

### 5.7.6 Working with the client and the expert.

Obviously, the client is one of the best sources of information in preparing any portion of a lawsuit, and the deposition of opposing witnesses is no exception. The client has a recollection of the relevant incidents which she obtained by living through the episode. And although that recollection can be aided or refreshed by the use of documents, it exists independent of documents. In advance of all of the depositions, therefore, a meeting with the client, perhaps with the main responsive pleading in hand, is mandatory to discuss the other side's position and the facts which would have to be true to support that position. If the other side claims contributory negligence as a defense, assume, with the client, that the claim is made in good faith. What then must the opposition believe happened? Are there other facts that they must believe? Are there witnesses that have not been considered? Can the client's memory of the episode be faulty, by omitting incidents or conversations, or by accidentally mis-remembering the sequence of events? Having such a conversation with the client enables pursuit of exactly those types of questions with the deponent. Will the opposition present additional witnesses at trial? Will they claim that the screws went in first, before the bracket was attached, instead of the other way around? Will they try to show that the client reviewed the competitor's pricing sheet before submitting her own bid, and not after?

In other words, enough time should be spent with the client to understand the potential weaknesses in the case and possible holes in the client's version of the facts. Then you can explore the opposition's reliance on those possible weaknesses at the deposition. Using questions such as, "Exactly what was the sequence of events leading to the injury?" can help to identify differences between the positions of the two sides and can be followed up with additional questions, such as, "What is the significance of the screws being put in after the bracket is attached?" or "If you assume that the board did not receive the appraisal until after it approved the loan, how does that change your conclusion on the adequacy of underwriting for this loan?"

Just as the client can help identify areas for discussion at the deposition, so can the expert. Contrary to common practice, do not use the experts only to help prepare for the opposing expert's deposition; they can be used to help identify questions about facts for the non-expert depositions as well. After all, expert opinions are only as good as the facts that underlie them. Indeed, the success or credibility of your expert's testimony at trial probably depends much more upon the ability to deal with contrary factual arguments than upon the ability to refute contrary theories. If the expert's testimony does not make sense to the jury, they have little choice but to reject the expert's opinions and conclusions. If it is instead a contest between the theories proposed by two experts, the jury is likely to choose that expert whose theory deals with all of the facts more logically. Imagine the fun to be had by having the opposing expert admit on cross-examination that she has accepted the truth of the factual statements made by her client, and then showing on cross-examination of the client that some of those facts were wrong.

How then should the expert be utilized in preparation for depositions of expert and lay witnesses alike? The expert must be asked to identify all of the factual assumptions made; to identify the facts which are needed to support her conclusions; and to identify all of the facts which, if proven, would weaken these conclusions. For example, in an antitrust case challenging a merger between two alleged competitors, the question of relevant market definition will almost always come up. One expert may assume that consumers will be sensitive to a price change of five percent in one product and switch to another, tending to indicate that the two products are in the same market. Therefore, at the deposition of the sales manager for the first product, questions must be asked about the consumer's buying habits and price sensitivity. By these answers, not only is the sales manager's information discovered, but it is also discovered whether the opposing expert has ready access to facts which are favorable to that side. Thus, preparing with the expert makes possible a more useful deposition of the fact witnesses.

## 5.8 ORGANIZING THE DEPOSITION OUTLINE

The deposition outline must obviously be organized in a logical way so that topics flow naturally from one to the other. As discussed in § 8.4, with the exception of a few planned traps, little is gained from a hopscotch approach to questioning witnesses. A systematic progression through materials and events, usually chronologically, but also by subject matter, allows maintenance of control of the material and of the witness.

Triple spacing the outline (whether in paper or electronic format) allows ease in moving back to the outline from an area of inquiry. The extra space also allows the addition of topics at the last moment as new ideas develop.

## 5.9 USING THE OUTLINE AT THE DEPOSITION

The outline should not be slavishly followed during the deposition. Any good deposition attorney listens carefully to the answers the witness provides and follows where those answers lead. And that is so even if the witness's answers suggest new topics not previously considered and, therefore, not on the outline.

Most lawyers follow the outline as long as doing so generates needed information. But when a witness's answer suggests a new topic or because a topic comes as an epiphany, mark the outline and either explore the new topic immediately or merely add the topic to a list of future topics to be explored. At other times topics will be abandoned if the witness's answers show there is nothing to gain by exploring certain areas. Most attorneys also check off topics on the outline as they complete the questioning on that topic. Then, before concluding the deposition, they take a few moments to review the outline to make sure they have left no topics uncovered.

Notice that we suggest that you outline topics, not write out questions. If the outline is a list of questions, it will not be long before the witness's answers and the outline questions part company. Using an outline of topics allows the shaping of questions that react to the witness's answers. Using written questions does not permit this flexibility. In addition, an outline that consists of a list of questions will often restrict the topics to be explored. The rigidity of the question-by-question format, and the need for the "right words" as reflected by such an outline, discourages exploration of nuances that lead to understanding the true meaning of the facts that a witness professes to know.

There are exceptions to the rule about not writing out deposition questions. Sometimes the evidentiary value of a question will depend on a particular wording of the question. For example, in putting a hypothetical to an expert witness, it may be necessary to be very precise with the assumptions being made. In this situation, it is much better to write out the question in advance rather than trusting in the power to compose the question extemporaneously during the deposition.

Another situation where questions are helpful is in laying the foundation for an exhibit. Most evidentiary foundations are more successful when particular "magic" words such as "fair and accurate" are used. Rather than run the risk of forgetting to use these magic words, it is better to write them out in advance. In addition, in some cases particular words have unique legal and factual significance. In those cases, the use of phrases such as "risk of loss" in a contracts case, or "substantial cause" in a torts case, in carefully framed questions can provide the predicate for case-dispositive motion practice or requests for admission. Another typical time when written questions may be helpful is when the purpose of the deposition is not discovery but obtaining admissions. There may be other situations where writing out the questions is better than relying on an outline, but as a general rule an outline is the better approach.

## 5.10 CHECKLIST FOR PREPARING FOR THE DEPOSITION

1. Review Federal Rules of Civil Procedure 26, 28, 29, 30, 32, and applicable local rules.

2. Contact all parties to see if agreement can be reached on the time and place of the deposition. *See* § 1.5.

3. If documents are needed in advance of the deposition, prepare and serve a request to produce if the documents are in possession of a party or a subpoena *duces tecum* if the documents are in the possession of a non-party. The request to produce may be served by first-class mail, but a subpoena *duces tecum* must be personally served. *See* § 1.11.

4. Consider and, if necessary, bring a motion for protective orders such as one limiting who may be present at the deposition. *See* Chapter 12.

5. Determine how the deposition is to be recorded— stenographically, videotaping, or sound recording—and provide the proper notice. *See* § 1.13.2.

6. Reserve a room and arrange for a court reporter for the scheduled date.

7. With sufficient time before the scheduled date of the deposition (usually ten days or more, but check local rules) prepare and serve a notice of deposition on all parties, usually by first-class mail or facsimile. The notice of deposition shall state the method of recording to be used at the deposition. If a subpoena *duces tecum* is to be served on the witness, the notice of deposition must include or have attached to it a list of the materials in the subpoena *duces tecum* that are to be produced at the deposition. Service of the notice of deposition is all that is necessary to compel the attendance at the deposition of a party or an officer, managing agent, or director of a party. *See* §§ 1.6, 1.10.1.

8.    If the deposition is of someone other than a party or an officer, managing agent, or director of a party, issue a subpoena (a blank subpoena is obtainable from the clerk of the court of the district in which the deposition will be taken, or an attorney may sign and issue the subpoena if she is a member of the bar of the district where the appearance is compelled or of the district where the action is pending) and arrange for personal service of it on the witness. The service of the subpoena must be accompanied by a tender of the witness fee and mileage allowance. *See* § 1.10.2.

9.    If documents are required for the deposition and they have not been produced in advance, attempt to have the documents voluntarily brought to the deposition. If there is no agreement, *see* number 3, above, about using compulsory process.

10.    Consider the stipulations that will be sought as a preliminary matter at the deposition and the most advantageous response that can be made. *See* §§ 1.13.4, 6.1.

## 5.11 A FINAL WORD ABOUT PREPARATION

No one is ever prepared for every question or every topic at a deposition: not the witness, not the witness's counsel, and certainly not the deposing attorney. If the progress and twists and turns could be forecast accurately, the amount of actual "discovery" would decline markedly. Therefore, instead of expending energy on anxiety about inadequate preparation, listen closely to the witness, follow up on interesting or incomplete answers, and try to understand the witness's answers and to uncover subjects the witness wants to avoid.

No one has ever taken a perfect deposition. Fortunately, justice does not depend upon perfection from lawyers or witnesses. From a full day of deposition testimony, perhaps twenty answers will have been worth extracting for possible use at trial; of those twenty, perhaps five will be used; and experience shows those five are most likely to have come in response to questions that were reactions to information provided by the witness that was unanticipated in the deposition outline.

The lesson? To prepare, get ready to listen to the answers and to follow up on those answers until what the witness is saying and why she is saying it are clear in the record. The achievement of that understanding represents one of the greatest services a lawyer can provide in litigation.

# CHAPTER SIX

# BEGINNING THE DEPOSITION

*A few strong instincts and a few plain rules*—Wordsworth

Some decisions regarding formalities and approach apply to every deposition, regardless of the issues in the case, the personality of the witnesses, or the substance of the information to be discovered. After thinking through these matters, an appropriate uniform approach for most, if not all, depositions conducted can be reached. Let's review these common areas and evaluate the options.

## 6.1 USUAL STIPULATIONS

Under the Federal Rules of Civil Procedure, lawyers may stipulate to changes in literally all of the rules governing depositions absent a contrary court order. Probably intoxicated with this power, it seems that at least seven out of ten depositions begin with one attorney, usually the deposing attorney, asking, "Usual stipulations, counsel?" as though these usual stipulations will change the procedures under the rules. In two of ten depositions it is the reporter who asks, "Usual stipulations, counsel?" In the remaining one, no mention of stipulations is made at all. In fact, the seven attorneys and the two reporters are behaving nonsensically because there are no "usual stipulations." There may be stipulations that have been found especially useful by some attorney, or those more commonly used than others in some county or courthouse, but there are no stipulations that are in such widely accepted use that they could meaningfully be called "usual."[1]

When asked to join in the "usual stipulations" at the start of a deposition, the best response is, "We can stipulate that this deposition is being taken pursuant to the Federal (or state) Rules of Civil Procedure.

---

1. In a few jurisdictions the term "usual stipulation" refers to a specific set of stipulations that the court reporter prepares and shows to the parties at the beginning of the deposition. These jurisdictions are a distinct minority.

Beyond that, what stipulations do you want to propose?" Quite often, the attorney proposing the "usual stipulations" will have only a vague idea of what she really wanted—something about reading and signing, and something about documents, and, oh yes, something about objections not being waived. In fact, each of these subjects is important and should be considered separately and carefully. Just as the "blue-plate special" is not the best order in a gourmet restaurant, a vaguely understood attempt at some general and usual stipulations is no way to select the rules under which a deposition will be conducted.[2]

In fact, most depositions will proceed quite smoothly without any stipulations being adopted in advance. Oftentimes it is best to handle matters that require stipulation as they arise, so their specifics are understood in context. For example:

> Q. Counsel, will you stipulate that this xerographic copy of the last will and testament can be substituted for the original, which we'll put back in the safe in our office?

> A. Yes, I have no problem with that.[3]

The most common types of deposition stipulations and the ones with the best claim to being "usual" are: "All objections except as to the form of the question are reserved until there is an attempt to introduce the deposition at some later proceeding," or "Objections as to matters other than form [or 'form and foundation'] are preserved," or "Objections to matters other than form are reserved, right, counsel?" Absent a stipulation to the contrary, in the federal system objections to the competence of witnesses and the competence, relevance, or materiality of testimony are preserved without the necessity of making an objection unless the objection can be obviated, removed, or cured if promptly presented. See FRCP 32(b) and 32(d) (3) (A) and (B). The parallel provisions of most states' rules of procedure will automatically apply unless their application is affirmatively stipulated away.

Another common stipulation that also vies for the title of "usual" is one waiving the reading, signing, and notice of filing of the deposition. FRCP Rule 30(e) makes superfluous such a stipulation regarding reading and signing, as the default position in the rule is that the

---

2. Imagine the consternation of the attorney who, having stipulated that the deposition could be taken before any of the five persons on a list provided by opposing counsel, without first investigating who those people were, discovered that she had agreed that it could be taken before the opposing attorney's secretary-stenographer. A subsequent motion to suppress the deposition was denied. *Laverett v. Continental Briar Pipe Co.* 25 F. Supp. 790 (E.D.N.Y. 1939).
3. This stipulation is consistent with Fed.R.Civ.P. 30(f)(1)(A) and with Fed.R.Evid. 1002.

reading and signing of the deposition is waived. It is for counsel, either taking or defending the deposition, to request that the witness read and sign the deposition, and even then, the witness must sign only when she makes changes to the deposition. The party taking the deposition, however, must still give notice of its filing to all other parties.

For depositions taken under a pre-1993 version of the Federal Rules of Civil Procedure, such as exists in many states, a stipulation to the waiver of reading and signing the deposition must be made, as the default position in those rules was a requirement of reading and signing. In either circumstance, it is usually tactically advisable for both deposing and defending counsel to want to have the deposition read and signed. For deposing counsel, if one of the purposes of taking the deposition is to create a source for inconsistent statement impeachment at trial, a signed statement, with or without corrections, has more persuasive force than a deposition where the deponent can claim for the first time at trial that the deposition transcript is inaccurate. An impeaching lawyer at trial with a read and signed deposition can highlight for the jury that the witness read and signed the deposition if the witness tries at trial to disavow the answers. ("Isn't it true that you also read your deposition after it was completed? And isn't it also true that you then signed the deposition on the last page? And this is your signature right here on the last page?") The only time it might make sense to waive reading and signing is when the witness will change a key answer if given the opportunity to review it in the less heated atmosphere following the deposition. Of course, there is no way to know this situation will occur when the decisions regarding reading and signing are normally made at the onset of the deposition. Further, if a witness does give an answer that needs to be corrected or explained, the defending lawyer can either ask clarifying questions at the time of the deposition, or insist that the witness have the opportunity to read and sign.

For defending counsel signing provides little benefit unless the deponent is a non-party whose potential trial testimony needs to be controlled. Reading, on the other hand, is very important. Witnesses do make mistakes and misspeak in the deposition. Usually attentive counsel will catch and correct these errors at the deposition, but not always. Reading over the deposition in the more relaxed atmosphere following the deposition allows counsel and the witness to correct these mistakes, which may be both as to form and substance of the deposition testimony. Court reporters also make mistakes, perhaps mishearing a question or an answer, Reading the deposition allows for correction of transcription errors. Correcting an answer does not cause the original answer to disappear; both the original and changed testimony may be *when both expert & fact witness*

admissible at trial. But where the witness has made an honest mistake, it is foolish to waive the right to correct it by stipulating to waiving reading and signing. A decision to waive reading should only be made at the end of the deposition when the questions and answers have been heard and considered and an informed decision can be made as to whether the stipulation is wise.

Waiving notice of filing is very much a matter of local practice. If the court reporter can be trusted to promptly provide to counsel a copy of the deposition, there is little reason to insist on being notified of filing. In fact, few courts still require filing. Instead, most have the taking attorney preserve the deposition until it is needed.

Where an expert is also a percipient witness (i.e., the treating physician), the parties may decide that the deposition on eyewitness information should be separate from testimony regarding expert opinions. If so, a stipulation can be made at the outset of the first deposition that it is being taken without compromising the right to take the expert deposition at a later time and stating that no expert opinions shall be elicited during the first deposition.

However, the fact that we can identify some special circumstances in which the parties may explicitly want to preserve certain rights and obligations obviously does not demonstrate that there is any use for a request for the "usual stipulations." Indeed, important concerns that are not adequately covered by the rules of procedure should be dealt with through explicit agreement and stipulation, not catch-all phrases such as "usual stipulations." As an example, in those jurisdictions following the pre-1993 version of the Federal Rules of Civil Procedure, there is one stipulation that is often useful and poses little danger. In place of requiring the deponent to return with his corrections and signature to the same court reporter who recorded the deposition, parties commonly stipulate that the signing may be before "any notary." The oath and its significance will be the same, so you need not worry about this stipulation.

## 6.2 SET-UP AND COMMITMENTS

At the beginning of the deposition a clear record should be made that the witness understands the deposition process and his rights and obligations. Here is a typical deposition introduction:

> Q.    Mr. Landsbergis, my name is Joanne Backus, and I will be taking your deposition. Have you ever been deposed before?

*prior depos/ ground rules*

A.   Yes, I have.

Q.   We'll talk about that previous case later, Mr. Landsbergis, but for now I would like to go over with you the ground rules for this deposition so that we can all be on the same page. Does that sound fair?

A.   Yes.

Q.   Good, now in this deposition I will ask you questions. My questions and your answers will be recorded by Mr. Emanuel, the court reporter at the end of the table. You understand that you need to speak up and to answer orally in giving your answers, so that Mr. Emanuel can hear you clearly? He won't be able to record a nod or shake of your head.

A.   Yes, I understand.

Q.   We're interested in finding out everything you know about the events and facts that underlie this lawsuit and for that reason we are looking for full and complete answers to the questions I'm going to ask. Is that understood?

A.   Yes.

Q.   Now, on occasion, I may ask a question that I don't state very well, or for some other reason you don't understand. If you don't understand my question for any reason, don't answer it. It is my job to ask understandable questions, so if you say you don't understand, I'll try to ask a better question. Okay?

A.   Yes, that's fine.

Q.   It will be my habit to take a break every hour and a half. Does that sound acceptable to you?

A.   Yes.

Q.   I also want you to understand, however, that if you need a break at any time, or for any reason, you should tell me or tell your attorney. We will finish your answer if we are in the middle of it, and then see what we can do about a break. Do you understand that?

A.   Yes, thank you. That sounds fine.

Q.   And you see that we have water and coffee here for you if you want. Feel free to get up and get whatever you need during the deposition. Okay?

A.     Yes, thank you.

Q.     I am sure that your attorney has told you this, but let me reinforce it: if you want to talk to your attorney, that's fine; I just ask that if there is a question pending or if you are in the middle of an answer you finish it before speaking to your lawyer. Okay?

A.     Yes.

Q.     Sometimes it happens that you will give an answer as completely as you can, and then later on, maybe five minutes later or maybe two hours later, you remember some additional information or perhaps some clarification in response to that earlier question. If that happens to you, please tell us that you would like to add something to the earlier answer, and we will do that right then while it's on your mind. Will you do that?

A.     Yes, I'll try.

Q.     That's good, and I'll try to give you opportunities at regular intervals in the deposition to provide any additional information or clarification as well. Is that fair?

A.     Fair enough.

Q.     In addition, sometimes it occurs to people that a previous answer is not completely accurate. If that happens, will you tell me and make any necessary corrections to your answers?

A.     I will.

Q.     Sometimes, when you are answering, you may think of some documents that might help you remember the answer, or might help you give a more accurate answer. If you do, tell us. We may have those documents here, or we may be able to get them to help you answer completely and accurately. Is that okay?

A.     Yes.

Q.     Are you taking any medication or drugs of any kind that might make it difficult for you to understand and answer my questions today?

A.     No.

Q. Have you had anything alcoholic to drink in the last eight hours?

A. No.

Q. Are you at all sick today?

A. No.

Q. Are you currently under a doctor's care for any illness?

A. No.

Q. Is there any reason you can think of why you will not be able to answer my questions fully and accurately?

A. Nothing comes to mind.

The primary purpose for this set of instructions, at least for the witness represented by counsel,[4] is not to ensure fair treatment of the witness but to make a record of the fairness of the deposition process, which in turn discourages attempts at trial to avoid the effect of deposition answers[5] and, at the same time, to begin the process of attempting to develop a rapport with the witness. Let's go through this introduction, comment by comment, and analyze what is actually going on:

### "Have you ever been deposed before?"

This sounds innocent enough, but if the witness answers that he has been deposed it can be used later to undermine the witness's claims in front of the jury that he was confused or uncertain about the deposition procedure. For example, in closing argument:

"Members of the jury, you heard Mr. Landsbergis admit in his deposition that he attended the pricing meeting in Chicago, and then try to deny it here on the stand in front of you. He claimed he was confused about the deposition procedures, and that he was very nervous.

---

4. For the witness unrepresented by counsel, such as the non-party witness. It is all the more important that you demonstrate to the jury later on that you were more than fair in your treatment and questioning techniques. Furthermore, without getting too deep into the ethical obligations involved, deposing counsel may well have a duty of fair treatment toward an unrepresented person, and a duty not to take unfair advantage of their lack of counsel. Where the deponent is unrepresented, the instructions concerning discussions with counsel should be amended to remind the witness that he could obtain counsel if he chooses.

5. "Unfairness" to the witness, of course, is not an option, and the lawyer should always be fair in dealing with witnesses. The question here, however, is whether the introductory instructions have that as their primary objective; they do not. In dealing with the unrepresented witness, general obligations of good faith and fair dealing would seem to impose an affirmative duty to inform the deponent of the nature of the process, what is expected of him, and what he is permitted to do.

But you also heard him testify that he had been in a deposition three other times. He was a veteran at depositions. He was not nervous. He was not confused. He was telling the truth at the deposition, he was at the meeting in Chicago, and his attempts to deny it here in front of you show that he is not very credible."

In addition, the fact that the witness has been previously deposed can lead to finding out about the nature of those testimonial opportunities and provide potentially relevant evidence for the current litigation. Some lawyers make the mistake, however, of foregoing the rest of the introductory instructions after getting a positive response to previous deposition experience. As should become clear, given the explanations of the purposes of these preliminary questions, previous testimonial experience should never preclude making the record we suggest above and explain below.

### "You need to speak up, and to answer orally."

This does indeed help the reporter, but it may also help the attorney taking the deposition, because it keeps the witness from letting his voice trail off toward the end of an answer that may embarrass him, and it reminds the witness of the special process of recording his answers. Some attorneys believe, however, that the attorney taking the deposition should do as little as possible to remind the witness of the fact that his answers are being recorded, so that the witness is more spontaneous and less guarded. If that approach is taken, the deposing attorney should watch for nods or shakes and merely confirm their meaning with, "You are shaking your head from side to side. Is your answer, 'No'?"

### "Interested in finding out everything you know, looking for full and complete answers"

The real goal, of course, is a reliable transcript of the witness's recollection of the facts of the case. The most common diversion from deposition testimony at trial is by witnesses who expand upon the facts of the case, and while not directly contradicting deposition testimony, leave a different impression of the events by adding facts and nuance to make their position more plausible. It is unclear whether the phenomena is better explained by knowing falsehood, or by the witness filling in on and reconstructing the events in question. That is, the witness knows what conclusions have been formed about the events and when thinking about them, reconstructs the events to be consistent with the firmly and honestly held conclusion. It is this reconstruction that shows up in trial testimony. When that occurs, of course, an acceptable impeachment will be on the theory of inconsistency by omission. This preliminary request for full and complete testimony is a precursor for that impeachment at trial. When the witness agrees to give full and complete testimony at deposition, and is given every opportunity to do so, expansion at trial is more telling on the issue of the witness's credibility. If at trial, then, there is an expansion of testimony the following examination can occur:

> Q. You told us on direct examination that you had a good view of the accident, correct?

> A. Yes.

> Q. You claim that was so for a number of reasons, don't you?

> A. I do.

> Q. You said that you were 40 feet from the intersection; that there was nothing between where you were standing and the accident; that although you were originally facing away from the intersection, your attention was focused by the squealing of tires; and that even though it was dark and rainy that night, there was a street light directly behind you that illuminated the intersection.

> A. That's right.

> Q. In fact, Mr. Jones, there was no street light at the intersection, was there?

> A. No, I remember the light.

> Q. Have you always had that memory, sir?

> A. Yes, I'm sure.

> Q. This isn't the first time you've given sworn testimony about this accident, is it?

> A. No, there was one other time.

> Q. You had your deposition taken?

> A. I did.

> Q. You swore at that deposition to tell the truth?

> A. I did.

> Q. The whole truth?

> A. That's right.

Q.  I told you at the deposition that we were interested in finding out everything you knew about the accident, right?

A.  You did.

Q.  And you agreed to give full and complete testimony, didn't you?

A.  I did.

Q.  You were told that if you realized that you had given an incomplete answer you could make the answer complete at anytime during the deposition, correct?

A.  I was.

Q.  And in fact, after every break I asked you if you wanted to complete or change a previous answer, didn't I?

A.  You did.

Q.  You never changed or corrected any of your answers at the deposition, did you?

A.  No.

Q.  You also had the opportunity to read your deposition and make any corrections or changes that existed?

A.  I did.

Q.  And in fact you made several corrections, didn't you?

A.  I did.

Q.  And then you signed your deposition, didn't you?

A.  I did.

Q.  Let me show you what has been marked as Exhibit 77. Exhibit 77 is your signed deposition, isn't it?

A.  It is.

Q.  Now again sir, it's a fact, isn't it, that on the day of the accident there was no street light, was there?

A.  Yes, there was.

Q.  Directing your attention to page 34, line 1 of your deposition, please read along with me.

Question:  Did you have a good view of the accident?

Answer:  I did.

Question:  How is it that you were able to see what happened?

Answer:     Well, I was just 40 feet from where it happened. I heard a squealing of brakes and turned and saw the accident. There was nothing between where I was standing, so I saw the whole thing.

Question:   What else gave you a good view?

Answer:     Just that. I was close and looking right at it with nothing in the way.

Question:   Were then any other reasons why you believe you had a good view of the accident?

Answer:     That's it.

Have I read the transcript correctly, sir?

A.    You have.

Q.    At your deposition you made no mention of this street light you claim was there today, did you?

A.    No.

## "If you don't understand my question. . ."

When trapped at the trial between his trial testimony and his prior answers at the deposition, the embarrassed or desperate witness often claims, "I didn't understand the question; I was confused." If the jury can see that the deposition question was in fact understandable, it may contribute further to the witness's loss of credibility. On the other hand, failing to understand and recognizing a failure to understand are really two separate events. Of all the preliminary instructions, this is probably the least useful.

Some attorneys prefer this instruction with a twist:

"Tell me if you don't understand one of my questions. If you answer a question, I am going to assume that you understood it."

This does not avoid the problem of the witness who fails to recognize that he does not understand, and the fact that the deposing attorney is going to make an assumption is really irrelevant. Her decision to make an assumption does not constitute any sort of admission by the witness or the opposing party.[6] Quite often, this "assumption" instruction merely impels opposing counsel to interject that the deposing attorney

---

6.  Furthermore, even if the deposing attorney did not mention this assumption, the normal human response is to assume that someone who answers a question has understood it, thus this stated "assumption" seems to add nothing but more legal verbiage to the task of gaining information.

must ask understandable questions; that to make the witness monitor the quality of the questions is unfair; that the deposing attorney can "assume" anything she wants, but that will not change whether or not the witness understood a question; and finally that the witness will answer the question as he understands it, not necessarily as the lawyer intends it. The opposing counsel probably has the best of this debate, and at the same time provides a tacit warning to the witness that the deposing lawyer, despite her friendly demeanor, will take every advantage in the deposition process, so the witness should be on guard.

### "If you need a break at any time. . ." "We have water and coffee here. . ."

If the witness needs a break, the witness is going to take a break whether the deposing attorney gives this instruction or not. The instruction's purpose, however, is to show the jury that this deposition was not a "third degree" interrogation in which the witness was questioned in the basement until exhaustion, under bright lights. In depositions where this instruction is given, and those where it is not, there is no detectable difference in the number of breaks taken by the witnesses. The question does, however, have the benefit of relaxing the witness, and of making a record of a fair proceeding.

The witness and his counsel will decide when he is too tired to go on, no matter what instruction you give. But this instruction sounds considerate to the jury later at trial, and makes it more difficult for the witness to say, "I did give that answer about stealing from the poor box, but I was very tired and you just kept pressing me without giving me a chance to breathe."

### "If you need to talk to your attorney. . ."

This instruction may actually have some effect at the deposition, as well as at trial. When the questioning gets intense and the witness gets anxious, many witnesses will want to check with their attorney before answering the tough question. This instruction gives the questioner a bit of leverage:

"Now, Mr. Smalkus, when we started, you agreed that you would answer my question before you talked with your attorney. Please give me your answer, and then we can take some time for you to talk with your attorney."

Although not a guaranteed remedy for dealing with constant discussion between question and answer, the instruction does help. At trial, the jury will again be shown the fairness of the deposition proceeding; that the witness had time to talk with counsel and yet he made these incredible admissions that are made even more reliable by this instruction. That alone makes this instruction worth giving.

### "If you remember some additional information or clarification. . ."

This instruction may actually help at the deposition. Witnesses cannot be expected to know the proper procedures or what they are allowed to do at depositions. This instruction provides concrete direction on how to correct or supplement an answer. Clarification taken together with the request for full and complete answers enhances the likelihood of obtaining all pertinent information from the witness, or, at least, a reliable record where the witness who expands upon or changes his deposition testimony can be taken to task as demonstrated above. This instruction is implemented by giving an opportunity after every break for the witness to make corrections or additions to previous answers. For example:

> Q.  Alright Mr. Smalkus, we are back on the record after our lunchtime break. Before we go ahead are there any of your previous answers that you would like to correct or expand upon?
>
> A.  No there isn't.

### "If you think of some documents that might help. . ."

Consistent with the goal of maximum discovery, this instruction encourages the witness to mention documents that occur to him. Of course, any document referred to by the witness that has not already been produced should be the subject of a Motion for Production of Documents.[7] Without the instruction, the witness may not know whether he is supposed to mention those documents. At trial, the fact that he received this instruction logically precludes the witness from saying, "Well, if I had the documents in front of me then I might have remembered this other bank account."

---

7.  When a "new" document is mentioned during the taking of a deposition, deposing counsel will frequently make an informal request on the record that the document be produced. Such a request has no formal value in guaranteeing the receipt of discovery material. The typical response by defending counsel is, "we'll take that under advisement." Such a response is code for, "you better file a motion for production or you will never see that document."

### "Are you taking any medications? . . ."

This question and the following questions about alcohol, feeling ill, and doctor's care cut off excuses that a witness might give at trial to avoid an unfavorable deposition answer.

The question about alcohol is worth asking again following the lunch break to forestall the excuse of "I was so upset by your questions in the morning that I went and had a couple of drinks over lunch."

Of course, a witness may actually be feeling ill or a personal injury plaintiff may be on pain medication that affects his memory and so on. When this happens, inquiry should be had into the extent of their problem.

Q.  Are you taking any medications or drugs of any kind that might make it difficult for you to understand or answer my questions today?

A.  Well, I had my wisdom teeth out two days ago, and I am taking something for the pain.

Q.  Do you know what medication you are taking?

A.  I have the bottle here. Let's see. The label says it is Hydrocodone. I think 500 mg.

Q.  When did you last take one of these?

A.  At 8:00 this morning.

Q.  How many did you take?

A.  Just one.

Q.  Have you taken any of these before?

A.  About five or six since I had the operation.

Q.  What effect do they have on you?

A.  They make my mouth quit hurting, and I get a little sleepy.

Q.  Do they affect your memory at all?

A.  Not that I can tell.

Q.  You don't have any problem remembering things?

A.  No.

Q.  How about understanding or answering questions— does the medication cause you any problems with doing that?

A.   No.

Q.   How about having your wisdom teeth out? Is that causing you any pain or difficulties now?

A.   Not since I took the pill.

Q.   Feeling fine now?

A.   Yes.

Q.   Will you be sure to tell me if you feel that your teeth or the medication are causing you any problems in understanding or answering my questions?

A.   Yes.

If after questioning it appears the problem will cause difficulties with the deposition—such as medication making the witness sleepy to the point that he is having difficulty staying awake—your best response is to reschedule the deposition.

A word of warning about the line of questions regarding doctor's care, medications, alcohol and drug use, etc.: these questions can be very off-putting, as they inquire into conduct or conditions the deponent may be embarrassed about or view as none of counsel's business. In addition, there are reasons other than these why a witness might not be able to give full, complete, and accurate testimony. For example, over a break a witness might learn about trouble in her business, a family illness, etc., all of which might cause an unreliable deposition. For that reason, it is wise to ask the overarching question. "Is there any reason why you cannot give full, complete and accurate testimony at the beginning of the deposition?" The inquiry should be repeated after every break by asking, "Is there anything that happened over the lunch break that will prevent you from giving full, complete, and accurate testimony." The off-putting effect of the more specific questions can also be avoided by use of this generic inquiry

## 6.3 SPECULATING OR GUESSING

Some attorneys like to ask the witness not to speculate or guess about answers. They argue that by putting this request on the record, it is harder for the witness later to try to avoid an unfavorable answer by claiming it was a guess or speculation. These attorneys also argue that the witness can be asked to disregard the instruction and guess and speculate if that is what is wanted.

Other attorneys recommend against an instruction not to speculate because it seems counterproductive and most jurisdictions have no rule that guessing is not permitted at depositions. Indeed, the speculation of a knowledgeable witness may be much more valuable than the limited actual information possessed by other witnesses. For example, consider these questions to the executive secretary in an office about his boss's activities:

Q. Mr. Smalkus, how much time did your boss spend on the Century account in May?

A. Well, I'm not exactly sure. You know, I don't keep track of his every minute.

Q. Yes, I understand that. Give me your estimate of how much of his time he spent.

A. Well, it would be more of a guess, I suppose.

Q. All right, give me your guess.

OPPOSING COUNSEL:

I'm going to object here. This isn't worth anything at all. I mean, all we're getting is guesses. He has already told you he's not sure.

Q. Mr. Smalkus, tell us what you know of your boss's time on the Century matter in May.

A. I don't know how much time he spent.

Q. Fine. Now, give me your speculation or guess.

OPPOSING COUNSEL:

Same objection. We've been through this.

Q. Answer the question, please, Mr. Smalkus. Give us your best estimate or guess as to how much time he spent on the account in May.

A. I guess it was about half of his time. I can't be sure, but we only had one other big account in the office then, and he seemed to be working on Century almost all the time. It could have been more than half.

While this testimony might not be admissible at trial, since it is a "guess" or "speculation," there is no question that it is clearly useful to know what the witness believes is the fact, because this witness presumably observed "the boss" daily. Speculation such as this can certainly lead to admissible evidence by suggesting document requests such as diaries and time logs, and inquiry at the deposition of other witnesses, thereby making the speculation within the permissible scope of allowable discovery.

So speculation not admissible at trial but at depos, okay (although subject to objection)

Topic

Open
clarify
fin

→

Topic

o
q

→ . . .

# CHAPTER SEVEN

## QUESTIONING TECHNIQUES

*It is not every question that deserves an answer.* — Publilius Syrus

The types of questions asked in a deposition can take many different forms. Speaking broadly, however, all of the questions being asked can be broken down into two different types: information-gathering questions and questions seeking admissions. Many attorneys err by asking only one or the other type of question. Effective attorneys know how and when to ask both types of questions.

## 7.1 INFORMATION-GATHERING QUESTIONING

In the information-gathering phase of a deposition, an effort is made to learn as much as possible about the witness's relevant knowledge. In this phase the focus is on encouraging the witness to talk—to lecture, to reminisce, to discuss, to evaluate—generally, to speak as freely as possible, without the constant intrusion of narrow questions that invite narrow answers. The focus should not be upon displaying the information possessed by the lawyer, but in learning the witness's version of the facts.

For ease of analysis, consider the questioning during a discovery deposition as having three phases: the open phase, the clarification phase, and the closing-off and pinning-down phase. Often lawyers will weave back and forth in these three phases or approaches, examining a topic first with open questions, then with clarifying questions on that topic, and finally by using more controlling questioning to pin down the witness on details or particularly helpful information.

One way to understand the three-phase deposition technique is to think of the process as a funnel. At the top of the funnel are open questions regarding any particular topic, utilizing open questions that encourage the broadest range of information on a given topic. The middle of the funnel is the clarification stage where information gathered at the top of the funnel is focused by the use of more specific but non-directive questions, beginning with such interrogatories as who, what, where, why, when, and how. The bottom of the funnel is the closing-off stage, where, by using questions that are directive (requiring a yes or no answer) or leading (suggesting an answer) the deponent is locked into his or her testimony regarding the topic. The funnel is repeated for each category of information within the purview of the deposition.

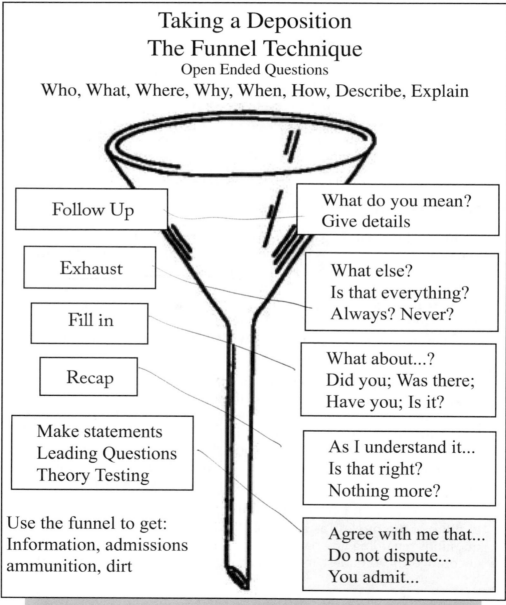

# Taking a Deposition
# The Funnel Technique
## Open Ended Questions
### Who, What, Where, Why, When, How, Describe, Explain

Follow Up

What do you mean?
Give details

Exhaust

What else?
Is that everything?
Always? Never?

Fill in

What about...?
Did you; Was there;
Have you; Is it?

Recap

As I understand it...
Is that right?
Nothing more?

Make statements
Leading Questions
Theory Testing

Agree with me that...
Do not dispute...
You admit...

Use the funnel to get:
Information, admissions
ammunition, dirt

### 7.1.1 The open phase.

In the open phase, questioning should be as wide open as the direct examination questioning of a trusted and competent witness at trial. Picture this aspect of the deposition like the wide mouth of a funnel, gathering up everything that might be useful to understanding and winning the case. The goal of these questions is to get the witness talking about the event and allowing the witness to choose the topics surrounding the event that are important to the witness's version of the facts of the case. The most open questions allow the witness to determine the scope of the information to be provided. Examples of these broadest of questions include:

(In a contracts case)

Q.   Tell me how this transaction came about.

(In a auto case)

Q.   Tell me everything that happened that caused this accident.

At the next level are the reporter's questions—who, what, when, where, why, how—and two more, "describe that for me," and "tell me about that" all of which accomplish the goal of encouraging the deponent to talk with slightly more narrow, but still non-directive, questions. Open questions cause the deponent to provide the information, making it much more difficult for him to "hide the ball" or drag the process out, hoping to exhaust counsel before substantial disclosures are made.

Imagine a personal injury automobile collision case where the defendant is being deposed. Examples of the reporter's questions are:

Q.   Who was with you?

Q.   Who was driving?

Q.   What you were doing just before the accident?

Q.   Where did the accident happen?

Q.   Why did the accident happen?

Q.   How did the accident happen?

Q.   What were you looking at?

Q.   What did you see?

Q.   What was the traffic like?

Q.   Describe the intersection for me.

Q. When did you first see the plaintiff?

Q. Tell me everything that happened after you saw the plaintiff.

### 7.1.2 The clarification phase.

Nevertheless, open-ended questions will not entirely suffice. While the open questions will suffice to elicit the appropriate topics for exploration, they do not necessarily provide the detail that is necessary for a full understanding of the facts as perceived by the witness. The details of the broad outline provided by the witness's answers to these broad questions must also be learned. The clarification phase fleshes out the details of the information provided by the witness. In other words, questioning now moves down to a narrower part of the funnel. Let's take the answer to one of the previous open questions and see how it can be narrowed down.

Q. When did you first see the plaintiff?

A. I saw him about 200 yards away approaching in the oncoming traffic lane.

Q. How fast were you going when you first saw him?

A. About thirty-five miles per hour.

Q. How do you know that was your speed?

A. I had looked at my speedometer about a half block before.

Q. Had your speed changed between the time when you looked at your speedometer and when you saw the plaintiff?

A. I don't think so.

Q. When you first saw the plaintiff, how long did you watch him?

A. Just for a second.

Q. Where did you look next?

Many of the questions are still open, but now they are becoming more focused on the particular topic. As the questioning on the topic progresses, the questions should become increasingly more narrow and closed.

Q. Did you look at your speedometer again between the time you first saw the plaintiff and the collision?

A.  No.

Q.  Did you see any other cars approaching in the plaintiff's lane?

A.  I think he was the only one.

Q.  Did the plaintiff have his lights on?

A.  You know, I can't really remember.

As the funnel narrows, questions become more directive and should start with verbs; words such as "did" and "do" and require yes or no answers. However, it is not a neat or uniform progression from open to closed questions. Often an answer to a closed question will require backing up and asking more open questions before moving on.

Q.  Did the plaintiff have his lights on?

A.  You know, I can't really remember.

Q.  How light was it at the time?

A.  It was starting to get dark.

Q.  Was there other traffic?

A.  Some, it wasn't rush hour or anything.

Q.  Did other cars have their lights on?

A.  I think so.

Q.  Did you have your lights on?

A.  At least my running lights, maybe the headlights too.

Q.  How do you know?

A.  That's my habit.

Q.  Alright, tell me more about your habit in turning on the lights in your car.

## 7.1.3 Closing off.

One of the goals at a discovery deposition is to prevent the deponent from reserving information for surprise use at trial. In addition, the typical inconsistency between deposition testimony and trial testimony is not that the information is different at trial, but that there is more of it. Witnesses frequently provide trial testimony containing more information about an event than was included during deposition testimony. As a result, a major function of information gathering is to get all the information possible and then to close off the information flow so

inadequacy a bigger concern than inconsistency

that, if at a later time information changes or grows, the witness can be impeached by omission. Three constraints hamper this goal: first, the questioning abilities of counsel; second, the witness's possible lack of candor; and third, time. A partial cure to these problems is the use of "closing off" questions to limit the witness to particular facts.

The usual method of closing off a topic is by asking "What else?" or "Anything else?" until the witness answers "Nothing" or "No." Depending on the topic being closed off, these "closing off" questions can take any number of forms: "Were there any other meetings?" "Have you now told me everyone who was present at the party?" "Did you do anything else to mitigate your damages?" and so on.

An important technique to remember is that recollection of additional information on a topic is enhanced by asking a question that assumes that such information exists. If, for example, an adverse witness has testified that there were a number of environmental factors at the scene of a car accident that impeded her ability to perceive one form of question is "What else limited your view?" This form of question encourages the witness to think of other interfering factors. If the goal were to show that the perception was not seriously limited, it is better to ask, "Is that it?" This formula offers the witness an easy way of saying there is no more.

More and more often witnesses are encountered who have been instructed in the strategic use of the phrase, "That is all I can remember at this time." Many clever attorneys believe that by arming their witnesses with such a shield, the attorneys will be able to rehabilitate the witnesses more easily with "refreshed recollections" at trial. Nevertheless, the witness's ability to claim later refreshment can be limited by cutting him off from some of the sources of refreshed recollection. Assume a construction site accident:

Q. Have you now told me the names of everyone who was on the site on the day of the accident?

A. That is all I can remember at this time.

Q. Mr. Summers, did you make any notes about who was on the site on the day of the accident?

A. No.

Q. Do you know if anyone else made such notes?

A. Nobody that I know about.

Q. Have you talked with your co-workers about this accident?

A. Yes, but it's just the people I've told you about that know anything about it.

Q. Are there labor sheets you could check to see who was working that day?

A. Sure, but I already did that for the company's lawyer. It's just the people we've talked about.

Q. Is there anything that might help you remember who was there at the site on that day?

A. Not that I can think of.

Q. Is there any document you can look at?

A. No.

Q. Is there anyone you can talk to?

A. Not other than those people I just told you about that I have already talked to.

## 7.2 EXHAUSTION

When questioning a witness on a topic, it is the goal to extract every important item of information from the witness before moving on to a new topic. In short, each topic should be completely and thoroughly exhausted. Doing so requires attention to the types of questions utilized for this purpose.

### 7.2.1 Breadth.

Exhaustion of a topic means covering the full scope of the topic as well as engaging in detailed questioning on every aspect of the topic. In other words, both the breadth and depth of the topic need to be covered. The usual approach is to stake out the breadth of the topic before exploring the depth.

Let's assume a shipping manager at a machine parts supplier is being questioned about the procedures for filling orders.

Q. What are your responsibilities as shipping manager?

A. I am in charge of all shipments going out of the company.

Q. What other responsibilities do you have?

A. If insurance is required on a shipment, I also arrange that.

Q. What else?

A.    I have to arrange the type of shipping used.

Q.    Any other responsibilities?

A.    I have to make sure that the amount of the shipping charges are passed on to billing.

Q.    What else?

A.    That's everything.

Notice that in addition to getting the full breadth of the witness's responsibilities, the topic is also closed off by asking, "what else?" The question is repeated until the witness says that is everything. If, however, you believe that there is more information regarding the topic, it is then appropriate to ask a series of directive questions to further exhaust the topic. For example, the shipping manager might be asked:

Q.    Do you also negotiate for the best shipping price?

A.    Yes.

Q.    And are you also the one who chooses the shipping company?

A.    Yes.

Q.    And if there is a problem with the shipping would you resolve that problem?

A.    Yes.

Q.    Now, what other duties do you have?

A.    That's all.

In this way, the witness's memory has been pushed to recall additional responsibilities, and he is himself allowed to determine when that information is exhausted. Consequently, the witness will find it difficult later at trial to add new responsibilities.

**7.2.2 Depth.**

Once the full breadth of a subject has been determined, the next step in effective questioning is to explore in depth the answers given. In other words, you now exhaust each topic within the subject. The image to hold in mind is, "Survey the landscape, then drill down." Assume again that the shipping manager is being deposed.

Q.    You said that it is your responsibility to arrange the type of shipping used. How do you go about doing that?

A.    Well, I usually get a quote from the rate books each of the shippers provides.

Q. What happens next?

A. I then draw up a shipping invoice for the cheapest shipper with service to that destination and contact them for a pickup.

Q. What else?

A. I will also fill out the insurance forms if insurance was requested.

Q. What else?

A. That's it. The shipper picks up the shipment and I am done.

Notice again that the questioner is closing off the topic, this time by asking "What else?" until the witness says that's it.

Exhaustion is accomplished by moving to the next topic (sending the shipping charges to billing) or, if more information about shipping is required, by further exploring this topic. For example, the next line of questioning might be about how the rate books are kept current or how the witness knows when to order insurance. The important lesson is not to move on to a new topic until everything about a topic is known that may be necessary for the litigation of the case.

After a witness has given all of the information he can remember, suggesting other information may help trigger his memory, as demonstrated in the transcript above regarding the duties of the shipping clerk.

If the goal is to limit the witness's recall or knowledge, then once the witness has said that is everything, move on to a new topic.

There is no magic formula for determining when the information gathering task is complete. The intelligence and judgment of questioning counsel will determine when enough is enough.

The exhaustion technique need only be utilized on those topics which are necessary to a fair determination of the case. The experience of defending depositions where the questioning lawyer spends endless hours exhausting the witnesses' knowledge about topics that have not the slightest relevance to any issue in the case is all too common in modern litigation, especially in commercial cases. Such an approach is expensive to the client and also runs the risk of losing sight of the forest for the trees. Exhaust where the issue is important, and move on where it isn't. This proscription is aided under newer formulations of discovery rules, including the Federal Rules of Civil Procedure, where depositions are time limited.

## 7.3 ELICITING CONVERSATIONS

Often a trial court will rule that some out-of-court conversations are admissible as non-hearsay under Federal Rule of Evidence 801(c) or (d), or under an exception to the rule excluding hearsay. If the witness at deposition has given only the "substance" or "gist" of the conversation, paraphrasing or summarizing what was said, the court may reject the evidence of the conversation because of the danger that it contains too much interpretation by the witness and not enough evidence of what the speaker said. Therefore, at deposition, a witness testifying about a conversation should be asked to state, in as close to the actual words as possible, what each speaker said and what the response was. Information about a conversation exists at three levels. At the first level is a word-for-word recollection of what was said by each participant; essentially a transcript. The second level consists of some exact words that are within the recollection of the witness, a partial transcript. The third level is, absent the actual words, the substance conveyed by each party to the conversation.

Another reason to insist on learning what the speaker actually said rather than the witness's summary of the words is that often the speaker's words will reveal more than a summary suggests. Consider this segment of deposition testimony concerning a conversation after an accident, as reported by a non-party witness:

> Q. Mr. Richkus, did anyone say anything at the scene of the accident?
>
> A. Well, when the owner got there, he was really upset. You know, it sounded like the driver was trying to explain what happened, but the boss just wouldn't listen. I thought he was going to fire him. He, the boss, I mean, kept yelling and screaming about the brakes and he was getting madder and madder. The driver finally sat down on the running board of the truck cab and he didn't say anything.

Compare that testimony with the following additional testimony where the attorney takes care to follow up to obtain actual language:

> Q. Okay, let's just go through this one piece at a time. Tell me first what the driver said to the owner or boss, what words he used, and what the boss said back to him.
>
> A. Okay. As best I can recall, the driver said, "The brakes went soft; they just didn't grab." And then the owner got really mad and started yelling at the driver.

Q.  What words did he yell at the driver?

A.  I can't remember everything he said, but I remember him saying, "Don't say that to anybody, don't say anything about the brakes. Just tell them it happened too fast." I don't know, I was kind of embarrassed about hearing this, you know. I mean, obviously, they didn't know I could hear them.

Q.  Did the driver say anything back to the owner?

A.  No. He just sat down on the running board of the truck and didn't say anything else that I could hear.

Q.  Where were you when you heard this conversation?

A.  I was standing at the back of the truck, about ten feet from them.

Q.  Who else heard this conversation?

A.  I'm not sure. Maybe the woman who was driving the Cadillac, because she was standing next to me. Both of us were waiting for the police to come.

Q.  Did anyone besides the Cadillac driver overhear this conversation between the boss and the driver?

A.  I don't think so.

Q.  Is that all that you heard of the conversation between them?

A.  Yes, then the police came and I was talking to them.

Q.  Do you remember anything else about that conversation between the boss and the driver?

A.  No, that's about it.

Q.  Did you make any notes about that conversation?

A.  Well, no, I didn't make any notes, but I told the police officer about what I had heard, and he was writing while I was telling him.

Q.  And that was Officer Davis that you mentioned before?

A.  Yes.

With the second example, there are specific statements, free of interpretation, which can be used later as party admissions. The litany for having a witness recount a conversation in which he was involved generally asks the following questions, in one form or another:

- Who was present (speakers and eavesdroppers)?

- Where did the conversation occur?

- What were you doing?

- What were the other people doing?

- What did you say to her and what did she say to you? or, What did she say to him and what did he say to her?

- Was anything else said at that time?

- Is there anything else you can remember about that conversation?

- Did you make any notes about that conversation? Are there any documents that refer to the conversation?

A note of caution is in order here: if the witness starts to talk about the conversation in generalities and impressions, take that answer. Avoid intimidating the witness by demanding specificity that may seem too onerous. Insistence on transcript makes the response, "I can't remember," a much more likely one. If the witness testifies about the substance of the conversation first, she can then be prompted, "Well, you said that the boss was angry. What did he say that sounded angry?" More limited questions about actual statements will seem less difficult and will likely receive a more complete response.

Another technique is to ask first, "What was said?" This simple question allows the witness to recount the conversation as it is remembered. After the witness has recounted everything she remembers, including responding to prods of "What else was said?" the conversation should be revisited. The second time through ask the witness what she first remembers being said, what was said in response, and so on until the conversation is concluded. By using this "two-bite" approach the witness is usually able to recall much more than if the conversation is only recounted once.

Whatever the approach used, if the conversation is important, exhaust the witness's memory, that is, learn everything that was said. This is accomplished using the same funnel approach as in the rest of the deposition, as has been described earlier. Sometimes placing the witness back in the surroundings of the conversation is a helpful memory prod: "Now, where did this conversation take place? How were you seated? What do you remember about the room? What could you see out the windows?"

## 7.4 LISTENING

Both information gathering and theory testing require the use of one of the most important but least noted deposition skills: listening to the witness. While preparation is to be applauded, an extensive outline or lengthy checklist of questions for the deposition or an attempt to take copious notes regarding the witness's testimony often interferes with concentration on the witness. When allegiance to an outline becomes the focus of the questioner, and taking notes an obsession, the result may be to take the focus of the questioner away from what the witness says and does in providing information. Remember, the goal in the deposition is not to complete the outline or take the best notes, but to learn about the witness's knowledge. Armed with lists, outlines, and notepads, counsel too often gets caught up in getting through those materials, with two unfortunate results: many of the answers by the witness are not fully appreciated because they are not heard, and information the witness provides in the form of non-verbal communication is unseen.

First, the distinction between hearing and listening must be appreciated. Reading while the television is on still allows a person to hear voices and sound effects but, because of lack of focus, actual listening does not occur. Word choices made by the dramatist, or the subtleties of language that the comedian depends upon, are not comprehended. Those things require much more attention than merely hearing sounds; listening is required.

At the deposition, involvement in checking outlines, refining notes, or reviewing a document while the witness speaks results in missing the subtle changes in meaning which the witness's tone of voice, hesitation, or word choice often provide. As an example, consider the message in the answer from the following exchange:

Q.    Did you see John again?

A.    Not on that day.

What is heard is that John was not seen by the witness on that day.

The listener who is focusing on the witness will immediately recognize the need to follow up with:

Q.    If not that day, when did you see John?

Other obvious cues, such as eye contact between the deponent and his attorney, silent coaching through head or hand gestures, a glance at a document, shifting in the chair, or any other physical gesture will be missed and, while not susceptible of accurate translation into a sign of truth or falsity, can often provoke further probing for information the witness may be screening.

Some attorneys have difficulty reconciling the need to keep track of items that a witness lists with the need to watch and listen to the witness. When asking the witness to name the people who were at the meeting or to list his reasons for taking an action, questioners then feel compelled to write the names or reasons down as the witness recites them. What should they do instead? The answer is simple: maintain eye contact with the witness. Eye contact with the witness while the answer is being given; probe for more ("Was anyone else there?") while still looking at the witness; and probe again ("Are there notes that might list more reasons?") while still looking at the witness. Then ask the reporter to read the answer back so a list of the people or reasons can be made and then reviewed one at a time. Shorter lists will not even require the resort to the court reporter, because information received both aurally and visually is more likely to remain in the mind of the deposing lawyer longer and more accurately than information merely heard. Attorneys sometimes rely in this way on an attorney or paralegal who is second-chairing them ("John, did you get those names?"), but the reporter, an official note-taker, can be used for the same purpose and will probably have more accurate notes. Once the information is obtained it can be highlighted by marking notes with circles, paper clips, or yellow stick-on squares as a reminder to come back and ask about each of those points until the witness's useful information is exhausted.

## 7.5 RECAPITULATING AND SUMMARIZING

Oftentimes an important fact or piece of information is buried in the middle of an otherwise useless answer. If the answer is read to the jury to impeach or control the witness, its impact will be lost on the listener. For example, assume the issue in the case is whether the defendant contractor had followed the manufacturer's instructions in assembling a prefabricated building:

> Q. Did you have the manufacturer's instructions before you started putting up the building?
>
> A. We have always worked very closely with Chief in putting up their buildings. Several of my crew have attended training sessions at Chief and we have worked

with their instructions a number of times, but I don't think we had a set when we started this job. But the crew members were very experienced in this type of work and knew exactly what they were doing.

You could extract the kernel of this answer with a quick summarizing question either right after the answer or at the conclusion of the topic:

> Q. Let me see if I got this correctly. You did not have a set of the manufacturer's instructions when you started putting up the building?
>
> A. Correct.

Of course, if opposing counsel has prepared the witness to give the long, rambling answer then any attempt at summarizing will draw more of the same. But most witnesses will respond to a reasonable summarizing question with a fair answer.

In one special situation, the witness must be pinned down and the groundwork must be carefully prepared. It often happens in a deposition that the witness finally concedes some important point, but only after much wrangling by both the witness and the defending attorney. See if the following exchanges ring a bell in a price-fixing case where the deposing attorney wants to establish that the two competitors had the opportunity to set prices at industry meetings:

> Q. Mrs. Vasys, as sales manager for Ajax Technology, you went to conventions and industry conferences and meetings, didn't you?
>
> A. Yes, probably once a month or so.
>
> Q. Representatives of your competition also attended those meetings?
>
> MR. ROBERTS:
>
> I am going to object here unless you take these meetings or whatever one at a time. I don't know what you are talking about, which one, or when.
>
> Q. Mrs. Vasys, can you answer my question, please? At these industry meetings that you attended, there were representatives of your competition, right?
>
> MR. ROBERTS:
>
> Same objection. Answer it if you can understand it, June.

A. Yes, well, I think that I understand it. There were… there are meetings during the year that I attend for the company, and our competition also sends their sales managers or, sometimes, their vice-presidents of sales.

Q. And there were meetings like this in 1989 and 1990, right?

MR. ROBERTS:

Meetings like what, counsel? That question doesn't make any sense. Ask a better question and we'll get out of here a lot sooner. I object.

Q. Please answer my question, Mrs. Vasys. Do you remember it?

A. Yes, I think so. We did have industry meetings and conferences in 1989 and 1990. Is that your question?

Q. Yes. And at some of those conferences, you met with sales representatives or officers of the World Technology Company, didn't you?

MR. ROBERTS:

Hold on now. I object. You are way beyond anything that the witness has testified to, and I think that you are trying to lead her to say things that she just hasn't testified to. You are just trying to tell your own story here. I object.

Q. Can you answer the question, please?

A. Well, during 1989 and 1990, there were several meetings where I met with the salespeople from World Technology, but…

MR. ROBERTS:

I object to this line of questioning. You are not being fair to the witness unless you go through these meetings one at a time. This testimony just doesn't mean anything at all.

Q. Mrs. Vasys, you hadn't finished your answer, had you?

A. No, I was just going to say that there were only a couple meetings where I spent any time with the vice-president of sales for World Technology.

The defending attorney saw exactly where this was going and tried, with mostly illegitimate objections, to disrupt the deposition. As a result, while the deposing attorney got the desired information, it is in bits and pieces and will not make a coherent transcript if it needs to be read at trial. Even if only used for impeachment at trial, the witness's answers are so chopped up that the point may be lost on the jury, and opposing counsel will be cued to make further objections to the use of the transcript.

The pinning-down technique that can help here is to leave the line of questioning on meetings at this point, and proceed to other areas. Then thirty minutes, or three hours, later, come back with the following:

> Q. Mrs. Vasys, I think that I am almost done here, and we can wrap up in just a few minutes. Let me check on some odds and ends. You finished business school in 1967?
>
> A. Yes, June of 1967.
>
> Q. And I think I have this right—yesterday you told us that you were assistant sales manager before you became sales manager—do I have that right?
>
> A. Yes, I was assistant sales manager for three years.
>
> Q. And as sales manager you met with the vice-president for sales of World Technology approximately twice in 1989 and 1990?
>
> MR. ROBERTS:
>
> I object. We have been over this enough.
>
> A. Yes, that's right.

At trial, for admissions or impeachment, this recapitulation is effectively used in place of the earlier, disrupted testimony. Even with the objection, it is much cleaner and clearer than the earlier testimony. The defending attorney could, of course, try to be disruptive at this point in the deposition also, but, given the context of the questioning (almost done) and its timing (late in the afternoon when he is too tired to fabricate illegitimate objections), there is a greater likelihood that it will all come out as planned.

When a transcript such as the above is used at trial the defending attorney has the right to introduce other portions of the transcript which "ought in fairness be considered with the part introduced."[1] The burden of finding and using the chopped-up portions of the previous

---

1. Fed.R.Civ.Pro. 32(a)(4) and Fed.R.Evid. 106.

deposition testimony, however, now falls on the lawyer responsible for the condition of the transcript rather than on deposing counsel.

## 7.6 GAINING ADMISSIONS

After completion of the information-gathering phase of questioning, either in a subject area or for the entire deposition, the process of theory testing can begin. While all of the deposition can be viewed as testing various pre-deposition factual theories, once all factual information has been gathered the process can proceed in earnest. Now the witness's testimony on specific facts which are necessary to support deposing counsel's factual and legal theories of the case, or on facts necessary to destroy or weaken the opponent's theory, can be explored with a good deal of focus.

For example, in a breach of contract case the plaintiff claims that he lost other business because the defendant did not deliver the parts and, implicitly, the plaintiff could not "cover" from other sources. Consider the deposition of the plaintiff's purchasing agent:

Q. Now, Mr. Shadis, before you began doing business with the defendant as the supplier of the fasteners, who supplied them to you?

A. Well, several sources. One was Jones' Cabinet Works. Another was Hinges and Hardware, Inc., in Paramus. We did some business with Barkers Builders' Supply.

Q. Were any of those companies still in business in February, when you say you were waiting for the defendant's fasteners?

A. Yes, as far as I know.

Q. Did you ever purchase your piano hinges from one of those companies, before you bought from the defendant's company?

A. Yes, but then the Janis Company, you know, the defendant, gave us a better price, so we switched.

Q. What communications did you have with any of those companies at that time?

A. I believe that I called Barkers.

Q. How many times did you call Barkers?

A. Once, I think.

Q. Did you have any contacts at that time with Jones' Cabinets or Hinges and Hardware?

A. No, I don't think so.

Q. How about anybody else in your company—did they call any of those suppliers at that time?

A. No, I'm in charge of purchasing.

Q. So despite being aware that these other suppliers existed, there was no effort made to obtain the parts you needed from them, is that right?

A. Yes.

In this simple, factual situation the questions are obvious. Nevertheless, the answers demonstrate that the plaintiff probably had other sources that he did not call to check the availability of parts for cover. Thus, the plaintiff's theory that substantial business was lost because cover was unavailable is weakened.

Notice that extensive use is made of leading questions in this "theory testing" situation, for the simple reason that the questioner has temporarily abandoned the goal of discovering new information and is trying to confirm specific and limited information necessary to the theory being developed. Non-leading questions can also be used, particularly if these are more likely to cause the witness to provide the desired answers.

The process of theory testing serves another purpose in the modern litigation setting, where the prospect of a jury trial becomes less likely every year. Because the deposition will likely be used by decision-makers in negotiations, mediations and arbitrations, the theory testing phase of the deposition can be utilized to demonstrate the relative weakness of the position being taken by the opposing party. For that reason the old saw of "saving the ultimate point for closing argument to the jury" is no longer appropriate. Questions that put the ultimate conclusion (theory of the case) to the opponent after laying out the factual predicate for that conclusion send clear messages about whether and for how much a case should be disposed of before trial. And, even if there is a trial, little is lost and something is gained. At some point before trial the case theories of both parties become apparent. Whether in negotiations alone or with the assistance of a mediator, the position of each party and the support for that position are made clear. As a result little is lost in "tipping your opponent to your case." What is gained is an unrehearsed answer to the deposing counsel's hardest question. This answer can be used at trial to limit explanations prepared and rehearsed by opposing counsel for trial testimony.

Ultimate point now appropriate in dep

# CHAPTER EIGHT

## STYLE, ORGANIZATION, AND OTHER MATTERS

*The partisan, when he is engaged in a dispute, cares nothing
about the rights of the question, but is anxious only to convince
his hearers of his own assertions.* — Socrates

The interrogating attorney can bring many styles to the deposition
and many methods of organizing questioning of witnesses. The attorney's techniques vary from witness to witness and from case to case.
The common thread, however, is the need for the attorney to find ways
to encourage the witness to talk and to tell his story completely, so that
no surprises pop up at trial.

## 8.1 STYLE

At a deposition, a lawyer should be assertive, bold, controlling,
deferential, effective, fair, generous, hospitable, intelligent, just, kind,
lucky, magnanimous, nurturing, original, professional, questioning,
retentive, studious, thorough, unexcitable, versatile, wary, xenopho-
bic, yielding, and zealous. Caveat: reading a long list of adjectives,
however, is not preparation for adopting the proper style for taking a
deposition. From deposition to deposition, witness to witness, case to
case, and from time to time at the same deposition, a lawyer can and
should display many of the characteristics from this list, but there is no
effective way to predict the most profitable demeanor for any given
deposition.

It is more helpful to set out the goals for the deposition and then
to examine the likelihood of achieving those goals using the attorney's
typical style. In general, a primary goal of a deposition is to find out
everything the witness knows that can harm or help your client at trial.
Therefore, during the open phase of questioning, which may well take
up two-thirds of the deposition, a demeanor that encourages the witness to talk is appropriate. Success will depend upon the degree to

which interest is displayed in the witness's story, eye contact is made while he answers, reasonableness and poise are demonstrated when his counsel argues and complains, and willingness is demonstrated to give the witness a chance to explain whatever he wants to explain. Finally, a lawyer should be mindful of all of the questioning techniques discussed in detail in Chapter Seven that are consistent with the fact-gathering phase of the deposition.

Specific witnesses will demand using variations on the strategy described above. With a non-party eyewitness, to an accident for example, an assertive, official demeanor may encourage cooperation. With a nervous deponent, unfamiliar with lawyers and the deposition process, a friendly, helpful demeanor may gain trust. Every witness will present a combination of characteristics and challenges, and several different approaches may be necessary before the goal of obtaining complete information is achieved. To illustrate, usually a witness will not become more forthcoming if deposing counsel starts an examination with an aggressive cross-examination style and then moves to a more friendly, open style.[1]

Nevertheless, some witnesses react to aggressive questioning and control with something like a "whipped dog" syndrome. These witnesses become meek and malleable, willing to agree to almost anything suggested by the deposing lawyer. Sometimes this defeated attitude is accomplished by shocking the witness with difficult or embarrassing questions at the beginning of the deposition; other times by pressing the witness who is unsure of his facts into repeatedly admitting, "I don't remember." Sometimes the witness will react in the opposite manner. Through persistent and aggressive questioning, the witness can be angered until he is tempted to lash out with intemperate responses that can often be quite revealing and helpful.

Even with the extensive caveat that witnesses come in endless varieties requiring varied responses, some generalizations may be helpful. First, honey draws more flies than vinegar; being pleasant and courteous to the witness is more likely to elicit responsive answers than being rude or nasty. Second, open questions usually are the best way to obtain information because they prompt the witness to talk and may also put the nervous witness at ease by permitting a broader range of acceptable responses. Certainly a conversational exchange with a wit-

---

1.  This is true for the same reasons that at trial constructive cross-examination (that does not attack the witness's credibility but rather tries to obtain those portions of the witness's story that are favorable to the cross-examining party) should ordinarily precede destructive cross-examination (that which attempts to diminish the witness's credibility).

ness encourages more information to flow than an interrogation. Compare the two questions below:

> Q. Was the Cadillac heading south on Kirby when it came through the yellow light at Madison?

> Q. Tell us about how the accident happened.

The first question contains at least five factual statements which the witness must analyze and accept or reject before she can answer. Each factual statement involves a test of memory; one involves a test of map skills ("heading south") and one involves judgment ("came through the yellow light"). These complicating factors reduce the witness's comfort in answering, and will naturally tend to make the witness reluctant to fully answer the question in a relaxed manner, thereby providing more complete information.

In contrast, the second question asserts no facts except that an accident happened. The question adopts no version of the accident, so no version is implicitly rejected. The question gives full freedom to the witness to tell a story and sets out no "right answers" in advance to intimidate the witness. Clearly, with a witness who is nervous or reluctant to speak in public, the second question is more useful in relieving pressure and encouraging conversation. It has the virtue of encouraging the witness to do what she does every day; have a conversation, as opposed to engaging in the unusual experience of responding to aggressive, complicated, formal, and perhaps intimidating questions. A witness, thus comforted, will provide information unimpeded by the discomfort of interrogation by an unfamiliar lawyer.

## 8.2 ORGANIZATION: BACKGROUND OF THE WITNESS

Most attorneys generally agree that some preliminary, non-confrontational questioning is useful after the stipulations are set up as discussed in § 6.1. In a deposition, establishing rapport with the witness should at least be attempted before beginning the intrusive questioning that compels pressing for details, and before squabbles with opposing counsel arise. Whether the tone is set through background questioning or through questioning on relatively unimportant introductory matters, the goal in the introductory stage of the deposition should be to draw the witness into a conversational mode.

Many attorneys start depositions by extensively questioning about the witness's background. With an expert witness, however, this technique may be counterproductive and a waste of time. Similarly, with a percipient or "eye" witness, this extensive background information may be irrelevant. If you accept the premise that depositions should not go on any longer than necessary because they are expensive for clients and inconvenient for witnesses, then there will be times when questioning the witness on background should be avoided, or at least delayed.

With the percipient witness, it should be determined early on (perhaps in preparation for the deposition) what background questioning will be useful. If a particular witness—normally a non-party witness—may be more forthcoming if relaxed, background questioning may be extended. While the answers may not be substantively useful, they will give the witness an opportunity to become accustomed to the deposition procedure while responding to non-threatening, non-challenging questions. The time spent in relaxing the witness will be repaid several fold by a more forthcoming witness and the ability to use time more efficiently.

In addition to relaxing the witness, a second purpose of background questioning is to assist in assessing the witness's personality, background, intelligence, ability, and so forth. Better judgments on how best to examine the witness can be made after assessing the witness's testimonial capabilities and importance to the lawsuit.

Four factors are important when deciding how much background questioning to do with a witness:

> 1. The role the witness plays in the facts of the case. If the witness merely had the bad luck to be standing on the corner and to observe the collision between the plaintiff's and defendant's car, it is unlikely that a great deal of background questioning is necessary. On the other hand, if the allegation is, for example, that the witness is the principal perpetrator of a complicated securities fraud, more background information will be required to effectively communicate with, evaluate, and place the witness appropriately within the litigation theory.

> 2. The importance of the witness's background to the issues in the case. When the witness's background helps to prove some issue in the case, then background questioning takes on a whole new meaning because the so-called "background" is actually a substantive issue in the case. For instance, in a securities fraud case where the broker is accused of taking advantage of a customer's naivete, the customer's educational history is more than just background; it directly addresses

the issue of how sophisticated or naive the customer was in relation to the information provided and consultations conducted by the alleged fraudulent broker.

3. The size of the litigation budget. Experienced litigators prepare a litigation budget as part of initial preparation and client counseling. An accurate estimate of litigation costs should be made at the outset of the litigation and communicated to the client early on. And, of course, as the projected costs change, those changes, too, should be provided to the client. Clients do not appreciate finding out that litigation is costing more than the amount at issue in the case. Attorneys operating on a contingent fee who regularly find at the end of the case that the time invested exceeds their fees will soon be seeking a different line of work. In short, good attorneys budget the amount of time to be invested in a case and try to adhere to that budget as the case progresses.

4. The amount of time to be spent questioning the witness on substantive matters. The seven-hour, one-day time limit on depositions provided in Rule 30(d)(2) imposes another deposition limitation which must be factored into the calculus of the time to be spent on background information. Unless the length of the deposition has been extended by stipulation or court order, the deposing attorney must make decisions about what topics must be covered during the available time and what topics can be jettisoned if the deposition begins bumping up against the Rule-imposed time limits. Questioning on the witness's background is a topic often dropped if other topics are likely to take the full seven hours.

Time spent during a deposition developing the witness's background has a cost, both in dollars and in opportunity cost (it is time that cannot be used in working on other topics in the deposition, other aspects of the case, or even other cases). A balance between the time spent in background questioning and the expected payoff from this line of questioning must be struck. Time spent learning important, useful information is time well spent. If not, then keep the background questioning short or omit it altogether.

As a general rule, it is helpful to know for any witness: (1) some personal background, *e.g.,* how old she is, if she is married, single, or divorced, does she have children and their ages, where she lives; (2) educational background, *e.g.,* how far she went in school, what her college major was, if any; and (3) relevant employment history, *e.g.,* what jobs has she held, her current employment, how long has she held this position, what her duties and responsibilities are.

It is usually best to begin background questioning with basic personal information (address, family, years in the town—information which establishes the witness's position in the community) and proceed chronologically through educational background and employment history. By proceeding chronologically, it is less likely that a period of time and events that the witness may not want to talk about—like the two months in the mental hospital—will be missed. Once the general chronological view of the background information is established, the witness can be asked to supply specific dates to make sure that he has not omitted any periods of time, as might happen if he is allowed to say, for example, "Well, three years ago I left my job at American, and then I started work at Century." While it might be true that the witness left the American job three years ago and also true that his next job was at Century, adherence to inquiry regarding a complete chronology would insure that the two interim months on drug rehabilitation will also be discovered.

By asking background questions and responding to the witness's answers in an interested, conversational, way, rapport with the witness will be built that carries over into the substantive portions of the deposition. While an opponent may be tempted to object that such questioning is beyond the proper scope of the deposition, or is a waste of time, the objecting attorney knows that such objections are useless. Even if the attorney objects just to interrupt, her contentiousness may backfire and further help to build the rapport between deposing counsel and the witness, who had been getting along just fine. It is fair to say that, for most witnesses (indeed, for most people), talking about themselves is a favorite pastime.

A percipient witness who is a party or who is identified with a party is less likely to relax and open up just because you have asked a few background questions. The witness's counsel will be cautioning the witness throughout the deposition, and any gains made in building rapport will have evaporated by the time the witness and his counsel return from a break in the hallway. Efforts to open up this type of witness must therefore be more subtle and persistent. Because such a witness is less likely freely to provide useful information during the substantive portion of the deposition, and because the exploration of background is not likely to yield significant positive results, background information can be relegated to the end of the deposition so that all available time, if necessary, can be devoted to substantive matters. This is especially so in modern litigation, where the background of a person is relatively easy to find through computer research made available with the receipt of a social security number.

That is not to say that the deposition of party witnesses or those associated with the opposing party should begin with the most important matters in the lawsuit. During witness preparation, the opposing attorney has undoubtedly cast the deposing counsel as the devil incarnate—ruthless, cool, calculating, conniving, and not to be trusted; a similar characterization to the one made by current deposing counsel when preparing her client for deposition. Because of this, the witness is likely at the outset to be wary of the deposing counsel and her motivations. Therefore, aggressive questioning is often least profitable at the beginning of the deposition. (However, this may not be true with experts, as is discussed in Chapter Nineteen.) An opportunity should normally be found to engage in some form of apparently harmless discussion. For example, while discussing the preliminary matters of the deposition, if the witness says that she has been deposed before, take a minute to talk about how long that deposition went and whether the case settled or involved testifying at trial. This exchange can have the same effect as background information in setting a conversational tone, using open questions that encourage the witness to be forthcoming.

## 8.3 GETTING AN OVERVIEW

When the substantive portion of the deposition is reached, the first task is to develop an immediate understanding of the witness's role in the important events in the case. For example, if this witness is an eyewitness to an traffic accident, the question: "Can you give us a general description of what you saw that afternoon at the intersection of Kirby and Madison?" will likely provide that information. At the outset it will be understood whether the witness saw all or part of the actual collision, or was merely a bystander to its aftermath, thereby establishing the witness's importance to the development of the facts of the lawsuit. If the witness is an executive in a company allegedly engaging in false advertising, the introductory question of, "Can we talk for a few minutes about what responsibility you have for the advertising of 'Fatso-Gone' weight reduction tablets?" will immediately provide information as to whether this executive is likely to be involved personally, in a supervisory role, or not at all in the facts at the heart of the dispute. Once the witness's role or knowledge of the relevant events has been established, exhaustion of all of the witness's information is a much

involvement ← personal
supervisory

easier task because it is unlikely that an important aspect of their relevant knowledge will be missed.

## 8.4 THE LOGICAL (OR ORGANIZED) TOUR OR THE "LEAPFROG" APPROACH

The issue of how to best elicit the witness's knowledge presents two clear alternatives: first, question the deponent in an organized way, moving from one topic to the next related topic until the entire field has been covered; or second, jump from one topic to some other, preferably unrelated topic, and then jump again, until all intended topics have been covered. Those who argue for the first approach argue that it leads to complete discovery of the relevant facts known to the witness, with less opportunity for missed information. Those who argue in favor of the second approach, the "leapfrog" approach, contend that it keeps the witness off-guard, prevents the witness from anticipating your goals, and reduces the opportunity for prevarication. Let's analyze each of these arguments. As will become clear, (if not already so by the titles of the two approaches) the authors have considerable trepidation regarding the so-called leapfrog approach, favoring instead what we choose to denominate the "logical and organized" approach.

First, the witness is more likely to relax, and be "off-guard," when she believes that she understands the nature and direction of the questioning. Conversely, her defenses will be up if she is anxious about the direction of the questioning. Thus, while increasing anxiety by leapfrogging may affect a witness in a number of ways, it will not lower her guard.

Second, leapfrogging does prevent the witness from anticipating what the next topic will be, but, within each topic, the questions still must be related to one another and build upon the answers given. If not, the deposition would degenerate into a chaotic exchange, and there would be no follow up or progression at all. Therefore, once the leap occurs with the first question in a new (perhaps disparate) topic area, the witness can adjust her mind-set to the new topic area and to some degree will be able to anticipate the questions. In addition, within the new topic, counsel must return to the methodical exploration of the relevant information with the new topic area. As a result, mere leap-frogging is unlikely to mask the deposition goals, still requiring the use of more sophisticated techniques designed to probe for information that a witness may be hesitant to provide. Probing the witness's answers with follow-up questions, seeking to exhaust the witness's knowledge, coming back to areas to check the consistency of information given, and asking general questions before coming to specific events are the types of techniques that will frustrate the witness's attempts to anticipate questions and block the goals of the deposition.

Third, the witness's opportunity to prevaricate or hide information depends more on the amount of time between his last answer and the next question—what is sometimes called the "pace" of questioning—than it does on the relationship between the topics. In other words, if the witness is motivated to shade the truth about whether the sales agreement included insurance for a shipment that has since been lost, that motivation exists whether the previous topic was changing the name of the business, the method of financing the sale, or the number of partners in the new operation.

Furthermore, at a deposition there is no jury to observe the witness's demeanor when, like Perry Mason, the leap occurs to the crucial question: "Isn't it true that you never intended to buy the hammers?" and the witness, taken totally by surprise, stammers, "Why, I … I … I couldn't … I just couldn't; I never liked the hammers; I lied about wanting to buy them; I hated the hammers and everything they stood for." At the deposition, if the witness's jaw drops open, his eyes roll back, and he is momentarily speechless, but he then recovers and delivers his version of the truth, little is gained (assuming the deposition is not being recorded on video) because the cold record transcript reveals little of the witness's demeanor.

Of course, gaining little is not the same as gaining nothing. If there are no negatives to the leapfrogging approach with a particular witness, it may be useful because once in a hundred times the witness's hatred of hammers will prove advantageous for the case. Sometimes witnesses are surprised into truthful testimony (harmful to them) or an unguarded admission that would not otherwise be obtained, but those instances are rare. In reality, a number of negatives are usually associated with the leapfrogging approach that diminish its value as a questioning style. First, when using the leapfrogging method, it is difficult for deposing counsel to keep track of which topics have been covered. If a logical pattern is consciously avoided, no logic dictates what has been accomplished and what remains. Of course, this problem is mitigated by using a detailed outline and checking areas off as you finish them. However, preparing such a complete outline involves considerable discipline, and its completeness depends upon "omniscience"—and we know that few attorneys can predict in advance all the topics that will be revealed in a deposition; after all, a primary goal of the deposition is to find out information previously unknown.

The leapfrog approach also makes it difficult to ensure that the witness's knowledge has been exhausted in an area, either because such exploration would be predictable or because the witness would anticipate the follow-up questioning. Thus, in leapfrogging, the natural inclination to follow the witness's answers with more detailed questions in an area is often forsaken because of the need to leap and surprise or confound the witness. As discussed earlier, leapfrogging from one major area to another major area does not avoid predictability within the areas, and, as a result, usually offers no real strategic advantage.

Finally, the leapfrog approach reduces the likelihood of discovering unanticipated areas of knowledge, which is one of the most important goals of a discovery deposition. Because leapfrogging involves moving from one area to another unrelated area, the most important tool in discovering new information is discarded: following little clues, chasing small leads, asking about odd words, pursuing hesitations, questioning illogical transitions, and insisting on some adherence to order and chronology.

Because we know that events happen in chronological order, that causes precede effects, and that motivations accompany actions, it is important to recreate and understand sequences of human behavior. By asking a deponent why something was done when it is learned that it was done, and by inquiring carefully about all of the actions surrounding a result to find the likely cause of that result, the truth is often uncovered merely by the follow-up probing questions regarding the chronological history of an event that disclose both sequence and failure of sequence (non-sequitur, which suggests inaccuracy). If in the discovery of the order of things fact two follows naturally from fact one, the sequence creates the likelihood that the sequence is complete and accurate. If, however, fact two does not follow from fact one there are several potential inferences, all of which need be probed. First, fact one may not be accurate. Second, fact two may not be accurate. Third, both may be inaccurate. Fourth, something happened between facts one and two that explains the sequence. Or fourth, there exists some relationship, at odds with the normal way of the world, that explains the sequence.

But leapfrogging as a questioning technique encourages working against those logical connections which identify patterns in human behavior in order to gain the limited benefit of surprise. When the witness has information that needs to be elicited, it makes little sense to abandon the logical tools of coherent, exhaustive questioning. Sometimes a question asked "out of the blue" will provide a valuable answer, but many more times leapfrogging will result in leaving areas undiscovered and connections unseen. If a witness is inclined to fabricate or obfuscate, that intention is less likely to be disturbed by surprise than by the inexorable march of logical exhaustion of information. In short, leapfrogging depends upon inspiration for its success; ordered questioning depends upon thoroughness. Thoroughness is a matter of preparation and execution, both of which can be replicated with practice; inspiration occurs less frequently, cannot be depended upon, and is therefore less reliable. So, plan to be thorough, and then hope to be inspired.

## 8.5 IMPEACHMENT AT DEPOSITIONS

Classically, impeachment of a witness's credibility was something that was set up at a deposition, but not executed until trial. Following this notion, if an opposing expert identifies a treatise as a reliable authority, and that treatise is consistent with the point of view of deposing counsel's client, that deposition testimony was put in a briefcase and saved for cross-examination at trial. If the company manager agreed at deposition that she wrote the series of memoranda on the contract negotiations, she was not confronted at the deposition with another memorandum she wrote that contradicts the first set of memoranda; that too was saved for trial. Getting the desired effect at the deposition—the witness looking befuddled and caught in a lie— usually insured that a repeat performance at trial was unlikely. By the time of trial, the witness would be prepared for the question and would have worked out an appropriate answer and demeanor in response to it.

This classic rule was consistent with the recommended goal for all discovery depositions: to obtain information, not to disclose how much is already known. But all of this wisdom rested upon the basic assumption that the end game for litigation was trial. As we have mentioned, and will discuss further in Chapter 13 on Witness Preparation, modern civil litigation should have as its premise that there will not be a trial. More likely in modern civil practice, the matter will be resolved by negotiation, assisted negotiation (non-binding mediation), mediation, arbitration or some other form of alternative dispute resolution. In fact, the reality of modern litigation is that the trial is the "alternative." And in the world of ADR the deposition has a prominent place. Decision-makers in civil cases review the depositions of favorable and opposing witnesses to evaluate the strength of the their litigation positions when making settlement decisions. Mediators and arbitrators often receive the facts of the case through reading depositions or at least designated portions of depositions. And many of these depositions and deposition designations are presented using video, where the demeanor of a witness can be observed almost as well as at trial. So, in the case where trial is unlikely, many of the functions of trial, including impeachment of witnesses, may be conducted at the deposition.

If it is virtually certain that there will be no trial, then the rules regarding impeachment at deposition or at trial might change. If a decision-maker considering settlement knows that the star witness for her company is impeachable because of inconsistent statements, that provides greater motivation for settlement. Impeachment at the deposition has much greater impact than a mere statement by opposing counsel that such potential impeachment exists. And that impact is enhanced when, as is now common, the depositions of the key witnesses to a litigation are recorded by use of video, where the stammering and befuddlement of the impeached witness is there to be seen. Likewise, the confrontation of an expert witness with a text that she considers authoritative but that contradicts the expert's conclusion will likely have a more significant impact on a mediator who is either guiding or deciding the resolution of the case. In addition, impeachment at deposition has the potential advantage of forestalling later, better-planned responses to that impeachment. Assuming opposing counsel is awake and well prepared, the fact that a witness has been set up for impeachment will be understood. If the impeachment has been held for trial, counsel then has the opportunity to work on, plan, and develop an explanation for the impeachment that has been planted. If, however, the impeachment is accomplished at the deposition, any explanation or excuse offered there does not have the benefit of hindsight and planned response. With trials as scarce as they now are, the former rules regarding saving impeachment for trial are thus in flux and the topic of considerable debate.

Even assuming that a dispute has a substantial chance to end in a trial, there are at least two possible circumstances where the impeachment of a witness during the deposition should be considered.

- An impeachment or disclosure which may by itself provoke settlement; and

- An impeachment which may dissuade an expert from testifying.

The first happens almost exclusively when deposing the opposing party, and then only when deposing counsel possesses material which directly contradicts the party. These are special circumstances, but they do occur and they can result in rapid settlement. Suppose, for example, that the owner of a company is suing for unfair competition, alleging that the defendant's business practices have cut his sales by half in the past year. Suppose, further, that the defense counsel has discovered, through a private investigator, that the manager suffered from alcoholism which limited his ability to manage. Revelation of that fact at deposition might settle the case; on the other hand, use of it at trial might embarrass the witness, and it might antagonize the jury, but it would not necessarily guarantee a verdict for the defendant. Counsel must weigh a potential case-dispositive benefit against a possible tactical advantage at trial, and impeachment of the party at the time of the deposition should thus receive careful consideration.

The second exception sometimes occurs with an expert who has not devoted substantial time to the matter. There may exist an opportunity at deposition to show the expert some of her prior writings that are inconsistent with the position she must take in this case and that make it difficult, if not impossible, for her to reconcile the conflicting positions, at least in the heat of the deposition. While an expert is no less (and no more) anxious to earn a high fee than any other professional, the expert recognizes that intellectual consistency is an important credential, and that her reputation for integrity must survive each trial even if the expert's client loses. If the expert has already sunk substantial time and resources into trial preparation, perhaps the expert will not be withdrawn (or withdraw herself) as a testifying expert; the better decision may be to preserve knowledge of the inconsistency for use during cross-examination at trial. But if the expert has not begun serious preparation, confronting the expert during deposition with barriers in her own writings that she must overcome may well dissuade her from continuing on the case.

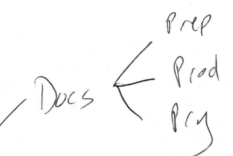

Prep
Docs ← Prod
Pcy

## CHAPTER NINE

## USING DOCUMENTS

*The historian, essentially, wants more documents than he can really use... .*— Henry James

In the complex commercial case, where depositions alone can consume far more resources than the entire remainder of preparation and trial, attorneys are commonly controlled and consumed by the documents produced in discovery and otherwise—by an apparent need to get through, to handle, and to discuss each and every document—even though the witness's testimony might replace dozens or hundreds of them. Documents should not control depositions; counsel should use documents to refresh, to direct, to encourage, but the preference should always be for the spontaneous testimony of the witness.

In general, documents come into play for the deposing attorney in three ways: first, the lawyer uses the documents she already has to prepare for and to organize the deposition; second, she uses them to prod the witness's memory or candor; and third, she uses them to identify documents that she does not have so that she can request them. In each of these areas, inexperienced counsel make mistakes that unnecessarily prolong and complicate depositions. These mistakes are not the kind discussed in court of appeals decisions; instead, they are the kind discussed at coffee breaks at bar association meetings when attorneys exchange stories about "depositions I have known and hated."

### 9.1 USING THE DOCUMENTS TO PREPARE

In the large, well-financed corporate case, it is routine for one of the assigned paralegals to receive a notice of deposition and immediately begin to gather all the "appropriate" documents. "Appropriate" is used with some caution here because what the paralegal actually does is gather the documents called for on some generic list. Typically, that *exactly!*

list will direct the collection of documents that the deponent wrote, received as the addressee or "copyee," or in which the deponent is mentioned. The paralegal consults the computerized database, calls up a list of those documents, and has the imaging system print them out automatically, or has a file clerk pull them from hard copy files and make additional copies manually. The paralegal then provides these documents in chronological order to the attorney, usually with some numbering system already applied. Next, a junior attorney reviews the documents to determine which ones have already been turned over in response to a document request, and, with respect to those that have not been turned over, whether any of them contains privileged material that should therefore probably not be used in preparing the witness.

In the process of responding to a document production request, counsel needs to identify those documents that contain communications protected by the attorney-client privilege or some other available privilege. A log is created in response to the opponent's discovery request that states the date of the communication, the nature of the communication (*e.g.*, a memorandum), the parties to the communication (identifying the claimed privileged relationship, *e.g.*, attorney-client), and the purpose of the communication (*e.g.*, to obtain legal advice). If the document contains some other protected material, such as Rule 26(b)(3) trial preparation material, a similar log showing the appropriateness of trial preparation material protection is provided. And finally, if the document contains some other material that ought be protected from discovery, such as trade secrets, a document is prepared claiming such protection and a Rule 26(c) protective order is sought from the judge. Next, the litigating attorney reviews the documents, both those to be withheld and those to be produced, noting matters for preparation of witnesses to be deposed by the opponent, as well as matters relating to the documents and the events reflected in the documents to ask about at the deposition of opposing parties and other witnesses. Even in the smaller document cases like personal injury matters, someone in the office, perhaps the attorney, normally conducts a "search and arrange" mission like this to find "all the witness's documents" for a deposition.

Trade secret

This apparently logical system for preparation contains a few holes. First, the witness's name will not appear on some relevant documents. For example, the blueprints or plan drawings in a construction case will not have the name or initials of the "clerk of the works" or the subcontractors, but they are certainly important at their depositions. Second, subject matter of the documents is probably a more compelling and useful arrangement than straight chronological order from first to last. Therefore, arrangement by topic, and then chronologically within each topic, to support questioning to exhaust the witness's knowledge in each area, is a better and more useful preparation tool. Third, arranging the documents by subject matter and chronological order helps to identify what the witness knows and when she knew it. Something else must be done to identify what she does not know, a most important goal in preparing to take a discovery deposition.

A relatively minor adjustment to this procedure provides better support for the deposition preparation process. First, undertake a review of those documents which the witness has written or received, covering the relevant period of time, to get some understanding of where the witness fits into the case. Next, consider the issues in the case which logically could have been affected by the witness's activities. Thus, if the witness was involved in sales during the relevant five-year period and the issues involve mislabeling and adulteration, it is a short leap to ask about complaints from customers, contacts with irate competitors, differences in price levels, and sales volumes. These topics come to mind because they involve the witness's position and the issues in the case and not because they are specifically mentioned in documents. The documents may or may not mention the topics, but they deserve inquiry nonetheless.

After giving some thought to issues about which this witness may have knowledge, search the documents for memoranda and letters and the like which deal with these topics, regardless of whether the witness's name is mentioned. Finally, within each topic, arrange the documents selected chronologically, so that they are available in an efficient way to help prod the witness's memory or honesty. Then, placing the documents for each topic into a labeled manila folder (or, just as likely in modern practice, in a computer file containing the documents in electronic format), counsel has them in an effective and usable form for use at the deposition, no matter when in the deposition the topic arises.

Many attorneys note questions on the face of their working copies of the documents, which seems efficient. Once again, however, remember that confirming the information already learned from the documents is only one objective; obtaining new information is usually a more important goal. A topic outline (as discussed in Chapter Five), independent from the documents, that helps direct the examination is much more useful and it, in turn, should refer to the collected documents as one part of the deposition plan. Following this method of preparation, the documents support the deposition but do not control it.

## 9.2 COMPELLING PRODUCTION OF DOCUMENTS FOR USE AT DEPOSITIONS

Frequently, document requests pursuant to Federal Rule of Civil Procedure 34 precede the deposition of key witnesses who will be deposed in the case. These documents, too, must be put in some usable form for reference during the deposition of those important witnesses. This can be handled in two ways. First, a subpoena or request to produce can direct the production of the documents before a deposition, so there is an opportunity to analyze the documents and determine appropriate lines of questioning in order to understand the documents. Second, if there are only a few documents involved, the deposition and the document production can be scheduled for the same time (or thirty minutes or so apart, if the document custodian and the substantive deponent are not the same person).[1]

If the request for production or subpoena called for "all documents relating to," as opposed to listing specifically identified documents, it may be necessary to depose the custodian of documents on the scope of the search for responsive documents to ensure a reasonable effort was made to discover and produce all appropriate documents. In such a deposition, use the typical "open-to-closed" or "funnel" technique of questioning, so document locations are not missed inadvertently. For example:

> Q. Ms. Arrowsmith, as secretary of the corporation, what responsibilities do you have for record keeping?
>
> A. I supervise all of the record-keeping procedures in the company, and all of the people involved in creating important records report to me.
>
> Q. What do you mean by important records?
>
> A. Well, the records that the company needs to operate, like sales orders, invoices in and out, bills of lading, inventory records, disbursements, receipts, everything that goes into compiling balance sheets, and other records.

---

1. Fed.R.Civ.P. 30(b)(5) states that a notice of deposition directed to a party witness can be accompanied by a request to produce made pursuant to Rule 34. Non-parties can be made to produce documents at a deposition by a subpoena *duces tecum* issued pursuant to Rules 30(b)(1) and 45(a). Of course, parties can also be required to produce documents prior to the deposition by a request to produce under Rule 34.

Q. You are talking primarily about financial records. What are the procedures for collecting and maintaining non-financial records, like correspondence and memoranda?

A. Well, those are not quite so rigorous. We do have a document retention policy that requires each office to keep files of all correspondence and memoranda for one year, at least; then we move the files to an inactive file area, unless there has been activity within the past year. After three years in the inactive file storage, those types of documents are destroyed. Our financial records, of course, we keep much longer; some of them we keep forever.

Q. What other methods are used for the retention of documents at your company?

A. None, that I'm aware of.

Q. Is there someone other than you in the company who would have such information?

A. No.

And this process would be accomplished with regard to electronic records as well. Counsel can depose the information and technology (IT) official of a company responsible for designing and maintaining the electronic document systems for the company to find out the nature of the system or systems used to maintain electronic documents (personal computers, cell phones, PDAs, and so forth), the type of electronic documents that are maintained, the method of electronic document creation, and the retention system which follows the electronic document from accessible data retention systems (*e.g.*, hard drives) to back-up systems, archives and final repositories. This information can be used to fashion an electronic discovery request or to insure that the proper searches have been made to obtain relevant electronic document discovery. (This "document information" could also be obtained by a Rule 30(b)(6) deposition specifying that counsel wants information about the creation, litigation collection, and custody of documents. Under that approach, the opposing party is obligated to collect the desired information from whatever sources are reasonably available, and present it through designees at the deposition.)

## 9.3 MARKING AND HANDLING DOCUMENTS AT THE DEPOSITION

Just like at trial, documents used at the deposition need unique names—exhibit numbers—so documents can be specifically identified. Not only do the people at the deposition need to know what piece of paper is being referred to at any particular time, but people using the deposition later (at a summary judgment motion, at another deposition, or at trial) also need to know that the piece of paper they are looking at is the piece of paper the earlier witness was talking about.

The great majority of courts today require, by pretrial order or otherwise, that documents for trial be pre-marked. The process of use of exhibits at trials and in motion practice is greatly enhanced if the same exhibit number for each exhibit is maintained throughout the litigation. If this occurs, Exhibit 17 will be the same for every witness, and in every deposition. As a result, gathering information for any use, motion *in limine*, summary judgment, trial, and so forth, is made easier and substantially more efficient. This is especially so when the transcription of deposition testimony is done in a digital format that is easily accessible. For example, in a case where there is a question about whether a particular document should be admissible as against a hearsay objection, the lawyers need only search the deposition transcripts by exhibit number, and all information necessary for making or opposing the motion *in limine* is readily available.

To make such a system work, exhibits should be marked with what will become trial exhibit numbers before the deposition begins, and this should be done in agreement with opposing counsel. This is important because many documents will be the subject of inquiry by both parties with the same or different witnesses. Put all of the documents in piles according to topic as described above, and then in chronological order within each topic. In most "big document" cases, the bulk of documentary discovery occurs before substantive depositions begin. If for some reason that is not the case, chronological numbering of the exhibits should be postponed until after all, or most documents have been exchanged.

Of course, this system will leave blanks in the sequence at trial where documents are not offered, but that is not a problem except to the most compulsive record keepers. Some judges, however, want the documents numbered at trial in the order in which they are offered. The reason for this preference is not clear. No instruction reminds the jury that "the numerical order of the documents provides a means of recalling the order of events at trial." Furthermore, the order of events in the "historical" scene that the trial is examining—the actions between the parties which gave rise to the dispute—is the important order. Therefore, documents should be arranged by topics and numbered consecutively, to give meaning to the numbering system. Of course, no matter what their number, documents will still be utilized at trial and otherwise in the order that suits the story being told by the witnesses, whose appearance one at a time normally prevents a straight chronological retelling of the events underlying the dispute.

Even if the court requires renumbering exhibits to follow the order of their use at trial, chronologically ordering and numbering documents for the depositions is useful to the attorneys because it provides a reference among the documents and gives them unique names. However, other systems are used.

Some attorneys like to number the documents anew for each deposition: Jonas Deposition Exhibit 1, Jonas Deposition Exhibit 2, Sugis Deposition Exhibit 1, and so forth. However, this approach can cause some confusion unless some care is taken. Often, a document is used at several depositions. Thus, Jonas Deposition Exhibit 7 may also be Sugis Deposition Exhibit 43. The attorneys on both sides must keep a meticulous "table of concordance," which, before computers, often provided a paralegal or secretary with many wearisome hours of work to produce a document that would appear as follows:

## TABLE OF CONCORDANCE

### SUGIS-JONAS DEPOSITION EXHIBITS

| Sugis 1 | Jonas 17 |
|---------|----------|
| Sugis 2 | Jonas 4 |
| Sugis 3 | Jonas 39 |
| Sugis 4 | Jonas 1 |

\* \* \* \* \*

### JONAS-SUGIS DEPOSITION EXHIBITS

| Jonas 1 | Sugis 4 |
|---------|---------|
| Jonas 2 | Sugis 9 |
| Jonas 3 | Sugis 42 |
| Jonas 4 | Sugis 2 |

If there are only two deponents, only two lists have to be prepared, with two columns. With the big document case, and the client who can support such extensive pretrial preparation, more record keeping is necessary. If there are three deponents, three lists are necessary with three columns, and so forth. With the current easy access to computers, a database program can take care of this record keeping rather easily, although the burden of putting the information into the database still exists.

After each deposition, someone must track what exhibits were used and what numbers they were given. If an imaging system is used for the documents, and all the transcripts are put on the system, then when the exhibit number is entered in the system as associated with a particular document, the concordances can be produced automatically. If a manual hard-copy system for the documents is used, the pages of the deposition transcripts at which documents are used are often included in the document control database or in a special exhibit control database, or at least in a word identification table at the back of the deposition. Then, once trial numbers have been assigned and that information is in the imaging system or the database utilized, the concordance has another column that shows the trial numbers. The final pretrial product, after all depositions are complete and all trial numbers have been assigned, looks like this:

### FINAL CONCORDANCE

| Exhibit Number | Sugis No./Used Tr. | Jonas No./Used Tr. |
|----------------|--------------------|--------------------|
| DX-1 | 73 / 153–157 | 14 / 43–44 |
| DX-2 | 74 / 168, 179 | 3 / 10 |
| DX-3 | 5 / 23 | 72 / 198–199 |
| DX-4 | 15 / 68 | 31 / 97, 201 |
| DX-5 | 46 / 109 | 62 / 153 |

If access to the document is desired at trial for examination of a witness with his prior testimony about an exhibit, an additional foundational step to relate the deposition document to the trial document is necessary.

> Q.   Ms. Vardas, you then wrote a letter to the president of the Shadis Company, didn't you?

A. I'm not sure what you are referring to. I don't think I ever wrote to him.

Q. In the same deposition we have talked about, Ms. Vardas, I asked you this question, didn't I? Page 73, counsel. "Isn't Vardas Deposition Exhibit 15 a letter from you to the president of the Shadis Company?" And you answered, "Yes, I wrote that to him." Wasn't that your answer?

A. Yes, I said that.

Q. Ms. Vardas, let me show you what has been marked as Defendant's Exhibit 142. That's the Deposition Exhibit 15 we've been talking about, isn't it?

A. Yes, it looks like the same letter.

Obviously, it makes a much cleaner trial examination if only one set of numbers is involved, yet another reason to assign trial numbers before the depositions of significant witnesses.[2]

Once a numbering plan is chosen and the arrangement of the working copies of documents chronologically within subject-matter categories accomplished, sufficient copies for all counsel, the witness, and the court reporter should be made. Some attorneys resist providing a copy to opposing counsel, thinking there is no reason to make the deposition easier for her. But in fact, it makes the deposition easier for the deposing attorney, too. If defending counsel has to ask for time to find her copy, or insists on examining the witness's copy before the witness can see it, the deposition is slowed, the flow of communication interrupted, and fewer, less forthcoming answers will be obtained. In the worst case, the defending attorney will review the document with the witness, pointing out various things as they go through it, thereby affecting the witness's testimony.

For the few extra cents it costs, a copy for the defending attorney should be provided. Once this practice is established it will likely recur throughout all the depositions in the litigation, thereby benefitting all involved. The only advantage lost is the unfair advantage of making it mechanically difficult for the other attorney to participate in the deposition. Of course, in many modern deposition practices, the numbering and use of exhibits is decidedly streamlined by having all exhibits pre-marked and stored electronically for use during the entirety of the

---

2. Once trial begins, you can supplement the computerized concordance to track rulings on admissibility of exhibits and transcript pages where witnesses testify about exhibits. In the 100-document cases, this may sound trivial. In the 30,000-document cases, it is not.

litigation. In that circumstance, each document in question is called up on the computer screens before the court reporter, witness, and all of the lawyers simultaneously and questioning can proceed. This process is an enormous time saver as it obviates shuffling and handing around documents, thereby wasting valuable deposition time resources.

If paper documents are in use, however, many attorneys put their pile of documents right up on the conference table, shifting them from the "to be asked about" pile to the "already asked about" pile as the deposition wears on. Beware, however, that this two-pile arrangement has the tendency to allow the documents to control the course and content of the deposition. This also may signal the defending attorney and the witness as to how much of the deposition is left, since they can watch the "to be asked about" pile dwindle. One simple solution is to put the "already asked about" documents back under the "to be asked about" pile whenever there is a break and opposing counsel and the witness are out of the room. Another is to keep the documents in a file box below table level, so that only deposing counsel knows how many documents are left to ask about.

When using a document, if it has not been pre-numbered, it should be handed to the reporter with a request that it be marked with a specific number:

> Mr. Reporter, would you please mark this next four-page document as Jonas Deposition Exhibit Number 17A through D?

The reporter will then affix a label to the document (often one color for plaintiff's exhibits and another color for defendant's) and write in the number and the date. Some reporters use a stamp and then fill in the blanks. The label or stamp affixed by the reporter has no evidentiary value; nothing is "received in evidence," that is, admitted into the trial record, at a deposition. The label or stamp merely serves to identify the document so there is no confusion about what is being discussed.

After the document is marked by the reporter or the pre-marked number is given aloud so it appears in the record, the document should always be referred to by its number. This can be accomplished without any particular formality or cumbersome phrasing, beginning with a statement for the deposition transcript that identifies the document:

> Q.   Ms. Vardas, let me hand you what has now been marked as Vardas Deposition Exhibit 43 which appears to be a letter from you to Ms. Jones at the Shadis Company

dated January 13, 2005. Counsel, here's another copy you may use. Would you look at that, please, Ms. Vardas?

A. Yes, this is the letter we were talking about.

Q. And is Exhibit 43 the same letter that you say you wrote after rejecting the Shadis Company offer?

A. No, there's another letter that I was thinking of.

Q. Let me show you another letter. Mr. Emmanuel, would you please mark this document as Vardas Deposition Exhibit 44 which appears to be a letter from you to Ms. Jones at the Shadis Company dated January 26, 2005? Now, Ms. Vardas, take a look at Exhibit 44. Counsel, here's an extra copy for you. Is this the letter you wrote after receiving the Shadis offer?

A. Yes, that's the one.

Q. Exhibit 44 is dated January 26, 2005, isn't it?

A. Yes.

Q. Now, could you tell us how this letter, Exhibit 44, relates to your rejection of the Shadis offer?

A. Yes, I can explain.

Q. Please do.

Later, perhaps at trial or when the parties are presenting their summary judgment motions, this care in keeping documents straight by using their "proper names" will allow all counsel and the court to know exactly to what document the attorney and the witness were referring.[3] Of course, if copies of the exhibits are attached to the deposition itself, there will be little chance of dispute at trial about which document was being examined at deposition, but use of the proper name of the exhibit, its number, will always provide a clear record.

If a document has more than one page, it is important that each page have some unique identification. Otherwise, the witness may come back later and claim that she was referring to a different page. If, in order to save time, the reporter is asked to mark the front page only and then the document's internal pagination is used, both the document number along with the page number should be referred to when

---

3. The availability of transcripts on computer disks has created another reason for proper reference to documents by their numbers: when the transcript database is being searched for references to the document, you will pick up more occurrences if the number has been used instead of "this document," "that letter," or "the first memo."

used with a witness. Also, care should be taken to ensure there is a record that the witness is looking at the same page as referred to by document and page number:

> Q. Ms. Vardas, would you please look at the fifth page of Vardas Deposition Exhibit 57. That's the page which begins with the language, "… and to tour the plant with Jonas and his employees." Do you have that page in front of you?
>
> A. Yes, I have it.

Sometimes, although trial numbers have not yet been assigned, the documents will have unique "Bates numbers"[4] on them, and many attorneys use those unique identifiers to refer to internal pages of voluminous documents.

All of these decisions on how to handle documents at a deposition are intended to reduce the possibility of confusion in the record. As with so many other areas of depositions, there are virtually no "rules" about how to mark exhibits; common sense is quite enough, once the goal is understood. Over time, however, it is preferable to develop a system for dealing with documents that is replicated, as a matter of habit, in every deposition, no matter the case or the witness. Habitual conduct has the advantage of creating consistently complete and accurate records of the use of exhibits during the deposition and for later use in motion practice, ADR, or at trial.

## 9.4 LAYING FOUNDATION FOR DOCUMENTS AT THE DEPOSITION

If the deponent later becomes unavailable for trial, and stipulations as to admissibility are not forthcoming, the deposition transcript may be the sole source for the foundational requirements for documents to be introduced in a later proceeding. Under the Federal Rules of Civil Procedure, lack of foundation may be a problem which the deposing attorney could cure. Therefore, opposing counsel should object if she is concerned about the foundation for the document. (This topic will be discussed more fully in Chapter Fourteen). If such an objection

---

4. These are called "Bates numbers" because Bates is the manufacturer of a popular handheld number stamping machine which is often used in manual document control systems to stamp sequential numbers, identical numbers, or "duplicate sequential," that is, two documents in a row with the same number, and then the next two with the next sequential number. Computer imaging systems can number documents automatically and print the documents with or without the assigned number. Even when done by computer, these are often called Bates numbers.

Foundation

arises, and the deposing attorney sees that additional information is necessary to lay the foundation for admission at trial, that examination should be accomplished at the deposition.

The easiest way to think about foundation in the deposition context is to confine it to five essential elements: (1) competence of the witness (does the witness have first-hand knowledge or the ability to opine regarding the foundational requirement in Federal Rule of Evidence 602);[5] (2) relevance of the document (does the document have any tendency to make an issue in the trial more or less likely);[6] (3) authenticity of the document (is the document in fact is what it appears or is claimed to be);[7] (4) does the document comport with the original documents rule (assuming the rule applies, is the document an original or if there is no genuine issue as to its authenticity, is it a duplicate);[8] and (5) does the document meet hearsay requirements for admissibility (does the document meet an exception to the hearsay rule or have a relevant non-hearsay purpose).[9]

We note, however, that the second of these elements, relevance, while "foundational" in the sense that it must exist for any evidence to be received at trial, is specifically excluded by Rule 32(d)(3)(A) from those matters which are waived if not raised. This means that silence from the defending attorney is not a waiver of this "foundation" objection to an asserted lack of relevance, and the objection can be raised for the first time at the trial stage.

With regard to the third element, authenticity, that is, that the "matter in question is what the proponent claims," frequently a great deal of time is saved by discussing categories of documents:

> Q. Mr. Shadis, with regard to Exhibit 76. Is Exhibit 76 an example of a form utilized by your company?
>
> A. Yes it is.
>
> Q. And Exhibit 76, this form document with "Shadis Co." in the upper right-hand corner, and "Invoice No." with a blank in the left corner, and then spaces for entering items and amounts, is that your standard form of invoice for bulk purchases of Shadis construction materials?
>
> A. Yes, that's the form we use.

---

5.  Fed.R.Evid. 601 (lay witnesses), 702 (expert witnesses).
6.  Fed.R.Evid. 401.
7.  Fed.R.Evid. 901, 902, 903.
8.  Fed.R.Evid. 1000.
9.  Fed.R.Evid. 801, 803, 804, 807.

> Q. And would all of your company invoices be in the same form?
>
> A. Yes they would.

After obtaining that answer, there is no need to ask about the form every time one of them occurs as a deposition exhibit. Similarly, the form for internal memoranda in an organization can be authenticated generically: "Was Exhibit 102 an internal memorandum, using the form you previously told us about?" and need not be asked about with reference to each exhibit that is a memorandum in the company form.

Finally, if a foundation objection is made and there is doubt as to what your opponent believes is missing, ask. If the opponent refuses to reveal the basis for the objection, it will be harder later, under Rule 37(d)(3)(B), to argue that the objection was made. It is virtually impossible to cure a lack of foundation if the objector refuses to identify what is lacking in that foundation.

If you are successful in laying a proper foundation, your opponent is left with making an objection to exclude the document at a later proceeding based on an argument that it is not relevant (an objection that need not be made at a deposition in order to preserve it) or pursuant to Federal Rule of Evidence 403, which allows exclusion of otherwise admissible evidence on the basis that it is cumulative, it will confuse the fact finder, or its prejudicial effect substantially outweighs its probative value. The need to make objections to preserve matters for later consideration may have been the topic of a request for a stipulation at the outset of the deposition, so that these objections are not waived even if they are not raised at the deposition. This type of stipulation is discussed at § 5.6.1. If the witness may not appear at trial, and the objection is either made or preserved if not made, the testimony at deposition that provides the basis, if one is available, for overcoming objections must be found in the deposition transcript. Lawyers who make an objection to an exhibit at a deposition may use the term "foundation" to cover both the foundation itself (competence, relevance, identification, and trustworthiness) as well as specific objections (hearsay, best evidence, and policy grounds). If an objection is made, be sure its basis is clear and address whatever infirmities can be cured during the deposition. (A further discussion of making and meeting objections at deposition appears in Chapter Fourteen.)

In addition to using deposition testimony to lay the foundation for the admissibility of a document, it is likewise appropriate to use the deposition as a vehicle for laying what we call a "negative foundation." During the course of document production it is often the case

→ Like Lisa Mead's investigation of SAD

that opposing counsel will produce a document which is particularly probative of the opponent's position, but may suffer from some evidentiary infirmity. During the deposition of the creator of the document or another witness, who is usually part of the same entity as the creator of the document, an examination can be had that shows the inadmissibility of the document, and lays the foundation for a motion *in limine* to exclude the document for use in later proceedings. For example, consider the situation where a company has been sued for gender discrimination. As a precursor to the bringing of the action a complaint was filed with the Equal Employment Opportunity Commission that in turn requested a reply from the now-defendant company. In response to the request an investigation was conducted by the defendant company's human relations department, which prepared a report that disclaims any discrimination on the part of the company and asserts that the now-plaintiff was discharged for poor work performance. The following, in pursuit of a "negative foundation," occurred at the deposition of the human relations officer, Ms. Wilson, by plaintiff's counsel:

Q. Ms. Wilson, were you the person who investigated my client's claim of gender discrimination at the Acme Paper Company?

A. Yes I was.

Q. Did you prepare a report of your investigation for Acme's Vice President for Personnel?

A. I did.

Q. Let me show you a six-page document which we have marked as Exhibit 23 which appears to be a memorandum prepared by you on January 28, 2004, and sent to Joyce O'Toole, Vice President for Personnel at Acme Paper Company. Do you recognize Exhibit 23?

A. Yes, that's the memorandum I just told you about that contains my report on your client's complaint.

Q. Why was Exhibit 23 prepared?

A. As I understand it, your client had made a complaint of gender discrimination against Acme and we had been asked by the EEOC to respond to that complaint.

Q. So when you conducted your investigation you knew that a complaint had been made by my client to the EEOC?

A. Yes, this has happened a few times in my ten years at Acme; someone complains to the EEOC, they ask for a response, and we respond.

Q. In the past when this has happened, has there ever been a lawsuit filed against Acme by the person who complained to the EEOC?

A. Yes, that has happened several times.

Q. Were you aware of that when you prepared Exhibit 23?

A. Yes.

Q. In addition to sending Exhibit 23 to Ms. O'Toole, does Exhibit 23 show any copies were sent to anyone else, and I refer you to the last page, page six of Exhibit 23?

A. Yes, a copy was sent to Jack Burns, Acme's General Counsel.

Q. Why was that?

A. Because there is always a possibility of litigation when an EEOC complaint is made.

Q. Am I correct then, that Exhibit 23 was prepared for two purposes; one, to respond to the EEOC, and two, in anticipation of possible litigation?

A That's right.

With this "negative foundation," Exhibit 23 can likely be excluded if offered by the defendant company. (The plaintiff could always offer Exhibit 23 as a party admission.[10]) Although it was part of the business of Acme to respond to EEOC inquiries, the memorandum was prepared in anticipation of litigation, which in all likelihood would disqualify it as a record of regularly conducted activity (business record) of Acme.[11]

*HS = out of trial stmt offered to prove the sm of the stmt*

## 9.5 INQUIRING ABOUT DOCUMENTS USED TO PREPARE FOR THE DEPOSITION

A favorite question of deposing attorneys is, "What documents have you reviewed in preparation for this deposition?" The witness typically will then disgorge a list of various types of documents ("the letters from the government about the spill site, internal memoranda

---

10. Fed.R.Evid. 801(d)(2).
11. Fed.R.Evid. 803(6).

concerning the clean-up efforts, diagrams and maps of the area …")
and defending counsel will make no objection. The attorneys in such
an instance believe they are applying the provisions of Federal Rule of
Evidence 612, which states, "if a witness uses a writing to refresh his
memory for the purpose of testifying … before testifying [at trial]," the
adverse party is entitled to see the document "if the court in its discretion determines it is necessary in the interests of justice." Indeed, if the
documents have not already been produced, defending counsel will
often agree to produce them without regard to whether they were required to be disclosed under the mandatory disclosure requirements
of Rule 26(a)(1)(B) or were called for by any subpoena or document
production request.

Inquiring about documents used by a witness to prepare for the
deposition raises two separate evidentiary concerns. If the documents
were selected by counsel for the purpose of preparing the witness to
testify, regardless of whether counsel was present when the documents
were actually reviewed, the identity of the documents may very well
fall within the trial preparation materials exclusion of Rule 26(b)(3)
(sometimes called the work product privilege). The selection of the exhibits to be shown to the deponent during preparation will, in all likelihood, reveal the mental impressions of the lawyer in the preparation of
the case. Neither the documents nor the fact that the witness reviewed
them are privileged in and of themselves, but "the selection process
itself represents … counsel's mental impressions and legal opinions
as to how the evidence in the documents relates to the issues and defenses in the litigation."[12] If the witness's testimony establishes that the
document actually refreshed his memory, however, many courts have
held that Evidence Rule 612 requires the witness to identify the document regardless of whether the selection process is work product.

When faced with this situation the courts have come to three different conclusions. On one end of the spectrum, if the witness has reviewed documents in preparation for his testimony, some trial judges
issue a blanket order that all such documents must be produced. These
judges reason that it is impossible to determine in any reliable way
whether a document that was reviewed actually "refreshed memory"
or not, so in fairness, if the deponent reviewed it, the document is certainly relevant to the deponent's testimony and it must be produced. In
these circumstances the "right" to production of the document occurs
once the deponent responds that such a review took place and the
documents are identified by the witness.

---

12. *Sporck v. Peil*, 759 F.2d 312, 315 (3rd Cir. 1985).

The middle position appears to be that if the deponent testifies that a document was reviewed and that it assisted the witness in recalling the events surrounding the lawsuit, then all such documents must be produced, at least to the extent that they refreshed memory. That is, if a ten-page document was reviewed and only the middle two paragraphs on page six actually refreshed memory, then all that need be produced is some identifying information regarding the document (*e.g.*, Memorandum of August 10, 2004, from J. Smith to D. Jones) and the two paragraphs from the document on page six. In this construct, before the document must be produced the witness must testify that her recollection had been refreshed regarding the matters underlying the lawsuit and the document must then be identified.

On the other end of the spectrum, before a document must be produced pursuant to Rule 612, it must be shown not only that the document refreshed the memory of the witness about the events underlying the lawsuit, but that the document refreshed the memory of the witness about testimony actually given at the deposition. These judges reason that unless there was actual testimony about the topic which was refreshed, there is no reason for the document to be produced under the rubric of Rule 612. Under this view of the law, then, the witness usually testifies first about a topic, and then if she responds that there was a document that refreshed her memory about the topic about which she has testified, that document (or portion of document) must be produced.

No matter which view a court takes about the refreshing documents that must be produced, another evidentiary issue concerns refreshing documents subject to privilege. Imagine that a party witness has reviewed copies of letters she had sent her counsel concerning key facts in the case before the deposition, and the letters refreshed her recollection about what occurred. Many courts have held that this may, pursuant to Rule 612, justify production of documents that would otherwise be protected under the attorney-client privilege.[13] This should serve as cautionary warning that a client should never be provided documents for refreshing recollection that are privileged documents that should be shielded from discovery. In fact, the best "rule" regarding documents provided to a witness in preparation for deposition testimony is to provide only those documents that either have already been produced or present no tactical disadvantage should they have to be produced to opposing counsel.

---

13. *See, e.g., Derderian v. Polaroid Corp.*, 1121 F.R.D. 13 (D. Mass. 1988).

In addition, inquiries about documents selected by counsel and used by the witness in preparing to testify can often be parried. For example:

> Q.	What documents did you review in preparation for this deposition?

BY COUNSEL:

> Counsel, Mr. Shadis reviewed a number of documents with me as we prepared for this deposition. That review, and the identity of the documents we reviewed, is protected work product as trial preparation material under Rule 26(b)(3). You may of course ask about whether he has seen particular documents before, and he will answer you as fully as he can without waiving the privilege.

Or:

> Q.	Mr. Shadis, are there any documents that you reviewed in preparation for your deposition testimony or otherwise that assisted in refreshing your recollection about the matters about which you have testified today?

BY COUNSEL:

> Counsel, Mr. Shadis has only reviewed documents that have already been produced in discovery, so you have already received them. Any selection from those documents by me is protected work product.

Of course, the deposing attorney can ask about documents which the deponent reviewed of his own accord, that is, without having been directed to do so by his counsel, and about documents used to refresh recollection on particular topics. However, the rules do not require the defending attorney to educate the deposing attorney on what questions might be helpful and allowed.

## 9.6 REQUESTING DOCUMENTS IDENTIFIED DURING THE DEPOSITION

Often during depositions, witnesses will refer to documents which have not yet been obtained by the opposing party, and deposing counsel then turns to defending counsel:

DEPOSING COUNSEL:

Vito, will you provide us with these documents we've been talking about?

DEFENDING COUNSEL:

Well, I don't think they were on any of your requests to produce, Ann, and they certainly weren't among the documents subject to mandatory disclosure under Rule 26(a)(1)(B).

DEPOSING COUNSEL:

I'm not saying they were. I'm just asking whether you will agree to provide us with the file of letters and the other materials, the memoranda, Mr. Shadis has referred to in the last hour or so.

DEFENDING COUNSEL:

We don't have them here.

DEPOSING COUNSEL:

When can you produce them?

DEFENDING COUNSEL:

I don't know. I'll have to get back to you.

DEPOSING COUNSEL:

Well, it's going to have to be soon, because you can see that we're probably going to have to have some more time with Mr. Shadis after we get the documents.

DEFENDING COUNSEL:

I'm not going to agree to that. You should have asked for the documents before you scheduled this deposition. We're not going to just hold it open and let you keep coming back again and again.

DEPOSING COUNSEL:

Well, we scheduled the deposition to fit your witness's schedule, and you know that. If you've held back some documents we have to ask him about, then we'll get an order for him to return.

DEFENDING COUNSEL:

Ann, we'll look at the transcript when we get it and do the best we can, consistent with our need to represent our client's best interests and to avoid subjecting him to harassment through repetitive depositions.

In fact, this unproductive colloquy occurs so frequently we ought to just give it a number, or a nickname, and whenever this situation arises we could just announce, "Document production argument number three," and it would be understood that all of the above worthless verbiage was intended.

Why is it worthless verbiage? Because it neither created nor waived any legal obligations. Defending counsel has merely agreed to look at the transcript and make a decision. If, after two months, he then decides not to produce the documents, he has not violated any agreement, stipulation, or order, and no motion to compel discovery is appropriate. In fact, all that is appropriate is a request to produce documents (or a subpoena, if it is a non-party deponent)—the same request to produce which would have been appropriate immediately after the deposition if none of this discussion had occurred. In other words, the exchange between counsel is really code for defending counsel saying, "File your document request motion" and deposing counsel responding, "You'll have it tomorrow."

Many times less contentious counsel does agree to produce the requested documents, but often the record is not crystal clear on what documents must be provided, nor within what time period. If, a month later, a few memoranda have been produced, the record supporting a request to the court for an order compelling further production is not as clear as it ought to be. A more likely scenario is that following the agreement to produce the documents, the deposition proceeds and both sides promptly forget about the matter. Only months or even years later, when reviewing the deposition transcript in preparation for trial, do both sides recall that they had made an agreement.[14]

How should the attorneys have handled the situation?

DEPOSING COUNSEL:

> Counsel, I don't think that document has been produced to us. Will you provide it without a formal request for discovery?

If defending counsel knows the document and is comfortable agreeing to release it without further review for privilege, he can agree at that time, since the scope of his obligation is clear. All that remains is to clearly identify the document to be produced. And if the document is readily available, it should be produced at that time to obviate

---

14. Such an agreement is an enforceable stipulation. Fed.R.Civ.P. 29.

*Ann: Send us something in writing & we'll take it under advisement*

the necessity of re-convening the deposition at a later time to explore the document in question. If defending counsel agrees to produce the document later, it eases his burden if deposing counsel writes a letter requesting it, because then defending counsel does not have to keep track of informal production obligations. In addition, in writing, the nature of the request will be unambiguous. Therefore, defending counsel's best response is:

DEFENDING COUNSEL:

> Ann, I don't think we'll have any problem producing this memo. Write me a letter to remind me of exactly which document you want, we'll review it, and give it to you if there's no privilege.

This places the burden of following up and identifying the precise document to be produced on the party seeking discovery, where it logically ought to be. As other documents are identified and requested, defending counsel can merely respond by saying, "Why don't you put that in your letter?"

Some attorneys insist upon a request for production in place of a letter after the deposition, although the advantage is not clear. We can hope an attorney's agreement to treat a letter as though it were a formal request for production would be sufficient, without any need for judicial intervention to determine the mutual obligations. Nevertheless, it is possible that attorneys find it easier to gain clients' attention if they can tell them, "These documents are subject to a request for production," than if they have to say, "Well, they wrote me a letter asking for them." Even if counsel does insist upon the request for production, deposing counsel should not debate the point. If the documents need not have been produced in response to earlier discovery requests, another request is appropriate; if the documents should have been produced earlier, then a motion to compel may be appropriate. In either event, arguing about the matter at the deposition achieves nothing.

One final note is in order. Threats to force the witness to come back for further deposition because of the need for additional documents are counterproductive and should be ignored. As discussed in § 10.3, your right to call the witness back for further deposition does not depend upon what counsel says, but upon whether you have had a fair opportunity for a complete deposition. Only the court reporter, who gets to transcribe additional pages of deathless attorney prose, benefits from the debate on this point.

## 9.7 REFRESHING RECOLLECTION

In order to be certain that a witness's knowledge has been exhausted at the deposition, it is sometimes appropriate to try to refresh the witness's recollection about a topic or event about which the witness testifies he has no memory, or an incomplete memory. When refreshing is attempted with a document (as it usually is), however, it should be done with care, because once a witness is shown a document, while it may refresh memory, it will also likely have a limiting effect. In other words, if a deponent testifies that he remembers only three subjects discussed at a meeting, and is then shown a memorandum which lists four subjects, the witness will adopt those four as the complete meeting agenda, regardless of how many subjects were really discussed. The key to avoiding this premature closure is to keep the document in reserve for as long as possible. Use the information in the document to probe the witness's memory, but bring the document out only at the end of that portion of the examination. Here is an example, based upon a document which shows that the prime contractor met with the roofing subcontractor at least three times about the change order on the roofing material. The subcontractor is being deposed for discovery:

Q. Now, Mr. Strongis, when did you discuss the materials with the prime contractor, Mary Jonas?

A. Well, we had one meeting on the site, and that would have been around the first of April, I suppose.

Q. Who was at that meeting?

A. Just me and Mary; oh, and maybe the clerk of the works, Harry Barker.

Q. What did Mary say about the roofing material at that meeting?

A. Well, I remember we discussed using a rubberized membrane covered with gravel, instead of the roofing felt shown in the drawings.

Q. What did you say in the conversation?

A. I can't remember anything specific, we just talked about the potential change in the plans.

Q. What else was discussed at that meeting?

A. Nothing else.

Q. Were there other meetings about the roofing material?

A.    Yes, I think there was one in the middle of May, because the membrane we wanted to use was not available.

Q.    Who was that meeting with?

A.    Someone from Mary's office, probably John Forsythe, and me.

Q.    Who said what?

A.    Well, I told John that the membrane from the Harrelson Company wasn't available when we needed it to dry in the building [seal the roof], so we really should plan on some substitute.

Q.    What did John say?

A.    He told me to write up the proposed change and submit it as soon as possible, and I gave it to him that day, or maybe the next day.

Q.    Was there more to that conversation?

A.    No, that was about it.

Q.    Were there any other meetings about the roofing material?

A.    Yes, I remember we talked once more about it, after we laid the roofing membrane. The question came up whether we needed to use more gravel, and we decided that we didn't.

Q.    Who talked about that?

A.    I think that this time it was Mary and John Forsythe and me. That was near the end of the entire outside job, so it would have been in August sometime.

Q.    Who said what at that meeting?

A.    Again, I don't remember specific words that were said, but I did say, in so many words, that I thought that the gravel in the plans was sufficient, and they asked about the lighter weight of the new membrane, and I told them that really wasn't a problem because we were putting down a lot of gravel anyhow. That was about it.

Q.    Were there any other conversations or meetings about the roofing material?

A.    You mean, before this lawsuit came up?

Q.    Right.

A.  No, I think you've got them.

Q.  Do you recall that there was a meeting at the end of July, about ordering more gravel?

A.  Oh, yeah, but that … well, that wasn't more gravel so that we'd have more per square foot; that was more to cover a projection that had been added, over the front entrance. We kept the per square foot number the same.

Q.  Who was present at that meeting?

A.  That was just me and John, I think, because it was no big deal.

Q.  Who said what?

A.  Well, just what I told you. I told John that we needed more gravel to cover the area that wasn't in the original plan, and he said go ahead and order and submit a change order right away. So we did.

Q.  What other meetings or conversations occurred regarding the roofing material?

A.  None.

Q.  Let me show you what has been marked as Strongis Deposition Exhibit 15 which appears to be a letter from Mary Smith in your office to the Smith Construction Company dated September 14, 2005. Is Exhibit 15 a letter that your office sent to the general contractor at the end of the job?

A.  Yes. Oh, yeah, I looked at this last night.

Q.  This letter lists one more meeting about the roofing materials, doesn't it?

A.  Yeah, its got two meetings that I mentioned, and then there's a meeting mentioned in here where the owner actually came down, in early July.

Q.  Who else was at that meeting?

A.  Well, Pierson, the owner, and me, Mary Jonas, and I think the architect, Penn Sharp, was there, too.

Q.  And who said what at that meeting?

A.  Well, of course, the owner, all he wanted to talk about was when we'd be finished, you know, when the building would be dried in. Sharp and Mary were looking at the weight limits for the roof. All I wanted to know was whether they would sign off on the sub-roof so that we could finish up, since the new membrane had come in and we were ready to go.

Q. What happened as a result of that meeting?

A. Oh, it all got worked out. The weight was good, and the sub-roof passed, so we could start.

By using the document in this way, the whole equaled more than the sum of the parts: the deponent remembered three meetings; the document had two of those meetings, plus a fourth witness did not initially recall. If the document had been used at the beginning of the inquiry about the subject, the information might have been limited to the three meetings referred to in the document. If the document wasn't used at all, the information would have been limited to the three meetings that the witness initially remembered. By holding back on the document until the witness's recollection was exhausted, information was obtained about all four meetings.

# CHAPTER TEN

# CONCLUDING THE DEPOSITION

*It ain't over 'til it's over.* — Yogi Berra

Normally there is only one opportunity to depose the witness; once the deposition is concluded it is difficult to call the witness back and reconvene the deposition. Therefore, it is wise to take a bit of time to think carefully about any areas of examination or particular questions that may have been overlooked.

## 10.1 INSURING COMPLETENESS

Before the deposition is concluded, a recess should be taken to consider whether the goals of the deposition have been accomplished to the extent possible. If there are friendly others present (a client, co-counsel, paralegal, and so forth), check with them as well. Do not rush to conclude the examination, which is probably what opposing counsel is encouraging.

Attorneys often ask a set series of questions at the end of the deposition:

Q. Now Mr. Tilts, are there any answers to my questions that you wish to change before we close this deposition?

A. Not that I can think of.

Q. Is there any information I asked about that you remember now but that you didn't recall when I asked the question about it?

A. No.

Q. Is there anything that you would like to add to what you have told us so that we can understand your perspective or viewpoint more clearly?

A. No.

Q. Thank you.

A witness rarely remembers anything new or changes an earlier answer. The value of these questions occurs when impeachment is necessary. If a witness attempts to avoid the consequences of an impeachment, it can be shown that an opportunity was given to correct and change any of his answers during the deposition. This opportunity to expand at the deposition makes it easier to hold the witness to the breadth and depth of his prior, inconsistent, impeaching testimony.

## 10.2 ARRESTS AND CONVICTIONS

Under appropriate circumstances a witness can be impeached by criminal convictions.[1] The court also has discretion, during the cross-examination of a character witness, to allow inquiry about arrests and other bad acts of the person whose character is being attested to. Such inquiry has the purpose of impeaching the credibility of the character witness by showing either that the witness does not really know the subject of the character evidence or, in the alternative, that the character witness has a faulty notion of what is means to have good character. For some strange reason, however, most deponents become quite resentful when asked if they have ever been arrested or convicted of a crime. It may be reasonably assumed that the witness will cease any cooperation with deposing counsel once questions about criminal convictions have been posed. Therefore, while witnesses should normally be asked about arrests and convictions, those questions should be reserved until the end of the deposition when cooperation no longer matters. But ask. In this day and age of numerous regulatory crimes, the possibility of a criminal conviction is more likely that one might think. Even if the information is not worth bringing out at trial, the mere prospect that testifying may bring about the revelation of a prior secret conviction may be enough to induce the opposing party to settle the case.

## 10.3 COMPLETING, ADJOURNING, RECESSING, TERMINATING, ENDING, CONTINUING THE DEPOSITION: WHEN IS IT ACTUALLY DONE?

In those jurisdictions that have not adopted the Federal Rules of Civil Procedure limitation of depositions to seven hours on one day, or

---

1. Fed.R.Evid. 609.

some similar limitation, the deposing attorney at the end of the deposition normally selects "appropriate" language from this shopping list of stock phrases:

1. The deposition is adjourned until next month.

2. It is suspended until a time to be identified in the future.

3. It is adjourned until such time as the court rules upon certain outstanding motions.

4. It is terminated pending further discussions between the parties on the production of documents.

5. It is suspended to permit a motion to be made for an order to compel discovery.

6. It is concluded, subject to the right to recall the witness for further questioning should that be required. Or,

7. "I have no further questions at this time."

What is the legal effect of using phrase four as opposed to phrase two? Young attorneys, or attorneys inexperienced at deposition, have probably spent collective centuries worrying over this question. In fact, none of these phrases has any specific legal effect at all. Unless there is an agreement to continue the deposition or there exists a court order to continue the deposition, Rule 30(b)(4) requires the officer to state on the record that the deposition is complete and to give any stipulations made by the lawyers.

All of these phrases, and any other similar phrases that regional creativity has brought into local practice, accomplish the same thing: the witness is excused to go home with no obligation to return unless ordered by the court or requested by agreement of counsel. In this matter, there is no arcane ritual to be followed to achieve a certain effect, no magic language to preserve one's rights and opportunities.[2]

But how about the situation where the deposing attorney has done all that she can, but she knows that new documents are on the way? Or that later witnesses may provide information justifying further questioning of this witness? Or that rulings from the court on claims of

---

2. In fact, Rule 30(d) is the only section of the Federal Rules which touches upon the procedure for concluding a deposition: on the grounds of bad faith, annoyance, embarrassment, or oppression of the deponent or a party, the court in which the action is pending or where the deposition is held may terminate the deposition (or may place limitations upon its continuation). If a party to the deposition demands suspension so that a motion for such an order may be made, the deposition "shall be suspended." Under Rule 37(a)(4), the court may impose costs of making or defending the motion upon the unsuccessful party or witness.

privilege may open new areas? What should she do to protect her right to come back later for further deposition questioning? And what about the defending attorney who believes that the deposing attorney is trying to "hold open" the witness's deposition just to irritate or discomfort the witness with the threat of having to return? How can he protect the witness without exposing either the witness or himself to paying costs for a motion to compel discovery?

The entitlement to have a witness return to answer more questions is governed, not by whether the deposing attorney selected the proper phrase at the end of the day, but by whether there is some justification for the return. In other words, if the court is later persuaded that it should deny the witness's privilege claims and orders the deposition to resume, the witness will have to come back regardless of the language used at the "end" of the last deposition session. Conversely, if the deposing attorney cannot demonstrate a sufficient reason for resuming the deposition, then the witness does not have to come back, no matter how careful the attorney was to say at the deposition, "Adjourned, subject to my right to recall."

Rule 30(a)(2)(B) requires court permission or a stipulation before a witness can be deposed a second time. If attorneys disagree on whether the deposition was completed, the simple and safe approach is to seek an order permitting the witness to be deposed again. When the deponent is a party (or party surrogate of some sort), a slightly more risky approach is simply for the deposing attorney to notice the deposition again, thereby putting the party in the position of either appearing for further deposition, applying for a protective order, or failing to appear. If the witness fails to appear, the matter is brought to the court on a motion to compel discovery. In any event, this process will resolve the question; arguing about the particular litany used at the "end" of the deposition does not.

# CHAPTER ELEVEN

## OBNOXIOUS OR OBSTRUCTIONIST OPPOSING COUNSEL

*[The enemy] must be hounded and annihilated at every step and all their measures frustrated.*— Joseph Stalin

Some attorneys believe it is their job in defending a deposition to prevent the discovery of information at virtually any cost. At least three reasons account for such behavior: first, the attorney is unprepared to defend the deposition and is desperate to avoid the substance of the case where he is ignorant; second, the attorney is inexperienced in depositions and trial, and therefore lacks the confidence to allow the facts to come out; and third, the attorney does not accept the premise of the Federal Rules of Civil Procedure that pretrial discovery of the opponent's information is favored[1] and trial by ambush, obfuscation, and surprise is disfavored.[2]

The obstructionist attorney is more likely to prey upon young or apparently inexperienced counsel, whom he believes he can intimidate, but he may try his tactics on any attorney in any deposition, from the small tort case to the multi-district commercial contract and RICO matter. Obstructionist behavior takes a number of forms. The most typical obstructionist tactics are:

1. speaking and meritless objections;

2. argumentative objections or questions or condescending or intimidating tone;

---

1. The goal of the discovery rules is to promote "free and open" exchange of information between the parties and to prevent surprise and delay. *See, e.g., Davis v. Romney,* 55 F.R.D. 337 (D. Pa. 1972); *U.S. v. I.B.M.,* 68 F.R.D. 315 (D.N.Y. 1974); *Wiener King, Inc. v. Wiener King Corp.,* 615 F.2d 512 (3d Cir. 1980).
2. From time to time, it seems that a "fourth category" attorney is discovered—the absolute jerk—but, like the "new" dinosaur that turns out to be the scrambled bones of previously known dinosaurs, the "jerk" usually turns out to be an energetic combination of two or all three of the previously known categories.

3. distracting coughing, throat clearing, and so forth;

4. distracting physical movement; and

5. baseless instructions not to answer.

Because this sort of behavior interferes with the legitimate goals of discovery, it has been the topic of numerous attacks and numerous responses by the organized bar, trial judges, rule makers and otherwise. Because the making of objections and instructions not to answer, and the manner in which these tactics were used, was the primary form of obstructive behavior, the Federal Rules of Civil Procedure contain clear dictates regarding how and under what conditions objections and instructions not to answer may be accomplished legitimately. Rule 30(d)(1) provides:

> "Any objection during a deposition must be stated concisely and in a non-argumentative and non-suggestive manner. A person may instruct a deponent not to answer only when necessary to preserve a privilege, to enforce a limitation directed by the court, or to present a motion under Rule 30(d)(4). [Seeking a limitation on the deposition][3]"

Strict adherence to this rule would prevent ninety percent of the obstructive behavior that occurs at depositions, and judges, especially those in the federal courts, are insisting on just that.

Individual federal districts and state courts have gone even further. There exist local rules that severely limit the form of objections that can be made. For example, local rules in several districts limit the making of objections to stating the word "objection." No grounds can be stated unless there is a request from questioning counsel for the basis for the objection so that it can be cured.

Finally, individual judges have fashioned discovery orders that severely limit defending counsel from any communication with the deponent during the pendency of the deposition. These rules are designed to prevent defending counsel from consulting with the deponent during questioning and providing testimony for the deponent. These discovery orders usually do and should allow, however, for consultation with the client necessary to discuss a potential claim of privilege or the ethically required remonstration with the client when the defending lawyer believes that the deponent has given false testimony.

---

3. The making of objections and instructing not to answer questions will be discussed more fully in Chapter Fourteen.

A few simple techniques will help to control the obstructionist attorney; if they do not control him, at least the techniques will help to complete the deposition despite the interference.

## 11.1 IRRITATING OR OBSTRUCTING BEHAVIOR

The first step in dealing with the obstructionist defending counsel is to decide whether she is merely being irritating and making the deposition more difficult or is actually obstructing and frustrating the ability to obtain information from the witness. In one situation, opposing counsel may make long speaking objections which do not have the effect of coaching the witness, or she may ask for clarifications of questions but not instruct the witness not to answer. In the second situation, opposing counsel may whisper in the witness's ear while a question is pending or instruct the witness to refuse to answer merely because she does not like the way the question is phrased. The effects on the deposition from the two types of behavior—irritating and obstructing—are different and the responses to the two should reflect that difference.

## 11.2 THE IRRITATING OPPOSING COUNSEL

First, let us examine the first situation described above—the irritating opposing counsel. The following are a few tactics to deal with this type of interference.

### 11.2.1 Size up the defending counsel.

Some lawyers are naturally "jerks" while others sometimes behave that way as a calculated strategy. Never forget, however, that every time opposing counsel asks for a question to be clarified or confers with the witness while a question is pending, it does not mean that the lawyer is being a jerk and is engaging in irritating or obstructionist tactics. Some lawyers ask for clarification because your question has genuinely confused them. They believe that the witness may be similarly confused or that the question is likely to lead to a misleading transcript on a matter of some importance to the lawsuit. Some lawyers confer with the witness while a question is pending because a legitimate issue of privilege must be cleared up before the witness can answer. Some objections are made because they are valid and legitimate.

Unless there were previous bad experiences with the opposing counsel or she has a reputation as one of the hated breed of obstructionists, it should be assumed, until proven otherwise, that opposing counsel is acting in good faith. Responding with the nuclear option to a polite request for clarification of a question is guaranteed to turn the deposition into an unpleasant experience for all involved. More importantly, it is also likely to interfere with the ability to obtain the maximum amount of information from the witness.

Treating opposing counsel as the enemy every time she opens her mouth may also result in ignoring a proper objection that should be cured to obtain the sought information in the most usable form. If it later becomes necessary to offer the deposition at trial and the court sustains the objection, important favorable evidence may end up being excluded. It may be that opposing counsel is being a jerk, or it may be that legitimate objections are being made (or perhaps both are true). Make this decision on an objection-by-objection basis, and do not rely on assumptions.

In short, if opposing counsel is behaving reasonably and is not disrupting the deposition, respond accordingly. A pleasant, courteous response on your part may engender the same sort of behavior from opposing counsel when later in the litigation the roles of counsel are reversed.

### 11.2.2 Keep the deposition goals in mind.

In all discovery depositions the primary goal is to obtain information, helpful or harmful, in order to prepare better for the disposition of the case. To state this goal more succinctly, it is to ask questions and receive answers. As we have said before, the ultimate goal of every deposition is to exhaust the witness's information about the case.

In order to accomplish this goal, especially when the time for deposition is limited, counsel must operate efficiently. By engaging in obstructionist behavior, the opposing attorney is inefficiently inviting argument about objections, encouraging worthless debate on procedural points, or calling on deposing counsel to refine and further refine questions that are understandable at first asking.[4]

Therefore, whenever anything is occurring at the deposition other than the asking of questions and the receiving of answers, it is probably also true that the goals of the deposition are not being advanced. Unless the "extracurricular activity" is more important than discover-

---

4. The Advisory Committee Notes to Rule 30(d)(2), limiting depositions to seven hours and one day, state that "if the deponent or another person [opposing counsel] impedes or delays the examination, the court must authorize extra time."

ing the opponent's case from this witness (something that is extremely unlikely), a return to asking questions and receiving answers is wise. The "cue" for analyzing the situation is clear: if deposing counsel is addressing opposing counsel instead of the witness, the primary goal of obtaining information has been abandoned.

### 11.2.3 Do not play his game: act, do not react.

This point is closely related to keeping the primary goal in mind. For whatever of the reasons that motivate his behavior, the obstructionist defending attorney does not want the flow of information at the deposition to go forward. In other words, his primary goal is directly opposed to your primary goal. Responding to his objections; debating points with counsel and the witness; unconsciously switching from open questions to closed, cross-examination style questions (as often occurs in response to a myriad of objections); becoming formalistic, objecting to routine and legitimate conferences between the witness and defense counsel which are not actually interfering with the deposition; and other such behavior on the part of deposing counsel is good evidence that the obstructionist counsel has accomplished his goal, and deposing counsel has lost focus on the goal of the deposition.

Instead, deposing counsel should merely ignore the obstructionist; literally refuse to acknowledge the conduct in any way or even look at the obstructor. By so doing and thereby demonstrating the futility of the conduct, the questioner may make the obstructionist eventually tire of the game and become much more docile. In short, behave as if opposing counsel were dead and no longer involved in the deposition. This approach requires discipline and patience, however, and it undoubtedly will throw the deposition off track somewhat, because the witness may well be confused about what is happening as the objector screams to be recognized. ("Won't you even give me the courtesy of looking at me and answering my question about why this is relevant?") Nevertheless, demonstrating the futility of obstructionist behavior at the outset will result in a much more effective remainder of the deposition.

Let's look at an example of this tactic of ignoring obstructionist opposing counsel:

> Q. Now, Mrs. Adomaitis, what makes you believe that your broker was not handling your stock account properly?

OBJECTION:

> Well, wait, let's just get our time periods straightened out here before we all get confused. What are you talking about? When she first believed that he was churning, or what?

Q.  Mrs. Adomaitis, please answer the question.

OBJECTION:

> Counsel, now, you haven't answered my question. I don't know when we are talking about here, and I'm sure that the witness doesn't either. That's just not the way to take an intelligent deposition, and I'm surprised your senior partners didn't tell you that, because maybe you just don't know. But you've got to have a time period for all these things.

Q.  Mrs. Adomaitis, do you remember the question?

A.  Well, no, I'm not sure that I do.

Q.  All right, let me ask it again. What makes you believe that your broker was not handling your stock account properly?

OBJECTION:

> Counsel, you are just trying to confuse the witness now, by not telling her when you are asking about her knowledge. Clearly, she knows a lot of things today that she didn't know back when this guy was handling her account, and it's not fair for you to just ask about what she knows or what she knew without saying "when." So, why don't you ask a better question?[5]

Q.  Mrs. Adomaitis, will you answer the question, please?

A.  Yes. I think that I was first, you know, a little suspicious when I saw some interest charges on my monthly statements, and he wasn't very direct when I asked him about them.

---

5.  "Why don't you ask a better question?" or "Why don't you ask the witness...?" are apparently among the most potent needles a defending attorney can jab into a deposing attorney. There are reported instances of attorneys getting into physical wrestling matches in the deposition room, spilling out into the hallway, over who has the right to suggest questions at a deposition; and there is one instance, transcribed in what has become a famous page of transcript in Washington, D.C., where the attorneys end a series of bitter exchanges about "suggested" questions with the taking attorney shouting at the defending attorney, "___ you, I'll ask whatever questions I want to!" This is probably not the most efficient way to obtain information from the witness.

The important things to notice here are that the attorney taking the deposition never responded to the challenge by the defending attorney and that she continually pressed the witness for an answer. If we were watching this little drama, we would have seen that the taking attorney kept her eyes on the witness at all times, never looking at defending counsel. No attention at all was paid to his inappropriate comments; she did not even say, "Your objection is noted," or "The question is proper," or make any other comment indicating she even heard him. The objection will be in the record whether she says it will be or not; the question is proper, or it is not; there is no need for comment. So she ignores him and takes almost all of the fun out of his game.

By watching the witness throughout defending counsel's comments and then immediately coming back to the witness with, "Can you answer the question?" you clearly send the message that those interruptions will not hide information and that the witness should not gain any courage from them.

The implicit message to the witness from deposing counsel is, "I will stay here until next Tuesday if it's necessary because of the jerk sitting alongside of you; so you decide—do we do this the easy way, or do we do this the hard way, because we are going to do it." Where the witness cannot really understand why the objection is important, or even understand it at all, this appeal has a good chance of success.

Having said this, sometimes merely acknowledging that opposing counsel has made an objection will cause the deposition to move forward. If opposing counsel feels it necessary for reasons of ego, or otherwise, to receive some sort of recognition that he has made a statement, and none is forthcoming, the disruptive behavior may continue until that recognition is given. A simple response, without looking at counsel might be, "Your objection is noted. Now, Mrs. Adomaitis, please answer my question." Remember, the objective is to get answers to questions, not to fight with opposing counsel.

### 11.2.4 Ask good questions.

One of the most effective ways to frustrate opposing counsel, who is waiting to pounce upon every minor flaw in questioning, is to ask good questions. While certainly every question cannot be planned at a deposition taken for discovery purposes, advance preparation about matters like form of questions and the proper handling of documents is always appropriate. If the advice of Chapter Seven is followed and questions are simple and open-ended, frequently beginning with who, what, where, why, when, how, describe, and explain, there will be little opportunity for legitimate objection. These questions not only frustrate obstructionist counsel because there is little opportunity to object, but they also send the message that deposing counsel is competent at what she does.

If, in the alternative, opposing counsel has a legitimate reason to object to questions on the grounds that they are compound, for example, argument in their defense is merely a further waste of time; the problem with the form of the question should be corrected by asking two questions instead of one. But there is no doubt that this type of success encourages the obstructionist opposing counsel. In reality, there is nothing obstructionist about making legitimate objections. It is incumbent on deposing counsel to take away that opportunity, thereby frustrating the defending lawyer who is intent on disruptive behavior. And, of course, if the allegedly obstructionist behavior is taken before the court, it does not help when the obstructor is correct on evidentiary and form matters.

## 11.3 THE OBSTRUCTING OPPOSING COUNSEL

While the approach for dealing with the merely irritating opposing counsel is to ignore him, this tactic does not work with the obstructionist, who actually precludes obtaining necessary information. Ignoring opposing counsel who coaches the witness's answers or who improperly instructs the witness not to answer only rewards what is clearly improper behavior. The question is how to control such behavior.

### 11.3.1 Relate to the witness.

The first tactic for controlling such behavior is to relate to the witness. Even when the witness is the chief executive officer of the opposing company, deposing counsel may well be able to develop a relationship with her that helps when her counsel becomes obnoxious and unreasonable. For example, when a simple question is asked and opposing counsel claims it is actually as complicated as the Theory of Relativity, the witness may be too honest or too embarrassed to agree. Consider the following exchange, which is rather common:

> Q.  Mrs. Lemontas, how long have you been in charge of sales for the Crabtree Company?
>
> OBJECTION:
>
> Counsel, you have got to be more specific than that. I mean, what are we talking about, in terms of "in

charge" of sales? That could mean, "How long has she been involved in selling any products for them?" or "How long has she supervised anyone in sales?" or any number of things. You have to ask a better question.

Q.   Mrs. Lemontas, do you understand my question, "How long have you been in charge of sales for Crabtree?"

A.   Well, yes, I think that I do.

Q.   Could you answer the question, please?

One might think that the responsible executive, as well as the lowly corporate employee, would carefully follow the defending attorney's lead in such a situation, but in fact the relationship is just not that simple. First, at the human level, the witness may feel a bit offended that she is being told by a lawyer that she does not understand something, especially when that something seems perfectly clear and understandable. Second, while she may be willing to sit quietly while the lawyer makes his speech about simple things being complicated, it is quite another thing to be called on herself to agree. That direct question, "Do you understand?" calls on her to lie or tell the truth, on the record, and that requires more deliberation than just sitting and letting the lawyer make his lawyer noises. Third, as she may already have learned in this deposition, the net effect of these kinds of arguments is that the information is eventually obtained, but it just takes longer. It wastes her time (and the company's money). This last consideration is especially persuasive with executives and professionals who have a healthy estimate of the value of their own time. Sometimes this fact can be brought rather forcibly home to the witness:

Q.   Doctor, I am sure your time is worth more than mine, but it appears that at the pace we are moving it will not be possible to finish up your deposition this morning. I will do my best, however, to tie it up by three o'clock or so this afternoon. So, let me again ask the question I just asked and to which your counsel objected.

### 11.3.2 Making your record and escalating the response.

Every once in a while it is useful to demonstrate to opposing counsel an awareness of his tactics, and that they are being tracked for later discussions with the court. Obviously, if his objections about "ambiguous" or "compound" or "confusing" are having little effect upon the witness's answers and the opportunity to gain information, there is no sense at all in having any discussion with opposing counsel. In such situations, treat him as merely an irritant and stick with rule number one, which is to ignore him.

Sometimes, however, such obstructionist tactics cause some trouble; they do not bring the flow of information to a halt, but they slow it down so the effect is felt. There may be concern that the witness's answers are being affected by the tactics. Each obstruction to the free flow of information can be easily noted on the record for later reference by saying something such as, "Let the record reflect that Mr. Barkauskas is again conferring with the witness before the witness has answered the question, and please mark this exchange for transcription for later motion practice."

If the interruptions escalate and become more serious and the low-grade noting-for-the-record approach does not discourage them, the next approach is to escalate the response and draw a line. A typical series of escalating responses is to:

> 1. Note for the record the improper conduct in which counsel is engaging. "Let the record reflect that counsel is conferring with the witness while the question is pending."
>
> 2. Have the court reporter mark the point in the record where the offending conduct is occurring. "Counsel, this is the third time in a row that you have conferred with the witness while a question is pending. You know that is improper and I am asking the court reporter to mark the deposition.[6]
>
> 3. Threaten to seek the assistance of the court. "Let the record reflect again that counsel is conferring with the witness while a question is pending. Counsel, if this conduct persists, you will leave me little choice but to ask the court for assistance. Of course, if I do that I will also ask that your client be held responsible for expenses [or the lawyer if you think that will be more persuasive]."
>
> 4. Take a break and talk with opposing counsel away from the witness. Counsel cannot afford to back down in front of his client; that is not the way to maintain good client relationships. Sometimes a reasonable request made in the hallway apart from the client will have better prospects for success. "Bill, this is getting out of hand. I don't want to break this off and see Magistrate Jones—you're busy and so am I—but you are putting me in a corner. If you don't stop the conferring, I am

---

6. Most court reporting machines have a key that places a mark in the margin of the tape. The purpose of this is so the reporter can quickly locate a particular question or answer.

going to have to call him."

5. Display anger. Use this tactic with caution. Depending on counsel's ability to display outrage and to intimidate opponents, it may cause opposing counsel either to back down or to become angry himself and even more outrageous in his behavior. Opposing counsel will never back down immediately—that would be conceding defeat in the eyes of his client—but may change his behavior later in the deposition. "[Slamming down the hand on the table] This has got to stop. What you are doing is outrageous and a complete violation of the rules. Either you stop it or I am going to get the judge to stop you!"

6. Note on the record the time consumed by breaks, conferring while a question is pending, and other disruptive contact. "Let the record reflect that counsel and the witness took a break while a question was pending and were gone for seventeen minutes." The Advisory Committee Notes to 31(d)(2), the rule limiting depositions to seven hours on one day, states the court must grant additional time if the witness or counsel engage in inappropriate, time-consuming conduct. In fact, transcription equipment has become so sophisticated that the amount of time in the deposition devoted to legitimate purposes (asking questions and receiving answers) and obstructionist conduct can be calculated so that the full seven hours of deposition testimony can be guaranteed.

7. Draw a line in the sand. Remember, however, if that line is crossed there is little choice but to follow through with the threat. "Counsel, if you confer one more time while a question is pending, I am adjourning the deposition while I seek a protective order and expenses. It's your choice."

8. Go to the magistrate or judge. *See* § 12.2.1.

### 11.3.3 Use the discipline of the rules.

While it may not always be evident, many lawyers feel somewhat constrained by a clear statement in the law that certain kinds of conduct are prohibited. Bringing to the offending lawyer's attention the prohibitions of Rule 30(d)(1) may control the improper conduct.

"Counsel, that last objection was argumentative and suggestive and clearly designed to coach the witness. I hardly need to point out to you that Rule 30(d)(1) of the Federal Rules of Civil Procedure states that 'Any objection during a deposition must be stated concisely and in a non-argumentative and non-suggestive manner.' Please do not violate that rule again."

### 11.3.4 Use a videotape deposition.

Where opposing counsel has a reputation for obstructionist behavior or previous experience with this lawyer has counseled that improper behavior is likely to occur, recording the deposition by videotape may stop the behavior before it starts. Rule 30(b)(2) gives the noticing attorney the option of recording the deposition by videotape, audiotape, or stenographically. For whatever reasons, lawyers who engage in the most outrageous conduct when only a court reporter is present will be on their best behavior when their actions are being recorded on videotape.[7] Perhaps their knowledge that the tape can be shown to the judge or magistrate accounts for this, but it works. For those opponents who obstruct not merely by objections and instructions not to answer, but by coughing, sighing, making faces and gestures, and other activity not shown on the transcript or on the head and shoulders shot of the deponent used in most videotaped depositions, a second camera, operated by a paralegal, can be brought to the deposition and aimed at the opposing counsel at all times. In this way there will be videographic support for a claim of any obstructive behavior by opposing counsel that will be indisputable.

### 11.3.5 The special problem of instructions not to answer.

Instructing a witness not to answer can be a perfectly proper response by opposing counsel to a deposition question. If the question calls for privileged information, or inquires into an area that the court has previously ordered off limits (by discovery order or protective order), or if opposing counsel is adjourning the deposition to seek an order terminating the deposition because of improper conduct, instructing the witness not to answer is legitimate. A problem arises, however, when opposing counsel gives the instruction, not because of a legitimate reason, but because he does not like the answer that will be given.

An instruction not to answer is a complete frustration of the ability to obtain information, at least on the topic covered by the question. The first step in dealing with such an instruction is to request opposing counsel to state the reasons for the instruction.

---

7. *See* § 1.13.2.

Q.   Mr. Glietus, when did you first learn about the problems with the computer design?

OBJECTION:

> Hold on. I have no idea of what you mean by first learning about the problems. You make it sound like all of sudden he learned this. He could have gradually learned about it.

Q.   Please answer the question.

OBJECTION:

> No way. I am not going to let him answer that question the way you are asking it.

Q.   Again, please answer the question.

OBJECTION:

> Are you deaf? I am instructing the witness not to answer.

Q.   Are you following your lawyer's instruction and refusing to answer?

A.   Yes.

Q.   Counsel, I ask you to state the reason for your instruction not to answer.

OPPOSING COUNSEL:

> Because your question stinks.

Q.   Rule 31(d)(1) states you may only instruct a witness not to answer in order to preserve a privilege, to prevent me from violating a protective order, or if you are adjourning the deposition to seek an order limiting or terminating the deposition based on harassment, annoyance, or embarrassment of the deponent. Which one of these are you relying on?

OPPOSING COUNSEL:

> I don't have to tell you that.

Q.   Are you refusing to give the basis for your instruction?

OPPOSING COUNSEL:

> Yes.

Q.   Counsel, I am sure you are aware that Rule 26(b)(5) requires that if you are claiming privilege as the basis for your instruction, you must expressly claim the privilege and describe the nature of the documents, communications, or things in a manner which will allow me to determine the applicability of the privilege. Rule 37(a)(2)(B) also requires that we confer to see if I can obtain the information called for by my question without seeking court action. Do you see any way for me to get that information or to get around this problem?

OPPOSING COUNSEL:

You guys who sit there and spout off statutes make me sick. If you don't have any more questions, I suggest we end this deposition now.

Once opposing counsel has given the instruction not to answer, it is difficult for him then to change his mind without losing face. The attempt is worth making, however, but a likely, more successful approach is to caucus with opposing counsel out in the hallway away from the witness. If you have been unsuccessful in getting the deposition back on track, a record of the curative effort must be made upon return to the deposition room.

If opposing counsel will not bend, it makes sense to finish the deposition before seeking the assistance of the court. If fact, most judges do not want to hear from counsel regarding discovery disputes until the deposition has been completed on all other topics. Assuming that the deposition continues on to other matters, and proceeds with less acrimony, it may even be possible to get an answer to the question that engendered the illegitimate instruction not to answer. If the deposition is adjourned to seek an order compelling an answer and the court refuses to grant the order, opposing counsel may oppose resuming the deposition. Finishing the deposition also allows time for calm consideration of the legal merits of the instruction outside the heated atmosphere of the deposition room. Merely state that you are going to proceed to other topics and are not waiving your right to return to the problematic topic or to seek an order compelling discovery.

## 11.4 OBSTRUCTING BEHAVIOR THAT ISN'T OBSTRUCTING BEHAVIOR

There are several common deposition tactics that, at first glance, appear to interfere with the ability to obtain information, but with experience are easy to avoid. Let's look at several of these.

## 11.4.1 Objection, vague.

Certainly, it is an acceptable tactic to ignore objections that do not coach the witness, unless of course, they are valid—in which case the question should be reconsidered or rephrased. Sometimes, however, opposing counsel and the witness have worked out a routine, particularly for questions that have been objected to as vague, which effectively stops the flow of information. Here is an example:

> Q.   Mrs. Lemontas, how large is the sales department at the Crabtree Company?

OBJECTION:

> Objection, vague.

> Q.   Mrs. Lemontas, do you understand the question?

> A.   No, I don't.

These responses are repeated every time opposing counsel makes a vagueness objection and are obviously rehearsed. The easiest method of dealing with this tactic is to ask the witness what it is that she does not understand about the question.

> Q.   Mrs. Lemontas, what is it that you do not understand about the question?

OPPOSING COUNSEL:

> She doesn't know whether you are talking about the number of employees in the sales department or how big is that physical area of the company.

> A.   That's right.

> Q.   I am asking about how many employees. How big is the sales department?

A variation of the vagueness game is when, as above, opposing counsel argues that the question can mean one of two or more things. A quick way of punishing this behavior is always to ask for all of the alternatives.

> Q.   Mrs. Lemontas, what is it that you do not understand about the question?

OPPOSING COUNSEL:

> She doesn't know whether you are talking about the number of employees of the sales department or how big is that physical area of the company.

> A.   That's right.

Q. Well, let's take both of them. First, tell me the physical size of the sales department.

A. About 2,000 square feet.

Q. And how many employees does the sales department have?

A. About thirty-six.

This tactic ends when opposing counsel realizes that every time all of the proposed interpretations are addressed and the questioning attorney is learning even more information.

### 11.4.2 Dictionary.

Sometimes witnesses play this game without any help from opposing counsel. Sometimes counsel alone plays it. Here is an example:

Q. What procedures does the purchasing department follow in placing orders for computer parts?

A. What do you mean by procedures?

Q. Well, I mean what does purchasing routinely do when it buys computer parts?

A. What do you mean by routinely?

Q. I mean regularly. Do you have a regular practice for ordering parts?

A. I am not sure what you mean by regular practice.

The witness may well be genuinely confused by the meaning of the questions. Or it may be that this is a sharp witness who is attempting to lure deposing counsel into playing the game of dictionary, thereby diverting attention from a question the witness would prefer not to answer. The way to respond to this game is to turn it back on the witness.

Q. Mr. Vitar, what precautions did you take when you learned that the boiler was overheating?

OBJECTION:

Objection, vague. What do you mean by precautions?

Q. Mr. Vitar, are you familiar with the word "precautions"?

A. Yes.

Q. What does that word mean to you?

> A.  Well, I guess it means what you do to prevent problems.
>
> Q.  Okay, using that definition, what precautions did you take when you learned that the boiler was overheating?

If the definition used by the witness and the definition of deposing counsel differ, then response to the question should first be elicited utilizing the witness's definition. Deposing counsel should then seek the information sought by the original question.

# Chapter Twelve

## PROTECTIVE ORDERS AND APPLICATIONS TO THE COURT

*They say that the first inclination which an animal has is to protect itself.* — Diogenes Laertius

### 12.1 PROTECTIVE ORDERS

Sometimes problems that might occur at a deposition can be anticipated, and proactive motion practice can eliminate them. Perhaps the deposition has been noticed for an inconvenient time or place, issues of privilege or the proper scope of discovery are likely, the opposing attorney's past behavior in the case suggests improper behavior may occur at this deposition, or there is concern that trade secrets will be revealed during the course of the deposition. When any of these or other potential problems are anticipated, one of the parties or the witness should seek a protective order resolving the problem before convening the deposition, with all its attendant costs and inconvenience for all involved.[1]

Rule 26(c) gives an indication of the wide variety of problems that may be the topic of a protective order. Under this rule, a court may make "any order which justice requires to protect a party or person from annoyance, embarrassment, oppression, or undue burden or expense," including one or more of the following:

"(1). that the ... discovery not be had;

"(2). that the ... discovery may be had only on specified terms and conditions, including a designation of the time or place;

"(3). that the discovery may be had only by a method of

---

1. In fact, if you fail to obtain a protective order in advance, you may not be allowed to object to the discovery during the deposition. *Mitsui and Co. (U.S.A.) Inc. v. Puerto Rico Water Resources Authority*, 93 F.R.D. 62 (D.P.R. 1981).

discovery other than that selected by the party seeking discovery;

"(4). that certain matters not be inquired into, or that the scope of the … discovery be limited to certain matters;

"(5). that discovery be conducted with no one present except persons designated by the court;

"(6). that a deposition, after being sealed, be opened only by order of the court;

"(7). that a trade secret or other confidential research, development, or commercial information not be revealed or be revealed only in a designated way; and

"(8). that the parties simultaneously file specified documents or information enclosed in sealed envelopes to be opened as directed by the court."

A protective order can be sought from either the court in which the action is pending or the court where the deposition is to be taken. Under Rule 26(c), however, a certification must be filed with the motion that there has been a conference or a good faith attempt to confer with other affected parties in an effort to resolve the dispute without court action. Many of the jurisdictions following the pre-1993 version of the Federal Rules of Civil Procedure also have rules imposing a similar requirement. The risk of bringing a motion for a protective order is that, if unsuccessful, the court may order the moving party or lawyer to pay the opposing party's reasonable expenses, including attorney's fees, for opposing the motion. Conversely, if the motion is granted, the opposing party may be required to pay the reasonable expenses, including attorney's fees, for bringing the motion.

While protective orders have traditionally been used defensively, offensive use is also possible. In advance of the deposition a protective order that supports inquiry into a certain area where objection and instruction not to answer by opposing counsel is anticipated can be a fruitful tactic. Such a use of the protective order promotes efficiency as it decides the issue for deposition practice without having to go through a deposition, endure the delay of the instruction not to answer, and then seek the court's intervention, which might require reconvening the deposition at significant cost and inconvenience.

A written request for a protective order can be simple in form and ordinarily does not require the support of lengthy case authority. Rule 26(b)(1) provides the primary authority for a motion for a protective order granting permission to inquire into an area. This rule allows discovery into all matters, not privileged, which are relevant or which are reasonably calculated to lead to the discovery of admissible evidence. Thus, the best support for a protective order motion seeking permission to inquire into an area is a strong factual argument that the area is relevant to the case independently or may reasonably lead to admissible evidence. A motion for a protective order seeking to preclude inquiry into an area should, conversely, demonstrate that the material sought to be protected is either privileged or is so clearly irrelevant that it could not reasonably lead to admissible evidence. If a protective order is sought because of previous improper treatment of deposition witnesses by the deposing attorney or other inappropriate conduct, relevant transcript excerpts from previous depositions should be attached to the motion. In a case where previous behavior has already been sanctioned by the judge, copies of those orders should be attached to remind the judge of the problem and the necessary curative judicial action in light of those prior discovery abuses.

Whether topics are open to discovery is essentially a question of fact the answer to which is determined by comparing the issues in the case to the materials sought to be discovered or protected, except when it comes to defining or recognizing a privilege. Because the determination of whether to issue a protective order is primarily fact-driven, extensive legal argument is not helpful in winning the motion. A party seeking discovery is better advised to argue that the information sought is relevant to the claims or defenses in the case or is likely to uncover other admissible evidence, such as the names of additional witnesses or the existence and location of potentially relevant documents, than to string out a series of case citations. As a matter of logic, the more relevant the material sought, the more likely it is that the court will allow or compel the inquiry.[2] If discovery is being opposed, the opposing attorney must demonstrate that the information sought is substantially unrelated to the claims or defenses in the case. Further, where possible, an additional demonstration that the questions invade the privacy of the deponent makes it even more likely that the court will grant a protective order.

In a case where the application for a protective order depends upon a factual determination by the court, the court may examine relevant material *in camera*, so that a finding can be made on privilege or trade secrecy (Rule 26(c)(7)), relevance, harassment, invasion of privacy, and so forth. Sometimes the court will permit counsel seeking discovery to

---

2.   This balancing test is analogous to the test under Fed.R.Evid. 403, where the court must weigh relevance against unfair prejudice. In the discovery context, the court is weighing relevance against the burden of production.

participate in such *in camera* inspections, while excluding the opposing party. This inspection is governed by rules of confidentiality which counsel must obey. The counsel producing the documents for *in camera* review should be on guard in this circumstance, even where discovery is ultimately denied, because the mere act of inspection by opposing counsel may provide leads for other discovery, and therefore confer an advantage (like a "fruit of the forbidden tree" problem in criminal law), even if discovering counsel does not violate confidentiality rules. In arguing against participation by discovering counsel in any *in camera* inspection, opposing counsel should make the court aware of these concerns. At the least, counsel opposing discovery should argue that inside counsel should not participate in such review.

## 12.2 APPLICATIONS TO THE COURT

While protective orders are used if a problem arises before the deposition is convened, the procedure for obtaining relief once the deposition has commenced or is scheduled to commence is to move for relief under several provisions of the rules. The type of problem determines what rule should be relied upon.

Modern discovery is intended to function largely without judicial intervention. Occasionally, however, either substantive problems or an attorney's posturing interfere with the appropriate flow of information. In such instances, the only recourse may be requesting relief from the court.

Born of necessity, the oral application to the court provides a vehicle for quick resolution of discovery disputes. Although "Let's get the judge on the phone!" may actually be wielded more often as a threat than as a real suggestion, it is generally an efficient way to resolve discovery problems where magistrates or even judges are willing to listen to disputes over the telephone. If the courthouse is relatively close, the attorneys may appear in person, but obviously that takes more time. Applications to the court, of course, depend largely on local circumstance. In some federal districts it is virtually impossible to reach a judge or magistrate on the phone. In these jurisdictions, resort to the court for resolution of discovery disputes during a deposition is essentially a written process. The lawyers are expected to accumulate discovery disputes and present them in an efficient way in a motion for the court's consideration. In other districts, judges or assigned magistrates are easily reachable by phone and prefer to dispose of discovery disputes as they occur without the necessity of formal motion practice, with its resulting need to prepare written orders.

### 12.2.1 Rule 30(d). Duration, termination, and suspension.

Under Rule 30(d)(3) of the Federal Rules of Civil Procedure, or Rule 30(d) of the pre-1993 version of the Rules, a party or the witness may suspend the deposition and request a court order to terminate or limit the deposition as provided in Rule 26(c) because the deposition is being conducted in bad faith or in such an unreasonable manner as to annoy, embarrass, or oppress the witness or party. The motion can be made either to the court in which the action is pending or the court in the district where the deposition is being taken. If either court terminates the deposition, only the court in which the action is pending may permit it to resume. Under the provisions of Rule 37(a)(4), the court can award expenses for either bringing or defending the motion.

### 12.2.2 Rule 30(d)(2).

This rule permits the district court by an order in the particular case to alter the time limits for conducting a deposition, which otherwise is one day of seven hours. The rule also permits the court to extend the time, if needed, for a fair examination or because the witness or another party has impeded or delayed the examination. The motion is made to the court in which the action is pending and, if the court finds that one of the parties has impeded, delayed, or frustrated the fair conduct of the deposition, it may impose sanctions on that party. It is for the purposes of motions such as these that modern court reporting systems have the ability to track the actual time during which examination of the witness is occurring, tracked separately from breaks, conferences with the deponent by defending counsel, or any other interruption. Most courts view the seven-hour time limit as the time during which the actual questioning of the deponent by the examining lawyer is ongoing.

### 12.2.3 Rule 30(g).

If the party noticing the deposition fails to attend and proceed with the deposition, or if the party fails to subpoena a witness who then fails to attend the deposition, the other parties attending the deposition may ask the court in which the action is pending to award them their reasonable expenses, including reasonable attorney's fees.

### 12.2.4 Rule 32(d)(4).

Errors and irregularities in the transcribing, preparing, signing, certifying, sealing, endorsing, transmitting, filing, or in the way the officer is otherwise dealing with the deposition must be raised by a motion to suppress the deposition or some part of it. The motion must be made with reasonable promptness after the defect is, or with due diligence might have been, ascertained.

### 12.2.5 Rule 37(a).

If a witness refuses to answer a question at a deposition or if a party fails to make a designation under Rule 30(b)(6), the questioning party or, in the case of a failure to designate under Rule 30(b)(6), the noticing party may move for an order compelling an answer or designation. Rule 37(a)(3) treats an evasive or incomplete answer as a failure to answer. Under Rule 37(a)(1), any motion concerning a party is made to the court in which the action is pending, while motions concerning the witness are made to the court in the district where the deposition is being taken. Under the pre-1993 version of the rule (still in operation in many state jurisdictions), motions concerning parties could also be made to the court in the district where the deposition was being taken. Rule 37(a)(2)(B) requires the filing of a certification that counsel have in good faith conferred or attempted to confer with the witness or party who has failed to answer or designate, in an effort to resolve the dispute without court action. The court may award expenses for bringing or opposing the motion pursuant to Rule 37(a)(4).

### 12.2.6 Rule 37(b).

If the court issues an order under Rule 37(a) compelling a witness to answer a question at the deposition or compelling a party to designate a witness pursuant to Rule 30(b)(6), and there is a refusal to obey the order, the court may impose a variety of sanctions against the witness or party. The court in the district where the deposition is being taken may hold in contempt a witness who refuses to obey an order to answer. The witness may also be held in contempt for refusing to be sworn. A party who refuses to answer a question or to designate after being ordered to do so is subject to the sanctions listed in Rule 37(b)(2). A party failing to abide by the order, the attorney advising the party, or both can be required to pay the reasonable expenses, including attorney's fees, caused by the failure.

### 12.2.7 Rule 37(d).

If a party or an officer, director, or managing agent of a party or a person designated to testify pursuant to Rule 30(b)(6) fails to appear at the deposition after being served with notice, the court in which the action is pending may make whatever orders are just, including imposing any of the sanctions listed in Rule 37(b)(2)(A), (B), and (C). The court can also require the party and the attorney advising the party, or both to pay the reasonable expenses, including attorney's fees, caused by the failure to appear. That the discovery is objectionable is no defense to the motion unless the party has a pending motion for a protective order.

### 12.2.8 An example.

Let's see how one kind of these disputes actually arises during a deposition and review the process for obtaining a hearing over the telephone:

> Q. Mr. Steponkis, let me ask you a few questions about the early days of your corporation. Who were the original shareholders?

> BY OPPOSING COUNSEL:

> Objection. That was ten years ago. It has nothing at all to do with this case. Let's try to stick to relevant questions here, Adrian.

> Q. Mr. Steponkis, will you answer the question, please? Who were the original shareholders?

> BY OPPOSING COUNSEL:

> Adrian, I just objected to that question. Now, you're not going to try to play hardball here, are you? Why don't you move on?

> Q. Are you going to answer the question, Mr. Steponkis?

> BY OPPOSING COUNSEL:

> I'm sorry, you are being so unreasonable, Adrian. I'm going to instruct the witness not to answer.

> Q. Mr. Steponkis, will you answer the question, please?

> A. No, I am going to follow the instructions of my lawyer.

> Q. Well, let me ask this, then. Were the shares originally held by more than ten people?

BY OPPOSING COUNSEL:

Again, this just has nothing to do with the issues here, and I instruct Mr. Steponkis that he need not answer this question.

Q.  Mr. Steponkis, how many people held the shares originally?

A.  I'm not going to answer the question, on the advice of my attorney.

Q.  Counsel, are you claiming some sort of privilege here? You realize, of course, that under Rule 30(d)(1) a witness may be instructed not to answer only to preserve a privilege, because I am violating a protective order, or you are adjourning the deposition so you can seek an order terminating or limiting the deposition. Which one of these reasons are you relying on?

BY OPPOSING COUNSEL:

I'm claiming that these questions have nothing to do with the claims or defenses in the case, or with discovering admissible evidence in the case, and are far beyond the scope permitted by Rule 26. So, the witness does not have to answer them.

Q.  Mr. Steponkis, let me see if I can get at the information in another way. There is some question whether the owners on the certificate of incorporation were all of the original owners. Let me show you that certificate, which is Steponkis Deposition Exhibit 13. Are those all of the original owners?

BY OPPOSING COUNSEL:

Same objection. You are way out of line here, Adrian. Just ask relevant questions and we will have no problems, but you're just not going to snoop around on some fishing expedition.

Q.  Mr. Steponkis, will you answer my last question about the certificate?

A.  No, I am going to follow my lawyer's advice and decline to answer the question.

Q.  Counsel, this is important to me, so before I call the magistrate let me confer with you, as required by the rules,[3] to see if there is anything further I can do or if there is some agreement or arrangement we can make so that I can get the information I need.

BY OPPOSING COUNSEL:

I think I have made my position very clear. I am not budging.

Q.   Well, since this is the last area I need to question the witness about, I might as well see if we can get the magistrate on the phone right now rather than waiting until the deposition is concluded.

[Since the deposing attorney has now asked about the same subject matter in three different ways, a solid record demonstrating that discovery in that area is being precluded by directions to the witness not to answer has been made. Counsel also has specifically asked whether the instructions not to answer were premised upon a claim of privilege, and the defending attorney refused to claim privilege or any of the grounds permitted under Rule 30(d)(1), relying instead upon a "beyond the scope of Rule 26 discovery" argument. Let's return to the deposition room:]

BY COUNSEL:

Mr. Reporter, would you please mark those last few pages, where I am asking about the original owners of the corporation and the certificate of incorporation? Then, let's just go off the record until I can get the magistrate on the telephone.

[Then, after the magistrate is on the telephone:]

Your Honor, we have a problem here in the Smith case, Docket Number C-93-1443. Plaintiff is taking the deposition of Mr. Julius Steponkis, the vice-president of the defendant corporation, and we have asked who the original shareholders were and how many there were. The defendant has instructed the witness not to answer on the grounds that the information being sought is beyond the scope of discovery under Rule 26. Let me now orally certify, as required by Rule 37(a)(2)(B), that I have in good faith conferred with opposing counsel in an attempt to avoid the need for court action. We have the reporter here, prepared to read the questions and objections, if you would like.

---

3.   Fed.R.Civ.P. 37(a)(2)(B).

MAGISTRATE:

> No, counsel, not at this point. Let me talk to defendant's counsel.

DEFENSE:

> Your Honor, what plaintiff's counsel has been doing here is egregious. These questions about original ownership have nothing to do with the issues in this case, and he knows it. He is just trying to fish around to see if he can bring other people into this controversy, people who have nothing to do with the problems that his client has experienced, so that he can inconvenience and embarrass them. Besides that, I know that he is working with other counsel in a different case against my client, and he may very well be intending to share the answers in this deposition with that other lawyer to give her an advantage in that other lawsuit. That's why I had no choice but to direct the witness not to answer these improper questions.

MAGISTRATE:

> Okay, let me hear the questions from the reporter.

[The questions are read back from the paper tape by the reporter.]

> Counsel, put me on the speaker phone, so you and the witness can all hear my ruling. The witness is directed to answer these questions, and other questions reasonably related to them. There is nothing privileged here and, as I understand it, defense counsel is not arguing privilege. These questions may not be on matters directly part of the claims or defenses in the case, but they are reasonably intended to lead to the discovery of admissible evidence, such as the identity of witnesses with knowledge of the initial purposes and profit-sharing structure of the company. If counsel in some other lawsuit can take advantage of these answers, that has nothing to do with whether the answers should be given in this case. Their use in the other case depends upon a determination of the judge in that matter on the relevance of the information to that other case.[4] I

---

4. However, the magistrate or judge ruling on this application has the discretionary power to order deposing counsel not to release the information obtained during the deposition to anyone, including counsel in another case. *See Scott v. Monsanto Co.,* 868 F.2d 786, 792 (5th Cir. 1989). Generally, courts find this "gag-order" power

find that these questions present a legitimate area for discovery, and, counsel for the defendant, you will not interfere by directing this witness, or other witnesses who may be asked about these topics, not to answer. Are there any other problems now, counsel?

BOTH COUNSEL:

No, Your Honor.

After closing the telephone conference with the magistrate, counsel can return to the deposition table and resume questioning. Deposing counsel should, of course, start right back into the deposition with the questions that were the subject of the application to the magistrate and to which he did not get answers. He may also want to "push the envelope" a bit, *i.e.*, press into areas where he thinks the defendant has something to hide or may claim privilege, under the assumption that the defendant's counsel is unlikely to provoke another hearing before the magistrate so soon after a loss. On the other hand, the magistrate may not be prepared to rule in favor of the plaintiff if another dispute arises immediately after the first ruling, either because the magistrate thinks that the plaintiff is pressing his luck, or because she is trying to alternate the parties receiving favorable rulings in order to give the appearance of evenhandedness. The best approach is to ask the questions that you had intended to ask and not get caught up in the "gamesmanship" of discovery.

---

relates only to matters obtained through discovery, and may not be used by courts to restrict the dissemination of material that counsel has obtained during pretrial from sources other than discovery under the rules. *See Seattle Times v. Rhinehart,* 467 U.S. 20 (1984); *Rodgers v. United States Steel Corp.,* 536 F.2d 1001 (3d Cir. 1976); *and International Products Corp. v. Koons,* 325 F.2d 403 (2d Cir. 1963).

# PART THREE

## DEFENDING DEPOSITIONS

### Chapter Thirteen

### PREPARING THE WITNESS TO BE DEPOSED

*Oh the nerves, the nerves; the mysteries of this machine called Man!*
*Oh the little that unhinges it: poor creature that we are!* — Charles Dickens

Perhaps forty percent of attorneys prepare witnesses for deposition by extensively reviewing the substantive facts of the case; maybe another forty percent do so by reciting an inordinately long list of "do's" and "don'ts" that even attorneys cannot remember (and therefore they are presented in writing, or on videotape, for the witness "to take home" after the last preparation session). That leaves only twenty percent of attorneys who realize that neither of these approaches deals with the primary factor affecting the witness's performance at the deposition, which is his level of confidence about his ability to perform in the deposition environment.

No matter how well prepared the witness is on the substance of his testimony, he will not present clear and persuasive testimony unless he remains calm enough to understand the questions and to respond appropriately and cautiously; by his demeanor he must demonstrate his confidence in the truth of his testimony. The primary goal in the preparation sessions should therefore be to take burdens off of the witness's shoulders so that he can focus only on the substance of his answers.

As a general rule, the witness interview regarding the substance that he knows should be separate and distinct from the session of preparation for the deposition. Sometimes, however, the witness's role is so minor or the witness is located at such a distance that it makes good economic sense to combine the two sessions. Separating the two sessions permits better preparation by counsel for the witness preparation session and also allows preparing counsel to have some idea of the witness's personality, intelligence, confidence, and anxieties before getting the witness ready for the deposition. Finally, having separate sessions also allows time for any follow-up investigation that might be necessary before the deposition.

The first task in preparing a witness for a deposition is reducing the witness's anxiety. Most witnesses dread the prospect of giving testimony at a deposition or trial. Anxiety and worry can overwhelm the witness as she conjures up scenes from "Law and Order" or "Boston Legal" and what happens to witnesses on such shows. If the witness is a party or has her employment on the line, her worries and concerns become even more heightened. In short, testifying at a deposition is not often a pleasant experience and anticipating the experience can be even more unpleasant.

Anxiety prevents witnesses from focusing on those things they must remember. When a witness is thinking about the types of embarrassing questions that might be asked instead of concentrating on what counsel is saying, the preparation session has gone far astray. Anxiety, because it is distracting, interferes with the witness's ability to understand and remember the advice of counsel. Therefore, if the session is going to serve its purpose—preparing the witness to testify—the witness's nervousness and worries about what is going to happen must be confronted and eased.

The witness preparation session, even if conducted after the witness has been previously interviewed about substance, should contain some inquiry about whether new or different facts have come to light since the last communication with counsel. The witness might have remembered more information, discovered or looked at a new document, or talked with another person who has knowledge of the event between the previous interview and the deposition preparation session. This "information gathering" should occur after addressing the nervousness of the witness, but before preparing the witness on the procedural and substantive matters relating to the deposition. The following discussion of witness preparation, however, assumes the attorney interviewed the witness for substance sometime before the witness preparation session and there is no new information that must be assimilated into the session. As a result, the focus is on the manner in which the witness will answer at the deposition, rather than finding out what will be said in those answers.

## 13.1 THE WRONG WAY

We start with a portion of a "conventional" preparation session.

> Q. So, John, how do you feel about this deposition coming up? You're not nervous about it, are you?

A.   Well, I guess I am, a little. I'm not sure exactly what to expect, you know, I don't want to make any mistakes.

Q.   Well, that's right, it's important that you don't make any mistakes, so I thought that we would go over your testimony again, what you know about the facts in this case. All right?

A.   Sure, that seems like a good idea. But, you know, I was just wondering, are they going to try to make me look stupid or forgetful or anything? I'm just not sure what to do if I get confused about what they're asking.

Q.   Well, it is very important that you be sure about what they are asking. Don't answer any question that's unclear to you, or that is ambiguous. They may try to make you look forgetful, so watch out for that.

A.   Well, you'll be there, right?

Q.   Yes, of course, I'll be right there, and I can object if they try to take advantage of you. Make sure that you pause, maybe take a deep breath, before every answer, so that I have time to object if I think it's necessary. Then, pay attention to what I say in my objection, because there may be something in the question that I think is unfair or improper, and you should be aware of that when you answer.

A.   Are they allowed to ask unfair or improper questions?

Q.   Lawyers do it all the time. They ask questions that have a double meaning, or they try to get the witness to admit things that he really doesn't mean, or they only put in part of the story; those kinds of things. So, we have to watch out for them, and only answer fair questions. Now, another thing for you to remember is not to volunteer information. By "volunteer," I mean answering with more than you were asked for. If the other attorney asks you, "Where do you work?" your answer should be "Strongis Ironworks," not "I've worked as a foreman at Strongis for the past seventeen years." You see, he didn't ask, "What is your position?" or "How long have you worked there?" So, just answer what is asked; those lengthy answers just cause trouble.

Let's just pause here and take a moment to examine whether the attorney is actually helping her witness. The attorney asked whether the witness was nervous in a way that suggested that it is wrong to be nervous. This caused the witness, at the outset of the preparation process, to feel he is not doing the right thing. When the witness answered that he was nervous because he did not want to make any mistakes, the attorney emphasized that it is important not to make mistakes. That certainly did not reduce the witness's anxiety level. Instead, the witness might be comforted to hear the following:

> "I know that you don't want to make any mistakes, but you should not worry too much about that. First, we are going to go over what I think will be the substance of the other lawyer's questions until you are comfortable with stating the facts, and we'll have a practice deposition where one of my partners will come in and ask questions as though she was the opposing counsel. You know, you will have a chance to read this deposition over once it is typed up, and I'll read it with you. If we see any mistakes, we can correct them. You really shouldn't feel that you need to be perfect. You'll make some mistakes, I'll make some mistakes, and the attorney on the other side will make some mistakes, but they just won't matter when we get to trial. Besides that, I'll be there, and if I think that anything is important enough to need correction right at the deposition, I'll make a note of it, and I can ask you questions after the other attorney is finished."

The whole idea here is to reduce the witness's nervousness. No one has ever given a mistake-free deposition, no matter how much he was cautioned not to make mistakes, so we might as well tell the witness that there are procedures for fixing mistakes, and that we, the attorneys, will worry about identifying mistakes that need to be fixed. In addition, it is usually helpful to let the witness know that most people are nervous when they have their deposition taken and that it is natural to feel that way. In follow-up questions, the basis for the witness's nervousness should be probed. If the witness is given the opportunity to express his concerns, the lawyer can address them. There is an additional benefit to such an inquiry, because at times the nervousness of the witness about a particular area of testimony will signal the necessity of especially careful preparation in that area.

Next, the witness expressed concern that the other side would try to make him look stupid or forgetful, and he said he did not know what to do if he got confused. Instead of providing reassurance, the attorney said, "Watch out for that." In other words, "You are right, that may happen, and it's your job to avoid it." The attorney could have said:

> "I'm going to be there to deal with any unfair questions, so you don't have to worry about them. I don't think they will try

to be unfair, because they just want to know what you know about this case. But if I think that a question is unfair, I will deal with it, and I will tell you what to do at that time."

Further, you should tell the witness directly what to do if he feels confused by a question. "Don't answer" is not sufficient because, absent an instruction from you not to answer, the witness will be pressed for an answer and will likely become more confused. In preparing the witness, she should be informed that if a question is confusing she should say, "I don't understand the question," and not feel embarrassed by doing so.

Next, the witness asked, "You'll be there, right?" Clearly, this question signaled the witness's lack of comfort with the proceedings. By responding that she will be there to object "if they try to take advantage of you," the attorney caused more problems than she solved. "Take advantage of you" is an ominous phrase, and like other such phrases it raises the specter of more problems than the witness has already imagined. The attorney then burdened the witness further by telling the witness to "take a breath" before every answer. Now, besides worrying about the content of his answers and losing some undefined "advantages," the witness must worry about timing as well. Then, the attorney told the witness to interpret her objections before giving his answer. This did not lift burdens from the witness's shoulders, but added more.

Furthermore, the attorney reminded the witness that lawyers ask unfair and improper questions all of the time but, again, she failed to give the witness any tools to deal with such questions. Finally, by instructing the witness not to volunteer information, and failing to provide any rationale, the attorney suggested to the witness hidden rules with hidden purposes. Again, none of this put the witness at ease.

## 13.2 BURDEN-REDUCING PREPARATION

Let's start the preparation session all over again; this time, the focus will be on taking burdens away from the witness and allowing him to focus only on the testimony.

> Q. Good morning, John. Thanks for coming in for a final session about this deposition. I imagine that you are feeling a bit nervous.
>
> A. Yes, I guess I am.

Q. Well, that's natural. It's just a little bit of extra adrenaline pumping, getting you ready to do your best. I feel the same thing every time I go into a deposition or a courtroom. Is there anything in particular that you are nervous about?

A. No. I've never been deposed before and I guess it's just fear of the unknown.

Q. That's understandable. Why don't I start by explaining the set-up for the deposition. The deposition will be in the offices of plaintiff's attorney, but I want you to come here one hour before the deposition so that we can go over there together. We'll take a cab from here so that we don't have to worry about parking. Is that all right with you?

A. Yes, that's fine.

Q. They have a comfortable conference room, very similar to this one, and there will be water and coffee throughout the deposition. And there will be a court reporter there. Do you know what a court reporter does?

A. Yes. I've seen them on "Law and Order."

Q. Well, the court reporter will be there to swear you in and to record the questions and the answers. Later on, the reporter will type up those questions and answers and send them to us so that we can read them and correct anything that we don't think is accurate. Any questions so far?

A. No.

Q. I will be sitting right alongside you at the deposition, and anytime you think that you need to talk to me, you just tell me. We can talk right there, or we can leave the room. You just tell me you want to talk with me, and I'll take care of it. Is that all right?

A.    Yes.[1]

Q.    Do you have any questions so far?

A.    No.

Q.    Well, if you have any questions at any time please feel free to ask. Sometimes we lawyers don't fully appreciate how foreign this process can be to non-lawyers.

A.    I will, thanks.

The above instruction allows the preparation session to start by immediately putting the witness at ease about several of his concerns. First, he knows that his anxiety is natural. Next, the logistics—where the deposition is and how he will get there—are taken care of. The witness is also told that it is appropriate for him to ask questions during the process. With this backdrop, counsel can then talk about what a deposition is, explain the deposition procedures to the witness, and assure the witness that counsel will be with him during the entire process.

How long this part of witness preparation lasts and what is said depends on the witness. Some witnesses have had their depositions taken before or are quite experienced with the way litigation works. Others are just not the nervous or worried type. But many witnesses are entirely ignorant of the whole process and are scared to death. Witness preparation should be tailored to meet the individual needs of the witness.

A caveat: false or insincere reassurances do not work. Comments like, "Don't worry, everything will be fine," do nothing to comfort the witness when the witness fears that the wrong answer may cause him to lose his job, his house, and everything else he holds dear. Far better to be honest, but upbeat and confident. Avoid false promises.

---

1.    Of course, when a question is pending the witness normally should answer before he talks with counsel. On the other hand, because the witness must be given the opportunity to discuss questions of privilege with counsel before being compelled to answer, this rule must have some flexibility. In general, as long as you do not abuse this procedure, it should be permissible for the witness to check with you if a particular question raises a problem. Where appropriate, you can prevent that interruption from becoming an issue by explaining, on the record, why the witness had a problem with the question: "Ms. Jones asked me whether we were still talking about the first transaction or had jumped ahead to the second transaction. I told her that I would ask you." Or, "Ms. Jones asked whether this last question got into a privileged area, and I told her that she could answer."

## 13.3 MAKING WITNESS PREPARATION STICK

Before we get into other specifics about witness preparation, a word about style is appropriate. Too often, witness preparation consists of the lawyer giving the witness a long, uninterrupted lecture which may go on for up to an hour and contains a set of so-called "rules" for the witness to follow during the deposition. At the end of the lecture, the attorney asks the witness if he has any questions and then sends him on his way. The attorney is then surprised to see the witness quickly forget everything discussed during the witness preparation session and start violating all of the "rules" the attorney thought she had so carefully impressed on the witness.

The question is how to make all of the suggestions made during the witness preparation session stick with the witness during the deposition. The answer is to follow the five important rules of witness preparation:

1. interact
2. confirm
3. repeat
4. illustrate
5. reinforce

### 1. Interact

Think back to your law school days and recall how interested you were in listening to the professors' lectures. For most of us they were boring. Think how your mind wandered during the lectures and how much you retained without going back and studying your notes. The same is true of witnesses. Straight lecturing is boring and not much of what is said will be remembered. But if the witness preparation session is more of a discussion with give-and-take between counsel and the witness, then it is more likely the witness will internalize and remember what was said.

### 2. Confirm

Confirming means constantly checking with the witness to make sure that what is being said is understood, and that the witness does not have any questions.

### 3. Repeat

Repeating information several times makes it more likely to be remembered than if the information is mentioned only once. Therefore, give key instructions more than once. But repetition does not mean merely saying the same thing twice. Instead, phrase the information differently but make the same point each time.

### 4. Illustrate

Illustrate means exactly what it says. Every time an important instruction is given to the witness, illustrate it by an example. This will make the instruction much more understandable to the witness.

### 5. Reinforce

Finally, reinforcing means actually having the witness practice following the instructions given. This helps impress the instructions upon the witness and makes it much easier for the witness to recall and apply the instruction during the deposition. Usually reinforcing means just reminding the witness when she violates an instruction, but it can also mean actually having the witness practice answering questions in the correct way. Constantly reminding the witness of deposition preparation instructions will make it easier for them to remember the instructions during the deposition.

## 13.4 ADDRESSING QUESTIONS ABOUT THE PREPARATION SESSION

Whether a lawyer's conversation with a particular witness is covered by the attorney-client privilege is beyond the scope of this book, but well before the witness preparation session it should be known whether the other side will be able to discover what counsel and the witness say to each other. The witness should be prepared on how to deal with these questions, so that he is not surprised by them at the deposition.

If the witness is covered by the attorney-client privilege, the witness should be told this:

> "Let me tell you right now that whatever we say to each other in getting you ready for your deposition is confidential. The other side is not entitled to learn about what we say here, so I want you to feel comfortable in saying whatever you wish.

Do you have any questions about that?"

If the witness is not covered, you should also explain this:

"I want you to understand that whatever we say here can be asked about during the deposition and you will have to tell them what you remember about our conversation. What this means is that we should not talk about anything or say anything to each other we would not want the other side to hear."

More important than the explanation of what the witness can or cannot say is that counsel should not say anything to the witness that would be better kept confidential.

## 13.5 ANSWERING QUESTIONS

Now let's address answering questions. This part of the preparation session is very important. The following is an example of the classic instruction:

COUNSEL: At the beginning of the deposition, you will be asked to swear to tell the truth, and then the plaintiff's attorney will start his questioning. The only thing that you have to remember during this whole time is to give the shortest correct answer to each question. Let's just take a minute here for me to explain what I mean by the shortest correct answer. There are seven answers that are the best response to ninety percent of the questions asked at deposition. Those seven are:

1. "Green," "Two o'clock," "In the basement;"

2. "Yes;"

3. "No;"

4. "I don't understand the question;"

5. "I don't know;"

6. "I don't remember;" and

7. "I'd like to take a break."

Each of these answers should be explained individually.

**1. "Green." "Two o'clock." "In the basement."** Counsel should explain the following to the witness about answer one: "If you are asked what color your car is, or when you came home in the afternoon, or where you keep your canceled checks, these short answers are best. You don't have to worry about what the questioner really wants to know, or where he is going. If he wants more information he will ask for it. The main reason that short answers are best is that attorneys are trained to chase down any paths that appear, just in case there is something relevant at the end. We don't have any desire to prolong this deposition unnecessarily, so it helps everybody if we keep the answers short and to the point."

**2. and 3. "Yes" or "No."** The following explains answers two and three: "You will find that most of the time the attorney will ask questions that let you answer 'yes' or 'no.' When he asks those questions, go ahead and answer that way. If he wants more information, it's his job to ask for it. If I want you to explain some answer more fully, I will talk to you at breaks, and we can ask some questions of our own at the end of his questioning, or I may ask you to expand on your answer right then. Let me worry about that. Just remember, it is not rude to answer with a simple yes or no."

**4. "I don't understand the question."** Witnesses frequently will answer questions without fully understanding what information is sought. The following explanation forestalls that behavior: "You do not have to try to answer any question that you don't understand. It's the other attorney's job to ask understandable questions, and we don't want to waste time guessing as to what he might mean. If he uses words you don't understand, tell him, 'I don't understand the question.' If he uses words that you do understand, but he uses them in a way you do not understand, tell him, 'I don't understand the question.' If the question just gets too long, or has too many different phrases in it, tell him, 'I don't understand the question.' Then, if he asks what you don't understand about the question, tell him that. You don't have to try to fix his question by saying, 'Well, if what you mean by 'no profit' is that we had no net profit after tax for that period, then my answer is such and so.' Just tell him that you don't understand the question and wait to see how he wants to clarify it."

**5. "I don't know."** This is often the hardest answer for witnesses to give, because they feel somehow as if they should know all the answers. The witness should be told: "You just don't have to feel that way. We haven't told the other side in this lawsuit that you have all the answers, and our case does not depend at all upon you having all the answers. What you do know, tell them; what you don't know, don't worry about. Just say, 'I don't know.' There is no need for you to try to guess what the answer is, or to try to figure out what it probably is, unless they ask you to do that.[2] If you don't have the answer in your mind, say, 'I don't know.'"

**6. "I don't remember."** Witnesses also find it hard to use this answer, perhaps because no one wants to admit that his memory is not perfect. The following assurance is often helpful: "You are not expected to have every answer or to remember every fact that the other attorney wants to ask about. If you don't remember at the deposition, and then later something reminds you of the answer, we can correct the transcript of the deposition or we can explain at trial that you remembered, if the question even comes up at trial. But, if you are asked for information that you can't remember at the deposition just say, 'I don't remember.' Then, if the attorney wants to try to help you remember by showing you documents or suggesting answers, he can do that. If those things help you remember, that's fine; if they don't, you just say, 'I still don't remember.'"

**7. "I'd like to take a break."** Finally, the witness needs to appreciate and learn to use the request for a break appropriately. The witness should be told: "Sometimes in the deposition you may be asked a question and you just are not sure what you are supposed to do. Maybe you think the answer should be private; maybe you think the answer is likely to be long and you need a chance to stretch and collect your thoughts; maybe you think the question is unfair in some way and you want to talk to me. If, for any reason, you want to take a break just tell me, or tell the other attorney, and we will take a break. I'll worry about whether it's a good idea or not. It is much better to take a break and talk together, to figure out how to make you comfortable with giving an answer, or to decide whether the question is objectionable, than it is to go forward and perhaps give the other side some information that really is your private business or that they are not entitled to. So, if you have any doubt as to whether you should answer, talk to me right then or say, 'I'd like to take a break.' The other lawyer may try to insist on an answer to her question before the break, but if you really need a break, just say so and it will happen."

---

2. Some attorneys in preparing witnesses for deposition tell the witness, "Don't speculate." There is only one problem with this advice: it's wrong. There is no rule against seeking the witness's speculation in a deposition, so long as that speculation is reasonably calculated to lead to the production of relevant information. For example, suppose the question is, "Who was the last person to adjust the temperature settings on the boiler?" The witness answers, "Well, I'd really have to guess, based on who was there." The next question could quite properly be, "Okay, what's your guess?" There is no basis here for directing the witness not to answer, since there is no question of privilege or harassment and the question is not patently beyond the scope of proper discovery. Yet, if the witness is told during preparation that he should not speculate, he may be confused when speculation is properly called for at the deposition itself.

These "shortest correct answers" are intended to simplify the witness's job—to reduce his burden at the deposition. When giving these instructions, continually reassure the witness: "It is not your job to wonder about the procedure or what the other attorney might say or do; that is why I'm there; I'll take care of all those matters, so you don't have to worry about them. All you have to do is give the shortest correct answer."

Consider, however, modern litigation, where trial is only a remote possibility, and settlement or some sort of assisted mediation is most likely. The seven shortest, best answers assume that there will be a trial, and they date from the time when trials of civil cases were common. Today, it must be assumed that those responses may be the only opportunity to provide all of the information that the opposing counsel needs to know from the witness in order appropriately to value the case, and that a non-trial disposition process should have to resolve the litigation fairly. If the ultimate user of the deposition is a decision-maker of the opponent on settlement, a mediator, or an arbitrator, consideration should be given to changing the rules of response.

When trial is not anticipated, and it seems most likely that motions practice or informal resolution of some sort will end the dispute, there are times when answers one, two, and three will not be the "best" answer that can be given to a question, because the goals have changed. If, in fair response to a question, an opportunity is provided to inform opposing counsel and the record of facts that are helpful to the deponent's position in the matter, that opportunity should be taken. In addition, and especially if the deposition is recorded on videotape, the short yes, no, green answers that don't volunteer any information can appear to be evasive. Recall the deposition of President Clinton. Deposing counsel was required to ask numerous questions to obtain even the most basic of information. When that performance was played to the public, the clear message was that the President was not forthcoming. (Of course that impression was aided by the denial of certain activity that was later recanted.) In another well-known example, Bill Gates's deposition testimony in the case of *U.S. v. Microsoft* was marred by his constantly stating that he could not recall information, even though there was a document, later shown to be known to him, that would have refreshed his memory. The clear impression left with the judge in that matter was that the witness was being intentionally evasive.

For the above reasons, the "best" answer in modern litigation may well be the answer that provides fairly responsive information to the question. A fair response to the question, "Did you go to college?" is not "Yes" but rather, "Yes, I graduated from Nita University in 1994 with a Bachelor of Science degree in civil engineering." This sort of response has several benefits. First, it is the sort of response that a person would give to such an inquiry if it occurred outside of a deposition, so it is an easy (more comfortable) way for the witness to respond, unencumbered by a lawyer's instruction to act in an unaccustomed way. Second, the answer will eventually save time as it requires one question by the lawyer, not four. Third, the witness can be better evaluated as a witness by a later decisionmaker as to matters of credibility, just as if at trial. Certainly the question about college at trial will not receive the answer "Yes" on direct examination of the witness. Fourth, any reader of a transcript or viewer of a video deposition will receive the information in a forthcoming and natural way that communicates credibility, or at least non-evasiveness, on the part of the witness. Fifth, the response sounds unguarded and complete and is less likely to engender probing by deposing counsel beyond the answer provided. If the witness responds in a natural and apparently complete way to all deposition questions, then at a later time, when a question is asked that might, but does not specifically, ask for damaging information, perhaps opposing counsel will not probe too closely. And finally, if a witness is prepared to give fair and natural answers to the questions posed to him at deposition, the preparation is likely to stick. Every lawyer has experienced the client who begins the deposition using the "best seven responses," only to abandon all instructions by the third hour of persistent questioning by opposing counsel that obtains all the information the witness has on any given topic, but merely in a more uncomfortable way. All witnesses (except perhaps experts paid by the hour) want to shorten the deposition process. As a result, eventually they will begin to respond in a natural, more expansive way, to the questions of deposing counsel, and attempts by defending counsel to stop that behavior will more than likely engender resentment in the witness towards the defending counsel.

Even if the likely end-game for the litigation is a trial, there are exceptions to the giving of the "best seven" responses.

First, if the deposition is of a party or a witness whose statements are attributable to the party as admissions, a more complete answer will make the use of those statements more difficult at trial by the opposing counsel. When looking for admissions, as described in an earlier chapter, short, specific answers are sought that can be read or shown to the jury during the trial. The fuller answer is harder to dissect for use as an admission, and will at least contain explanatory material regarding any fact contained in the answer that might be harmful. As to these witnesses, it will usually be best to prepare them to answer fully, with appropriate explanatory material, all of the most difficult questions in the lawsuit. In that way, even if a fact is isolated as an admission, there will be explanatory material that will be provided to the jury regarding the so-called admission under Federal Rule of Evidence 106.

Second, if the witness is one who will likely be unavailable at trial, and whose testimony will be provided to the jury by reading or showing the deposition testimony, the witness should be prepared to give complete answers where those answers are helpful to the party sponsoring the witness. There is no advantage to having such a witness fail to disclose helpful information. In addition, the demeanor of the witness for trial purposes should communicate that the witness is being open and forthcoming. These witnesses should be prepared, then, just as if they were being prepared for trial, and counsel who would normally call this witness at trial should be ready to conduct what is essentially the direct examination during the course of the deposition.

Finally, as will be discussed later in this chapter, when a deposition is recorded by videotape, the likelihood that the "best seven" responses will be viewed as evasiveness is accentuated. If there is a chance that the video will be played, in any substantial part, at a trial, the more complete, fair response is usually preferable to the short responses dictated by the "best seven."

## 13.6 EXPLAINING THE ISSUES

Witnesses who have an interest in the outcome of the case will naturally try to give answers helpful to their chosen side. This does not mean they will be dishonest or less than fully truthful, but they will try to phrase their answers in the most helpful way possible and to emphasize those facts they believe contribute to a winning outcome. In addition, during the course of a dispute, what most witnesses do is reconstruct the events in question. During the reconstruction, there is a natural filling-in of information that is consistent with the witness's point of view about the case. The reconstruction therefore, unintentionally shades the facts so they become more consistent with that point of view. Again, these witnesses are not fabricating. They would all pass a lie detector test.

The danger exists, however, that witnesses may misunderstand or not fully grasp the position of the side they wish to help. As a result, they end up emphasizing facts which actually help the other side and do harm to their own side's position.

To avoid such problems, some time should be spent explaining the issues in the case and each side's position regarding each issue. This does not mean giving a long legal explanation to the witness or attempting to have the witness achieve a lawyer's level of understanding. Instead, the goal is to help the witness develop a basic grasp of what the case is about.

If the witness is also the client, counsel will undoubtedly have educated her early in the case and updated her many times since. But, in corporate and similar cases, lower-level employees and others not directly interested in the outcome may have only vague ideas of what the lawsuit is about.

This sort of explanation should be presented issue by issue. Long summaries are not necessary; the discussion should cover manageable amounts of information by focusing on one issue at a time. Then, for each issue, give each side's position or what it is trying to prove. If the witness's role in the facts giving rise to the litigation is limited, limit the discussion just to those issues in which the witness was involved. Like every other aspect of witness preparation, explanations of the issues should be tailored to fit the witness's intellectual abilities. Do not make the explanation more complex than the witness can understand and remember. The following is an example of an explanation of the issues to a non-party witness:

LAWYER:

> Let's now talk about what this case concerns and how you fit into it. As you know, this is an antitrust action. Dr. Rimard is claiming Hospital Pathology, Inc., has unfairly taken all of the pathology business for itself and has prevented Dr. Rimard from getting any of the business. Have you heard about that?

WITNESS:

> Yes, there has been a lot of talk in the doctors' lounge about the case.

LAWYER:

> The reason your deposition is being taken today is to find out whether Hospital Pathology uses general practitioners such as yourself to steer pathology patients to themselves and away from Dr. Rimard. Dr. Rimard is claiming that, when a patient requires pathology work, the hospital automatically refers the patient to Hospital Pathology without letting the patient or the patient's

primary care physician know about alternative sources of pathology services. Hospital Pathology, on the other hand, is claiming it and the hospital always give a patient and the primary care physician a choice about what pathology services to use.

WITNESS:

Okay.

LAWYER:

Your deposition is being taken today because you are a primary care doctor, and Hospital Pathology wants to find out what your experience has been with the referral of patients for pathology services. Does this all make sense?

WITNESS:

Yes.

## 13.7 WHAT TO DO WHEN OBJECTIONS ARE MADE

In a preparation session, witnesses often ask what to do if a particular topic comes up, or if the opposing counsel asks irrelevant questions, or if she asks the same question over again. The attorney's typical response is, "Well, if she does that, I'll object." Unfortunately, the attorney usually does not tell the witness that he will have to answer the question anyhow.

The witness must be told that usually he must answer the question, even if it is objectionable, and that counsel will specifically direct or advise him not to answer when appropriate. Discuss privileged areas with the witness and describe the ways in which such issues could come up. Tell the witness that, if he has any question about whether an answer will involve privileged matters, he should request to speak with counsel before he answers so that he does not inadvertently waive the privilege.[3] If the privilege problem is identified by counsel without

---

3. Of course, as mentioned earlier, the questioning attorney may object strenuously if the defending attorney consults with the deponent while a question is pending. Because there is no better way to protect legitimate privileges, however, this consultation before the answer is given is appropriate. If the deposing attorney raises such a fuss that you cannot consult with the witness effectively, you can take a break and take the witness out in the hallway to discuss the possible privilege. Sometimes we call this the "elbow rule," since you take the witness by the elbow and lead him out of the room; normally, this effectively prevents answers from being given until the witness has adequate counsel.

the consultation with the witness, an objection such as the following should be made: "Mr. Smith, objection; there may be a matter of privilege involved here; give me a moment with the witness, please." Consultation can then be had with the witness.

During the preparation, the witness should be informed that if privileged matters come up, an objection will be made coupled with an instruction not to answer based on privilege. The witness should also be informed that objections will be lodged to questions that are designed to harass, annoy, and embarrass the witness, and that he may be instructed not to answer so that a protective order can be sought. Finally, the witness should know that if a question calls for information covered by a protective order already in existence, it may again be necessary to instruct him not to answer.

At that same point in the preparation session, the witness should be informed that opposing counsel will frequently follow up on a direction not to answer by asking the witness directly whether he will answer the question. The witness should be prepared to state, "On the advice of my counsel, I decline to answer the question."

Beyond these three situations, however—privilege, harassment/annoyance/embarrassment, and protective orders—the witness needs to understand that he is expected to answer all questions truthfully, and preferably in accordance with the approach outlined above, even when an objection has been made.

The witness should be prepared to hear the objection "assumes facts not in evidence." This objection is often heard at depositions, even though, technically, nothing is yet in evidence because this is still discovery. Therefore, this objection, if taken literally, could probably be made to all questions at depositions. Often, however, the objecting attorney is concerned about a question that is in some sense compound, that is, contains within it the suggestion that a certain fact has already been established by the testimony of this deponent. Then, in answering the explicit question, the witness seems to be giving approval to or adopting the implicit fact. For example, a witness might be asked, "Well, when your company was doing so poorly with respect to environmental compliance in the late 1980s, you were still in charge of the governmental regulation group, weren't you?" By answering that she was still in that position, the witness seems to be accepting the characterization of the company's environmental performance. Putting the burden on the witness to avoid such an interpretation by giving a two-part answer ("We weren't doing poorly, and yes, I was still in the government regulation group.") is patently unfair. Perhaps a better objection would be "compound" or "complex" (or even "misleading," in the manner of, "are you still an environmental criminal?"), but "assumes facts not in evidence" certainly calls attention to the problem, although somewhat inartfully.

Once the witness is prepared regarding the meaning of objections, provision should be made to facilitate their making. Too frequently a witness will listen to a question, decide the information that the questioning counsel is seeking, and begin the answer almost before the question is completed. This, of course, is how conversations occur, and it is difficult for a person to change a life's worth of conversation experience for the purpose of a deposition. This phenomenon creates several problems. First, the witness will frequently answer a better question than was asked. The lawyer perhaps should have asked the better question but, in reality, failed to do so. Second, if the answer begins as the question ends, defending counsel must act quickly before a damaging answer is provided. For that reason witnesses may be told that the process of questions and answers in a deposition has five steps:

1. listen to the question;

2. think about what information the question calls for;

3. think about the answer;

4. formulate the answer; and finally

5. answer the question.

This process, if followed, will likely provide appropriate answers and provide at least a second or two for counsel to lodge an objection. A witness should not be explicitly burdened with "waiting a moment before answering in order to allow objection" because that heightens, rather than reduces, the witness's anxieties. Witnesses should be given less, not more, to worry about. The slowing down of the process of answering questions is almost always beneficial to the witness. And in the deposition that is recorded in a written transcript (as opposed to on videotape) the immediate audience is a piece of paper. Silence between the question and the answer is not reflected in a written transcript. Once the witness understands this fact, the likelihood of providing clear and precise answers is greatly enhanced.

## 13.8 HOW TO HANDLE DOCUMENTS IN PREPARATION

In the reasonably small case where there are twenty or thirty crucial documents, they should be carefully reviewed with the witness before her deposition. Witnesses are sometimes unnerved by facing documents relating to their testimony which they have not seen in months or years. The pre-deposition review assures the witness that her testimony is consistent with the important documents and that letters written long ago will not trap her out on a limb.

Larger cases pose a different problem, however. Faced with hundreds or thousands of "crucial" documents, the witness will not be able to use them in any effective way to prepare for the deposition. In a complex case, therefore, the documents must be culled for those that are most important to the witness's testimony. This means giving the witness only the key documents relating to her expected testimony and not overwhelming her with boxes of material of varying importance.

Some lawyers also provide witnesses with summaries of what other witnesses have said in their depositions. This practice has some attendant risk because, if the witness's recollection of the events about which testimony will be given is refreshed by these lawyer-prepared summaries, a judge may very well order that those memoranda be turned over to opposing counsel pursuant to Federal Rule of Evidence 612.

Simply giving documents to a witness for review does not, of course, ensure she will actually look at them. Therefore, counsel must still go through the documents with the witness at the preparation session. Here, the task falls to the preparing lawyer to organize and review those documents and to prepare the witness by leading her through the events, using the documents to assist where necessary.

Assuming that there are several issues on which the witness is likely to be questioned at her deposition, the documents should be arranged chronologically within each issue. The documents will assist in preparing an outline that can be used by counsel as a road map to the preparation session for each issue. (This same outline, obviously, can become the primary basis for arranging the witness's direct examination at trial.) In preparation, the witness should be asked to describe the events pertinent to each issue, seeking clarification where the witness's description seems at variance with the documents. After this exercise, the witness should have some confidence that she has not forgotten something important shown in the documents. The more complex the case and the more issues about which the witness has information, the longer the preparation will take. Sessions can extend for days. One rule of thumb, for both deposition and trial preparation, is three hours of preparation for each hour of anticipated testimony.

Preparation in this fashion is a time-consuming task for counsel, but it greatly eases the load on the witness.

As has been discussed elsewhere, a standard question at depositions is, "Have you reviewed any documents in preparation for this deposition?" This question is based on the rule that at trial the questioner is entitled to know whether the witness has used documents "at or before trial" to refresh her recollection. This logic fails because "reviewing a document" and "refreshing recollection" are different activities. If a witness reviews a document under the direction or in consultation with her attorney and the witness finds the document to be consistent with her recollection, or finds that she still has no recollection, then the document has not been used to "refresh her recollection" and no basis exists, at deposition or trial, to reveal that those documents were reviewed with the attorney's assistance. That review remains protected work product. This issue should be discussed with the witness in the preparation session. In response to the question regarding document review she should answer truthfully, "Yes, I have reviewed documents with my attorney in preparation for this deposition," but a follow-up question regarding what documents were reviewed should be met by defending counsel with a direction to her not to identify particular documents (on the grounds of attorney work product) unless the questioning attorney can establish that some document did in fact refresh her memory on some relevant point.

## 13.9 PRACTICING ANSWERING QUESTIONS

The heart of witness preparation is having the witness actually practice answering questions. Only through practice will the witness fully understand how to phrase the answers to questions to get her meaning across accurately, how to respond to an aggressive cross-examination style, how to behave during the deposition, how to apply the instructions given about the form and content of answers, and how to deal with the many other nuances that occur during the deposition.

Not every likely deposition question can be rehearsed. nor is it necessary to do so. It is important, however, to identify the key areas on which the witness is reasonably certain to be examined and to have the witness practice answering questions on those topics. But remember, this is not just a time for practicing answering, but also a time to refine and improve the answers given by assisting the witness with word choice, chronology, and accuracy. While the substance must come from the witness, the attorney is entitled—even obligated—to assist the delivery so that the witness is correctly understood. Listen to the witness's answers and give suggestions about how they can be phrased to better state the witness's knowledge. Then have the witness practice answering again until the response is accurate and clearly states what the witness intends. Here is an example of what should occur:

LAWYER:

> Okay, let's imagine again I am the lawyer for Hospital Pathology and let me ask you some questions about your efforts to generate pathology patients. Ready?

WITNESS:

> Yes.

LAWYER:

> Dr. Unitas, please tell me all of the things you did to get pathology patients of your own.

WITNESS:

> Well, I contacted all of the hospitals and told them I had left Hospital Pathology and was now accepting patients of my own. And I also sent a letter to all of the primary care physicians telling them about the availability of my services.

LAWYER:

> Is that all?

WITNESS:

> That's about it.

LAWYER:

> Okay, let me become your lawyer again. Those were good answers, but I think we can phrase your answer better. Didn't you tell me that when you went out on your own, you sat down and tried to figure out the best way of generating patients?

WITNESS:

> That's true.

LAWYER:

> And as I recall, you also did some research on how to start your own practice and made some phone calls to doctors to let them know you were now taking patients?

WITNESS:

That's true.

LAWYER:

Did you ever tell other doctors at parties and Medical Association meetings that you were now out on your own and accepting patients?

WITNESS:

Sure, it would come up and I would let them know.

LAWYER:

Let's see if you can incorporate this information into your answers. Here is an example of what I mean. If you were asked the question of what did you do to generate patients, based on what you've told me, a more complete and accurate answer would be this: "When I started my own practice I thought about the best way of getting patients, so I did a lot of reading on the subject such as books and articles in medical economics journals. I also talked with other doctors who were practicing on their own and received a number of suggestions about how they were able to generate patients. Another thing I did is to carefully study how Hospital Pathology went about getting patients. When I went into practice, I systematically visited all of the hospitals in the area, where I met with the surgeons and other hospital staff to let them know of my availability. I explained my background and experience to them even though I had worked with many of them through the years and they were well familiar with my skills. I also sent a personally signed letter to all of the primary care physicians in the area again explaining I was available to take patients and about my experience. Finally, when I determined that a personal contact would be helpful, I followed the letter up with a phone call to the physician in which I emphasized the same things.

I think you have told me in previous interviews everything I just included in that answer, but you can add other things you did that I left out or subtract anything I got wrong. Okay?

WITNESS:

Yes. That's a better answer. That's what I really meant.

LAWYER:

> Let's try it again. Imagine again I am the lawyer for Hospital Pathology. Tell me everything you did to generate patients when you went out on your own.

Note what is going on here. The lawyer is actively suggesting how the answer should be phrased and is not relying on the witness to think of what should be said. The lawyer is being very careful to suggest only those facts the witness has previously related or has confirmed as true. The information must come from the witness or documents, otherwise the danger of improper "coaching" arises. Most importantly, the lawyer does not just suggest a better way to answer, but has the witness actually practice until the lawyer is satisfied.

The witness's answers during the deposition will never be as perfect as they were during the preparation session, but they will be better for having been practiced. Even if not phrased exactly the same way as in the witness preparation session, the witness is now better aware of what facts should be included in the answer and is more likely to give the information in a persuasive manner when asked the question.

In the above vignette it was assumed that the preparing lawyer would first assume the role of the deposing counsel and from time to time step out of that role to assist the witness in completing and formulating answers. This process can be confusing to the witness and, of course, takes the preparing lawyer out of the role she will ultimately play at the deposition, that of defending counsel. For that reason, whenever possible, the role of questioning counsel during the preparation session should be assumed by another lawyer. Preparing counsel can then stay in the role of defender and stop the questioning whenever the witness needs assistance in the manner or content of answers. This process is much easier on the preparing lawyer as it makes the witness's answers (and not the next question to be asked) the clear focus of the session, thereby making the preparation session qualitatively better and more efficient. Finally, it is during this preparation session that the witness can be given suggestions as to how to insert in her answers the information that the opponent, or some later decision maker, needs to know to make a fair evaluation of the case. These answers should be carefully planned so that when the opportunity arises during the deposition, the witness will give opposing counsel the bad news about the small likelihood his client has of prevailing in the lawsuit.

## 13.10 GETTING USED TO AGGRESSIVE CROSS-EXAMINATION

The witness should not suffer the shock of an aggressive cross-examination for the first time during the deposition. Instead, let the witness get comfortable with this type of questioning during the witness preparation session so the witness will be more comfortable when it actually occurs during the deposition. If the witness knows what to expect, the witness is less likely to become angry or intimidated when the opposing counsel tries this tactic. If another lawyer is not available to role play for the entirety of the preparation practice session, every effort should be made to use one for this limited exercise of acclimating the witness to an aggressive examination. To the extent possible the person playing the role should be as much like deposing counsel as possible in style and demeanor. Consider the following example:

LAWYER 1:

Sometimes aggressive questions may make you upset. The important thing for you is not to get angry or intimidated by what is happening. Just remain cool and answer the questions as best you can. Let me show you what I mean by this. Pretend we are at the deposition and Mary, my partner here, is opposing counsel. Go ahead, Mary.

LAWYER 2:

Now Doctor, you never ran any advertisements in the Nita Medical Association Journal saying you were available to accept patients?

WITNESS:

No.

LAWYER 2:

You know every doctor in the area receives a copy of the Journal?

WITNESS:

Yes.

LAWYER 2:

A three-by-five-inch ad would only cost $250?

WITNESS:

I don't know what the advertising rates are.

LAWYER 2:

You never checked?

WITNESS:

That's right.

LAWYER 2:

You would agree this is an inexpensive way of making sure all of the physicians in the area would know about your services?

WITNESS:

Well, quite frankly, I don't think many doctors read those ads or take them seriously. I have talked with lots of doctors through the years and I have never heard of any of them bothering to read those ads. And when I talked with other doctors who had started their own practices, none of them thought it was a good idea to run an ad like that.

LAWYER 1:

O.K. Let's take a break from the questioning for a moment and talk about what just happened. You are doing the right thing. Just remain calm and answer the questions. But, with the last question, Mary asked whether you would agree that the ads are an inexpensive way of making sure all of the doctors know about your services. If you don't agree, just say "I don't agree." What you did was natural. You wanted to explain why you didn't think so. Don't give the explanation unless it is asked for. Okay?

WITNESS:

Yes. I am afraid I was starting to get angry.

LAWYER 1:

That won't help you focus. You may say more than you should, and more or less than you mean, when you speak from anger. Keep calm and listen to the question.

Keep the examples of aggressive cross-examination short. Even though the witness understands intellectually that your colleague is merely playing the role of opposing counsel, being treated in such a hostile fashion is still irritating. The idea is not to make the witness angry with her own lawyers, but only to prepare her to deal with this type of questioning. Using one of your colleagues to conduct the cross will reduce the possibility of any damage to your relationship with the witness.

## 13.11 USING VIDEOTAPE TO PREPARE

Some witnesses require intensive work to prevent speech habits or mannerisms from distracting from their testimony first at deposition, then at trial. While they might not always believe an attorney's comments about their demeanor or speech habits, they will find it difficult to argue with videotape showing those problems. Stuffy corporate executives, pompous experts, and mumbling fact witnesses can all have their performances improved markedly if they are shown videotape of the problems.

Lengthy taping sessions are not necessary; the witness will more likely improve in his delivery from taping a fifteen-minute segment, then reviewing and discussing it, and then taping another segment with further suggestions for improvement. For key witnesses, communications consultants can assist in identifying and curing problems that interfere with the witness effectively presenting his evidence.

The question arises, of course, whether such videotape rehearsals are discoverable: they are, after all, verbatim statements by the witness. Nevertheless, the better rule is that these videotapes, just like an attorney's notes on preparation sessions, constitute attorney work product and are protected from discovery. The order of questioning, the subjects prepared, the suggestions from the attorney or consultant—all reflect the attorney's approach to and preparation of the case. The fact that videotape technology provides an especially effective way of accomplishing preparation does not reduce the protection courts should accord such effort by the attorney. While courts should uphold a claim of work product protection, counsel and the client should be prepared to discuss such preparation if the court decides otherwise.

A more subtle question is whether using videotape to prepare a witness for deposition or trial makes that witness more vulnerable to effective cross-examination at trial on the use, if not the content, of video preparation. Assume that your opponent has discovered the use of videotape (or suspects its use) in a witness's preparation session; consider the following approach to cross-examination on such "rehearsals," which can be attempted with no risk during the deposition of the witness.

Q.    Mr. Shadis, you spent quite a good deal of time reviewing and preparing your testimony with your lawyer before you came to court, didn't you?

A. Yes, I did, I suppose.

Q. And you went over and over that testimony, your story, because you wanted to get it just right, isn't that true?

A. Well, we did go over it several times, yes.

Q. Several times, until your attorney thought it was just right?

A. Well, until she was satisfied that it was clear.

Q. In fact, you gave these answers again and again in your attorney's office, so you could get them just the way she wanted them?

A. Well, as I've said, we went over my testimony.

Q. And then she actually videotaped you giving your answers, didn't she?

A. Yes, we used videotape to prepare.

Q. And then you reviewed the videotape, and looked at what you said, and how you said it, and what words you used, and how you looked while you were answering, right?

A. We did review the videotapes, yes, but I don't see anything wrong with that.

Q. Then your testimony here this morning is actually the result of very careful rehearsal, isn't it?

A. I don't think I would use the word rehearsal.

Q. You prepared as though you were playacting, and delivering lines that had been written for you, isn't that right?

A. No, no, I think that presents the wrong picture entirely.

No matter how the witness protests, the impression that the jury receives when this same examination is performed at trial is that they have somehow been "conned" by having a set piece of theater presented when they thought that they were hearing the spontaneous testimony of the witness in his own words.

The witness can dispel this impression, however, if he makes it clear to the jury why this videotape preparation was necessary:

A. No, no, I think that presents the wrong picture entirely. I am nervous about testifying here; I've never done it before, and I don't speak in public often. I don't think that it would be fair if that nervousness made me mix up my testimony and kept me from telling the jury what really happened. So my attorney and I decided that we would try to do everything that we could, including going over my testimony several times on videotape, to get the truth of what happened across to the jury.

The simple fact is that if a witness needs the assistance that videotaped practice can provide so effectively and efficiently, the concern about disclosure at trial should not by itself be a sufficient argument against that assistance.

## 13.12 FINAL INSTRUCTIONS

Never conclude the witness preparation session without taking care of all of the necessary housekeeping details. Let's look at a few of those details.

### 13.12.1 What to wear.

As was discussed in § 2.3.1, depositions influence the settlement value of a case by giving opposing counsel a chance to assess the impression a witness will make upon a judge or jury. A strong favorable witness—a witness whose testimony is believable and who can withstand the rigors of cross-examination—will cause the opposing party to demand less or pay more in settlement than a witness who vacillates, is tentative, has memory problems, or otherwise makes a poor impression.

The witness's appearance is one of the factors affecting the impression a witness makes. If the witness is attractive (we are not talking about being handsome or beautiful, but about the impression made) and is dressed appropriately, this will enhance the witness's credibility. What dress is appropriate for a particular witness depends on the image to be projected and deserves careful thought by defending counsel. Whatever the image desired, instruct the witness on how to dress for the deposition, perhaps after consultation with a professional communications consultant.

### 13.12.2 What to bring.

When defending a deposition, one of the less pleasant experiences occurs when a witness suddenly reaches into his pocket and pulls out a set of notes never before seen by the defending counsel. Not only are these notes a surprise when seen for the first time, but it may be determined that the witness has scribbled on them all sorts of damaging comments about the strength of the case. If the witness used the notes to refresh his memory, little can be done to keep them away from opposing counsel.

The scene just described happens more times than defending lawyers wish. Often, after the witness preparation session, a witness will go home and start worrying about what questions will be asked the next day. The witness logically thinks that a few notes will help him keep events straight. Then, if he forgets, he can also refer to the notes during the deposition. The witness may also figure it would not hurt to write down counsel's comments about some of the problems in the case.

The easiest way to prevent this scenario from occurring is to instruct witnesses to bring nothing to the deposition—no notes, documents, or anything else. Don't, however, rely only on these instructions. On the day of the deposition, be sure to ask whether the witness has any notes or other papers and, if so, take them away before the deposition begins.

### 13.12.3 What to look at and who to talk to.

The witness can surprise defending counsel in many ways during the deposition. After being carefully prepared until he can provide satisfactory answers, he may start coming out with new and unexpected information during the deposition. During a break the source of this new information should be inquired about as well as why he never mentioned it before. It may then be discovered that, after the witness preparation session, he decided to do some last-minute investigation on his own. Instead of going home and having a quiet evening and a good night's sleep, he telephoned other witnesses or went to the office to track down new documents.

Sometimes the investigative efforts are for the good—new, helpful evidence turns up or the witness is better able to answer the hard questions during the deposition. But the danger is, of course, that his lawyer has never had the opportunity to discuss the new information with him.

These nasty surprises can be avoided, or at least limited, by instructing the witness at the witness preparation session about who he should talk with and what he should look at between the end of the session and the time of the deposition. Again, on the day of the deposition a final check should be made to see whether he has followed your instructions.

### 13.12.4 Where and when to meet.

It hardly needs saying that the witness should not leave the witness preparation session without knowing where and when to meet counsel for the deposition. It is frequently desirable to meet at defending counsel's office to do some last-minute preparation and then drive over together. Work out these matters with the witness in advance. If meeting the witness where the deposition is to be taken, be sure to give instructions about not talking with opposing counsel if the witness should arrive before his lawyer. And do show up early so this will not be a problem.

### 13.13 CONCLUSION

The basic rules for preparing a witness to be deposed are simple:

- Try to reduce the witness's anxieties.

- Try to lift burdens from the witness, rather than to put burdens on the witness.

- Try to assure the witness that defending counsel is there to handle any problems that might come up.

- Try to persuade the witness that any procedural problems will be minor and will not interfere with effective testimony.

- Try to get the witness to a comfort level with the content and the form of the answers to be given.

# CHAPTER FOURTEEN

## DEFENDING THE DEPOSITION

*They have no lawyers among them, for they consider them as a sort of people whose profession it is to disguise matters.* — Sir Thomas More

The attorney defending the deposition must support and protect the witness, preserve certain objections in the record for the court's later ruling, and protect the client from the disclosure of privileged and other protected information. The first step in fulfilling these responsibilities is to determine whether the deponent is, indeed, a client.

## 14.1 DETERMINING WHETHER THE WITNESS IS A CLIENT

Determining whether a witness is a client is usually quite simple: Has the witness retained the lawyer to represent him? More difficult problems arise, however, when the party who has retained counsel is, for instance, a corporation and the witness is an officer of the corporation or, at the opposite extreme, is a low-level employee at the bottom of the organizational chart. Even though these individuals may not be clients, they may nevertheless be covered by the attorney-client privilege and work product protection that extend between counsel and the corporate client.

Whether the privilege and the work product protection extend to such a witness depends upon whether the jurisdiction in question is a "control group" jurisdiction or an "Upjohn" jurisdiction, which may well be a question of state law, as there are no defined privileges in the Federal Rules of Evidence. In a "control group" jurisdiction, the attorney-client privilege extends only to those individuals in the corporation or organization who can make decisions on behalf of the entity or have the authority to bind the entity in any way. Some of these jurisdictions limit the "control group" to such persons as the directors or officers of the entity. In "UpJohn" jurisdictions (so-named after the 1981 Supreme Court case of *UpJohn v. United States*), communications between counsel and any employee for the purposes of obtaining information necessary to provide legal advice to the entity are covered by the attorney-client privilege. To further complicate matters, the witness's legal interests may be different from, and possibly inconsistent with, those of the corporate party. For instance, the defendant bank and its president may both be accused of wrongdoing and each may have an interest in showing that the other committed malfeasance.

Determining whether a witness is a client and whether he is covered by the attorney-client privilege is difficult, complex, and beyond the scope of this book. The answer may depend on the rules of professional responsibility as well as on state and federal law.[1] The important thing is, when in doubt, research the applicable law to determine whether the witness is considered to be protected by the attorney-client privilege accorded to the party who is clearly a client, and whether counsel may properly represent the witness at the deposition.

When the deponent is a client or someone else who can properly be represented by counsel at the deposition, the witness retains the protection of all of the benefits of the attorney-client relationship. For example, the preparation sessions are privileged, and the deponent can consult privately with counsel during the deposition (although only rarely is this proper when there is a question pending). Counsel for the deponent is responsible at the deposition for:

1. supporting and protecting the witness;
2. entering into any necessary stipulations;
3. preserving the record;
4. conferring with the witness;
5. stating objections;
6. instructing the witness not to answer when appropriate;
7. adjourning the deposition to seek a protective order; and,
8. follow-on questioning of the witness and clarifying and correcting answers.

Even when the witness is neither a client nor covered by any attorney-client privilege, many of the same roles are performed in the deposition room that would be performed on behalf of a client. With

---

1.   *See* Fed.R.Evid. 501 (matters of privilege, when jurisdiction is based on a federal question, is determined by the common law as "interpreted by the courts of the United States in light of reason and experience"). In diversity actions and actions where state law supplies the rule of decision, matters of privilege are determined by reference to state law.

friendly witnesses, counsel may be providing emotional support and protection. Even with witnesses who are hostile, counsel has the responsibility to make necessary objections and clarify the record. The important difference between witnesses covered by the attorney-client privilege and those who are not is that any conversations between counsel and the uncovered witness may have to be disclosed upon questioning of the witness by opposing counsel. Unless otherwise specifically noted, the remainder of this chapter assumes that the deponent is being represented by counsel.

## 14.2 SUPPORTING AND PROTECTING THE WITNESS

Anyone who has ever been deposed can attest that it is almost always an anxiety-provoking, unpleasant experience. Most witnesses are nervous about the prospect of being deposed. If witnesses are parties, they are worried about whether they are answering correctly or in a way that might cause them to lose the case. Even when not a party, they may be concerned that their answers might cause them to lose their jobs or that people whose opinion they value may think they did something wrong. The interrogating attorney often challenges and argues with the witness, asks personally embarrassing questions, and even suggests, directly or indirectly, that the witness is a scoundrel and a liar. In short, being a witness at a deposition is a horrible experience.

One of the most important tasks of defending counsel is to provide emotional comfort and support to the witness. The job is to make an unpleasant situation as bearable as possible. In large part, this can be accomplished merely by insuring that the witness perceives counsel as being there to take care of him and to look after his interests. Witnesses rely upon their counsel to make sure that nothing bad happens.

This is not just a matter of handholding and client service. A witness who feels secure and protected will feel more comfortable in defending his or her actions, fending off the questioning attorney's efforts to shake his story, and avoiding unfortunate admissions. It is not only good client service, but also good deposition strategy to have the witness see the lawyer as his guardian during the deposition. Keep in mind, however, that there are limits to what a lawyer can do to protect a deponent. Witnesses are frequently called upon to answer questions that may be embarrassing or, more likely, that call for information about the case that is harmful to their position. Care should be taken to inform the witness of such eventualities. If the witness is not so warned, when the witness cannot be protected from answering a question that the witness would rather avoid, there may be a break-down in the protective relationship built between the witness and defending counsel.

At the deposition, defending counsel and the client-deponent will be seated next to each other, normally across from the questioner. In order to participate effectively in the deposition, defending counsel should take a position slightly forward of the deponent, that is, closer to the table, so as to be always in the deponent's view. By taking that position, counsel can halt the witness's answer merely by slightly raising a hand, thereby preserving the opportunity to make objections or to instruct the witness not to answer before answers are given. Sometimes defending counsel may want the witness to wait before answering to provide a moment to think about the question, its propriety, and its ramifications. By holding up a hand between the witness and the reporter and saying, "Give me a moment, please," the attorney gains some reasonable time to consider whether an objection or direction not to answer is called for. No rule requires that counsel must, without thought, immediately object upon a question being asked; just as the questioner is entitled to pause and consider between an answer and his next question, so should a defender be allowed to think about possible objections to questions.

By staying up at the table at the witness's elbow, counsel will also stay much more involved in the deposition, and the witness is less likely to fall into a "conversation" with deposing counsel which can lead to ill-considered volunteering. When objections are made, the witness will be able to both see and hear defending counsel, and will more readily perceive the significance of the objection.[2] In that position, at the witness's elbow, counsel is also positioned to exercise two of the most important—albeit, limited—rights at the deposition: consultation

---

2. In the authors' opinion, attorneys in trial or deposition may not object for the primary purpose of coaching a witness or otherwise affecting the witness's testimony; but a good-faith objection—that is, one which has an arguably valid basis in evidentiary considerations—does not become improper merely because the witness, on hearing it, may adjust his answer.

For example, consider a good-faith objection that a question is ambiguous:

Q. Tell us about the regular procedure.

OBJECTION: At what time, counsel? The question is ambiguous. I object.

The witness will certainly review the "regular procedures" in his mind to determine whether there have been changes since the relevant time. That review by the witness does not render the objection improper or unethical. On the other hand, an objection clearly raised to cue the witness, and for no valid evidentiary purpose, is improper:

Q. Did your company earn any profit the first year of operation?

with the client-witness at the table and recessing the deposition briefly for a conference in the hallway.[3] Protecting the client is not confined to the deposition room.

Be cautious about allowing the witness to converse with opposing counsel before the deposition begins, while everyone is filling up their coffee cups and getting comfortable. Even if substance is not disclosed, these casual moments with opposing counsel tend to lower the witness's guard. As a corollary to this, never leave the witness alone in the deposition room. Follow the rule that the witness is never left without counsel: if counsel must leave the room for a telephone call or a restroom break, take the witness out of the room as well. During restroom breaks, instruct the witness not to speak with anyone—opposing counsel, paralegals, friends, strangers, or secretaries. Even though it is clearly inappropriate, deposing counsel frequently try to engage the witness in conversation when defending counsel is absent or occupied. Although deposing counsel always try to defend those conversations as "merely trying to make the witness comfortable," they are improper when the witness is represented.

## 14.3 ENTERING INTO STIPULATIONS

The wisdom of various stipulations has been discussed in § 6.1.

## 14.4 PRESERVING THE RECORD

Depositions usually result in a transcript or video recording of the testimony that can be used for various purposes, including use at trial.[4] Like an appellate record, the deposition transcript may be clear and understandable or a muddled jumble of words incomprehensible to both judge and jury. The question to be answered is which is better— clear or muddled. Is the client's best interest served by a clear record, or is the client better off if the transcript is a mass of confusion? The answer to this question may change with the topics under examination and also with whether the deponent's answers are favorable or unfa-

---

OBJECTION: I object. I don't understand the question. I don't see how anyone could understand the question. It's completely ambiguous as to what you mean by "profit" and "operation." Can you understand the question, Mrs. Banis?

THE WITNESS: No, I don't understand the question.

*See* Rule 30(d)(1).

3. *See* § 14.5.

4. *See* Chapter Sixteen, "Using Depositions."

vorable to the client's position. Helpful answers should be clear and understandable; harmful answers are better left obtuse and incomprehensible. Making this decision—clear or muddled—requires counsel to be alert during the deposition and to listen carefully to the answers being given.

Such answers as "It was from here to there," or "It was right here at this point on the map that I first saw the other car," are useless if the deposition is later used at trial. Even though everyone in the deposition room could see exactly where the witness was pointing when these answers were given, the judge or jury will be left without a clue as to where "here" and "there" are or to which point on the map the witness was referring.

If that is the way you prefer it—the judge and jury in the dark— because the answer is harmful to your claim or defense, sit quietly. However, if the answer is helpful, then you should state for the record what is occurring. "Let the record reflect that the witness is indicating from his chair to counsel's chair, a distance of approximately five feet," or "Counsel, let's have the witness mark with the letter A where he is pointing on the map which has been marked as Deposition Exhibit 12." However, it must be absolutely clear that, while defending counsel has no affirmative duty to clarify a record that is muddied by deposing counsel's ineptitude, defending counsel may not contribute to such muddiness by baseless objections, inappropriate demeanor, improper preparation of the witness, or other unethical behavior. See Chapter Eleven for further discussion.

## 14.5 CONFERRING WITH THE WITNESS

One reason to sit next to the witness is to enable counsel and the witness to confer quickly and easily about a question or answer when necessary. Assuming such conferences are not abused to obstruct discovery, there is no limit on the number of times or frequency with which they can be used unless, of course, are precluded by a discovery order. More and more judges are issuing discovery orders that do not allow conferences between the defending lawyer and the witness during the pendency of the deposition, even during breaks and recesses, except when necessary to discuss whether to assert a privilege or when required as a matter of professional responsibility to ensure that the witness is not committing perjury.[5] Assuming, however, that such

---

5. *See, e.g., Hall v. Clifton Precision*, 150 F.R.D. 525 (E.D. Pa. 1993); *Chapsky v. Baxter v. Mueller Division*, 1994 WL 327348 (N.D. Ill. 1994).

conferences are permissible for other reasons, and the relationship between opposing counsel has been a professional and courteous one, the following can occur.

After the witness has answered a question, defending counsel can lean over and remind the witness she should not volunteer information beyond that called for by the question, or that she should not attempt to argue the case, but should merely state facts. This conference is off the record because it is whispered and inaudible to the reporter and opposing counsel. Obviously, if this type of conference follows every important question and answer, deposing counsel will begin to "make a record" by commenting on each conference, with the result that the witness will grow uncomfortable and the judge, if asked to rule on this behavior, may grow skeptical. So long as this "right" to confer is used judiciously and not for the purpose of obstructing legitimate discovery, it can be an effective and proper means of controlling the witness so that her answers are responsive without being overly generous.

Even where some topics are off-limits in a deposition because they are privileged or because the court has previously issued a protective order, defending counsel can use these "mini-conferences" to remind the witness that the questions are getting close to those topics. This may prevent the witness from inadvertently providing protected or privileged information in an answer to an upcoming question and thereby waive the protection of the order or the privilege.

Occasionally at a deposition, a witness will need some lengthier counseling—she has forgotten the basic rules of listening to the question and answering accurately and briefly, she has adopted the role of advocate rather than witness, or she is allowing the deposing attorney to goad her into intemperate remarks. In such situations, after an answer is completed, the "elbow rule" should be invoked: take the client-witness by the elbow, state, "We're taking a break here," and guide her from the room into the hallway or a vacant office to straighten her out.

Deposing counsel will probably try to prevent this interruption by saying something like, "You can't do that," or "You can take a break after I finish this line," or "Let's break after this next question," but no response to those suggestions is required. The questioner cannot prevent counsel and the deponent from leaving. The "elbow rule" should be used as soon as the witness is starting to get out of control. At a minimum, deposing counsel will get no information from the witness while the witness is out of the room, so march her out and re-instruct her in the proper behavior of a deponent.

As stated, these conferences can be held *sotto voce* at the table or out in the hallway without much concern that they will lead to a ruling by a judge that discovery has been illegitimately frustrated. Sometimes, however, counsel and the client-deponent must confer before an answer is given—when privileged information might be disclosed in an answer or when the witness is unsure about how he may answer without divulging confidential or personal information. In such a case, there is little choice but to confer with the witness while the question is pending in order to determine whether the witness should be instructed not to answer the question on grounds of privilege.

In fact, there is no added interruption by this conference since the alternative is for an objection to be lodged and the witness instructed not to answer in order to protect her opportunity to find out if a privilege objection must be raised. After that objection and direction, the exact same conference as just discussed would necessarily occur between counsel and the witness.

## 14.6 STATING OBJECTIONS

The process of making and responding to objections at depositions probably consumes more energy, causes more frustration, and wastes more time than any other aspect of discovery. Perhaps because of their lack of confidence in their own knowledge of the rules of evidence, or because they are unsure about what objections are waived and what objections are preserved, attorneys at depositions object and battle over objections, by actual count, 517 percent more than is necessary to represent their clients properly.

Consider a typical exchange in the deposition of an opposing party:

> Q. Now, Ms. Vardas, you've told us that you ran this company for the last seven years. During that time, how profitable was your company?

DEFENDING ATTORNEY:

> I object. You are misstating her prior testimony. Also, we don't know what you mean when you say, "how profitable." You know that's a term that hasn't been defined, so your question is ambiguous. Nobody can understand it. Besides that, none of this is relevant to this case. I mean, what does this have to do with your claim that the company somehow mislabeled? Besides that, you haven't shown any personal knowledge.

DEPOSING ATTORNEY:

> The question is not ambiguous; it is perfectly clear. Anybody could understand it, and you know that. Besides that, we've been over this before and I'm not misstating anything. The witness can tell me if she understands the question or not. And you know perfectly well that this has a lot to do with this case. Those profits properly belong to us, or at least a share of them do. So, why don't you let her answer?

DEFENDING ATTORNEY:

> Well, I have a right to understand the question so that I can protect my client's interests. You're trying to trap her with these trick questions, and that's not fair. Why don't you just ask a reasonable question without trying to force your views on her? Besides that, your question assumes facts not in evidence. It sounds like you are referring to some document. If you have a document, you should show it to her.

DEPOSING ATTORNEY:

> I'll ask whatever questions I want, and not what you want me to ask. I'm not trying to trap anybody, and I resent your suggesting that. Why don't you just state your objection for the record, and let's get on with the deposition. Ms. Vardas, would you please look at what I am having marked as Vardas Deposition Exhibit 73? Would you please read the first paragraph into the record?

DEFENDING COUNSEL:

> Objection. Come on, counsel. You know that the document speaks for itself.

Of course, we all know that this is not the end of it. This time, or the next, this discussion may go on for pages, without resolution, without purpose, and without profit to the clients. In such discussions, there is no light, only heat, and there is therefore no possibility that one or the other of the attorneys will suddenly throw up his hands and say:

> You're right. I've been a fool. I do hate myself when I get like this. How pigheaded of me not to see that your question [or your objection] was perfectly proper and clear! I'll pay for the extra pages of transcript that all took.

In fact, if an attorney ever said such a thing at a deposition, not only would his reputation around town suffer badly, but the opposing attorney would immediately suspect some sort of clever ruse, and probably become even more argumentative.

To cure this problem and to put objections in their proper role at a deposition, we must first look at the purpose of discovery in our system. Rule 26(b)(1) explicitly states about discovery:

> Parties may obtain discovery regarding any matter, not privileged, that is relevant to the to the claim or defense of any party, including the existence, description, nature, custody, condition, and location of any books, documents, or other tangible things and the identity and location of persons having knowledge of any discoverable matter. For good cause, the court may order discovery of any matter relevant to the subject matter involved in the action. Relevant information need not be admissible at the trial if the discovery appears reasonably calculated to lead to the discovery of admissible evidence. All discovery is subject to the limitations imposed by Rule 26(b)(2)(i), (ii), and (iii).

The rules are consistent to the effect that, absent a protective order, "a party may obtain discovery."[6] The history of the rules and their amendments makes it clear that discovery, not suppression, was being promoted. The "sporting theory of justice" and "trial by ambush" were intended to fall under the changes made by the discovery rules.[7] Yet we continue to raise generations of young lawyers to believe that a deposition is successfully defended only if substantial and important information is hidden from the opponent. In fact, as was discussed in Chapter Thirteen on preparing the witness, there are many reasons in modern practice why information should be volunteered during a deposition so as to encourage fair disposition of a case that will likely never go to trial.

The results are discouraging. Defending attorneys, if unsure of the rules of evidence and procedure, raise and argue objections which would be preserved even if they were not raised and which will merely have to be raised again in the designation process or at trial. Deposing attorneys, if motivated by a misplaced pride of authorship of their questions, respond vociferously to sound and unsound objec-

---

6. The matter of discovery against experts is the single exception and is dealt with separately in chapter 19, "Expert Depositions."

7. "The pretrial deposition-discovery mechanism established by Rules 26 to 37 is one of the most significant innovations of the Federal Rules of Civil Procedure." *Hickman v. Taylor*, 329 U.S. 495, 500 (1947).

tions alike, even though the witness has not been instructed not to answer and no judge is present there to rule on their responses. No profit can be gained from this arguing: no ruling will be obtained and there has been no real obstruction, to this point, of discovery. Furthermore, these counsel are not serving their clients well as the clients pay the attorney's fees and the transcript costs for all of this time and useless verbiage. All in all, in the objection and response pattern at depositions we probably see the trial attorney at his worst.

The rules clearly state what objections must be made at the deposition and how to make them. They also identify those objections that are not waived if counsel does not raise them during the deposition. Following those rules will help avoid many of the problems just described.

## 14.7 OBJECTIONS THAT DO NOT HAVE TO BE MADE AT THE DEPOSITION

Rule 32(d)(3)(A) states that objections to the competency, relevancy, or materiality of deposition testimony are not waived by failing to make them at the deposition unless the objection could have been cured. Similarly, Rule 32(d)(3)(B) only states that curable objections are waived by failing to make them at the deposition. In short, you need not assert any objection that cannot be cured at the deposition; you can assert them for the first time when one of the parties attempts to introduce the deposition at trial or in support of or in opposition to a motion.[8] What kinds of objections cannot be cured? Again without attempting to be definitive, the usual non-curable objections are:

### 14.7.1 Relevancy (including materiality).

Obviously, relevance is a matter which cannot be cured by further questioning or by rephrasing the question; it may be disclosed, but it is not cured. It depends solely upon the relationship between the facts sought and the issues in the case.[9] Furthermore, Rule 26(b)(1) allows discovery of relevant information and defines it to include information which may not itself be admissible but which is reasonably calculated to lead to the discovery of admissible evidence.

---

8.   At least one court has said that it is improper to make objections at the deposition to competency, relevancy and materiality. *Hall v. Clifton Precision*, 150 F.R.D. 525, 528 n.3 (E.D. Pa. 1993).

9.   *See* Fed.R.Evid. 401: "Relevant evidence means any evidence having any tendency to make the existence of any fact that is of consequence to the determination of the action more probable or less probable than it would be without the evidence."

### 14.7.2 Prejudicial.

Whether, under Federal Rule of Evidence 403, the probative value of the evidence is outweighed by the danger of unfair prejudicial effect cannot be determined until trial when the evidence is weighed in relationship to all of the evidence in the case.

### 14.7.3 Hearsay (unless the testimony can be placed within a hearsay exception).

Hearsay is not a curable objection and therefore you do not waive it if it is not made at the deposition. If a statement is hearsay under Federal Rule of Evidence 801, no amount of further questioning will convert the statement into non-hearsay. If, however, the hearsay statement can be placed into one of the hearsay exceptions of Federal Rules of Evidence 803 or 804, then the objection might be cured at trial. Whether the statement is admissible under a hearsay exception depends, of course, on the statement.

### 14.7.4 Confusion of the issues, misleading to the jury, undue delay, waste of time, or needless presentation of cumulative evidence.

As with unfairly prejudicial evidence, these objections under Federal Rule of Evidence 403 can only be evaluated in the context of trial or a motion *in limine* and not at the discovery stage. Therefore, you do not waive these objections by failing to make them at the deposition.

### 14.7.5 Competency.

Federal Rule of Evidence 601 provides that every person is competent to be a witness unless otherwise provided in the rules. However, when state law supplies the rule of decision for an element of the claim or defense, then the competency of a witness will be determined in accordance with state law. Rule 32(d)(3)(A) expressly states that you do not waive objections to lack of competency if you do not make them at the deposition.

## 14.8 OBJECTIONS THAT MUST BE MADE AT OR BEFORE THE DEPOSITION

Objections to problems which can be cured must be made or they are waived. Neither taker nor defender should assume that improper questions or procedures will be considered later, at trial, by the judge. If the problem is "non-trivial," the objection should be made at deposition, as soon as the problem arises.

### 14.8.1 Objections as to notice.

Rule 32(d)(1) states that all errors and irregularities in the notice of deposition are waived unless prompt written objections are served on the party giving notice. The purpose of this provision is to prevent technical irregularities from destroying the utility of depositions at trial. If the irregularities are not corrected and present some substantial question of the deponent's rights, the objecting party should seek a protective order; otherwise, if he merely fails to attend, he may have to justify his noncompliance with the notice at a hearing on a motion to compel discovery.[10]

Counsel will usually have agreed upon a time and place for the deposition, and the fact that the witness showed up is usually a demonstration that the notice has been adequate. Sometimes, however, the notice should contain some additional information—the subject of a 30(b)(6) deposition, or the specifications for the subpoena *duces tecum* accompanying the subpoena to a non-party witness—on which counsel may not agree. Because these are matters of notice which can be corrected—cured or obviated—during the deposition, they must be raised or any such objections are waived.

### 14.8.2 Objections as to qualifications of the officer.

Rule 32(d)(2) states that unless an objection is made before the deposition begins, or as soon thereafter as the disqualification becomes known or could be discovered with reasonable diligence, any objection to the qualifications of the officer before whom the deposition is being taken is waived. Occasionally, the reporter provided by the reporting service is not a notary in the jurisdiction in which the deposition is being taken. Sometimes this occurs because the notarial powers are granted for limited geographic areas, like counties, and the reporting service was not aware that the deposition was across a county line. Nevertheless, this can be easily cured by having a notary come in to swear the witness. As a technical matter, the "officer" notary would then have to remain in the room, because the deposition is to be recorded "in the officer's presence."[11] By stipulation, of course, the parties could waive this requirement so the officer could leave.

---

10. *See* 7 James W. Moore, *et al., Moore's Federal Practice* ¶ 32.43[1] (3d ed. 2000).
11. Fed.R.Civ.P. 30(c).

### 14.8.3 Objections to cure problems.

Rule 32(d)(3)(B) requires that failure to object at the deposition waives errors of any kind occurring at the deposition which might be obviated, removed, or cured if promptly presented at the deposition. This includes, but is not limited to, errors in the taking of the deposition, in the form of the questions or answers, in the oath or affirmation, or in the conduct of the parties. The vast majority of deposition objections are made under this provision.

What follows is a collection of the objections that are within the definition of Rule 32(d)(3)(A) and the methods by which the objections can be "obviated or removed" if made at the time of the deposition. For purposes of our discussion we will describe the process of "obviating or removing" an objection as curing the objection.

### 1. Objections as to competency of witnesses.

There is a wide range of witness competency issues covered by the Federal Rules of Evidence. Within the rubric of witness competence are the following issues:

**Testimonial capacity**—Before a witness can give testimony in a trial, deposition, or other proceeding, it must be shown that the witness has testimonial capacity. The appreciation by the witness of the necessity to tell the truth coupled with the ability of the witness to recall events and relate them are prerequisites to the providing of testimony.[12] If an objection is made to the general competence of the witness to provide testimony, and the deficiency is curable, questioning counsel can show as a matter of preliminary inquiry that the witness knows what the truth is, Federal Rule of Civil Procedure 30(c), and appreciates the necessity to tell the truth, or such other facts as will cure the defect. Absent the objection, the witness is presumed to be competent. Likewise, if examining counsel has reason to believe that a witness does not have the ability to recall events, or to provide testimony about them, an objection must be made or it will be waived, if there is a cure. If it is believed that a deponent lacks testimonial capacity before the beginning of the deposition, the objection should be lodged at that time. If the lack of testimonial capacity only becomes apparent during the course of the deposition, a motion to strike the witness's testimony on that basis can be lodged at that time, thereby giving opposing counsel the opportunity to develop testimony from the witness that cures the objection. If, however, the objection merely

---

12. Fed.R.Evid. 601, 603.

reflects a difference of opinion between counsel, no cure is possible and no waiver occurs.

**Firsthand knowledge**—Before lay witnesses can give testimony about an event, it is necessary that it be demonstrated that they have firsthand knowledge about the topic of their proposed testimony. If an objection is made that a witness lacks firsthand knowledge of the matters of proposed testimony, questioning counsel can show by the testimony of the witness that in fact the testimonial pre-requisite is met, by showing the time, place, and circumstances where the required firsthand knowledge was obtained.

**Character witnesses on substantive matters** (reputation, opinion, or conduct)—A character witness may testify as to the character of a party for substantive purposes by providing reputation, opinion, or specific instances of conduct evidence regarding a party, when the character of a party is an essential element of a civil claim or defense.[13] An objection to the competence of such a witness can be cured by showing that the witness has sufficient familiarity with the party about whom the character evidence is offered to form an opinion; sufficient familiarity with other people who know the party to be able to provide reputation evidence regarding the character of the party; or firsthand knowledge of the specific instance(s) of conduct.

**Character witnesses on credibility** (reputation or opinion)—A character witness may provide opinion or reputation evidence regarding the character of another witness regarding truthfulness or untruthfulness.[14] An objection to the competence of such a witness can be obviated by showing that the witness has sufficient familiarity with the other witness, about whom the character evidence is offered, to offer an opinion; or sufficient familiarity with other people, who also know the witness about whom character evidence is offered, to be able to testify by way of reputation evidence on the issue of honesty.

**Lay opinion testimony**—A lay witness may provide an opinion only if it is rationally based on perception, helpful to the jury, and not an expert opinion.[15] If a lay opinion is objected to, questioning counsel can lay a factual predicate to show that the lay opinion is in fact rationally based on perception and provide sufficient foundation to show that it is helpful to a fair determination of the case. If the proposed lay opinion is objected to as really being an expert opinion, that objection too can be answered by taking further testimony from the

---

13. Fed.R.Evid. 602.
14. Fed.R.Evid. 608(a).
15. Fed.R.Evid. 701.

witness that either demonstrates that the opinion is not outside the ken of the lay witness, or, in the alternative, that the witness possesses the attributes that qualify him or her as an expert witness. (Of course, the newly identified expert witness would then have to satisfy all the other requirements under Federal Rule of Evidence 702 and Federal Rule of Civil Procedure 26.)

**Expert opinions**—An expert witness may only provide an opinion if it requires special knowledge, the witness has that special knowledge (is an expert), the opinion will assist the trier of fact, the opinion is based on reliable and verifiable data of the sort normally relied upon by such an expert, and she is utilizing reliable principles and methods.[16] Objections to qualifications of an expert witness can be obviated by eliciting further testimony about them. Likewise, whether a principle or method is reliable so as to meet the *Daubert/Kumho Tire* standards can be shown with testimony that meets the requirement of Federal Rule of Evidence 703 and those cases. Many judges, when considering motions to exclude expert testimony on Federal Rule of Evidence 703 or *Daubert/Kumho Tire* grounds, will want all matters relevant to such a motion to have been explored during expert depositions, thereby saving the time and expense of having an evidentiary hearing to take the testimony of the very same expert witnesses who, if allowed, will then have to be deposed again.

### 2. Competence, relevance, and materiality of evidence.

Within this category there exist a number of potential curable evidentiary issues that must be raised during the deposition or are waived:

**Character evidence for substantive purposes** (conformity)— Character evidence offered to show that a party acted consistently with that character trait is admissible in civil cases only when character is an essential element of a claim or defense, such as in defamation cases.[17] As such, character evidence for conformity purposes is severely limited in civil cases. It may be, however, that the proposed character evidence regarding prior acts shows such consistently and regularlity that if an objection was made the proposed evidence could be shown to be admissible as habit or routine practice evidence.[18]

---

16. *See* Fed.R.Evid. 702, 703; *Daubert v. Merrill Dow,* 509 U.S. 579 (1993); *Kumho Tire Co. v. Carmichael,* 526 U.S. 137 (1999).
17. Fed.R.Evid. 405(b).
18. Fed.R.Evid. 406.

**Character evidence for a substantive purpose** (other than conformity)—Character evidence regarding a party by way of specific instances of conduct may be offered to prove such matters, when relevant, as identity, intent, motive, opportunity, preparation, plan, knowledge, or absence of mistake or accident.[19] If an objection is made to a question regarding specific instances of conduct based on calling for improper character evidence, the objection can be cured by resort to the nature of the claim or defense involved to see if any of the permissible uses for character evidence in Federal Rule of Evidence 404(b) is material. If any of them is, the evidence can be further developed to show that it meets the requirements of quantum of proof required by Federal Rule of Evidence 104, and is not otherwise excludable pursuant to Federal Rule of Evidence 403.

**Habit/routine practice**—Evidence of instances of conduct that are shown to amount to a regular response to a repeated situation is relevant to show that a party acted in conformity with that habit or routine practice in a particular instance.[20] A timely objection to prior act evidence will allow the questioning counsel in a deposition to develop the facts of the prior acts to show that they have occurred in the same way with such frequency, in response to repeated situations, so as to meet the requirements of habit (for individuals) and routine practice evidence (for institutions).

**Subsequent remedial measures**—Evidence of a subsequent remedial measure is not admissible to show negligence, culpable conduct, a defect in a product or its design, or the need for a warning, but may be admissible (competent) for other purposes. If an objection is lodged as to subsequent remedial measures, questioning counsel could inquire as to whether the party who performed the subsequent remedial measure is contesting ownership, control, or feasibility of precautionary measures, or could treat the problem as one of relevance and ignore it until the testimony comes up at trial.

**Offers of compromise**—Offers or acceptances of compromise are not admissible to prove liability, the validity of a claim, or the amount claimed.[21] Making the objection will allow deposing counsel to show that there was no controversy at the time of the offer (a precursor to invoking an objection to an offer of compromise) or to show that the objected-to evidence is admissible to contest the credibility of the persons involved or to negate a relevant contention of delay.

---

19. Fed.R.Evid. 404(b).
20. Fed.R.Evid. 406.
21. Fed.R.Evid. 408.

**Payment of medical or similar expenses**—Evidence of furnishing or offering to furnish payment for medical expenses is not admissible to prove liability.[22] In response to an objection, counsel may try to demonstrate that the offer has another admissible purpose, such as establishing the credibility of the party offering to make such a payment in the circumstances surrounding the offer.

**Liability insurance**—Evidence of liability insurance is not admissible to prove the liability of the insured or the proper amount of damages, if any, that are due in a cause of action.[23] If an objection is interposed as to questions seeking this evidence, inquiry can be made as to whether the holder of the insurance is contesting agency, ownership, or control, or as to whether the fact of insurance creates some sort of credibility issue regarding the witness (*e.g.*, the witness is an agent for the insurer of the defendant for whom the witness testifies favorably). Although inadmissible at trial, the insurance coverage may nevertheless be discovered because it fosters settlement.

**Privileges and trial preparation materials**—If a question calls for information that is privileged, an objection must be interposed before testimony that contains privileged information is answered, or the privilege is waived. Once that objection is interposed, and after objecting counsel has specified the privilege and its applicability as required by the Federal Rule of Civil Procedure 26(b)(5), questioning counsel can cure the objection by demonstrating that the privilege does not apply, that there has been a waiver of the privilege by some action of the privilege holder either individually or by an agent, or that there exists some exception to the application of the privilege.[24]

If the question calls for protected trial preparation materials,[25] a similar process should be employed. The objection should be made, followed by an instruction not to answer. At that point, opposing counsel has the opportunity to show that the material in question does not fall within the trial preparation protection of Federal Rule of Civil Procedure 26, or there exists sound reason for invading that protection such as the evidence not being available to deposing counsel by other reasonable means.

---

22. Fed.R.Evid. 409.
23. Fed.R.Evid. 411.
24. For example, if there is a claim of physician patient privilege and the plaintiff/patient has put his or her medical condition in issue by the nature of the lawsuit that privilege will be raised. In the case of a claim of attorney-client privilege, questioning could show that the communication is excepted from the claimed privilege because the communication was made for the purpose or in furtherance of a crime or fraud.
25. Fed.R.Civ.P. 26(b)(3).

**Expert opinions** (reliability of theory/methodology)—A qualified expert witness may only give opinion testimony if it is based on sufficient data and the scientific principles relied on and the methodology utilized are reliable.[26] An objection to the competence of an expert opinion can be obviated by showing compliance with Federal Rule of Evidence 702 and the *Daubert/Kumho Tire*[27] standards which require a showing of reliability of scientific or other principle, and the use of a demonstrably reliable methodology. This can be done by showing (a) the theory or methodology has been tested; (b) the theory applied or the methodology utilized has been published and subject to peer review; (c) the known error rate for the methodology; (d) the standards and controls for the use of the methodology; (e) the theory or methodology is generally accepted; or (f) any other indicia of reliability of the theory or methodology.

**Expert opinions** (bases)—An expert opinion can be based on information and data of a type that is reasonably relied upon by experts in a particular field, but generally that data or information may only be made known to a fact finder if the data or information is otherwise admissible.[28] An objection to the competence of bases evidence relied upon by an expert will allow exploration as to whether the data or information is generally considered reliable within the expert's field, thereby justifying the expert's reliance on that information in forming an opinion. In addition, the objection can be further cured by showing that the relied-upon data or information is otherwise admissible and may therefore be revealed to the jury.

**Hearsay**—The hearsay rule precludes admission of out-of-court statements that are offered for the truth of their content.[29] An objection to the admissibility of such a statement can be cured by showing that (a) the statement is not offered for the truth of the content of the statement, but for some other admissible purpose; (b) the statement meets the requirements of non-hearsay statement, admissible for the truth of the content of the statement;[30] or (c) the statement meets an exception to the hearsay rule.[31] Deposing counsel may want to establish the grounds for arguing at trial that an exception to exclusion applies, but the hearsay is discoverable even where no exception applies.

---

26. Fed.R.Evid. 702.
27. *Daubert v. Merrell Dow*, 509 U.S. 579 (1993); *Kumho Tire Co. v. Carmichael*, 526 U.S. 137 (1999).
28. Fed.R.Evid. 703.
29. Fed.R.Evid. 801, 802.
30. Fed.R.Evid. 801(d).
31. Fed.R.Evid. 803, 804, 807.

**Authentication** (voices)—A witness may testify to an admissible oral statement of another person once it is established that the witness can authenticate the voice of the other person.[32] An objection to authentication will call for questioning counsel to demonstrate that the witness has familiarity with the voice of the other person or that there is sufficient circumstantial evidence to identify the voice of the person. Such familiarity may be obtained either before or after the communication in issue and may be acquired solely for the purposes of litigation.

**Authentication** (instruments)—An instrument such as a writing, document, photograph, or tape recording is admissible only if its identity and authorship can be established.[33] An objection to the authentication of an instrument can be cured by showing sufficient evidence to prove that the instrument is what it is purported to be by establishing its identity and authorship. If authentication of the instrument depends on familiarity of handwriting, that familiarity cannot have been acquired for the purpose of litigation.

**Original documents rule**—In order to prove the contents of a document (including writings, recordings, or photographs), where the contents of that document are directly in issue, the proponent must produce an original of the document, unless its production is excused.[34] An original documents rule objection can be cured by showing (a) the rule does not apply to the document in question; (b) the document is an admissible duplicate; or (c) the production of the original document is excused.

### 3. Objections to the form of the question or answer.

By the clear terms of Federal Rule of Civil Procedure 32(d)(3)(A), objections to the form of questions or answers at a deposition are waived unless made at the time of the deposition. These objections are made appropriate at a deposition by the terms of the Rule 30(c), which provides that the examination of witnesses may proceed as if a trial. The following are the generally recognized objections as to the form of the question or answer. It should be noted that, except with regard to leading questions, there is no federal rule that governs these objec-

---

32. Fed.R.Evid. 901.
33. Fed.R.Evid. 901—In addition to being authentic, an instrument must be relevant and comply with the hearsay and original document rules to be admissible at trial. In some instances an instrument will also present issues of privilege.
34. Fed.R.Evid. 1000.

tions. They are all cognizable within the general authority of the court to regulate the mode of witness questioning.[35]

**Leading**—A leading question is one which suggests the desired answer to the deponent in such a way that there is concern that it is the lawyer who is testifying. Leading questions are generally not allowed on direct examination, and are allowed on cross-examination. In the normal deposition of the adversary's client or witnesses, there is little logical objection to leading questions. Of course, they are not an efficient way to learn new information; they serve instead to confirm information already known.[36] An objection to a leading question can be cured by rephrasing the question or demonstrating that the leading question is necessary to adequately develop the testimony of the witness.

To preserve the objection, it must be made at the deposition. Should counsel defending the deposition of a party he represents choose to ask questions at the end of the testimony taken by deposing counsel, those questions should normally be non-leading.

**Ambiguous/vague**—An ambiguous question is one that is susceptible to at least two interpretations. A vague question is so unintelligible as to make it likely that it either confuses the deponent or that a response to the question will create an unclear record. The objection can be cured by rephrasing the question or by demonstrating the understanding by the witness of the question.

**Argumentative**—An argumentative question is one that is asked not for the purpose of obtaining information from the witness but rather to make argument regarding the facts of the case in the guise of a question, hoping for witness agreement. An argumentative question will often seek to get witness agreement to inferences to be drawn from the facts. For that reason the objection may frequently be accompanied by an objection that the question is calling for an inadmissible lay opinion, or conjecture. The objection can be cured by rephrasing the question so that it is clear that it is seeking facts versus inferences.

**Asked and answered**—A question may be objected to as asked and answered when it calls for the repetition of testimony from a deponent who has previously provided an answer to the same question by deposing counsel. The objection to such a question can also be stated as calling for cumulative evidence. The objection is cured by making clear the thrust of the question is different from that which has already

---

35. Fed.R.Evid. 611(a).
36. Fed.R.Evid. 611(c).

been asked during the deposition. In a deposition it is often a tactic to ask an already-asked question in a different way to test the credibility of the witness and the information that has been provided.

**Assuming facts not in evidence**—A question is objectionable if it assumes, in the asking, facts that have not already been proved through the testimony of the deponent or by other competent evidence. The objection is cured by asking the witness about the fact that was assumed in the objected-to question and verifying that the witness knows the fact. The main body of the objected-to question can then be asked in sequence. For example, the question, "When you went to the store, what did you buy?" might assume that the deponent went to the store although she has not testified about going to the store. It could be improved by asking, "Did you go to the store? What did you buy?"

**Compound questions**—A question is objectionable if it asks for two or more items of information at the same time, so that it is impossible to understand the meaning of the answer to the question, or the answering of the question will create a misleading or confusing record of the deponent's testimony. The objection is cured by breaking the component parts of the question into single fact inquiries.

**Misquoting the witness**—A question is objectionable when it includes a factual predicate purportedly based on previous testimony by the deponent, but in fact misstates the previous testimony of the deponent. The objection can be cured by having the witness repeat earlier testimony or by having previous testimony of the witness read back to clarify what was said.

**Narratives** (questions and responses)—A question can be objected to if it is unfocused as to the particular information that is sought so as to be overbroad. A question that calls for a narrative creates a danger that a deponent will fail to include all of the information within the broad scope of the question, so that reliance on the answer to the question as being complete is unfounded.

An objection can also be interposed as to the narrative form of the answer, which makes it difficult to interpose timely substantive objections to the broad and oftentimes rambling testimony of the deponent. Questions that call for narrative responses are generally good discovery devices in a deposition as a starting point regarding any particular topic. The danger of the question not eliciting all relevant information within the scope of the question is cured by asking more specific questions in follow-up to the narrative. If the narrative fails to elicit all the witness knows about a topic, and if defending counsel wants opposing counsel to know about those facts, the topic can be exhausted at the end of the deposition when defending counsel can ask questions of the witness.

**Non-responsive answers**—An answer by a deponent that exceeds the scope of the question or fails to respond to the question is subject to objection and motion to strike by questioning counsel. If, in fact, the answer of the witness was non-responsive but provided relevant information, defending counsel can ask about those matters at the end of the deposition when there is an opportunity to inquire of the witness.

## 14.9 THE FORM OF OBJECTIONS AND INSTRUCTIONS NOT TO ANSWER

### 14.9.1 Form of objections.

Since the landmark case of *Hall v. Clifton Precision Tools* in 1993,[37] the manner and form of objecting at depositions has received increased scrutiny from judges, commentators, and rule makers. Lawyer conduct, which used the making of objections and instructions to the witness not to answer legitimate questions as a means to coach witnesses and interfere with the right of deposing counsel to ask for and discover relevant testimony, has been the subject of criticism by individual judges, legal scholars, and the organized bar. The result has been changes to the Federal Rules of Civil Procedure, further regulation in the district courts by promulgation of even more restrictive local rules, and the fashioning of discovery orders by individual judges that govern the conduct of counsel during the taking and defending of deposition testimony.

The Federal Rules of Civil Procedure have made clear the proper manner for the making of objections and the limited circumstances in which a lawyer defending a deposition can instruct a witness not to answer. As to the making of objections, Federal Rule of Civil Procedure 30(d) provides:

> (1) Any objection during a deposition must be stated **concisely and in a non-argumentative and non-suggestive manner**. (emphasis added)

Taken together with Federal Rule of Civil Procedure 32(d)(1)(3)[38] the rule envisions that objections be made stating the word "objection"

---

37. 150 F.R.D. 525 (E.D. Pa. 1993).
38. Fed.R.Civ.P. 32(d)(3)(A) suggests the purpose of an objection at deposition is to obviate or remove the objectionable nature of a question or response.

and a brief statement of the specific legal grounds for the objection. In this way objecting counsel makes clear the basis for objection without coaching the deponent, and questioning counsel has a fair opportunity to cure the objection.

### 1. Objections to the form of the question

An example of a proper objection to a question that assumes a fact not in evidence is:

> "Objection: assumes a fact not in evidence."

This objection is neither argumentative nor suggestive, and still, by stating precisely what is wrong with the question, gives the questioning counsel an opportunity to cure the objection.

Alternatively the objection could be made by stating:

> "Objection: that question assumes that my client has testified to [insert fact] which he has not, and further assumes that he knows [insert fact] which he does not, and further assumes that the fact exists, which is plainly not true."

While this objection makes clear the grounds of the objection, it is argumentative and clearly suggests several answers to the witness. It is classic of what are typically called "speaking objections" and is designed not only to interfere with the taking of discovery by being argumentative, but also to instruct the deponent, in the form of an objection, as to how the deponent should answer the question.

On the other end of the spectrum, the objection could be made by stating:

> "Objection."

or

> "Objection to the form."

This objection would be neither argumentative nor suggestive, but would not provide sufficient legal grounds to allow opposing counsel a fair opportunity to cure the objection.

### 2. Substantive objections

An example of a substantive objection that is in compliance with the letter and the spirit of the Federal Rules of Civil Procedure is:

"Objection—improper lay opinion"

Faced with this objection, deposing counsel can instruct the witness to answer as even inadmissible opinions are likely to lead to relevant evidence. In the alternative, counsel can ask the witness sufficient questions to show that the lay opinion was rationally based on the perception of the witness and likely to be helpful to a trier of fact and therefore an admissible lay opinion. (Fed.R.Evid. 701.)

Alternatively, this objection could be made by stating:

> "Objection: you're asking my client to guess as to the meaning of what it is that he saw and that's asking for an inadmissible opinion, not much more than a guess that he doesn't have to give if he is uncomfortable in doing so, but if you want him to guess, he can go ahead and guess, but I don't see any value in it."

This objection states the grounds for the objection so it could be cured, but is certainly both argumentative and suggesting to the witness that he should either say that he would prefer not to guess or make clear that what he's doing is guessing. Alternatively, the objection could be made by stating:

> "Objection: foundation"

or

> "Objection."

These objections are neither argumentative nor suggestive. Their failure is that they provide no clear guidance to deposing counsel as to what could be done to cure the objection.

It should be noted, however, that there are some local rules that limit counsel to stating the word "Objection." or "Objection: form." These local rules are usually silent as to whether questioning counsel has the right to be informed as to the specific grounds for the objection so as to be provided the opportunity to cure the objection. Presumably such a request would have to be answered by objecting counsel with the specific grounds for the objection that has been interposed. In addition, there are individual discovery orders routinely issued by judges where local rules such as those described above are not available to impose similar restrictions on the form of objections at deposition.

### 14.9.2 Privileges and trial preparation materials.

When, during a deposition, questioning counsel seeks privileged information, the failure of defending counsel to object <u>and</u> instruct the deponent not to answer will likely result in the waiver of the privilege. At the time of the asking of a question that calls for privileged information, defending counsel should immediately interpose an objection, instruct the deponent not to answer, and seek a recess for the purpose of discussing with the deponent the propriety of claiming a privilege. Most questioning counsel will honor such a request, but even if there is a protest, a recess must be taken. Although the privilege belongs to the client and can be waived by the client, counsel should always assume that the deponent seeks to invoke her privilege and act accordingly. The same procedure should be followed for the protection from discovery of trial preparation materials[39] during the course of the deposition.

Once the client decides to invoke a privilege, defending counsel must provide sufficient information so that questioning counsel can determine whether the assertion of the privilege is proper, and so that a judge would have sufficient information to rule on either a protective order to enforce the claim of privilege or a motion to compel seeking to overcome the claim of privilege.

Federal Rule of Civil Procedure 26(b) provides:

> "(5) Claims of Privilege or Protection of Trial Preparation Materials. When a party withholds information otherwise discoverable under these rules by claiming that it is privileged or subject to protection as trial preparation material, the party shall make the claim expressly and shall describe the nature of the documents, communications, or things not produced or disclosed in a manner that, without revealing information itself privileged or protected, will enable other parties to assess the applicability of the privilege or protection."

For example, in a case where the plaintiff claims that the defendant defrauded him when he entered into a contract for the sale of goods, plaintiff's counsel may ask the deponent/defendant whether he spoke to anyone before he decided to enter into the contract that underlies the cause of action and the defendant may respond that he spoke with a lawyer. Any attempt to determine the content of that conversation should be objected to by defending counsel, who should also instruct

---

39. *See* Fed.R.Civ.P. 26(b)(3) (limiting discovery documents and other tangible things prepared by or for a party in anticipation of trial) *and* Fed.R.Civ.P. 26(b)(4)(B) (limiting discovery relating to consulting expert witnesses).

the deponent not to answer the question. If, after conferring with his client, defending counsel asserts the attorney-client privilege on behalf of the deponent, defending counsel should be prepared to provide the following information, although in most circumstances what is typically provided are items 1, 2, and 7. The other areas are usually inquired about by the deposing counsel.

1. the name of the client;

2. the name of the person spoken to;[40]

3. the date of the communication;[41]

4. the place of the communication; [42]

5. people present during the communication;[43]

6. any person to whom the subject matter of the communication was given either orally or in writing;[44]

7. the general nature and purpose of the communication (*e.g.,* oral or written communication for the purpose of obtaining legal advice.);[45]

8. whether the communication was recorded and, if so, to whom the record was shown and where it currently exists.[46]

Once this information is received by deposing counsel, he can ask questions about any of the factors listed above in order to attempt to show that the communication does not meet the attorney-client privilege because of waiver or because it meets an exception to the privilege. Armed with that information, counsel can seek a motion to compel disclosure of the communication as not privileged, or seek *in*

---

40. This information will insure that the person spoken to was either a licensed lawyer or an agent of a licensed lawyer.

41. This information will assist in determining whether the attorney-client relationship was in existence at the time of the communication.

42. This information will assist in determining whether the communication occurred in a place where there was a reasonable expectation that it would be confidential (*e.g.,* in the lawyer's office, as opposed to a crowded restaurant).

43. This information will assist in determining whether there were people present during the communication whose presence might obviate the privilege.

44. This information will assist in determining whether the privilege was destroyed by the communication of the alleged privileged information to someone not also protected by the privilege.

45. The communication must have been one that sought legal advice and may not have been for a purpose that destroys the privilege, such as the preparation for or furtherance of a crime or fraud.

46. The provision of a record of the communication to a non-privileged entity, or the failure to keep it safely, may be evidence that the communication was not intended to remain confidential.

*camera* inspection of a written communication (or a recording of an oral communication) by the judge to determine whether the privilege is properly claimed, if there has been waiver, or if an exception to the privilege exists.

The same process would be utilized regarding a claim that the information sought during the deposition is not discoverable because it is trial preparation material pursuant to Federal Rule of Civil Procedure 26. Defending counsel, after objecting and instructing the witness not to answer, must provide sufficient information to set out the nature of the trial preparation material protection claim so that deposing counsel can ask questions going to the validity of the claim, and so a judge can make an appropriate ruling should there be a motion to either protect disclosure of the material in question or to compel its production.

In addition to attacking the validity of objecting counsel's claim that the material or information sought are indeed trial preparation materials, questioning counsel may also attempt to show that there exist valid reasons for invading the claimed trial preparation materials protection. The protection of these materials from discovery can be invaded upon a showing of (1) substantial need for the material; and (2) the inability, without undue hardship, to obtain the substantial equivalent of the materials by some other means.[47] Typical of such a situation is when one party has obtained a statement from a witness with a unique information set, who has since become unavailable by death or whose location cannot be found after a diligent search.

## 14.10 THE TACTICS OF MAKING AND MEETING OBJECTIONS

### 14.10.1 To object or respond or not.

The first issue facing the defending lawyer once a deposition begins is whether to object at all. In a well-conducted deposition, the only objections that need be made are those for which waiver would create a potential problem later on in the litigation, whether in motion practice, alternative dispute resolution procedures, or at trial. And if there has been a stipulation that all objections except as to the form of the question or answers are reserved, it is arguable that even those objections need not be made.

---

47. Fed.R.Civ.P. 26(b)(3).

We have already discussed how the making of objections as to the form of the question can assist in making sure that the record is accurate as to the facts as known by the deponent. What must be acknowledged as well is that objections, whether they be to the form of the question or as to substantive matters, can really perform the function of improving the quality of the lawyering by opposing counsel.

The objections to the form of question recognized by the law of evidence are really guideposts for effective examination. When an objection is made, for example, to a compound question, it makes it clear to opposing counsel that, unless the compounding parts of the offending question are parsed into one question at a time, there will likely be a confusing and not terribly useful record. When a substantive objection is made with regard to a question or an answer,[48] the objection may point out an evidentiary problem with the testimony, which, through appropriate further questioning, can be cured, thereby insuring use of the testimony at a later time. So if the questions of counsel are likely to be improved, or substantive objections likely to be cured, by the making of objections by defending counsel, the better practice might be to not make them.

As to questioning counsel, it needs to be understood that not every objection that is made is done only for the purpose of distracting the questioner, or to interfere with the free flow of information. As stated above, often a well-placed objection to the form of a question will in fact have the effect, if the opportunity is taken by questioning counsel by rephrasing, of improving the quality of the examination. In addition, a substantive objection can provide the opportunity for questioning counsel to cure a potential objection to later use of the evidence in the litigation. That being said, there are times when the questioning counsel will need to stand his or her ground to insure that the deposition record will be as useful as possible. There are several typical tactics that need be understood.

It is self-evident that during a deposition there is no one present to rule on objections. As such, just the fact an objection is made does not mean that the question is a bad one, or that the evidence it seeks is not discoverable. It is also unlikely that questioning counsel can persuade the objecting lawyer that the objection is not well-stated. If an objection is made to the form of the question, and questioning counsel does not agree with the objection or believe that rephrasing is necessary

---

48. Even in situations where there has been a stipulation that preserves substantive objections until the time the deposition is attempted to be used in motion practice or trial, those objections can still be made.

to protect the record, the appropriate response is to ignore objecting counsel and inform the witness that he may answer the question.

Another typical circumstance regarding objections to the form of the question occurs when defending counsel merely states, "Objection: form," and does so with regard to many questions. If there is truly nothing wrong with the form of the questions, it is likely that defending counsel's purpose is not to preserve objections, but rather to interfere with the free flow of information at the deposition. A good tactic with such defending counsel is merely to inquire, "What is wrong with the form of the question?" Failure to state what is wrong with the form of the question will likely result in waiver of the objection because a fair opportunity to cure that objection will not have been provided. The lawyer who is merely attempting to interfere will typically not have an answer to your question and will be deterred from the tactic in the future.

With regard to substantive objections, the mere fact that evidence or testimony sought by a question may later be found to be inadmissible at trial is not conclusive for deposition practice. The standard for the scope of all discovery is whether the sought-after testimony is reasonably calculated to lead to the discovery of admissible evidence, not whether it is admissible in and of itself.[49] A question that seeks to find out from the deponent what other witnesses present during a relevant event said at that event, although perhaps inadmissible as hearsay at trial if offered through the testimony of the deponent, can certainly lead to fact investigation of those witnesses, whose depositions can be taken or whose testimony can be presented at trial.

Further as to substantive objections, some lawyers will lodge such objections by stating,

"Objection: foundation."

These lawyers, too, may be seeking to interfere with questioning rather than preserve an objection. With these lawyers it is usually wise to ask, "What is wrong with the foundation?" Because the legitimate purpose of an objection is to allow questioning counsel to cure it, defending counsel must respond or waive the objection. If interference is the goal, there will be little wrong with the foundation, and defending counsel will be discouraged from offering further interfering objections.

One further issue deserves some comment. There are some lawyers who believe that they have the right to consult with their clients before the client responds to a question, or discuss an exhibit before the de-

---

49. Fed.R.Civ.P. 26(b)(1).

ponent is questioned regarding that exhibit. These tactics have resulted in local rules[50] and individual discovery orders[51] that have severely restricted the ability of defending counsel to consult with their clients once the deposition has begun. Local rules and discovery orders prevail, of course, but in circumstances where there are no such rules, the default position seems to be that consultation with a client is not appropriate while a question is pending or while a particular line of questioning is being pursued.[52] The consultation with counsel should be anticipated and perhaps one of the "usual stipulations" can be that there will be no consultation with the deponent by defending counsel while a question is pending, except with regard to the claiming of a privilege or trial preparation material protection.

When consultation occurs during the pendency of a question, an objection should be made and the transcript marked for the purpose of later seeking sanctions or a court order precluding the conduct. Deposing counsel should then continue to question the witness. With regard to consultation regarding exhibits, such consultation can be lessened if deposing counsel, when referring to an exhibit, makes copies for both the deponent and counsel, so there is no need for the deponent and counsel to collaborate over the exhibit.

### 14.10.2 Whether and when to involve the judge.

The short answer to this question of whether and when to involve the court is, only when absolutely necessary. Although there exist regional differences, most local rules require that there must be an effort by counsel to resolve discovery disputes, and a certification to that effect, before a motion to compel discovery can be made. The clear message of such rules is that lawyers should act professionally and comply with reasonable discovery requests, at deposition and otherwise, and that most disputes should be capable of resolution by counsel acting in a professional manner. That being said, agreement is not always possible.

---

50. *See, e.g.,* N.J. Civ. P.R. 4:14-3(f) ("Once the deponent has been sworn, there shall be no communication between the deponent and counsel during the course of the deposition while testimony is being taken except with regard to the assertion of a claim of privilege, a right to confidentiality or a limitation pursuant to a previously entered court order.").

51. *See Hall v. Clifton Precision Tools,* 150 F.R.D. 525 (E.D. Pa. 1993).

52. A full examination of this important topic is beyond the scope of this work. The authors believe that consultation while a line of questions is pending is improper except with regard to claiming privilege, enforcing trial preparation materials protection, enforcing an existing protective order, or seeking a protective order. *See In re Stratosphere,* 182 F.R.D. 614 (D. Nev. 1998).

The only time that it would normally be necessary to involve the judge with the making and meeting of objections at deposition would be when defending counsel objects in a manner that is suggestive, argumentative, or conducted in such a way as to interfere with reasonable discovery. The allegation to any of these matters must be supported by the deposition record, and, before a judge is likely to take any action, it must usually be shown that deposing counsel has made all legitimate efforts to achieve legitimate discovery during the deposition. Only then can a successful motion to compel be brought, seeking appropriate sanctions.

Much the same can be said with regard to instructions not to answer. Because the legitimate grounds for such an instruction are limited to privilege or trial preparation materials preservation, the existence of a protective order, or the opportunity to seek a protective order, Fed. R.Civ.P. 30(d)(1), the legitimacy of such an instruction is usually fairly easy to determine. If there is a claim of privilege or trial preparation materials protection, properly stated, and questioning counsel has developed information regarding the appropriateness of the privilege, its applicability, waiver, or the existence of an exception to the privilege; or with regard to trial preparation materials some reason to overcome protection exists, all that is necessary to raise the matter for judicial review in a motion to compel testimony, Fed.R.Civ.P. 37(a), is present on the deposition record. In the case of a protective order, a motion to compel will determine whether the disputed sought-after discovery is precluded by the protective order. And finally, an instruction not to answer for the purpose of seeking a protective order will be litigated in the form of that request. Fed.R.Civ.P. 26(c).

That being said, where there is an instruction not to answer a question, it is always appropriate for deposing counsel to attempt to get the sought-after information in a form that does not invade either privilege, trial preparation material preservation, or protective orders. In many circumstances the instruction not to answer may go to the form in which the information exists (*e.g.*, in a memo from client to lawyer) as opposed to the content of the information that may exist independent of a privileged context.

Should the judge find that objections or instructions not to answer have in fact interfered with legitimate discovery, there exist a number of potential sanctions. Federal Rule of Civil Procedure 30(d) provides:

> "(3) If the court finds that any impediment, delay or other conduct has frustrated the fair examination of the deponent, it may impose upon the persons responsible an appropriate

sanction, including the reasonable costs and attorney's fees incurred by any parties as a result thereof."

In addition to the sanctions provisions of Rule 30, a district judge has enormous discretion to provide any sanction that meets discovery abuse, up to and including dismissal of claims or defenses.[53]

**The rule for making objections.** The rule for making objections at a deposition is basically the same as for trial: only object if you will gain by the objection; that is, when unfavorable evidence to your position may be made inadmissible. For example, if the witness is asked about what occurred at a meeting with your client without first being asked whether he was present at the meeting, you could properly object that there has been no showing of personal knowledge. But should you make such an objection? Certainly you should if you know that the witness was not at the meeting or even if you are unsure and you expect the answer to be unfavorable (*e.g.*, "They discussed how to breach the contract."). If the questioning attorney then cures the objection by asking if the witness was present and the answer is no, any statement about what occurred at the meeting will be inadmissible at trial. On the other hand, if you expect the answer to be favorable ("There was a discussion of how to avoid breaching the contract.") or you know the witness was present at the meeting, you gain little from the objection. Worse, you can harm your client's interests by making what would be an admissible, helpful answer inadmissible if the witness should become unavailable and you wish to introduce the answer at trial. The questioning attorney may also, in the face of a curable objection, end up making the witness's answers more persuasive and harmful. Assume that the witness is now unavailable for trial, but at the deposition the following occurred:

Q. Mr. Vilas, what was said at the meeting that occurred in the corporate offices on May 5, 1994?

OBJECTION:

Objection. No showing of personal knowledge and lack of foundation.

Q. All right, were you present at the meeting?

A. Yes.

Q. Who else was present at the meeting?

A. Johnson from corporate and Ted Smith from purchasing.

---

53. Fed.R.Civ.P. 30(b).

Q.   When did this meeting take place?

A.   Ten o'clock in the morning on May 5, 1994.

Q.   Where exactly did it take place?

A.   In the boardroom on the second floor of the corporate building.

Q.   Were you able to hear everything that was said during the meeting?

A.   Yes.

Q.   Did you leave at any time during the meeting?

A.   No.

Q.   Do you remember clearly what was said at that meeting?

A.   Yes.

Q.   What was said at that meeting?

If defending counsel had not objected, it is possible that the questioning attorney would have learned what was said at the meeting and moved on to a new topic. By objecting, however, the questioning attorney clearly established the witness's accuracy of recall about what happened. In the event this portion of the transcript is read to the jury, the testimony is now likely to be much more persuasive than if the objection had never been made.

Having given the general rule—do not object unless you will gain by the objection by keeping unfavorable evidence from being admitted at trial—there is one difference between objections made at deposition and those made at trial. Objections made at trial will be ruled on by the judge before the questioning proceeds further. In contrast, no judge is present at the deposition to rule on objections and the questioning will proceed subject to the objections. Therefore, if in doubt, make the objection. If you later decide that the objection was not valid, nothing requires you to assert it at the time the judge rules on objections (and there will be no opportunity to assert it later unless one of the parties attempts to introduce the deposition testimony). But if the problem with the question is curable and you fail to make an objection, the objection is waived forever.

## 14.11 INSTRUCTIONS NOT TO ANSWER

When defending a deposition, one of the most difficult decisions to make is whether to instruct or direct a witness not to answer a question. Rule 30(d)(1) sharply curtails the situations in which such an instruction is proper: "A person may instruct a deponent not to answer only when necessary to preserve a privilege, to enforce a limitation directed by the court, or to present a motion under Rule 30(d)(4)." Rule 30(d)(4) refers to adjourning the deposition to seek an order terminating or limiting the deposition because it is being conducted in bad faith or in such a manner as unreasonably to annoy, embarrass, or oppress the deponent.

The decision is difficult because if you make the wrong choice, the penalties can be great. If you instruct the witness not to answer a question which the court later determines is proper, the attorney or her client can be required to pay the reasonable expenses, including attorney's fees, of the questioning attorney in obtaining the order compelling an answer.[54] On the other hand, if you allow the witness to answer the question, you risk both losing the protections of the privilege or court order, at least for that question, and waiving them for the future as well.

The calculus of deciding whether to instruct the witness not to answer runs as follows: (1) If I instruct the witness not to answer, how likely is it that opposing counsel will bring a motion to compel? (2) If opposing counsel brings a motion to compel, how likely is it that the court will sustain the motion and compel an answer? (3) If the court sustains the motion, how likely is it that I or my client will be required to pay the reasonable expenses of opposing counsel bringing the motion and resuming the deposition? and (4) How important is it to prevent discovery of the information to which the question is directed compared to the amount and probability of having to pay the opposing side's expenses? If you are giving the instruction not to answer so as to adjourn the deposition to seek a protective order, then your calculation must focus on how badly the protective order is needed and the prospects for the court granting it.

Having decided to instruct the witness not to answer, the actual instruction should sound like this:

> Q.   Now, Mr. Vasys, did you ever receive any advice from your attorney concerning whether it was proper to terminate the contract?

---

54. *See* § 12.2.1 and § 12.2.5.

OBJECTION:

> I object to the question on the grounds that it asks for information covered by the attorney-client privilege, and I instruct the witness not to answer.

Q.  Mr. Vasys, will you answer the question, please?

A.  No, I'll follow my counsel's advice.

Several additional comments are in order. First, one of the matters that must be covered in preparing a witness to be deposed is what to do when an instruction not to answer is given. You must instruct the witness that the question is not to be answered, and if he is asked whether he will answer, the response is "No." Second, you should place a hand on the witness's arm and speak directly to the witness when giving the instruction. If the witness then starts to answer, you can start squeezing the witness's arm, which is usually an effective way to get the witness to stop talking, and quickly interrupt by cutting the witness off with a stern "Don't answer that question." Third, Rule 26(b)(5) requires that, when instructing a witness not to answer based on a claim of privilege or work product, you must do so expressly and shall "describe the nature of the documents, communications, or things not disclosed in a manner that, without revealing information itself privileged or protected, will enable other parties to assess the applicability of the privilege or protection." In the example given, the question itself makes evident the nature of the communication. Finally, be alert to questioning counsel's tactic of coming back later in the deposition, often toward the end when everyone is tired, to an area about which you have instructed the witness not to answer. Unless you have decided that the previous instruction not to answer was a mistake, you should persist in closing off the inquiry.

Instructions not to answer for purposes of adjourning the deposition to seek a protective order occur for many different reasons. The questioning attorney may be abusing the witness by yelling at her, the questions may be asking for trade secrets, the questioning attorney may be asking questions about matters that have absolutely nothing to do with the issues in the case, a 30(b)(6) deposition witness my be asked questions about subjects not listed in the notice of deposition or subpoena, and so forth. While Rule 30(d)(1) suggests that you should immediately adjourn the deposition to seek a protective order, the lawyers often agree to complete the deposition before filing their motions. An exception occurs when the questioning lawyer engages in abusive tactics; then you should adjourn the deposition immediately.

A problem that often occurs is when, at least in the eyes of the defender, the questioning attorney has gone so far beyond the scope of the complaint and answer that the information sought no longer "appears reasonably calculated to lead to the discovery of admissible evidence," which is the outer bound for discovery defined in Rule 26(b)(1). Problems arise when what the questioner believes is "reasonably calculated" is seen by the defender as unreasonable and intrusive. The result is an argument between counsel that probably accounts for most of the heat and none of the light at discovery depositions.

The practical solution is this: defending counsel should recognize her own bias in favor of a narrow interpretation here, and therefore should give the questioner a bit of latitude; the questioning attorney should recognize he need not turn over every rock in the field in order to find enough worms to go fishing.[55] If the questioner still wants what the defender will not give, the areas should be postponed until the defender can bring the matter to the court in a motion for a protective order.

## 14.12 QUESTIONING AND CLARIFYING AND CORRECTING ANSWERS

Traditionally, defending counsel did not ask any questions at the deposition of the party witness or a friendly witness. The reason was simple. If the witness was friendly or a client, the best place to ask questions was in the privacy of the lawyer's office where opposing counsel could not overhear what was being said. It was thought that there was no sense sharing information with the other side when there was no requirement of doing so. But all of this assumed that the end game of the litigation was a trial, when undiscovered information could be used to surprise the opponent and when there was less time to construct a theory to answer this surprise evidence.

In modern practice, as discussed in previous chapters, the end game for most modern litigation is some disposition mechanism other

---

55. Controversies on scope can be better understood if we recognize that attorneys at a deposition take such positions in large part because they believe their clients expect them to, and not because they believe in the need for the discovery or the protection. Thus, the deposing attorney is intent upon pressing her inquiries to the limits of reasonableness because she does not want her client (or senior partner, or government supervisor) to think she gave away the store; the defending attorney has the same concerns about allowing too much latitude. In fact, these are exactly the kinds of judgments trial attorneys get paid to make, and if their focus were on the genuine needs of the litigation, rather than on how their actions would be second-guessed later on, the purposes of discovery would be better served.

than a trial. In these dispute resolution arenas the deposition is a primary source of information and, as such, should contain all the favorable information for the client. It is for that reason, as discussed in Chapter Thirteen, that clients and favorable witnesses are prepared to find the opportunity to divulge the favorable information they possess during their questioning by opposing counsel. If, however, that opportunity does not arise, then defending counsel should be prepared to ask the questions necessary to be sure that opposing counsel appreciates the strength of the client's case. Even assuming a traditional approach to litigation in a circumstance where a trial is likely, there exist exceptions to the "rule" about defending counsel not asking any questions at a deposition.

When a witness refuses to cooperate or to be interviewed informally, such a witness should be questioned by defending counsel at the deposition for the same reason that the other side is asking questions: to find out what the witness knows. When the witness is uncooperative with both sides, both have an incentive to ask questions. Even though the other side has noticed the deposition, the "defending" counsel may also question the witness. Defending counsel will also want to question a deposition witness, even though friendly, if she expects the witness to be unavailable for trial and the deposition will be the vehicle used to get that witness's information to the jury. In such a circumstance, the friendly witness should be prepared to testify through sessions just like those that would be used to prepare her for trial.

Sometimes the opposing party will notice the deposition of its own party or of a witness friendly to that side. This usually indicates that the witness will be unavailable for trial and the deposition is being taken to preserve his testimony. Prudent counsel will prepare to cross-examine the witness in the same way they would if they were noticing the deposition.[56]

Defending counsel should also question a friendly witness when that witness is likely to testify at trial and has given an answer that is capable of several interpretations, one of which could be considered as inconsistent with the trial testimony that the witness will be called to give. In that case, clarifying questions are wise because, as part of the deposition transcript, those clarifications can be read to the jury pursuant to Federal Rule of Evidence 106 (the rule of completeness) if an impeachment is attempted, as they are part of the same writing or recording and should be considered contemporaneously with the evidence they clarify. In addition, once the clarification at deposition has

---

56. *See* § 17.3.

occurred, opposing counsel will likely avoid a losing battle at trial and not bother to attempt the possible impeachment.

Finally, defending counsel may want to "question the witness" using an off-the-record conference if the witness has misstated an answer or has given a confusing or incomplete answer which might later cause trouble. An example of how this might be accomplished is as follows:

> Q. Mrs. Matulis, what marketing plans did you have for the Green Boy lawn sprinkler for its second year on the market?

> A. For the second year? There, we intended to consolidate our first-year market penetration by using point-of-purchase manufacturer's rebate coupons, and, I think, that was when we were going to heavy-up our spot TV advertising, probably doubling our television budget.

DEFENDING COUNSEL:

> Mrs. Matulis, have you finished your answer?

> Q. Yes, I have.

DEFENDING COUNSEL:

> Let me talk to you a moment, then. [Aside and off the record, whispered.] I thought that you told me last night that the increased TV advertising was intended to begin in the first quarter of the third year of sales. You've just said it was going to start in the second year.

WITNESS:

> [Still off the record.] Oh, oh. No, I didn't mean to say that. I meant that we were planning in the second year. Can I correct that?

DEFENDING COUNSEL:

> Of course. Just say that you want to correct your answer.

THE WITNESS:

> [Aloud.] Let me correct something I just said. I was a bit confused. During the second year, we were making plans for that heavy-up in television advertising, but the heavy-up itself did not begin until the third year of sales.

> Q. Is there anything else about your answer you would like to correct or change?

A.    No, I think that is accurate now.

Alternatively, defending counsel could wait until the attorney taking the deposition had finished questioning. The defending attorney could then ask:

Q.    Do you recall earlier answering a question by counsel by saying that you began marketing the heavy-up in the second year?

A.    Yes.

Q.    Was that a correct answer?

A.    No.

Q.    What was incorrect about your answer?

If deposing counsel asks the witness about the content of the conversation with counsel, the attorney-client privilege protects that information from disclosure and defending counsel should object and instruct the witness not to answer. Of course, the deposing attorney could ask whether the change was made as a result of the conference, a slightly different and probably legitimate question.

In the last example given, the correction occurred after examining counsel had completed her questioning. Nevertheless, if the witness has misstated an answer it is most efficient to clear it up at the same point in the transcript, rather than pages or days later.

The examining counsel may follow up any questions by defending counsel or by other parties with "redirect" examination, to be followed by "recross" and further redirects and recrosses until everyone reaches the point of exhaustion.[57]

---

57. Fed.R.Civ.P. Rule 30(c) provides that "Examination and cross-examination of witnesses may proceed as permitted at trial under the provisions of the Federal Rules of Evidence... ."

## 14.13 CONCLUDING THE DEPOSITION

Under Rule 30(e), the deponent or a party must demand before the conclusion of the deposition the right to review the deposition transcript or recording and to make corrections. As discussed elsewhere,[58] it makes little sense to give up the right to correct mistakes the witness has made in answering, or the court reporter in transcribing, or for deposing counsel not to have a signed transcript. Therefore, both counsel should always demand the right to make corrections before ending the deposition.

---

58. *See* Chapter 15 and § 6.1.

## CHAPTER FIFTEEN

## REVIEWING, CORRECTING, EDITING, AND SUPPLEMENTING THE TRANSCRIPT

*You can't always get what you want, But if you try sometimes, You just might find, You get what you need.* — The Rolling Stones

### 15.1 REVIEWING, CORRECTING, AND EDITING

Under Rule 30(e), a party or the witness must request before the completion of the deposition the right to review and change the deposition. The witness then has thirty days, once the deposition officer has given notice that the deposition is available for review, to carry out the review, and to make and sign any changes. In those jurisdictions following the pre-1993 version of the Federal Rules of Civil Procedure, the parties and the witness must waive the right to review and make corrections to the deposition, and the parties must waive the right to sign the deposition. In those jurisdictions, the witness must join in any waiving of the right to read the deposition if the parties wish to do so; a failure to have the witness join in the waiver may make the deposition unusable at trial even though the witness is now unavailable. Obviously, if the deposition is of a party then only the parties need waive the reading. No penalty attaches under either the current rules or pre-1993 version of the rules if the witness fails, under the thirty-day period for doing so, to review the deposition or, under the pre-1993 rules, to sign the deposition; the court will treat it as admissible to the same extent as if the witness had reviewed it and, when necessary, signed it. Normally both sides have an incentive for the witness to review the deposition, a matter more fully discussed in § 6.1.

In practice, the correcting and editing process usually begins when the reporter creates the transcript and sends it to the attorney who defended the witness at the deposition. That attorney then arranges for the witness to read the transcript, either at the attorney's office or at a convenient location for the witness. If the witness reviews the transcript on her own, she should note changes and then review the changes with her attorney.

Many attorneys have the misconception that the witness may only "correct" mistakes made by the reporter or transcriber, but may not make substantive changes. In fact, under both the current version of Rule 30(e) and the pre-1993 version, the witness may make changes to both "form and substance," but shall give the reasons for doing so. The witness, however, may be subject to further examination, especially if the changes are so extensive or so substantive that they destroy the utility of the deposition.[1] Counsel should exercise caution before allowing the witness to make changes in deposition answers and should avoid making wholesale changes in the deposition transcript. Changes in the original transcript are treated as though they resulted from examination by counsel for the witness at the deposition. Thus, the deposing attorney can obtain an order permitting further examination of the witness.[2] Moreover, the additional examination may inquire into the reasons for the changes.[3] The deponent may also bear the costs and attorney fees associated with re-examination.[4]

Indeed, in the extreme case where a witness makes extensive changes to the transcript which render the deposition virtually useless, the court may, on application of the deposing attorney, order that the original transcript be deemed an accurate record of the deposition testimony, as though the witness had waived reading and signature.[5] For example, a *pro se* Title VII civil rights plaintiff crossed out the answer to almost every deposition question. The plaintiff noted in the margin, "This question was never asked," or "Plaintiff never gave this answer." After an evidentiary hearing at which the court reporter confirmed the accuracy of the transcript, the court imposed sanctions under Rule 37(b)(2), and ruled that the original transcript would be considered an accurate representation of the plaintiff's testimony, as though the plaintiff had waived reading and signing.[6]

In practice, the standard procedure for correcting the deposition transcript is for the witness and defending counsel to review the transcript and create a sheet which notes the page and line numbers of

---

1. *See Colin v. Thompson*, 16 F.R.D. 194 (D.C. Mo. 1954).
2. *See, e.g., DeSeversky v. Republic Aviation Corp.*, 2 F.R.D. 113 (D.C.N.Y. 1941); *Colin v. Thompson*, 16 F.R.D. 194 (D.C. Mo. 1954).
3. *Sanford v. CBS, Inc.*, 594 F. Supp. 713, 715 (N.D. Ill. 1984).
4. *See, e.g., Lugtig v. Thomas*, 89 F.R.D. 639 (N.D. Ill. 1981).
5. *See Barlow v. Esselte Pendaflex Corp.*, 111 F.R.D. 404 (M.D.N.C. 1986).
6. *Baker v. Ace Advertisers' Service, Inc.*, 134 F.R.D. 65, 73 (S.D.N.Y. 1991).

the deposition testimony and the corrected testimony (*errata* sheet). The witness then signs the *errata* sheet and also may have the signature notarized. The *errata* or corrections sheet is then returned to the officer/reporter who, under Rule 30(e), will attach the sheet to his certification under Rule 30(f)(1). The certificate will also indicate within it whether any changes were made. The corrections are included in the final bound transcript of the deposition. A typical *errata* sheet under either version of the Rules looks like the following:

### Corrections to Vardas Deposition of May 17

Page 17, ll. 2–5:

> "should have been considered a possible sort of supplier, but never really came to a close on supplying," should read, "should have been considered a possible source of supply, but never really came close to supplying."

Page 43, l. 13:

> "now that I see a difference" should read, "not that I see a difference."

Page 51, l. 20:

> "Harry Schmidt and Russell Trover" should read, "Harry Schmidt, Russell Trover, and Jane Vilnius."

Page 73, ll. 15–18:

> "and lumber. I cannot remember the other person at the meeting. It may have been George Estus, but I am not certain" should read, "and lumber. The other person at the meeting was George Estus."

Page 114, l. 10:

> "No" should read "Yes."

Page 165, ll. 7–10:

> "if you understand the document, and I can read it to you and we'll discuss" should read, "if you understand the document, and I cannot, read it to me and we'll discuss."

The best practice always is to satisfy Rule 30(e) by including the witness's reason for the change after the new answer even though the reason for the change is readily apparent from the context and the change itself. This prevents opposing counsel from moving to strike the correction because of a failure to give the reasons for the change. For example, the page 114 change above might read:

Page 114, l. 10:

> "No" should read "Yes." Reason: The deponent did not understand that the question had been phrased in the negative.

Some attorneys prefer to provide the changes in a brief form which requires the reader examining the changes to refer back to the original transcript more often in order to understand the context. For example, two of the above changes in this case would instead be:

Page 43, l. 13:

"now" should be "not"

Page 165, ll. 7–10:

> "I can read it to you" should be "I cannot, read it to me"

A better practice, however, is to include enough of the unchanged material that the reader can understand the significance of the change without referring back.

An important point that some attorneys do not appreciate is how corrected answers are used at trial. In impeaching the witness or presenting a party admission, the deposing attorney is entitled to read the original, uncorrected transcript. The defending attorney can then request, under Federal Rule of Civil Procedure 32(a)(4) and Federal Rules of Evidence 106, that the corrected response be read immediately thereafter. In such a situation, the corrections are simply additional statements by the witness and the original testimony does not lose its testimonial value, but remains the prior statement of the witness. While the corrections and the trial testimony may be inconsistent with the original deposition statement, this merely means that both of the later statements can be impeached by the original deposition statement.

## 15.2 SUPPLEMENTING THE DEPOSITION

The Advisory Committee Notes to Rule 26(e) clearly state that, with two exceptions, a witness has no duty to supplement her deposition by correcting or adding to the answers given. The first exception is depositions of expert witnesses. The depositions of such experts must be supplemented if the answers are in any way incomplete or incorrect, provided that the new information has not previously been made known to the other parties during the discovery process or in writing.

Second, the court may order any witness to supplement her deposition if it deems appropriate.

The duty to supplement under Rule 26(e) extended to:

> 1. the identity and location of persons having knowledge of discoverable matters;
>
> 2. the identity of expert witnesses who will testify at trial, as well as the subject matter and substance of their testimony; and
>
> 3. new information that the party acquires so that the party knows that an answer in the deposition was incorrect or, even though correct when given, is no longer true and a failure to amend the answer would be in substance a knowing concealment.

Under the current Rule 26(e)(1), a party must supplement the information provided under the mandatory disclosures of Rule 26(a) "if the party learns that in some material respect the information disclosed is incomplete or incorrect" and the new information has not been given to the other parties through the discovery process or in writing.

Of course, as with almost all discovery rules, the parties can stipulate to different obligations for supplementation.[7] Therefore, when defending a deposition counsel should recognize that a casual agreement—to provide further information, to produce additional documents, or to check on the accuracy of an answer—does in fact impose an enforceable obligation.

---

7. Fed.R.Civ.P. 29.

# PART FOUR

## USING DEPOSITIONS

### Chapter Sixteen

### USING DEPOSITIONS

*How use doth breed a habit in a man!* — William Shakespeare

Testimony from depositions, especially that of parties to the lawsuit, can be used in many ways in pretrial and trial. Such testimony can be used to support or to oppose motions (such as summary judgment and other motions), as a source of admissions, as a substitute for the testimony of absent witnesses, to control witnesses at trial, and to prepare for trial. Therefore, using depositions primarily as a source of impeachment material fails to extract the most value from the process.

## 16.1 MOTIONS FOR SUMMARY JUDGMENT

A common use of witness statements from depositions is to use them like affidavits, to support or oppose motions for summary judgment.[1] Deposition testimony consists of statements made under oath, so those statements have all the trappings which give weight to an affidavit; therefore, logically, they should be regarded in the same way.

Some attorneys are concerned about asking open questions at depositions of the opposing party's witnesses because they feel this gives opposing counsel the opportunity to create a record to use for summary judgment purposes, and perhaps in some small part because they believe that, if they do not discover unfavorable information, the other side will not discover it either.

---

1. *See* Fed.R.Civ.P. 56(c) (the court will consider depositions along with the affidavits, pleadings, admissions, and responses to interrogatories in determining whether a genuine issue of material fact exists). Fed.R.Civ.P. 56(e) ("the court may permit affidavits to be supplemented or opposed by depositions, answers to interrogatories, or further affidavits," and the response shall be "by affidavits or as otherwise provided in this rule ... ."). *See* also *Weldon v. Kraft, Inc.,* 896 F.2d 793 (3d Cir. 1990); C. Wright & A. Miller, *Civil Procedure* § 2142 (West 1994).

In simple fact, opposing counsel has the opportunity to create a favorable record in any event, either through her own questioning at depositions or through affidavits from the party or friendly witnesses if the subject is avoided at the deposition (although some courts see post-deposition affidavits to oppose motions as sandbagging, and will not permit it). Therefore, there is no impediment to proceeding with the normal "funnel" approach at the discovery deposition, using open questions to try to uncover all the relevant information in possession of the witness. The idea that unfavorable information can be left undiscovered should be discarded. The safest assumption, especially when dealing with witnesses who are parties or closely identified with parties, is that the opposing attorney already knows all of the information they have that hurts the client, and deposing counsel might as well find it out, along with any additional information which may lessen its impact.

Occasionally, when one side has to defend a motion for summary judgment early in the pretrial schedule, depositions are scheduled explicitly to permit response to the motion.[2] At such a deposition the deposing attorney's focus is clearly on discovering "genuine issues of material fact." The emphasis, however, remains on "discovering," since relying solely on a cross-examination style with narrow, leading questions may leave entire areas of dispute unrevealed. Just as in a normal discovery deposition, the last portion of the deposition may be used to sharpen positions and issues with more leading questions, so that the answers are narrower and the court may see the "genuine issues" and the "materiality of the facts" more clearly. The approach for summary judgment or simple discovery is the same.

Deposition testimony can always be used to support or oppose any motion where the court would consider affidavit evidence. As previously noted, a deposition, being under oath, resembles an affidavit and courts will generally give the same weight to the two.

## 16.2 PREPARING FOR TRIAL

Perhaps the most important use of depositions is in preparing to cross-examine witnesses at trial. The late Irving Younger, in his famous lecture, *The Ten Commandments of Cross-Examination*, gave as his fifth commandment, "Never ask a question to which you do not al-

---

2.  Rule 56(f) specifically provides, among other things, that where it appears that a party opposing a motion needs discovery beyond affidavits to support its opposition, time for depositions may be allowed.

ready know the answer." ("If you didn't see him bite it off, how do you know my client did bite off the plaintiff's ear?" "I saw him spit it out.") One of the ways to know the answer is through the witness's deposition.

Many trial lawyers construct their cross-examinations based on the answers given in the witness's deposition. The difference, however, between the deposition answers and trial is that the questions asked at trial can be reorganized to make the intended points in the most effective way possible. For example, a critical point for trial may not have been covered until toward the end of a deposition, but nothing prevents beginning the cross-examination with this point. Not only may the order of points and questions be changed, but unimportant or harmful information in the deposition may be deleted and inartfully phrased questions may be rephrased.

When dealing with important admissions by a witness, the cross-examination questions should mirror the deposition questions as closely as possible in meaning, if not actual wording, so that an attempted impeachment will present clearly inconsistent answers to the judge or jury. A minor change in wording between the deposition and trial may permit an intelligent witness to avoid the sting of impeachment and may make the cross-examiner look foolish in the process. Consider the following example:

> Q. Isn't it true, sir, that you never even bothered to read the contract?
>
> A. No, that's not true.
>
> Q. Are you telling this jury that you did read the contract?
>
> A. Yes.
>
> Q. Well sir, do you remember having your deposition taken?
>
> A. Yes.
>
> Q. Showing you that deposition, do you see on page 14, line 6 that you were asked, "Did you read the contract before you signed it?" and your answer was "No"?
>
> A. Yes, but that's different than what you just asked me. You asked whether I had ever read the contract and I did read it about two weeks after the signing.
>
> Q. Well, then, let's move on.

Many trial lawyers, when preparing both their direct and cross-examination outlines for witnesses, will annotate the outline with the page and line of the deposition confirming the expected answer. Such an outline, this one for cross-examination, might look like this:

> Was going approximately 50 mph as approached the intersection. (28:16)
>
> Started braking about 200 feet away. (30:14)
>
> Baby was crying in the back seat. (12:4)
>
> Was expected to be at work at 8:00 A.M. (72:12)
>
> Was running late that morning. (73:19)

Thus, if impeachment is necessary on cross-examination or a witness's memory needs to be refreshed on direct examination, the exact page and line of the deposition can be quickly located. In modern deposition practice deposition transcripts are created in a digital format. By use of this technology the answers that form the basis for cross-examination can be bar-coded so that, if the witness varies his testimony, a simple swipe of the bar code can display the deposition transcript on monitors throughout the courtroom. Similarly, if the deposition is recorded using digital video, the answers can be bar-coded to display the video deposition and the witness can be seen and heard delivering her self-contradictory testimony.

Depositions should usually be abstracted or summarized shortly after they are taken to facilitate preparing for motions and trial, as well as for locating impeaching answers in the heat of trial. Paralegals or new associates usually do the abstracting, but experienced attorneys also do it as a way of becoming more familiar with what was said during the deposition. Clients are more likely to read abstracts than full transcripts, and they may be able to participate in trial preparation more fully as a result.

There are a number of methods of abstracting depositions, such as the full summary method and the subject method. The first is a straight summary of the deposition; the second organizes the summary by topics. Some attorneys, instead of abstracting, now rely on computer searches for key words and phrases, having used a reporting service that provides a computer disk of the deposition. This method is more expensive and requires bringing a computer to trial, but in modern practice many courtrooms have installed equipment that merely requires plugging in a laptop computer that has the relevant information stored on disk or hard drive. Of course, as with any technology, there should be back-up computers and, if all else fails, hard copy of the deposition transcript. Use of the available technology can sometimes be quicker and more efficient than reviewing a lengthy abstract. A typical summary abstract might look like the following:

| | |
|---|---|
| 14:6 | Formed own construction co. after graduation from college. |
| 14:12 | Had only 5 to 10 employees for 1st 10 years. |
| 14:16 | Now has 50 employees. |
| 14:20 | Does all engineering work and bidding on contracts. |

A typical subject abstract of the same topic would look like this:

> Formed own company after college (14:6) where he does all the engineering and bidding work on the contracts (14:20). The company has grown from 5 employees to 50 in 10 years (14:12, 14:16). He has plans to grow it to 100 (43:25) and then to sell it to his younger sister and brother-in-law (45:13).

Many times witnesses will be testifying at trial months and even years after they gave their deposition testimony. It is not uncommon for their trial testimony to change in minor ways from what they said at the deposition, not because of any intent to lie or deceive, but because memories fade. Nonetheless, these deviations in the hands of a skillful attorney can be used in a way to discredit a witness's integrity and honesty, along with their memories.

Many of these problems can be avoided if all witnesses expected to testify in a trial or other proceeding are asked to review their depositions carefully before they take the stand. Trial counsel should emphasize the dangers of changing their testimony from what they said in the deposition during preparation of every witness for trial.

### 16.3 SEVEN WAYS TO USE A DEPOSITION AT TRIAL

Whether you have originally taken a deposition for discovery or trial purposes, you can use it at trial in many ways. Among the most common uses are:

1. as the testimony of an absent witness;

2. as a basis for a proffer;

3. as a source of admissions;

4. as a means of refreshing recollection;

5. as the testimony of a witness who is unable to testify because of lapse of memory;

6. as a means of impeaching a witness; and

7. as a means of accomplishing a "phantom" impeachment.

Each use of a deposition has a different foundation, deriving from the evidentiary rules which control that use. Since depositions are out-of-court statements which the attorney may be offering for their truth, the rules restricting the use of hearsay are often involved in determining the proper foundation. Here are examples of each use of a deposition at trial.

### 16.3.1 The testimony of an absent witness.

In many cases by the time of trial some witnesses will have become unavailable, even though you may not have anticipated this when the absent witnesses' depositions were taken. In that event, the depositions may be used to replace the live testimony of the missing witness under Rule 32(a)(3) and Federal Rule of Evidence 804(b)(1). Here is what that process would sound like in court:

PLAINTIFF'S COUNSEL:

> Your Honor, Mr. Theodore Barker was scheduled to be our next witness, but he has been called out of the state due to an illness in his family. Counsel for the defendant has been kind enough to stipulate to Mr. Barker's unavailability, and to the fact that this is his deposition testimony.[3] In place of Mr. Barker's live testimony, we would like to read certain limited portions of his deposition testimony for the jury. In total, there are about fifteen pages, Your Honor.

THE COURT:

> That's fine, Mr. Moreland. I presume that these portions

---

3. By this statement reciting the stipulation, counsel has laid the foundation for use of the deposition under Fed.R.Evid. 804: the witness is unavailable, not through the fault of the proponent of the evidence, and this is in fact his deposition. If opposing counsel refuses to stipulate, it may be necessary to offer evidence establishing the witness's unavailability.

have been redacted pursuant to the pretrial rulings?[4]

PLAINTIFF'S COUNSEL:

Yes, Your Honor, and defendant's counsel also has had an opportunity to review the portions we intend to read. And with the court's permission, we would like to have Mr. Richkus, a paralegal who works with us, read Mr. Barker's answers from the witness stand as I read the questions.

THE COURT:

All right. There being no objection, you may proceed.

PLAINTIFF'S COUNSEL:

Mr. Richkus, if you will go up to the witness stand, we can start with page 27, at line 17.

Q.    (By defendant's counsel:) Mr. Barker, what was your position with Vitas Industries in 1987 and 1988?

A.    I was the vice-president for purchasing for the company.

Q.    What were your responsibilities in that position?

A.    I oversaw the purchasing of all materials that we required to manufacture all of our products. That included everything from the copper wire that we wound around the cores to make the armatures for the generators to the decals that we put on the transformer boxes telling about the high voltage.

Q.    During that time, from whom did Vitas Industries purchase refined copper?

A.    We had several suppliers, but the main ones for those two years were Chilean Copper Conglomerate, Incorporated, and Python Industrial Metals.

PLAINTIFF'S COUNSEL:

Now, Mr. Richkus, will you please turn to page 43 in the deposition of Mr. Barker? We'll begin with line 4.

Q.    Mr. Barker, why do you think that Chilean Copper and Python Industries were engaged in some kind of

---

4.   Normally during the pretrial proceedings parties will have designated the deposition portions which they intend to use and presented objections for ruling by the court. In addition, any objection to the witness's unavailability would have been raised as part of the mandatory pretrial disclosure scheme. *See* § 16.4. The portions that the court rules are not admissible are "redacted," or deleted.

agreement to fix copper prices to your company, as is alleged in the complaint in this case?

A.    Well, during that time, I often tried to get one or the other of them to give me a better price, you know, to bid against a price I had from the other. But they'd never break the line. Right in lockstep, all the time. On my other metal purchases, I could make deals by going from one supplier to the next, but on copper, those two never gave even a penny off.

DEFENDANT'S COUNSEL:

Your Honor, at this point, we ask that the next two questions and answers be read, pursuant to Rule 32(a)(4), because they contain material which, in fairness, the jury ought to be allowed to consider along with this last answer.

THE COURT:

Well, let me just look at that material for a moment. Yes, I agree, we'll have that read at this point, please, Mr. Moreland.

PLAINTIFF'S COUNSEL:

Yes, Your Honor.

Q.    Mr. Barker, isn't it true that there was a terrific demand for copper during that period, and a shortage of supply due to unrest in the government of Chile?

A.    Well, there were some political problems down there that made the supply of copper a little less predictable. But we were getting all that we needed.

Q.    And isn't it also true, Mr. Barker, based on your experience in the purchase of metals, that no one discounts their prices on metals during periods of shortage, because they can clear their inventories without price reductions?

A.    Yes, I suppose that is true in general, but I still think that Chilean Copper and Python were fixing prices.

The process continues until all selected portions of the deposition have been read. At that point, opposing counsel may read in as her cross-examination additional portions of the deposition, either with another "witness" on the stand, or perhaps with this same one, to lessen the likelihood of jury confusion.[5]

Some courts rule, erroneously, that 32(a)(4) material can just as well be presented during cross-examination. If the conditions of these rules have been met, that is, that the proffered material is so closely related to what has already been read, the jury "ought in fairness" to consider the two selections together, then they should be presented together, and not separated by the remainder of the main examination. These rules promote the jury's understanding of the evidence; the fact that the additional material could be presented on cross-examination does not mean that is the best way for the jury to understand it.

### 16.3.2 As a basis for a proffer.

Often you must persuade the court that certain evidence is relevant or certain lines of questioning have a good-faith basis. Sometimes you can use depositions to provide this foundation for going forward. Consider the following example from a cross-examination:

> Q.  Mr. Taras, isn't it true that you never saw the plaintiff before he went into the hospital?
>
> A.  No, that's not true at all. I saw him several times. We were good friends, and visited a lot.
>
> Q.  Mr. Taras, you were good friends a year before the plaintiff's car accident, weren't you?
>
> A.  Yes, yes, of course.
>
> Q.  And you are good friends now, aren't you?
>
> A.  Yes, that's true, of course.
>
> Q.  But at the time of the accident, you and the plaintiff were not even on speaking terms, were you?
>
> A.  I don't understand what you're saying. He's my friend and I see him all the time.
>
> Q.  Mr. Taras, you used to play poker with the plaintiff once a week, didn't you?
>
> PLAINTIFF'S COUNSEL:
>
> I object, Your Honor. This is irrelevant and prejudicial, and I request that counsel be directed to move on to

---

5.  The use of Rule 32(a)(4) deserves comment. This rule allows additional portions of depositions to be read into the record which ought "in fairness to be considered with" portions which have been read by the other side.

another area.

DEFENSE COUNSEL:

Your Honor, may we approach the bench?

THE COURT:

Yes, step up, counsel. Now, where are you going with this, Mr. Kaunas?

DEFENSE COUNSEL:

Your Honor, based on this witness's deposition testimony, which I can show you here at pages 34 and 35 of the deposition transcript, I believe that he will testify that he and the plaintiff used to play poker once a week, but that two weeks before the accident they had an argument over a poker hand, and that they didn't speak to one another for several months. That testimony impeaches his testimony on direct that he visited with the plaintiff in the weeks after the accident and could see the pain and limited movement that the plaintiff now claims he had.

THE COURT:

Let me see the deposition. All right. Based on this deposition testimony, I am going to overrule the objections and permit the questioning. You may proceed, Mr. Kaunas.

DEFENSE COUNSEL:

Mr. Taras, the question is, didn't you and the plaintiff play poker once a week before the accident?

A. Yes, but he was never very good.

Q. But just a week or so before the accident, you stopped playing poker, right?

A. Yes, that's true.

Q. You had an argument about a poker hand, didn't you?

A. Yes. He never had a pair of aces. He had one ace, and he took the other from his pocket.

Q. And because of that argument, you and the plaintiff didn't talk to each other for almost a year?

A. Yes, that's the truth. It was silly. I've had aces in my pocket, too.

Q.   And you didn't spend time with him and visit with him right after the accident, did you?

A.   No, I didn't. But he has told me that he was really in a lot of pain then.

### 16.3.3 As a source of admissions.

You can introduce admissions of a party opponent in a deposition under Rule 32(a)(1) and (2) as though the statements were given as live testimony from the stand. Rule 32(a)(2) specifically authorizes using the deposition of a party, an officer, director or managing agent of a party, or a person designated to testify under Rule 30(b)(6). Further, Federal Rule of Evidence 801(d)(2) defines admissions by a party opponent to include not only the party's own statements, but also statements made by the party's agents, employees, and persons authorized to speak on behalf of the party. All of these statements are classified by the Federal Rules of Evidence as non-hearsay and are admissible as substantive evidence.[6]

Thus, a plaintiff may use portions of the defendant's deposition to establish the plaintiff's *prima facie* case, without calling the defendant as an adverse witness. Assume in the following assault and battery case that an element of plaintiff's case is the fact that the guard was an agent of the company at the time of the assault.

(QUESTIONING BY PLAINTIFF'S COUNSEL:)

Q.   And what was the defendant Sugis wearing when he came out of the building and struck you with the nightstick?

A.   He had on a guard's uniform, you know, like a rent-a-cop kind of outfit, that said, "Ace Security" on a patch on his shoulder.

BY COUNSEL:

Your Honor, at this time we would like to read a section of one page of the defendant Sugis's deposition, which is a party admission under Federal Rule of Evidence

---

6.   Rule 32(a)(1) states that depositions can be used for any purpose permitted by the Federal Rules of Evidence. Party admissions, direct or vicarious, should not be confused with "statements against interest," which are defined by Federal Rule of Evidence 804 as exceptions to the rule excluding hearsay if the declarant is unavailable. This confusion has probably persisted much longer than it otherwise would have because of the unfortunate habit of some courts of using the hybrid phrase, "admission against interest."

801(d)(1). The depositions have been stipulated as authentic.

THE COURT:

With that stipulation, you may proceed, but let's keep it short, since you have this witness on the stand.

COUNSEL:

Yes, Your Honor. The portion appears on page 17 of the deposition. Quote:

Q.  Mr. Sugis, when you saw the plaintiff marching down the street with the group carrying the antiwar signs, what were you doing?

A.  I was at my desk in the lobby of the Metropolitan Building.

Q.  Why were you there?

A.  I was on the job; that's my responsibility, to provide security for the clients of the company.

Q.  You say, "the company." Is that the Ace Security Company?

A.  Yes. That's who I work for, Ace Security.

Of course, use of a deposition as an admission is not limited to matters that are elements of the *prima facie* case. You can use selections for any purpose, as long as they are relevant and otherwise unobjectionable.

Rule 32(a)(4) applies to this use of depositions also. Thus, in the above situation involving Ace Security, counsel for the company might say:

ACE DEFENSE COUNSEL:

Your Honor, may we read the next two questions and answers, under Rule 32(a)(4)? Let me give you a copy.

THE COURT:

Well, let's see. Yes, I see what you're saying. Yes, you may read the next two questions and answers.

ACE DEFENSE COUNSEL:

Thank you, Your Honor. Let me quote:

Q.  Mr. Sugis, what time was it when you went out onto the street and had this confrontation with the plaintiff?

A.   Well, it was about 9:30 in the morning.

Q.   And what shift were you working for Ace Security at the Metropolitan Building?

A.   I was on the midnight to 8 shift, but, you know, I heard there was going to be this demonstration, so I kind of stayed around so that I could see these people with their signs and things.

### 16.3.4 As a means of refreshing recollection.

You may refresh a witness's recollection with anything from a simple leading question to a photograph, a snatch of song, or a letter from Mom. The question which the court must decide is not, "What was used to refresh recollection?" but rather, "Is the witness actually testifying from refreshed recollection?" Depositions are useful tools to refresh recollection, since they have often been taken months or years closer to the relevant events. The foundation at trial for using depositions in this way is essentially the same as that for any attempt to refresh present recollection:

Q.   Now, Ms. Vardas, what was the next step in trying to persuade United Lumber and Hardware to finance the expansion of your business?

A.   Well, I think that I met with Mr. Shadis at the bank. No, that wasn't it. Maybe … I'm sorry, I'm just not sure what was next. There were a number of meetings.

Q.   Is there anything that might help you remember?

A.   I think that we discussed this, you know, at my deposition. It seems to me that we went over this in the deposition.

Q.   Okay, let me hand you your deposition, and ask if you would turn there to page 73. Read that to yourself, please, and tell me when you've finished.

A.   All right … yes, I've read it.

Q.   Now, just let me have the transcript back, please. Having read that portion of your deposition, do you now recall what the next step was in trying to negotiate financing through United Lumber and Hardware?

A.   Yes, I do. I met with their accountant, and brought my accountant and architect with me. It was at that meeting that United told me, "Go ahead with obtaining the permits and negotiating with your general contractor. We'll work something out."

Notice Rule 32(a)(4) does not apply here, since no deposition, writing, or other recorded statement is being offered; only the refreshed memory of the witness provides the evidence.

### 16.3.5 As the testimony of a witness whose memory cannot be refreshed.

When a non-party witness[7] or your own client testifies at trial and cannot remember what color the traffic light was even though the witness testified in her deposition that the light was red, another method of introducing the statement, other than impeaching the witness with the deposition testimony, is available. Federal Rule of Evidence 804(a)(3) defines a failure of memory as unavailability for purposes of admitting statements that would otherwise be hearsay.[8] The witness's deposition testimony then becomes admissible as substantive evidence under Federal Rule of Evidence 804(b)(1), the provision allowing the use of "former testimony."

The foundation under Federal Rules of Evidence 804(a)(3) and 804(b)(1) is quite simple. You need merely show the witness's memory is currently inadequate for the matters on which the deposition is being offered and the deposition was in fact given. An example of cross-examination (but the same thing could also occur on direct examination using non-leading questions) using the deposition testimony in this way follows:

Q.  Now, isn't it true that, as his friend, you were advising the defendant not to break this contract with the plaintiff?

A.  Well, I don't remember doing that.

Q.  You don't remember having a conversation where you told Mr. Shadis that you thought it was a fair contract and that he shouldn't breach it?

A.  No, I don't remember that.

Q.  Mr. Barker, in that same deposition we discussed earlier this morning, you were asked this question and you gave this answer—page 46, counsel: "Question: What

---

7.  We focus here on non-party depositions because the deposition of an adverse party can be used as an admission, regardless of his present recollection or his availability, as we have discussed above.

8.  Rule 32(a)(1) states that a deposition may be used by any party for any purpose permitted by the Federal Rules of Evidence.

did you discuss about the McLean contract? Answer: Well, I told Shadis that he seemed to be getting his money's worth, and that it looked to me like Vardas was doing a good job. I mean, he asked if I thought it was a fair deal, and I said, 'Yeah, it looks fair to me'." That was your answer, wasn't it, Mr. Barker?

A.    Yes, that's what I said.

### 16.3.6 As a means of impeachment.

Under Rule 32(a)(1) you can also use depositions as prior inconsistent statements to impeach a witness at trial. In fact, under Federal Rule of Evidence 801(d)(1)(A), deposition testimony used to impeach a witness with a prior inconsistent statement is classified as non-hearsay and may be considered by the judge or jury as substantive evidence as well as reflecting on the witness's credibility.[9] Such testimony may also qualify under 801(d)(2)(A) as an admission of a party opponent.

Early on, we discussed the commitments extracted at the outset of the deposition in some detail and made the point that those commitments were made to aid in control and impeachment at trial. Now, presented with the opportunity to impeach at trial, that groundwork comes into play. A full-blown impeachment of a non-party witness at trial follows, at the first time an impeachment of the witness has been necessary:

Q.    Mr. Lapitis, on your direct examination you said that you saw the traffic signal when the defendant's Cadillac started into the intersection, is that right?

A.    Yes, sir, I said it and it's true. I saw that light.

Q.    Isn't it true that the light was red for the defendant?

A.    No, like I said, it was green for him. No question about it.

Q.    No question about it?

---

9.    In contrast, prior inconsistent statements not under oath can be used only for impeachment, *i.e.*, reflecting on the witness's credibility, and cannot be considered as substantive evidence. Thus, if the defendant's running of a red light is an element of the plaintiff's *prima facie* case, a letter in which the witness wrote, "the light was red" can impeach his testimony that the light was green, but it cannot prove the light was red to satisfy the plaintiff's burden on that point. A deposition from the same witness in which he previously testified the light was red can impeach his trial testimony that the light was green and can also provide the necessary substantive element that the light was red.

A. No question about it.

Q. Mr. Lapitis, you remember coming to my office a few months ago?

A. Yes, I remember that.

Q. You came there to have your deposition taken, right?

A. Yes. Well, I got a subpoena, so I showed up like I was supposed to.

Q. And the defendant's attorney was there, wasn't she?

A. Yes.

Q. In fact, you met with her before the deposition, didn't you?

A. Well, yes, she asked me to come to her office the day before, so I went in and talked with her.

Q. When you came to my office for your deposition, we met in a conference room; do you remember that?

A. Yes.

Q. And the defendant's lawyer sat right next to you during the deposition, didn't she, and talked with you?

A. Yes, she was very nice.

Q. I told you that you could have breaks when you wanted them, and we had coffee and water there for you, isn't that right?

A. Yes, it was very pleasant.

Q. There was a court reporter there who gave you the same oath that you took here in court today?

A. Yes, that's right.

Q. And you promised then to tell the truth?

A. Yes, I swore to tell the truth as best I could.

Q. And you did tell the truth in your answers, didn't you?

A. Yes, I did.

Q. And after the deposition was over, the court reporter typed up my questions and your answers into a booklet, and he sent you that booklet, didn't he?

A. Yes, I went over it with the defendant's lawyer.

Q. And after you made corrections of some errors, you signed the corrections and sent the booklet back to the court reporter, right?

A. Yes.

Q. Let me show you that deposition, Mr. Lapitis, and I'd like you to look at page 76, the correction page. That's your signature right there at the bottom?"

A. Yes.

Q. Mr. Lapitis, at that deposition, page 16, line 32, I asked you this question and you gave this answer: "Question: Sir, what color was the traffic light for the westbound car, the defendant's Cadillac? Answer: For the Caddy, let me see, for the Caddy it was red." I have read your answer correctly, haven't I, sir?

A. Well, yes, that's what I said then.

Q. And you did not change that page of the deposition when you read it later with the lawyers, did you, Mr. Lapitis? Take a look at the page of corrections here.

A. No, we didn't change it.

That completes the impeachment, and under Federal Rule of Evidence 801(d)(1)(A) that puts in front of the jury the substantive evidence the light was red for the Cadillac, as well as the evidence that this witness has told two different stories under oath.

Sometimes, especially when there is nothing about the stories to distinguish them—that is, to make the favorable deposition statement apparently more truthful than the later, trial testimony—impeaching counsel might want to provide the motive:

Q. Mr. Lapitis, since the deposition, you have met with the defendant's counsel a couple times, haven't you?

A. Yes.

Q. You met with her to review the deposition and you met with her to prepare for your testimony today in court, isn't that right?

A. Yes.

Q. And both those times, you discussed what you were going to say here today, didn't you?

DEFENDANT'S COUNSEL:

Objection, Your Honor. This calls for hearsay and attorney work product.

PLAINTIFF'S COUNSEL:

Your Honor, these are conversations with a non-party witness. There's no privilege here. And these conversations are relevant and admissible for impeachment, and therefore they are not hearsay.

THE COURT:

Objections overruled. Please answer the question, Mr. Lapitis.

A.    Well, yes, we discussed what was going to happen at trial, and what questions I'd be asked.

Q.    And you practiced your answers to those questions, didn't you?

A.    Well, yes.[10]

### 16.3.7 As a means of accomplishing a "phantom" impeachment.

The "phantom" or "ghost" impeachment is so-called because no impeachment actually occurs, but the witness answers truthfully because he thinks impeachment is possible. This success of this tactic depends upon convincing the witness at trial that the cross-examiner has absolute mastery of the facts in the deposition, coupled with ability to call them up virtually instantaneously.[11]

Some attorneys put the witness's deposition in bright covers with the witness's name two inches high across the front so that, perhaps during the direct examination, but certainly during the cross, the witness comes to recognize the cross-examiner has that deposition readily available. Then, when impeaching during the cross-examination

---

10. One caveat is appropriate here, however. This impeachment for bias depends for its success upon the latent (or patent?) mistrust which lay jurors have for attorneys—their belief that an attorney can make a witness say that red is green. If the cross-examiner establishes this as a premise, he indeed weakens that particular witness's testimony, but he also weakens the testimony of all of his own witnesses. And, since he is an attorney, he risks weakening his own credibility as well if the jury analyzes this form of impeachment logically.

11. In *The Art of Cross-Examination*, Francis Wellman writes, "A witness, in anger, often forgets himself and speaks the truth." Wellman, *The Art of Cross-Examination*, 4th ed. at 135 (Macmillan Publishing Co. 1962). A similar phenomenon occurs with the phantom impeachment.

you would make conspicuous use of the brightly bound volume using notes in your examination notebook to go directly to the right page and line without fumbling.

After a number of such impeachments, the witness will become "disciplined," that is, will be much less willing to fight over testimony. At that point, you may be able to force the witness to tell the truth by making apparent use of the deposition, even though the deposition does not contain testimony on the point in question. If you have a good faith basis for believing a particular fact is true—for example, that the witness's car is green—but that fact is not in the deposition, you might conspicuously leaf through the deposition, settle on one page, appear to read it for a moment, and then say to the witness who has been watching:

> Q.   And, sir, your breathing problems started long before you began work at Dustco Brake Manufacturing Company, didn't they?

The witness, now believing that the date of onset of his problems is pinned down in the deposition, because the attorney has not been wrong yet, would rather admit the truth the car is green than lie and be impeached again.

## 16.4 THE DESIGNATION PROCESS AND OBTAINING RULINGS ON OBJECTIONS

Discovery depositions, unlike examination at trial, contain many misstatements, false starts, irrelevancies, and arguments between counsel. The procedures for cleansing the transcript of such problems have arisen not so much from the rules of procedure as from common practice and common sense. The designation and counter-designation conventions are intended to avoid arguments at trial about objections and to provide all parties with the opportunity to respond to deposition testimony which has been selected for use at trial.

If the case is sufficiently complex, at some point before trial most courts will order the parties to designate those depositions or portions of depositions each intends to offer at trial. In U.S. district courts, Rule 26(a)(3)(B) requires as part of the mandatory pretrial disclosures that each party designate those witnesses whose testimony is expected to be presented by means of a deposition, except for impeachment testimony, and, if the deposition was not recorded stenographically, also to provide a transcript of the deposition portions to be used. Each party must make these disclosures at least thirty days before trial unless the court orders otherwise. Each party then has fourteen days, unless the court sets a different time, in which to file a list with any objections to the use under Rule 32(a) of the deposition testimony designated by any other party. You must be careful to include all objections you intend to urge since any not listed are waived. The only exceptions are for objections made under Federal Rule of Evidence 402 (relevancy) and 403 (prejudice, cumulative, and so forth) or if the court permits the objection to be added later for good cause shown.

In those jurisdictions following the pre-1993 version of the Federal Rules of Civil Procedure as well as those under the current rules, no required procedure for the actual designation and ruling on objections exists. Some general observations apply, however. Simultaneous designations are common: first, each side identifies the portions of depositions it intends to offer, either by making a list of witnesses, pages, and lines (the procedure under the current Federal Rules) or by marking on a copy of the transcripts with a particular color; red for plaintiff's designations and green for defendant's designations, for example. The parties then exchange the lists or transcript volumes and make counter-designations, either with additional lists, or by marking with additional colors; blue for plaintiff's counter-designations, yellow for defendant's. (Of course, the parties keep duplicate color-coded copies, so that each can know what it designated and counter-designated and what the other side designated and counter-designated.) That normally is the end of it—counter-counter-designations normally do not occur.

Once the designation and counter-designation process has occurred, the court will usually order a submission on objections to any designated portions and then may hold a hearing to resolve them. Some judges prefer to postpone a ruling on these objections until trial, but that does not provide the attorneys with any certainty as to what portions will be admitted. On the other hand, ruling pretrial on all objections to the designated portions can be very time-consuming and will result in the court spending time on objections to portions which may never be used at trial.

The best procedure may be to ask the court to review designations a few days before their intended use at trial, after the jury has left for the day. That will be close enough to the presentation so that the attorneys will have a relatively firm idea of what they actually want to use at trial, and yet far enough in advance so that they can plan based on the judge's rulings.

As a practical matter, however, courts are very unwilling to set aside time for ruling on these objections to designated portions, and seem to hope that if they postpone looking at the designations long enough those designations may never surface at all. To a great extent this is true, because, far in advance of trial, attorneys tend to designate more than they will ever need. By refusing to turn to rulings on designations until near trial, or during trial, the courts may be dealing with the attorneys when they are able to evaluate their needs more realistically.

After the parties have made their designations and registered their objections, no other designations or objections should be considered by the court for admissions or testimony of an absent witness. (Uses for impeachment, proffers, and refreshing recollection of course remain unaffected.) Even for use of the depositions under Rule 32(a)(4), those materials ought to have been counter-designated, since that rule deals with use in response to an opponent's original use. The court should allow additional deposition material to be used only on a showing by the proponent that the need to use that portion of the deposition could not reasonably have been anticipated.

## 16.5 PRESENTATION OF DEPOSITION TESTIMONY AT TRIAL

We have already discussed one method of presenting written deposition transcript in court by having an associate or paralegal read the answers from the witness stand.[12] Although suitable for lengthier portions of the written deposition, this method is much too cumbersome for short excerpts and, of course, is inapplicable to videotaped depositions.

Using an associate to read answers from the stand, however, is clearly preferable to the attorney standing and reading pages to the jury; even though it is a "re-enactment," the give-and-take of questioning of a live witness has a dramatic content that is not present in a straight reading. You should consider, however, some subtle problems.

The court will expect the deposition readers, attorney and employee, to avoid inserting emotional content into the deposition through exaggerated intonation or pauses. Nevertheless, the jury itself will "add" content to the deposition reading by reacting to the appearance and personality of the witness-reader. In the instance where a friendly witness is unavailable and you are reading his deposition, you will want to select a witness-reader who presents an appropriate and attractive demeanor in terms of age, appearance, and bearing. Thus, if

---

12. *See* § 16.3.1.

your absent witness is a middle-aged executive, select a middle-aged reader dressed in a suit and tie; if the witness is an assembly line worker, select a reader who looks as though he could make a living with his hands, and perhaps have him wear a sports coat and open shirt; if the witness is a woman who owns a small business, select a reader who presents the appropriate appearance of experience, competence, and success.

Obviously, the opponent must guard against abuse by the attorney presenting the reader. If the actual deponent is a twenty-five-year-old high school dropout who happened to be present when his boss discussed contract terms, it is misleading to present to the jury a reader of his deposition who looks and speaks as though he has a graduate degree in business administration. The opponent should object, under Federal Rule of Evidence 403, that use of that particular reader will mislead and confuse the jury by inviting it to associate greater credibility with the testimony than would have occurred had the actual witness been available. The court may have a hard time appreciating this objection because it will not have seen the actual deponent, but the attorney could present the educational background of the witness from the deposition, so that the court has some understanding of her concern.[13] Sometimes you suspect your opponent is taking the deposition because the witness will be unavailable for trial and is deliberately choosing to stenographically record the deposition because the witness would be less persuasive on videotape. While expensive to do so, under Rule 30(b)(3) you can defeat your opponent's strategy by arranging for the deposition also to be recorded by videotape. At trial, when your opponent presents the deposition to a jury, you have a right under Rule 32(c) to insist on having the videotape recording shown instead of your opponent using associates or actors to read the stenographic version.

The opponent of the deposition testimony may have no advance notice of the identity of the reader selected by the other side, so it would be wise for you to keep a "generic" bench brief in your trial notebook. This brief would remind the court of its power to control the mode of presentation of this deposition testimony and of the need to prevent confusing and misleading the jury.

---

13. As mentioned, courts already understand that the weight given the testimony can be affected by the manner in which it is read, and they will instruct readers to avoid adding any emphasis or drama. The same concern logically applies to adding substance or weight by selecting readers from "Central Casting."

# PART FIVE

## SPECIAL TYPES OF DEPOSITIONS

### CHAPTER SEVENTEEN

### DEPOSITIONS FOR USE AT TRIAL

*It took me forty years on Earth, To reach this sure conclusion: There is no Heaven but clarity, No Hell except confusion.* — Jan Struther

One talent of attorneys who are "good deposition takers" is that they are able to hear, as the deposition record is created, how the deposition testimony will sound months later when portions are read at trial. Testimony read from a transcript is not as interesting to a jury as testimony presented by live witnesses; therefore care must be taken to make the deposition testimony as clear and interesting as possible for its later use.

Any deposition can be used as a substitute for the live testimony of a witness if for some reason the witness becomes unavailable to testify at trial.[1] One inherent risk of taking a deposition of a potentially adverse witness is that, if the witness later becomes unavailable to testify at trial, the deposition taken for discovery purposes may end up being read into evidence by opposing counsel. Thus, questions asked to gather as much information as possible later come back to haunt deposing counsel when the other side uses the answers. This becomes an even greater problem when deposing counsel has refrained from aggressively cross-examining the witness during the deposition, planning to reserve such attacks until trial to avoid giving the witness experience on how to respond. If the witness has become unavailable, then the other side can present the deposition testimony to the jury mostly unchallenged.

But depositions sometimes are taken specifically in anticipation that a witness will not be available at the time of trial. These are called "preservation depositions," "trial depositions," or "depositions *de bene esse*." The plan is to present the witness's direct testimony through deposition. For instance, if a witness is moving to another state or is expected to die before the trial, the deposition is not being taken only for

---

1. Fed.R.Civ.P. 32(a)(3); Fed.R.Evid. 804.

discovery purposes, but also to perpetuate the witness's testimony for use at a later time.

Usually counsel will want to take such a deposition of friendly witnesses; that is, witnesses expected to testify favorably. Because the witness is friendly, he can be prepared for his deposition in the same way he would have been prepared to testify at trial. Occasionally, however, a witness is known to have important information that may be favorable, but neither side is quite sure and the witness refuses to be interviewed. When it is expected that the witness will be unavailable for trial, the hard decision must be made of whether to take the witness's deposition and thereby preserve potentially favorable testimony, or forgo taking it because of the risk that the testimony will turn out to be unfavorable and the deposition will ultimately be used to the client's detriment.[2] Of course, the other side can short circuit all of these plans by noticing the witness's deposition.

When a witness refuses to be interviewed or when it is otherwise impossible to pin down a witness's story in advance, the deposition must, by necessity, be a combination of discovery (finding out what the witness has to say) and perpetuation (putting the testimony in a form that can be used for trial). The risk, of course, is that all of the information will be harmful and there is nothing to put into shape for trial.

Despite the risks of preserving unfavorable testimony, it will often be necessary to take a witness's deposition in anticipation of that witness being unavailable for trial. Preparing for and taking these depositions is at least as important, and sometimes more so, as taking a discovery deposition.

## 17.1 PREPARING TO TAKE THE TRIAL DEPOSITION

In preparing to take a deposition for purposes of perpetuating the witness's testimony for later use at trial, remember that reading the deposition testimony almost always renders juries slightly comatose. Even placing an associate in the witness box to play the role of the witness only minimally increases the interest level of the jurors. Thus, if finances and logistics permit, consider recording the testimony on videotape.[3] The jury's attention span and retention are likely to be much greater than with the use of a stenographic deposition.

---

2. In some states, attorneys control this risk by conducting a discovery deposition first, then proceeding with a "trial" or *de benne esse* deposition if the evidence is favorable and should be preserved.

3. *See* Chapter Eighteen, "Videotape Depositions."

The deposition of the potentially unavailable witness should be scheduled as early in the litigation as possible. This is especially so if the witness is in precarious health or is known to be planning to leave the country.

If the witness is friendly and cooperative, preparing him or her for the trial deposition or *de bene esse* deposition is the same process as preparing a witness to testify at trial. Counsel should carefully explore the witness's story and attempt to resolve any internal discrepancies or weaknesses. More importantly, counsel should review the expected questions and the witness's answers and make suggestions for improving the presentation through better word choice, order, or emphasis. Documents and graphics should be incorporated into the presentation. Finally, potential cross-examination should be discussed and the witness should be given a flavor of what it is like by undergoing some cross-examination during the preparation session. Remember, however, the preparation conference with the witness will not likely be privileged unless the witness is a client or an agent of a client.

One difference between preparing a witness for a trial deposition and preparing that witness to testify at trial is that there will be no jury or judge at the deposition to evaluate the witness's demeanor. Thus, the witness's dress is not particularly important. Nor is whether the answers sound memorized, and so on, except to the extent that it might cause opposing counsel to try to find out what was said to the witness in advance. But the transcript gives no indication of demeanor or tone and therefore preparing on these matters is unimportant. (Obviously, this is not true for a videotape deposition, where preparation on dress and demeanor is very important.)

For the same reason, it does little harm to write out your questions in advance. The transcript will not show whether counsel is reading questions or composing them on the spot. Nor does it much matter with most friendly witnesses whether counsel is making eye contact with them while asking the questions or looking down at the script of the examination questions. Writing the questions gives counsel the opportunity to make sure they are correctly worded and that all of the important topics are covered with the witness. The negative aspect of writing out the questions is that if the witness deviates from the prepared answers, the questions may prove useless. Also, written questions may sound prepared rather than the sort of thing that would be asked in a natural oral exchange. However, reviewing the questions with another person, such as a secretary, can usually protect against the use of stilted lawyers' language.

## 17.2 TAKING THE TRIAL DEPOSITION

The examination of a witness whose deposition is being taken to perpetuate the testimony is conducted as if the witness were testifying at trial, with several important differences. First, because the jury or judge will not have an opportunity to observe the witness's demeanor and to make judgments about credibility on that basis, other indices of veracity should be explored. The most important is a longer and more complete accreditation of the witness. Providing details about the witness's personal background is helpful, such as whether the witness is married, has children, and has lived in this community for a number of years. Similar information about the witness's education and employment history will also aid the jury. If the witness's testimony relates to his or her job, add some detail about the job and the witness's experience. Finally, if the witness is neutral and has no ties to either side of the dispute, this should be emphasized.

Because there is no opportunity to ask the questions again at trial, it is important that counsel's questions and the answers be clear and understandable. Carefully thinking through the best method of explaining complex matters and even writing out the questions help ensure that the jury or judge will understand the witness's testimony when it is read at trial. An effective trial lawyer learns how to "self-monitor." In other words, counsel must learn to listen to her own questions and the witness's answers and judge whether they are clear, understandable, and successful in bringing out all of the witness's important information.

Techniques such as using tone of voice and facial expressions to convey meaning do not work for stenographic depositions. Make sure that all questions and answers are understandable without reference to these factors. Similarly, hand gestures and other body language do not come across in a transcript.

If it will be necessary for the witness to give distances or illustrate movements, plan in advance how to do this in such a way that the jury listening to the testimony later will understand what is going on. Thus, counsel should clarify all hand gestures and descriptions, such as "from here to there," by stating such clarifications as, "let the record show that the witness has pointed to an object ten feet from the witness chair." Questioning counsel may do this, because opposing counsel is there to correct any misstatements. ("We'll stipulate that the object is at least eight feet away from the chair.")

When opposing counsel makes an objection at a deposition being taken for discovery purposes, counsel will normally not respond in any way to the objection except to request that the witness answer the question. Where there is no intention ever to introduce the testimony at trial or use it for a summary judgment motion, it does not really matter that the question was objectionable; the only interest is the answer and the facts provided by that answer. However, this is not the case with a deposition being taken for use at trial.

Counsel should avoid objectionable questions by carefully reviewing the testimony in advance. If objections are then made at the deposition, the advance review will put counsel in a better position to decide whether to rephrase a question. If the objection is valid, or if it might be sustained, rephrase the question. If in doubt as to the basis of the objection, do not hesitate to ask opposing counsel to state the grounds. There will not be an opportunity to ask the question again at trial if the objection is sustained and the witness is unavailable. Even if the objection is of doubtful validity, rephrase the question once it is answered the first time. Then, if the objection ultimately turns out to be unfounded, a choice between the two phrasings can be made in deciding which will be read to the jury. If the objection is sustained, the second, good question and answer will still remain.

Sometimes it is necessary to take a deposition for use at trial when there has been no opportunity to interview the witness in advance. In those situations, it may be necessary to first ask discovery-type questions to find out what the witness knows. Once the witness's knowledge has been explored, questions can be formulated covering the desired information in a form more suitable for trial presentation. For instance, if the witness, in answering a question about what happened, provides a long answer with neutral information and a few items of importance, several additional questions should be asked to highlight the favorable information. That the useful questions are separated by several questions and answers with unhelpful information does not matter. When the deposition is read at trial, the irrelevant questions and answers can be omitted and only the useful ones presented.

Remember also that leading questions are only permissible in limited circumstances: preliminary matters, an adverse party, a witness identified with an adverse party, a witness who has demonstrated hostility, or when leading questions are necessary to develop the testimony of the witness, such as with a child witness or with an expert witness where leading questions may be necessary to translate the technical to the understandable. There should be no question about who is an adverse party, but it needs to be established through questioning that a witness is hostile or identified with an adverse party. The foundation for asking leading questions is usually laid at the beginning of the trial deposition.

## 17.3 DEFENDING THE TRIAL DEPOSITION

Nothing in a notice of deposition indicates whether the deposition is being taken for use at trial, for discovery, or for both. But any time a notice of deposition is received from the other side for a witness who is known to be friendly to that side, it is probably being taken to preserve testimony. It generally makes no sense to take the deposition of a witness who can be interviewed out of the presence of opposing counsel, unless the witness is likely to be unavailable for trial. If this occurs, be prepared to cross-examine the witness in the same way as would occur at trial.

If the witness is friendly to the other side, there probably has not been an opportunity to interview him and to determine what the witness has to say. Thus, before the proponent of the witness conducts the deposition to preserve direct testimony for use at trial, opposing counsel may notice a deposition for discovery purposes so that cross-examination can be conducted and preserved. Unless it can be determined from other sources what the witness will be saying, it will be difficult to prepare cross-examination before conducting some discovery.

The usual procedure in preparing to cross-examine is to conduct information-gathering questioning to determine what the witness knows and to develop possible areas for cross-examination and impeachment. While normally counsel would worry about preserving unfavorable testimony, such information is likely to be brought out on direct examination, unless opposing counsel is equally ignorant of what the witness will say. The task is to discover the testimony favorable to the client that opposing counsel may fail or has failed to bring out, as well as all information that tends to discredit the witness. Then, before concluding the deposition, a break can be taken during which a trial-type cross-examination can be constructed for execution when the deposition re-convenes. When the deposition is read or (in the case of a video deposition) played at trial, only the trial-type examination will be delivered to the jury.

Besides cross-examining, appropriate objections must be made. Since any objection to a problem which can be cured is waived if not made, counsel must be alert in the role of opposing counsel. The transcript will be read at trial and this is the only opportunity to make curable objections.[4]

Naturally, the same strategic considerations that govern objections at trial also govern in defending the trial deposition; therefore, some objections will not be made for tactical reasons. For instance, objecting to a lack of foundation is rarely helpful unless the questioner cannot establish the necessary foundation.[5] Otherwise, the opposing lawyer is likely to ask the necessary questions resulting in the evidence being more persuasive than it would otherwise be.

## 17.4 USING THE DEPOSITION AT TRIAL

How deposition testimony is presented to the trier of fact is very much a matter of local custom and procedure. In a bench trial, the offering party usually will merely designate the pages and lines that the court is to consider, and the judge (or the judge's clerk) will read the testimony at some later time. In a jury trial, however, the testimony is almost always read to the jury and the actual deposition transcript is never given to the jury to consider during its deliberations.

The procedure for reading the deposition to the jury also varies from jurisdiction to jurisdiction. Some courts have the bailiff read the designated portions to the jury while in others one of the attorneys for the offering side reads it. The preferred method with many attorneys, however, is to have a person—usually an attorney—sit in the witness box to read the deposition answers while another attorney reads the questions. This makes the deposition reading resemble actual trial testimony as much as possible. As discussed before, some attorneys attempt to select an associate or other person to play the role of the witness who presents the desired image to the jury.[6]

Before the deposition can be presented at trial, two steps are necessary: first, editing; and second, ruling on objections.[7] The judge must rule on objections only if objections have been made in the designated portion. Usually the judge's ruling is done as part of the pretrial conference or during the trial.[8]

Deposition readings are invariably a tedious experience for the jury. One study of jury comprehension noted that "[t]he jurors' re-

---

4.  See § 14.8.
5.  See § 14.10.2.
6.  See § 16.5.
7.  See § 16.4.
8.  Ibid.

sponse to reading of depositions into evidence was uniformly negative. They found it boring, difficult to follow, and uninformative."[9] The more mercifully brief the experience, the more likely the jury will understand, remember, and be persuaded by what they hear. If lawyers will be reading the testimony, they should animate their voices and, within reason, emphasize those questions and answers they particularly wish the jury to focus upon. While the reading of depositions is boring, reading in a monotone turns it into torture.

A mistake many lawyers make is reading the entire deposition to the jury, not because all of it contributes to their cause, but because of desire for context or completeness. This should not be done. Carefully edit depositions for reading so that only those questions and answers are presented that will contribute to the jury's understanding and persuasion. The other side can request that additional portions be read, but whether this occurs as part of counsel's reading or during the opponent's case is discretionary with the judge.[10] Use brevity as the guiding principle.

Most of the above applies equally to the presentation of deposition testimony that has been recorded on videotape. There are, however, some significant differences. In the video deposition, demeanor matters; both the demeanor of the witness and the demeanor of the lawyer. All those factors important to demeanor at trial apply to the video deposition. The witness must look at the fact finder. In a video deposition that is the camera. It is for that reason that the examining counsel will frequently sit in a position so the camera is directly over counsel's shoulder. In that way, when the witness naturally speaks to the questioner, she is also speaking to the jury through the eye of the camera. Proper courtroom attire, at least for the witness, is required and should be consistent with the witness's place in the litigation and the image sought to be portrayed of the witness. Unlike in a paper transcript, pauses between questions and answers appear on the video as being evasive, as they do in trial. Attorneys "appear" in video depositions through their voices. Questions must be clear and precise, with inflection appropriate to the information being solicited. As to objections, most videographers ask and many judges require that counsel state the word, "objection," whereupon the video stops and the nature of any objection and response is recorded in a paper transcript. Once the judge rules on the objections, then the video is edited to be consistent with the court's ruling. Although better than reading a deposition,

---

9. Special Committee of the ABA Section of Litigation, Jury Comprehension in Complex Cases, 37 (1990).
10. Fed.R.Civ.P. 32(a)(4).

head-and-shoulder shot video depositions are not scintillating. Consideration should be given to the use of visual aids and other devices that enhance juror interest and understanding at trial. And, above all, if there exists the possibility of having the witness actually appear at trial, that option will usually be preferable.

# CHAPTER EIGHTEEN

## VIDEOTAPE DEPOSITIONS

*A picture may instantly present what a book could set forth only in a hundred pages.* — Ivan Sergeyevich Turgenev

Presenting a witness on videotape, for impeachment or in place of live testimony, has much greater impact than testimony read from a transcript. Because of that greater impact, special care needs be taken to create the visual record that conveys the desired message. As a corollary, in defending the videotaped deposition, the client must be protected from sometimes subtle techniques which can unfairly diminish his performance and credibility.

## 18.1 WHEN TO TAKE A VIDEOTAPE DEPOSITION

Testimony from a live witness in the witness box is almost always preferred to presenting evidence through depositions, video or otherwise. An actual person on the stand answering questions holds the jury's interest better and is more understandable and persuasive than listening to the reading of a deposition. Juries also expect that the testimony of key witnesses, particularly that of a party, will be presented live. The assumption is that a party or witness must not think the case important if they are not willing to testify at the trial. This preference for live testimony is reflected in the requirement in most jurisdictions that deposition testimony may only be used if the witness is unavailable.[1]

Sometimes, however, a witness cannot be available for trial or strategic considerations dictate using deposition testimony rather than a live witness; some examples include when a witness is seriously ill or elderly, a company executive is required to be out of the country at the time of trial, or a key witness is beyond the subpoena powers of the court and refuses to appear voluntarily. Expert witnesses present

---

1. Fed.R.Civ.P. 32(a)(3); Fed.R.Evid. 804(b)(1).

a particular problem. The best are usually busy, as well as expensive. The problem of coordinating the expert's schedule with the court's is oftentimes insurmountable, and the expense of having an expert witness waiting to testify is more than many clients can bear.

Even though a witness's testimony must be presented by deposition, some of the advantages of live testimony can be captured by using a videotape deposition. The jury can see the witness testifying as well as hear what the witness is saying. The jury can evaluate the witness's demeanor and credibility almost in the same way they could if the witness were in the courtroom sitting in the witness box. In short, videotape technology now provides the ability to bring distant witnesses into the courtroom and have the jury hear their testimony as if the witness were testifying live.

## 18.2 ADVANTAGES OF VIDEOTAPE DEPOSITIONS

Just as live witnesses are more interesting and persuasive than deposition testimony, so too are videotape depositions in comparison with stenographically recorded ones. Consider the following advantages of videotape depositions:

**Videotape depositions permit the jury to see the witness's demeanor.** Videotape allows the jury to judge a witness's sincerity and trustworthiness almost in the same way it can with live testimony at trial. Reading a stenographic deposition deprives the jury of this opportunity.

**Videotape depositions allow the jury to see the witness's physical condition.** A videotape deposition can capture the physical condition of a witness who is terminally ill and who is expected to die or become too infirm to testify by the time of trial. For example, a videotape deposition of a plaintiff with asbestosis allows the jury to see the effects of the disease on his health in a way the bare transcript of a stenographic deposition cannot.

**Videotape deposition testimony is more entertaining and easier to follow.** Reading stenographic depositions is often the most boring part of the trial. Stenographic deposition testimony is usually presented by one or two lawyers reading the questions and answers to the jury. No matter how well it is presented, juries repeatedly confirm that the reading of written deposition testimony leaves them confused and bored. While not as easy to follow as live testimony, videotape depositions are an improvement over the reading of depositions. The jury gets to watch as well as listen and is more likely to follow the testimony and remain interested in what is occurring. It is well known among social scientists that information presented to two senses (sight and hearing) is much easier to comprehend and believe than information presented to the ears alone.

**Videotape depositions allow for the better presentation of exhibits.** Consider what happens in a stenographic deposition when a witness refers to an exhibit, for example an anatomical diagram about which a doctor is testifying. The witness might say, "The fracture occurred here," and the lawyer will then attempt to make the record clear by saying, "You are pointing to the upper portion of the ulna?" and so on. If the deposition is read at trial, a copy of the exhibit must be shown to the jury with the hope the jury can understand from the deposition testimony at what part of the exhibit they should be looking. The procedure is cumbersome and there is always a risk that the jury will not understand to what part of the exhibit the witness is referring.

A videotape deposition solves most of these problems because the camera can take a close-up of the exhibit and show the viewer exactly where the witness is pointing when she testifies, "The fracture occurred here."

**Videotape depositions permit the witness to demonstrate large pieces of equipment, work with materials, and show a scene when these cannot be brought into the courtroom**. Sometimes counsel may want the jury to see how the plaintiff in a products liability case was operating the machine when the injury occurred or how, for instance, a piece of scaffolding was assembled. When the exhibit is too large or inconvenient to bring into the courtroom, the best way of having the jury understand the witness's testimony is through a videotape deposition taken where the witness can demonstrate exactly what happened. Similarly, a videotape deposition permits the witness to visit the scene of an accident or a construction site to point out where events occurred. Of course videotapes can also be used as an exhibit during the testimony of a witness appearing at trial.

**Videotape depositions can show tests and experiments being conducted while in the laboratory when they cannot be shown in court.** Where an expert witness has conducted a series of experiments but will be unavailable to testify at trial, a videotape deposition permits the jury to see exactly what the expert did and what results were reached.

**Videotape depositions can be more effective for impeachment; the jury can see as well as hear the prior inconsistent statement.** The dramatic impact of impeachment is heightened when the jury cannot only hear, but also see the witness actually speaking the words of the prior inconsistent statement. While it may be cumbersome to set up and use the videotape deposition (unless the videotape is recorded in a digital format and the sections likely to be used are bar-coded as described earlier), under the Federal Rules of Evidence the inconsistent statement need not be presented while the witness is on the stand so long as the witness is given the opportunity at some time to explain or deny the statement and the opposing party is afforded a chance to interrogate the witness about it.[2]

**Videotape depositions highlight an opposition witness's evasion, fumbling, or pauses before answering.** Some witnesses do not perform well in the courtroom. They come across as evasive or disingenuous, and the jury will not likely believe their testimony. This is wonderful if they are important opposing witnesses. Presumably opposing counsel in such a situation will make the same evaluation of the witness and, if the witness is beyond the subpoena power of the court, prefer to present the testimony by stenographic deposition rather than live testimony. But either party can choose to use a videotape deposition, thereby allowing the jury to see the witness and make the same judgment about the witness's credibility as if it were live testimony.

**Videotape depositions can be edited for use during the closing argument and, with the court's permission, during the opening statement.** Courts increasingly permit the use during opening statement and closing argument of selected portions of videotape depositions that will be or have been admitted in evidence. Consider the effect on the jury of actually showing them a key question and answer in the deposition during opening so that the witness is placed in the desired light before giving testimony, or in the closing rather than asking them to recall what was said at some earlier point in the trial.

**Videotape depositions are more likely to control the behavior of disruptive opposing counsel.** As noted earlier lawyers who are willing, in front of a court reporter, to disrupt the deposition and act completely inappropriately are often much more reluctant to do so when their actions are captured on videotape. Even for those lawyers who are not deterred by the presence of the camera, the existence of the tape will make it much easier when sanctions against counsel's behavior at deposition are requested, as the judge will be better able to evaluate obstreperous counsel and the effect of that behavior on the discovery process.

---

2. Fed.R.Evid. 613(b). This requirement does not apply to admissions of a party opponent.

## 18.3 DISADVANTAGES OF VIDEOTAPE DEPOSITIONS

While videotape depositions have many important advantages over stenographic depositions, they do have drawbacks. When considering whether a deposition should be taken stenographically or by videotape, carefully consider both the advantages and disadvantages of each and decide which method provides the greater benefits in light of the objectives of the deposition and its potential later use. The drawbacks of videotape depositions are:

**Videotape depositions are usually more expensive than stenographic depositions.** They require more effort to arrange, and may involve editing costs as well. In addition to the cost or rental of the equipment, an operator must be paid, a special room may be required, and the tape may require editing before it can be presented at trial. Rules 26(a)(3)(B) and 32(c) as well as the deposition rules of many states also require that a stenographic transcription be prepared of the portions of the deposition to be offered at trial in order to facilitate making rulings on objections and to ensure accuracy.

Videotape depositions can be comparable in cost to stenographic depositions if the deposing lawyer already owns the necessary equipment, the deposition can be taken without arranging additional space, and the lawyer acts as the operator. Even where an accompanying stenographic transcription is required, the parties often agree the deposing lawyer's secretarial staff may do the typing.

**Videotape depositions are more likely than stenographic depositions to have technical or mechanical problems.** Videotape equipment occasionally breaks down or malfunctions, the operator forgets to turn on the tape at the proper time, or no one notices the tape has run out. When this happens in the middle of a deposition, the results can be disastrous, particularly if the malfunction or error is not discovered until the deposition is completed and the witness has departed. Careful checking of equipment before the deposition begins and using a monitor while the deposition is occurring help minimize the problem, but the risk is always present.

**Videotape depositions are more difficult to use for trial preparation.** One of the more important uses of depositions is to help in trial preparation. They can be used to review what evidence is available for and against a position, to plan the deponent's cross-examination, or to sketch out the closing argument. Using a stenographic deposition is often more convenient than reviewing a videotape when preparing for trial. Not only does it take more time to review the tape (reading is faster than speaking), but the necessary video equipment must be available, it is difficult to go back to an earlier question and answer, and it is harder to keep track of what has been said. An accompanying stenographic transcription can be made available, but its preparation will add to the deposition's expense.

**Videotape depositions are a waste of money if the deposition is being taken for discovery purposes only.** The expense of a videotape deposition need not be incurred if discovery is the only anticipated purpose for the deposition. The strength of videotape is in presenting evidence at trial, or to a mediator or arbitrator. Usually, however, if there is no intention to show the tape at the trial or other proceeding, then a stenographic deposition is easier to take and even easier to use for trial preparation. One exception to this rule, of course, is where the videotape is being used to record or control the behavior of an obstreperous opposing counsel.[3]

**Videotape depositions require special equipment and extra arrangements for use in court.** Reading a stenographic deposition in court does not require any special preparation or equipment, but the same is not true for videotape depositions. There must be a monitor and deck (although many jurisdictions now have them as part of the courtroom equipment), lighting and viewing conditions must be checked, extension cords need to be available (seemingly by the dozens), and everything must be situated so that the entirety of it does not obstruct movement in the courtroom. Furthermore, an allowance for equipment malfunction must be made (backups of everything), and everything must be set up and running before the tape can be shown.

**Videotape deposition witnesses may be more attractive or less attractive than the person used to read the answers from a stenographic deposition.** Where the deposition is of a witness testifying favorably for the other side but who will also provide harmful testimony on cross-examination or through impeachments, the pleasant manner of the witness may dilute the impact of that harmful testimony. In such a situation, the persuasive impact of the deposition may be higher if it is read to the jury by someone who is less appealing than the actual witness who would appear on the videotape.

**Videotape depositions are more difficult and cumbersome to use for impeachment purposes than stenographic depositions.** Videotape depositions are not usually taken for discovery purposes, but to perpetuate testimony because a witness is expected to be unavailable to

---

3. Many lawyers who are willing to act in an outrageous manner during a stenographic deposition feel constrained to behave reasonably when their actions are being recorded on videotape. *See* Chapter Eleven.

testify at trial. When, however, the witness does end up testifying and testifies differently than at the deposition, using the videotape deposition to impeach can be difficult, unless the recording is digital and has been bar-coded as explained earlier. Any potential downside can be avoided either by using a stenographic transcription of the videotape, in other words, converting the videotape deposition to a stenographic form, or by presenting the impeaching portion of the case at a later time in the case, such as during rebuttal. Another option that allows much greater flexibility is presenting the video deposition on laser disk or DVD. This allows instant access to any portion and great control of the displayed material. The cost of such storage and retrieval is declining rapidly, and the juxtaposition of the live testimony and the video impeachment is impressive.

**Videotape depositions may preserve evidence harmful to your side more effectively than stenographic depositions.** All depositions have the potential of preserving helpful evidence, but there also exists the potential of preserving harmful evidence. When harmful evidence is preserved on videotape, the impact of showing the tape to the jury will be higher than if the questions and answers are read from a transcript.

**Videotape depositions allow an opponent's witnesses to hone their performances if they later testify at trial.** Sometimes a videotape deposition is taken of an opposing party's witness because it is expected the witness has helpful information but will not be testifying at trial. Remember, however, the witness can always decide later to testify and use the videotape as a guide on how to improve. If the witness made a poor impression on videotape, for instance, because of poor eye contact or appearing to be evasive when answering questions, the videotape will help him to correct these problems.

**Videotape deposition witnesses may not talk or film well.** Remember Richard Nixon in the 1960 presidential debates—poor preparation and hot lights made him look like a gangster and may have lost him the election as well. And then there was the performance of President Clinton, whose false sincerity caused him many problems (among them, perjury). The videotape of the deposition of Bill Gates in the *U.S. v. Microsoft* case has become a textbook on how not to perform on a video deposition. When a witness cannot testify at trial, consider how they will appear and sound on the tape. Some witnesses are more persuasive and credible if the jury cannot see and hear them. Reading a stenographic deposition will not give any hint of a witness's halting answers, furtive looks, and nervous manner, but a videotape deposition reveals all these flaws and more.

## 18.4 THE LAW

The Federal Rules of Civil Procedure favor the use in jury trials of videotape depositions over stenographic depositions. Under Rule 32(c), on the request of any party, deposition testimony offered other than for impeachment purposes must be presented in non-stenographic form, *e.g.*, videotape, if available, unless the court for good cause orders otherwise. In bench trials, deposition testimony may be offered in stenographic or nonstenographic form. Whenever a videotape deposition is used at trial or, for instance, in support of a motion for summary judgment, the offering party must provide the court with a transcript of the portions being offered.

Rule 30(b)(2) states that videotape depositions may be taken as a matter of right unless the court orders otherwise. The only requirement is that the notice of deposition shall state that videotape will be used to record the testimony. The cost of the videotaping is borne by the taking party, but any party may arrange for a transcription to be made from the videotape.[4] Any party may also, after giving notice to the witness and other parties, designate another method, in addition to the noticed method, for recording the testimony. In short, even if the taking party notices the deposition to be taken by stenographic means, any other party may, as of right, require that the deposition also be videotaped. The cost of videotaping shall be at the requesting party's expense and is also arranged by that party.[5]

Rule 30(b)(4) specifically instructs that the appearance or demeanor of the deposition witness shall not be distorted through camera or sound-recording techniques. In other words, the videotaping must be done through fair and accurate means.

Rule 26(a)(3)(B) states that if a party is intending to use videotape deposition testimony at trial, this fact must be disclosed to opposing counsel, as part of the required pretrial disclosures, at least thirty days prior to trial or by a date set by the court. In addition, a transcript of the pertinent portions of the deposition testimony must be provided to the other parties.

Many states have adopted specific rules or legislation concerning videotape depositions, but in those jurisdictions following the pre-amendment version of the Federal Rules the parties may stipulate in writing, or the court may upon motion order, that a deposition be tak-

---

4. Fed.R.Civ.P. 30(b)(2).
5. Fed.R.Civ.P. 30(b)(3).

en by videotape.[6] The stipulation or order shall also designate: before whom the deposition is to be taken; the manner of recording, preserving, and filing the deposition; and other provisions necessary to assure that the recorded testimony will be accurate and trustworthy.

## 18.5 SCHEDULING THE VIDEOTAPE DEPOSITION

Videotape depositions are scheduled in the same manner as other depositions, but be aware that editing may be necessary before final use of the tapes at trial. Also, the potential for mechanical or technical problems is always present. Therefore, take the deposition sufficiently in advance of trial to leave adequate time for any necessary editing or to retake the deposition if technical difficulties do occur.

As previously discussed, most videotape depositions are taken of a party's own witness who expects to be unavailable for trial. Since the deposition will be the only opportunity for opposing counsel to cross-examine the witness, it makes sense to schedule the deposition on as short notice as possible and as early in the litigation as feasible. Short notice and early scheduling may reduce the opposing counsel's abilities to prepare effectively for any cross-examination.

The converse of this is that, if a notice of a videotape deposition is received from the party sponsoring the witness, it should be anticipated that the witness will be unavailable for trial and counsel will need to be fully prepared to conduct any cross-examination of the witness at the deposition. To prepare adequately for cross-examination, counsel must consider all discovery that might provide her with potential sources of cross-examination before the deposition occurs. Counsel may even want to postpone the videotape deposition either by agreement or by requesting a protective order from the court until preparation is complete.[7] While expensive, it may also be desirable, either by agreement or with the court's permission, to conduct a stenographic deposition before taking the videotape deposition. Since this would be the procedure if the witness were to be testifying at trial, a strong argument can be made that a similar procedure should be followed when a videotape deposition is noticed. The stenographic deposition transcript can then be available for trial-type preparation of the video deposition.

---

6. Fed.R.Civ.P. 30(b)(4).
7. Fed.R.Civ.P. 26(c).

## 18.6 PREPARING TO TAKE THE VIDEOTAPE DEPOSITION

Videotape depositions being taken for use at trial more resemble a movie of a trial than they do a traditional deposition. Like a witness's trial testimony, the videotape deposition should be entertaining and persuasive, but to accomplish these objectives preparation must be done as carefully as it would be for a trial examination.

Effective videotape depositions must be carefully planned productions. Keep in mind that when the tape is being shown, the jury is concentrating on every word and action occurring on the screen in a way that does not occur with live testimony. When counsel is examining a witness at trial and briefly stops to search for a document, the jury can look at the judge, opposing counsel, the witness, or entertain itself in other ways as long as the interruption is short. With a videotape deposition the television monitor becomes the center of attention and that same pause to find a document seems to last forever.

### 18.6.1 Hire a capable operator to conduct the videotape deposition.

Using an experienced and capable operator to record the deposition avoids most of the difficulties that can occur with the use of videotape. An experienced operator can provide guidance in planning room setup, lighting, positioning the camera, editing, and the many other considerations that do not exist with a stenographic deposition, but which are crucial to taking an effective videotape deposition.

Many court reporting firms now advertise themselves as having videotape capability, but before making the decision to hire one be sure to check on what actual experience they have had. Get the names of several lawyers they have worked for in the past and check with these lawyers on the quality of the work.

### 18.6.2 Decide on taping options.

When counsel decides to take a videotape deposition, she becomes the director of a movie. Like any director, she must decide on how the movie will be shot. And like any director, counsel will also need to make compromises between keeping expenses reasonable and making the deposition entertaining and persuasive.

**Type of camera and format**—Some variety of digital recording is now the standard format and should normally be used for the videotape deposition, with VHS tape cassette as the second choice. Depositions have turned to video recording using digital cameras because of the ease of later access this medium provides. A camera with a date/time generator, required by some courts, will provide increased security against tampering or unauthorized editing of the tape and can also be added to any accompanying stenographic transcription of the tape.

**Single camera versus multiple cameras**—In deciding on the recording, an important decision is whether to use a single camera or multiple cameras. Multiple cameras allow a variety of shots and angles that help to maintain the jury's interest. But multiple cameras are also more expensive and invite the other side to complain about unfair editing, cutting, shot selection, and other distortion of the evidence. This choice may be co-opted by local rule. Many courts limit the manner of recording a video deposition to a head -and-shoulders, one-camera shot of the deponent, using color tape. This sort of local rule may decide the following issues regarding distance, panning, camera angle, zooming, and whether the video is made in color or black-and-white. Departures from a mandated protocol require a court order.

**Distance**—Most videotape cameras have zoom lenses which permit a range of shots from full to close-ups. Even without a zoom lens, the camera can be positioned to capture a range of shots from the entire room to a close-up of the witness's face. Before deciding on the taping distance, check whether local court rules or practice require a particular method. Depending on the opponent, counsel may also want to attempt to agree before the deposition on camera placement and the types of shots to be used. Finally, it is worth running some test shots to see which type of shot is most flattering to the witness.

**Panning**—Unless the preferred camera distance will take in both the examining attorney and the witness, counsel should decide whether the operator should pan back and forth between the lawyer as the question is asked and the witness for the answer or remain focused on the witness the entire time. Panning is more entertaining and is better able to hold the jury's interest. If, however, the deposition is of an opposing witness, remaining on the witness will show the witness's reaction to the question.

**Camera angle**—As with taping distance, counsel should select a camera angle that is most appropriate for the witness. Usual choices are either straight-on or at a three-quarters angle. Usually an angle shot is best for a favorable witness while a straight-on shot is best for an opposing witness.

**Zooming**—Zooming can be used both to provide visual interest to the videotape and to show close-ups of exhibits, demonstrations, or the witness's features while a critical answer is being given. The danger of zoom shots is that, unless agreed upon in advance, the court may consider them misleading to the jury and require deletion of portions of the tape. Close-ups of exhibits and demonstrations are normally permitted, but counsel should use other types of zoom shots with caution and attempt an advance agreement with opposing counsel.

**Black and white or color**—Juries are used to watching color television at home and they expect the same in the courtroom. Color also usually makes witnesses more attractive and better holds the jury's interest. On the other hand, black and white is better for showing detail in an exhibit and is often less flattering to a witness.

**Arrangement of microphones**—Think about the number and arrangement of microphones before the deposition. Normally there is one microphone for each participant. If this is not possible, work out an agreement with opposing counsel in advance about sharing the available microphones.

Always check the microphones before the deposition to ensure they can adequately pick up the voices of all the participants. Directional microphones attached to the camera can be a particular problem. If the witness is some distance from the camera, or if someone off the camera is speaking, such as opposing counsel, the voices may not be picked up clearly and it may be difficult to identify who is speaking.

### 18.6.3 Selecting a suitable location for the deposition.

Unlike a stenographic deposition, the jury will see the location where a videotape deposition is conducted. As with everything else connected with the deposition, the surroundings should present the witness in the best possible light. For instance, a cluttered or messy background with stacks of old files and paper coffee cups distract the jury and cause it to think less of the witness's testimony. Often the court reporting firm will have a room where the deposition can be conducted, but this should be checked with the same thoroughness that would be given any important trial issue. Even where the opposition is conducting a discovery deposition on video, an offer to provide the office for the deposition of the witness may be accepted, allowing some control over the surroundings.

**Size**—The room should be large enough to permit all of the participants to be comfortably seated and to hold all of the necessary equipment. Allow adequate room to position the camera and for the operator to move about.

**Lighting**—Always check whether the lighting is adequate. Also check whether the lighting causes glare, whether curtains or shades should be open or closed, and whether additional lighting is necessary.

**Temperature**—If the deposition room is too hot, a witness's perspiring will show on the tape and may cause the jury to believe he is nervous or lying. Make sure the room is cool enough, particularly if additional lights will need to be brought in.

### 18.6.4 Planning the questions.

Since the videotape deposition will be used in place of live testimony at trial, the deposition questioning should be as carefully organized as if it were occurring before a jury. In fact, because jurors are used to perfect dialogue on television, any variations from this "norm" will adversely effect the persuasiveness of the presentation. A videotape deposition is not the place for stream-of-consciousness questioning or for asking questions on the fly. The goal is to present the fact finder with a clear, persuasive, and memorable story. To do so requires careful planning of the questions.

**Organizing and drafting the questions**—How to draft and organize trial testimony is essentially the same question as, "How should direct examination be conducted?" As such, it is beyond the scope of this book, but the witness's testimony should be presented as if the witness were in the witness box.[8] The witness's background is usually brought out at the beginning of the testimony, questioning should move smoothly and logically from topic to topic, and the witness's story is normally presented in a chronological fashion.

**Avoid interruptions**—Long pauses and interruptions during a videotape deposition are far more noticeable than if the same thing occurred at trial. The jury focuses on the television screen and anything that occurs becomes the center of attention. Therefore, maintain a quick pace and avoid interruptions as much as possible.

One method of avoiding pauses and interruptions is by carefully outlining your questions. Using an outline will not be distracting to the jury if the camera is focused only on the witness, and will prevent counsel from having to grope for the next question.

---

8.  *See* Steven Lubet, *Modern Trial Advocacy*, Chapter Four (NITA 2004).

**Dynamic questions and visual aids**—The usual videotape deposition shows what in the television industry are called "talking heads," and talking heads are boring. Make every attempt to enliven the testimony without sacrificing the witness's credibility. Putting more modulation in questions and making the questions as dynamic as possible is one method of doing this. But do not stray far from normal courtroom demeanor or the videotape may appear false or contrived, when counsel appears one way in the courtroom and another way on the television. A test tape can identify these problems and allow for correction of any underplaying or overplaying of the counsel's role.

Exhibits and visual aids help to make otherwise flat testimony more interesting. If possible, space exhibits throughout the testimony in order to maintain interest to the end. Concentrations of exhibits can be as boring as uninterrupted testimony.

Exhibits should be arranged so they are quickly accessible during the deposition and are in the order in which they will be used. Delays can also be avoided during the deposition by pre-marking exhibits and having extra copies for opposing counsel and the court reporter.

**Minimize objections**—Objections during the deposition can be edited out before the presentation of the videotape at trial, but such editing can be expensive and can make the testimony appear choppy. Therefore, carefully review planned questions and expected answers before the deposition to avoid objections. While an excessive number of objections may cause the judge to place the editing costs on the objecting party, the party offering the deposition most often will bear the cost, particularly if the objections are sustained.

### 18.6.5 Preparing the witness.

Factors that often are not important in a stenographic deposition become critical in a videotape deposition. For instance, a stenographic deposition does not show the witness's dress or demeanor, the tone with which questions are answered, or a witness's movements and nervous habits. However, all of these factors should be explored with the videotape deposition witness a day or more before the actual deposition to minimize the witness's anxiety, just as would be done for trial testimony.

**Dress**—Usually dark clothes and pastel shirts film best, but a test shot is advisable. Avoid checks and small prints that do not come across well on the camera. In general, the witness should dress as if for court.

**Demeanor**—The witness should be courteous and responsive to all questions. Evasiveness, particularly on cross-examination, will be readily apparent to the jury and should be avoided. Similarly, jousting with opposing counsel and displays of anger or irritation will come across poorly, and you should coach witnesses to avoid this type of conduct.

**Movement**—Natural movements in the courtroom may come across in a videotape deposition as jerky and distracting or as signs of nervousness. Advise witnesses to avoid unnecessary or distracting movements or gestures. One particular area to caution about is drumming on the table, particularly if table microphones are being used. On tape, the drumming sounds like a stampeding herd of elephants.

### 18.6.6 Preparing the operator.

Without close cooperation between the questioning attorney and the video operator, a videotape deposition can quickly turn into a disaster. Start working with the operator from the earliest possible moment to make sure that the operator fully understands his role and what is needed from him to make the presentation as persuasive as possible.

**Check equipment in advance**—Have the operator thoroughly check all of the equipment in advance to make sure it is in operating condition. Waiting until a few minutes before the deposition to discover that a key cord is missing is courting disaster.

**Camera set-up and lighting**—Discuss with the operator the lighting needs for the room and the camera angles and distances to be used during the deposition. Check these out in advance to make sure the image on the videotape is what is desired and that the operator understands all of counsel's instructions.

As part of the review, a check should be made of all exhibits, especially those, like x-rays and photographs, that might not tape well to insure clear recording. If they do not, enlargements, positive images of x-rays, or other steps to ensure exhibits come across on the videotape in a comprehensible way must be considered and undertaken.

**Arrange operator cues**—The operator should know when to zoom in on an exhibit and when to shift angles or distances. Work out a series of cues which the viewer will not notice, but which the operator will clearly understand. Similarly, the operator may need to give cues to counsel. One such important cue to be arranged in advance is the signal by the operator that the tape is coming to an end. If the necessary cues are few and the viewer will easily understand them, it may be better to place them on the tape. For instance, when the witness points to an exhibit, it will appear quite natural for counsel to say, "Why don't we have the camera do a close-up of where you are pointing?"

**Arrange for a deposition officer**—As a matter of economy, the operator should also be a notary public able to serve as the deposition officer. But if one is not available, be sure to arrange for a notary to be present to swear the witness and "preside" over the deposition.[9]

### 18.6.7 Working out agreements.

Resolving with opposing counsel as many matters as possible before the deposition helps avoid expense and disruption of the deposition and facilitates future use of the deposition at trial. Agreeing on such matters as the number of cameras, the angles and distances of shots, and whether to shoot in color or black-and-white are all matters that are best resolved by agreement beforehand.

One particular area that should be discussed in advance is the lawyers' conduct during the deposition. Deciding on the ground rules helps maintain the quality and usefulness of the deposition for both sides. Some topics that should be covered are:

> • All the participants should avoid speaking while another participant is still speaking. The lawyers should avoid stepping on the witness's lines.

> • Objections should be made only after the examining attorney has finished the question or the witness has finished the answer.

> • Fingers drumming on the table, rustling papers, or other distracting noises should be avoided.

## 18.7 CONDUCTING THE VIDEOTAPE DEPOSITION

Most details of conducting the video deposition can be worked out during the preparation stage, but thinking through how the deposition will actually progress is important to its success. As noted earlier many of these issues may be decided by local rule concerning the manner and mode which video depositions must take.

---

9.  *See* § 1.13.1.

### 18.7.1 Beginning the deposition.

The taping of the deposition should follow a set sequence to anticipate the jury's curiosity about what is happening and to satisfy the requirements of Rule 30(b)(4):[10]

> 1. Start out with a full shot of the room. Have the deposition officer give his or her name and business address; announce that this is a videotape deposition; and give the name of the witness, the date, the time, the place of the deposition, and the title of the case. This should be repeated at the beginning of each new videotape of the deposition.
>
> 2. The deposition officer should identify every person present for the deposition while the camera focuses on that person using a full or medium shot.
>
> 3. The officer should swear in the witness.
>
> 4. If the camera will be panning between the examining lawyer and the witness, the camera should start with a full shot of the lawyer asking the first question and then go to a medium or close-up shot for the remainder of the question. All further questions and answers should be medium shots unless it is necessary to do a close-up of an exhibit or demonstration.

### 18.7.2 Questioning.

**Maintaining interest**—Remember that long questions and answers are difficult for a jury to follow and understand. Therefore, keep questions short and simple in the same manner as a stenographic deposition. Similarly, break up lengthy answers with questions calling for clarifications or additional information.

**Information-gathering questions versus perpetuating questions**—Sometimes a videotape deposition is taken for discovery purposes as well as for perpetuating testimony. For instance, counsel may believe that a particular witness who is beyond the subpoena powers of the court has helpful information, but the witness has rebuffed attempts to interview her. One response is to take a videotape deposition so that any useful information from the witness can be presented in the most persuasive manner at trial.

With such a witness, first ask information-gathering questions necessary to find out what the witness knows. Once familiar with the witness's story, go back to the beginning and ask only those questions you

---

10. See § 1.13.3.

would ask at trial. Editing the tape for use at trial is easier, and the final tape will appear less choppy if the information-gathering questions are grouped at the beginning of the deposition rather than intermixed with questions for perpetuating the testimony.

**Demeanor and conduct**—Care should be taken by counsel to present a pleasant and authoritative image, just as in the courtroom. Displays of irritation or anger are rarely appropriate. The jury will appreciate a courteous approach even more if the witness is acting in an obnoxious manner.

The jury will also be favorably impressed with appropriate and logical questions and the maintenance of a suitable pace to the examination. Long pauses and a disorganized approach will present an image of incompetence and demonstrate a lack of preparation. Finally, both counsel and the witness should avoid distracting movements or sounds that will be magnified on the film.

**Going off the record**—One way of controlling interruptions and delays on the tape is to go off the record when it appears the witness will need to look for an exhibit, read a long document, or otherwise slow down the questioning process. When going off the record, it is appropriate to give a short explanation of why that is happening. "While you review those x-rays, Doctor, why don't we go off the record." The explanation should be repeated when going back on the record. "Doctor, while we were off the record you were reviewing the plaintiff's x-rays. Are you prepared to discuss them now?"

### 18.7.3 Concluding the deposition.

Rule 30(b)(4) requires that at the end of the deposition, the officer shall state on the record that the deposition is complete and shall set forth any stipulations agreed to by the parties.

### 18.7.4 Post-deposition review.

Under Rule 30(e), if the witness or one of the parties makes a request before completion of the deposition, the witness shall have thirty days after having been notified by the deposition officer of its availability, to review the videotapes of the deposition and to make written changes.[11] Making corrections to a videotape deposition is more difficult than writing an errata sheet for written deposition testimony. First, the "incorrect" testimony will not be erased from the tape (just as the

---

11. *See* § 15.1.

"corrected" testimony is not erased from the written copy). Thus, the jury will see the videotape of the testimony at the deposition, while the jury only hears the corrected version of a stenographic deposition as it is read in court. Visual testimony clearly has more impact.

If a stenographic record of the video deposition has been created,[12] that transcript can be corrected using the standard rules and procedures for a written deposition transcript. However, without a written transcript the attorney and the witness will have to review the deposition videotape and create a "corrected script," which indicates the time or footage of the material to be corrected, and states the correction and the reason for the changed testimony. As a general rule, counsel should have a transcript of the videotaped deposition made simultaneously. This will save money in the long run, because it obviates the need for repeated real-time viewings of the video.

## 18.8 PREPARING TO USE THE VIDEOTAPE DEPOSITION AT TRIAL

### 18.8.1 Transcribing.

In those jurisdictions that require a stenographic transcription to be prepared, it will be necessary to have the videotapes transcribed or arrange to have a court reporter attend the deposition (who can also serve as the deposition officer). It is usually cheaper to have the transcription made from the videotapes or from audiotapes made simultaneously with the videotapes.

A stenographic transcription is useful even when not required. Taking a simultaneous audiotape recording of the proceedings will permit secretarial staff to prepare a transcription at a lower cost than having a court reporter prepare one.[13]

### 18.8.2 Editing.

While videotape depositions are more entertaining and will hold the jury's interest better, than stenographic depositions, even the best videotape deposition can be terribly tedious. The jury's exposure to all depositions, both videotape and stenographic, should be kept as short

---

12. Fed.R.Civ.P. 30(a)(4).
13. The Advisory Committee Notes to Rule 26(a)(3)(B) suggest that the transcription required by this rule and by Rule 30(b) can be prepared by a lawyer's own secretarial staff.

as possible, consistent with the jury hearing the necessary testimony and being persuaded of its truthfulness. This can be accomplished through prudent editing.

As a practical matter, many more questions are asked at a deposition than are necessary for the effective presentation of that evidence at trial. In selecting the testimony to be presented at trial, whether from stenographic or video recording, each question and answer should be critically examined with an eye to deleting any that do not advance the theory of the case.

### 18.8.3 Ruling on objections.

The pretrial conference is the usual and best time for the court to rule on objections, but this is a matter of local practice and court rules. Whatever procedure is used, do it sufficiently in advance of trial so that any portion of the videotape ruled inadmissible can be deleted. Of course, in order to preserve the matter for appeal, a complete original tape or disk of the testimony, without deletions, must be maintained.

Having the judge watch the tape to rule on objections is a time consuming and wasteful procedure, and most judges will refuse to do so unless the objection is to the taping itself or the conduct of the deposition. But if the objection is to a question or answer, the court can much more conveniently make these rulings by examining a stenographic transcription of the tape. Once the excluded portions have been edited, the tape should always be reviewed to ensure that the editing was done correctly.

### 18.9 USING THE VIDEOTAPE DEPOSITION AT TRIAL

The usual method of showing a videotape deposition to a jury is to position a monitor and tape deck in front of the jury box for viewing. Like all other aspects of the trial, showing the tape should proceed as smoothly as possible. A few simple steps will make this possible:

- Check out the equipment in advance to make sure it is in proper working order.

- Know how to operate the equipment or have a competent operator present for showing the tape.

- Check out the courtroom in advance to determine how far away from the jury box the monitor should be positioned, where the electrical outlets are located, whether you will need extension cords, and whether glare on the monitor screen or other problems cause the jury difficulty in viewing the tape.

• Determine whether the judge will require a separate monitor.

Try to show the tape following a break so you have an opportunity to set up the necessary equipment without disrupting the trial. During the actual showing, either counsel or the judge should explain to the jury what they are about to see and that the witness is unable to testify at the trial.

Leave the courtroom lights on during showing unless darkness is necessary to prevent glare on the television screen. A dark room and the hypnotic effects of television are too much of a temptation to sleep.

Often the lawyers, having already seen the tape, will leave the room or prepare for the next witness during the videotape showing. Do not do this. If counsel is asking the jury to pay attention to the tape, they should demonstrate that the tape is worth watching by also paying attention.

Since appellate courts will rarely take the opportunity of reviewing the videotape testimony shown to the jury, it is wise to introduce into the record a stenographic transcript of the tape for purposes of appeal.

There is a temptation in presenting videotaped depositions to use the biggest television screen available in order to make an impression and to capture the jury's attention. Several negative aspects of this approach should be considered.

A large screen is where Americans, including jurors, watch movies; it is where Star Wars and Indiana Jones take us on fantastic flights from reality. The simple fact that the image is larger than life serves to remove it from reality and, since the jurors probably do not have such a giant screen television in their homes (although home TV's get larger all the time), its unfamiliarity also makes its images less real. Furthermore, the big screen tends to dominate the room, even the courtroom, so that the video portion of the trial might well be seen as completely separate from the rest of the trial. Additionally, the high-technology approach of the big screen television may distract the jurors from the content of the testimony. Finally, the time and effort needed to set up the large screen television is an intrusion which may be resented by the court and jury; it certainly raises greater expectations in the jury that the video will be entertaining and significant.

In comparison, the use of several small televisions avoids most of these problems. Average size televisions are where Americans, including jurors, get their news every evening. The technology is so commonplace that little attention is paid to the medium and it is so unobtrusive that it can be present in the courtroom throughout a trial without distracting the jurors' attention or diminishing the import of other portions of the trial presentation. Several small televisions give each juror a clear view, and additional sets can be provided to allow the judge and opponent to view at the same time without any awkwardness. Many of the issues regarding display of the videotape are solved by so-called "high-tech courtrooms" that come fitted with monitors, computer jacks, evidence cameras, and the like. In using of these courtrooms, care should be taken to review the judge's particular rules regarding the use of the equipment.

## 18.10 DEFENDING A VIDEOTAPE DEPOSITION

We have previously discussed some of the considerations concerning defending a videotape deposition. For instance, if your opponent schedules a videotape deposition of a witness before adequate opportunity to prepare a cross-examination has been had, a request for continuance of the deposition date or notice of a stenographic discovery deposition should be considered.

The major concern in defending a videotape deposition is to ensure the taping is fair and is not done in such a way as to make either the witness or counsel appear in an unfair and unflattering light. Be vigilant against distorting camera angles, close-ups of the witness that show the pores on their noses and every drop of perspiration, and other such tricks. If opposing counsel is less than fully trustworthy, consideration should be given to requiring continuous taping of the deposition with a time/date counter to avoid any later disputes about whether material has been inappropriately deleted.

Finally, while appropriate objections should be made, courts have been known to saddle the defending attorney with the cost of editing out an excessive number of objections. Even more draconian is the practice of some courts of not permitting the tape to be edited, but allowing the jury to see the behavior of the defending attorney. Therefore, be particularly aware of how objections may appear to the judge or jury.

# CHAPTER NINETEEN

## EXPERT DEPOSITIONS[1]

*An expert is someone from out of town who
carries a briefcase.* —Anonymous

## 19.1 PREPARING TO DEPOSE THE EXPERT

Preparation for the deposition of the opponent's expert should begin with a review of the expert report and the "voluntary disclosures" required under Rule 26. Graduate students are inexpensive, talented support in this preparation. Despite tantalizing anecdotal evidence, the *curriculum vitae* is least likely to provide effective cross-examination material, and the information can be easily checked outside the deposition. Conferences with consulting and testifying experts provide rich sources of questions for the deposing expert at the deposition. Two timelines—one that shows the historical events giving rise to the lawsuit and the other that shows the history of the opposing expert's involvement from first contact through the anticipated completion of the work—are important tools during preparation and at the deposition itself.

### 19.1.1 Expert discovery.

As the attorney's thoughts turn toward discovery of the facts and opinions held by the opponent's experts, he should not overlook the discovery devices that are available in addition to depositions. Most federal courts routinely require Rule 26(a) voluntary disclosures, which provide some information about the expert, along with expert reports, which provide much more information about the expert's opinions and bases (if they are done properly). Of course, those expert reports will

---

1. This chapter is adapted from Chapters 6, 7, and 8 in *Effective Expert Testimony*, 2d ed. (NITA 2006).

normally not be obtained until perhaps ninety days before trial, and therefore they cannot be relied upon to guide other discovery efforts or trial preparation. Interrogatories are a poorly conceived device for obtaining useful information for two simple reasons: (1) there is no practical opportunity for follow-up questioning, so incomplete or less useful answers can be clarified; and (2) the responses, while signed by a party, are prepared by attorneys. More properly, the attorney should recognize that, just as one party's word processor creates the interrogatory set, the other party's word processor creates the response to that interrogatory set. This society is rapidly reaching the time (awaiting perhaps only the widespread availability of high-speed modems) when word processors will merely talk to one another and accomplish useless interrogatory discovery without the cumbersome intervention of attorneys. With regard to requests for admissions, their usefulness is minimal before the expert deposition, but they can be particularly useful to pin down specific opinions, assumptions, and bases if more specificity is needed for trial.

Again, turning to graduate students and their role as non-consulting experts, one technique counsel can use is to assign the students the role of preparing the expert report of the opponent. The student will have to research the facts and the case from the perspective of the opposing party and can provide counsel with questions, learned texts, and treatises the opposing expert may use in preparing her report. Counsel should read these texts and treatises to gain expertise for questioning the opposing expert in deposition.

Graduate students are invaluable because they provide an inexpensive source of sophisticated labor to review the transcripts of prior testimony, which have been identified through the 26(a) disclosures. With the availability of computerized legal research, the attorney should not feel limited by the four-year period for which Rule 26 mandates the opposing party must disclose expert trial or deposition testimony. (The mandated contents of the report are a "floor," not a "ceiling," for disclosures.) Later at deposition, the attorney should feel free to ask the expert about testimony given beyond those four years, just as he may ask about publications authored beyond the ten-year period stated in Rule 26. Before deposition, the attorney is clearly free to direct his graduate students or other assistants to investigate earlier testimony and earlier publications and to read them all with the issues of the present case in mind. If the attorney has been so fortunate as to find other counsel who have opposed this expert in their cases, they may be able to provide him not only with transcripts but also with copies of exhibits prepared by that expert, or at least used by the expert, which will foreshadow the expert presentation that the attorney is likely to face at deposition and trial. All of this discovery is conducted "outside the rules," to the extent that it is not governed by rule-imposed deadlines or limitations.

Graduate students or other assistants, operating under the loose direction of the attorney or the consulting expert, can also create a complete resume for the opposing expert even before one is received through the discovery process. Publications by the expert, available in specialized libraries, normally provide substantial biographical detail; web sites maintained by educational institutions often proudly boast of the credentials of their faculty; and prior testimony is likely to contain sworn statements or adopted exhibits detailing the expert's credentials. Thus, before a formal *curriculum vitae* has been obtained from the expert, the attorney's informal discovery may have provided him with even more complete information. All of that information can then be run down by graduate students to determine its truthfulness and accuracy. As a result, the trial lawyer's dream of unmasking the expert as never having graduated from Hometown U as claimed may still become reality, but the foundation for such deadly cross-examination will have been laid months earlier before formal discovery even began. (In order to avoid the nightmare of having the same cross-examination happen to his expert witness, the attorney should consider having his graduate students conduct the same kind of search on the credentials of experts he is considering or perhaps has already hired.)

Online research can also be used to find additional instances in which the opposing expert has testified and to find additional cases where the same expert issues have arisen. For example, LexisNexis has a number of ways to search cases to get information dealing with:

- the opposing expert's actual testimony;
- for whom she usually testifies;
- whether her testimony has ever been refused;
- other experts who may have given opinions on the same subject;
- multiple copies of resumes that may have been submitted electronically as exhibits to dispositive motions.

It also provides for searching of news information on the expert and other public record information, including where she lives, property she owns, and other on-line licensing information that might be available. LexisNexis also has a verdict and settlement reporting feature that may also contain information on a given expert or area of expertise. In addition, Google searches may reveal web pages that contain resumes or other publication information not provided in discovery.

From such information, the attorney can often identify material to be used on cross-examination—changes on resume or exaggeration of credentials, the identity of other experts who disagree with the approach being taken, the existence of literature from reliable authorities that contradicts assumptions or approaches being used, and even data problems that challenge the opposing expert's ability to come to the conclusions she is presenting. As an example, in the *Daubert* case, the expert in question, Dr. Done, was amalgamating data from several studies that had been found by experts in other cases to be insufficient as a basis for epidemiological analysis. Done's ability to reach valid conclusions based on the agglomeration of otherwise inadequate data became the central issue in the appeal of the *Daubert* case. These individual prior cases might have been discovered by computer searches directed at the issues rather than at Dr. Done. LexisNexis has a "*Daubert* tracker" feature that can greatly assist in providing updated information relating to *Daubert* issues that have been raised in the subject area of the experts' field of speciality. For instance, you can find cases that will not only help you to prepare to defeat a *Daubert* motion, but also to prepare for a deposition of your opposing expert to help you gain admissions that may keep the expert from testifying.

Clearly, if the attorney has already committed to having a testifying expert, the attorney will spend substantial time with the expert, learning the areas of her field that are relevant to the case and understanding the adversary's position before taking the opposing expert's deposition. The attorney's own expert is of invaluable assistance in reducing the opposing expert's advantages, in shaping the case, and in preparing for all phases of discovery.

---

### Rule 703—Bases of Opinion Testimony by Experts

The facts or data in the particular case upon which an expert bases an opinion or inference may be those perceived by or made known to the expert at or before the hearing. If of a type reasonably relied upon by experts in the particular field informing opinions or inferences upon the subject, the facts or data need not be admissible in evidence. Facts or data that are otherwise inadmissible shall not be disclosed to the jury by the proponent of the opinion or inference unless the court determines that their probative value in assisting the jury to evaluate the expert's opinion substantially outweighs their prejudicial effect.

---

### 19.1.2 Location of the deposition.

If it is possible, the attorney should hold the deposition in the expert's own office or building. The deposition may be interrupted from time to time as the expert's regular work intrudes, but the attorney will have the opportunity to learn more about the expert, her approach to matters, and her other interests. The titles of books on the expert's shelves, the identity of her colleagues down the hall, the photographs of handshaking politicians on the wall—all of these give some additional clues to the personality and allegiances of this witness. They may not amount to much—if anything at all—but once again, why give up a possible advantage, no matter how small?

An additional reason to hold the deposition at or near the expert's office is that her files will be more accessible, and the attorney may have the opportunity to see and use underlying materials at the deposition for which he would otherwise have to wait. Certainly, the normal exchange of expert interrogatory responses and underlying data may provide a good deal of material before the deposition, but the attorney is not interested only in what the expert and the opposing counsel have concluded are the underlying support. For example, it is also quite enjoyable and profitable to review the material that the expert considered but rejected because it did not provide support to the expert's opinion. If the attorney is in the expert's office, he is more likely to obtain such materials. On the other hand, if he is insecure about his own level of knowledge, there are advantages to seeing after his own comfort and convenience. Controlling where the expert sits and what she looks at during the deposition (what view she has from the conference room window), and protecting the session from interruption, can all lead to a more complete and accurate understanding of what the expert has to say.

A party who identifies an expert as a likely witness at trial will normally be obligated to present that expert for deposition within the jurisdiction of the forum court or at the expert's normal place of business. By agreement (including the expert's agreement), the expert deposition may be held almost anywhere. If faced with a dispute, the forum court is likely to defer to the expert's convenience, especially if the expert is only occasionally a witness and is normally engaged in the practice of her profession. In other words, it is appropriate for the deposing attorney to choose his preferred location for the expert's deposition and to negotiate to gain that location, but he is limited in his ability to insist upon it.

### 19.1.3 Preparing for the deposition.

There is a lot the attorney can do to prepare himself to take an opposing expert's deposition. Two or three weeks before the expert deposition, the attorney should begin his preparation by immersing himself in the relevant information—the data, the reports, the statistics, the engineering data, the depositions of the fact witnesses, the expert's writings, the expert's teachings, the findings of the graduate students—all the information that may provide grist for the deposition mill. The attorney should participate in discussions with the consulting expert and assistants (graduate students or others) in which he raises possible lines of deposition inquiry and expert response so he not only practices following up but also becomes familiar with the "scientific, technical, or other specialized knowledge" that is the subject of the expert's opinion. In further preparation, counsel should be reviewing legal theories, which have probably by this point been sharpened by motions to dismiss and motions for summary judgment.

On the defense side, the elements of the affirmative defenses should be analyzed. In addition, the attorney should research the law of evidence to determine whether there are any particular standards that must be met by the opinion of the opposing expert. For example, in a medical malpractice case, must the opinion include knowledge of the local standard of care, or in a legal malpractice case, must the opinion display knowledge of the level of practice within a particular legal specialty like antitrust counseling or products liability prosecutions? There may be cases where the methodology to be employed by the expert is dictated by statute or prior cases. In a patent case where she is computing damages due to infringement, the expert may be required to state them in terms of reasonable royalties that were lost by the patent-holding party.[2]

With a lay witness, the review of legal theories would be sufficient for that portion of deposition preparation, but with an expert the lawyer must proceed to review the "scientific, technical, or other specialized" theories being offered by both her expert and the expert to be deposed. Herein lies a great part of the challenge and charm: for a short time during the deposition, it is the lawyer's goal to be as expert as the expert in the narrow slice of her field that is involved in the case. The lawyer should indeed adopt the persona of the ignorant (but interested) student as he deposes the expert, but that ignorance is largely feigned. The lawyer must be sensitive to the nuances of the expert's opinions,

---

2. *See Georgia Pacific Corporation v. U.S. Plywood Corporation,* 318 F. Supp. 1116, 1121 (S.D.N.Y. 1970), *modified,* 446 F.2d 295 (2d Cir. 1971), *cert. denied,* 404 U.S. 870, 92 S.Ct 105, 30 L.Ed.2d 114 (1971).

to those small changes in assumptions or facts that result in major changes in conclusions, and to those studied choices of words that are an attempt to mask or avoid weaknesses or unfavorable alternatives. The lawyer is seeking to become attuned to the relevant science to the point where he can identify occasions when the expert has substituted judgment for knowledge, assumptions for facts, faith for understanding, or opinion for truth. The consulting expert is the lawyer's greatest ally in this preparation; the testifying expert may be less useful because of concerns about exposing her to worries about unfavorable theories and marginally provable fact. In developing this very narrow but intense understanding of the relevant science, the lawyer must position himself to unmask what is non-science—those factors of judgment and discretion, of bias and prejudice, of interest and ignorance which allow the opposing expert to disagree with the proponent's expert while wrapping that disagreement in a cloak of apparent scientific certainty.

### 19.1.4 Brainstorming on themes and facts.

One device the attorney can use to get to that level of preparation is to brainstorm the case with his graduate students, associates, and consulting experts. Brainstorming is the process of encouraging a group to call out, without argument or disagreement, facts that are good or bad for the case; scientific approaches that are helpful or harmful; areas of expert strength or weakness; data that is supportive or unsupportive; or themes that are attractive or unattractive. It is often helpful to brainstorm around a whiteboard or easel in order to capture the contributions of the group and to discover connections, themes, and theories, that will provide the attorney with a unifying theory of attack or will identify areas of his ignorance.

The purpose in avoiding argument or critical comment about contributions in a brainstorming session is twofold. First, the recipient of a negative comment will be reluctant to voice his thoughts on the next point; second, even an ignorant comment may spark an insight by another member of the group—a valuable insight that may be lost if the original ignorant comment is suppressed. Therefore, until the ordering or ranking portion of the session has been reached, the person facilitating the brainstorming session must actively work to avoid negative comments from all members and to encourage universal participation. One additional way to help structure the brainstorming session is to impose a time limit to the brainstorming. The time limit will provide assurance to the more compulsive types in the group that the creative process will eventually come to an end and will allow them to participate with an eye toward more structured analysis.

After the brainstorming has been completed, organization begins. One way to organize the facts, opinions, data, and approaches is to place the material on a time line. The time line can be constructed according to when key facts occurred in the case; or it can be constructed to reveal when opinions were reached by the opposing expert in relation to the acquisition of information about these facts. Time lines are also useful for telling the lawyer what he knows and what he does not know. Look at the time line and ask what caused the events to occur and also what facts, approaches, and opinions do not appear or were not used by the expert or by the party on the other side. Policies and procedures, which may have been in place but were not followed, may not show up on the time line, but the time line should signal the lawyer to ask about whether those policies and procedures existed. ("Time line," as used here, refers to a horizontal array of information organized chronologically from left to right.)

### 19.1.5 Time lines.

During deposition preparation, the lawyer should prepare a time line and redraft it until he is comfortable that it displays known and relevant information organized correctly by date. Reduce this time line to a size that can be kept available during the deposition, so when the expert refers to events, the lawyer can locate them on the time line easily, add them to the time line if necessary, and determine their relationship to the other historical incidents that make up the dispute being litigated. *Post hoc ergo propter hoc*, "after which therefore because of which," is indeed a logical fallacy (just because bullfrogs come out after it rains does not mean it rained bullfrogs); however, causes do precede effects (bullfrog [cowfrog] eggs precede bullfrogs), and until the chronological relationship of events is understood, the cause-and-effect relationship may remain undiscovered. One additional reason to prepare a time line is it can be used as a jumping-off point for creating a storyline—what the lawyer tells the jury that will appeal to their common sense as to what happened, why it happened, and how it compares with their intuitions and experience. Preparing a two-paragraph, chronological statement that answers the question "What is this case about?" encourages the lawyer to focus on the forest and not on a selected tree or two.

### 19.1.6 The fourteen document rule.

As further preparation for taking the opposing expert's deposition, the attorney must review and become intimately familiar with the important documents in the case—those that support his client's position and those that challenge it. Especially where the attorney is working with documents recording scientific information—laboratory notes, chemical analysis, engineering diagrams, critical path flow charts, econometric calculations, medical charts—there is extraordinary comfort in having at the deposition a well-annotated copy of the document in question, where the annotations are a result of careful review by the attorney and the consulting expert. Such review begins with the consulting expert explaining the document to the attorney line by line, entry by entry, number by number, describing sources for each entry and providing meaning to each entry. As the consultant guides the attorney through the document, the attorney should annotate his copy, so eventually he is able to present an explanation of the document in the same detail as the consultant. At deposition, it is not the attorney's goal to disclose his thorough knowledge of the documents, but that thorough knowledge allows him to recognize instances where the opposing expert has inadequate or mistaken knowledge and may be relying upon the document with consequently mistaken conclusions.

When the entire case is presented to the jury, there will be no more than fourteen documents that will sway the jury's verdict—in part because it is too difficult to consider more documents than that and to keep them separate; in part because the jury will be satisfied to select one document from a group as representative of the case and will use it while ignoring the others; and in final part because, while lawyers tend to overcomplicate cases, juries act to reduce them once again to their proper dimensions. (In other words, some cases are as simple as "who hit who first?") In the deposition preparation, the attorney must deal with more than the ultimate fourteen documents—he might not be able to identify which fourteen those are—but he should not overcomplicate his preparation or the deposition by attempting to master (and then to question) all aspects of all documents. Clearly "all documents" will not be the subject of cross-examination at trial. Life is too short!

---

**Expert Depositions in a Nutshell**

✦ Opinions
✦ What did you do; why did you do it; how did you do it; what result did you get; what effect did that have on your opinion?
✦ Learned treatises
✦ What assumptions did you make?
✦ What did you not do?
✦ Curriculum vitae

---

### 19.1.7 The goal of expert deposition.

As a final step in preparing to take the deposition of the opposing expert, the lawyer must determine his goal. There are times when he will be taking the expert's deposition purely for discovery—to learn the opinions and bases, the methodology, and the conclusions that she is preparing to state at trial. When such pure discovery is the goal, the lawyer should remind himself that open questions are his sharpest tool: who, what, when, where, how, why, tell us, describe, explain. These questions force the expert to speak in more than monosyllables and, in the best of deposition worlds, encourage the building of a rapport between the attorney and the opposing expert as counsel plays his role of ignorant but interested student.

Another goal—not inconsistent with pure discovery but normally pursued after the discovery portion of an expert deposition—is theory testing: laying before the opposing expert different portions of the expert's explanations and opinions to learn in advance of trial the opposing expert's avenues of challenge to the attorney's expert case or to produce admissions, concessions, and narrowing of issues. For example, the attorney could ask the opposing expert, "Professor Jones, am I correct then that you have no fault with the use of a critical path methodology in determining the cause for the construction delay? Instead, your only disagreement with plaintiff's expert involves the proper reading of the blueprints to determine the number of structural steel units that should have been purchased?" In a medical malpractice case where the question is whether the plaintiff's epilepsy was caused by a motorcycle accident, the attorney might ask the opposing expert, "Doctor, your opinion is the plaintiff's epilepsy is idiopathic—of unknown origin. Of the factors that are potential causes of epilepsy, which factor do you believe is the most likely cause of the plaintiff's epilepsy, even though you cannot select one as the cause?" The lawyer might ask the opposing expert, "If the cause of the plaintiff's epilepsy is not idiopathic—and please accept that for the moment, at least hypothetically—then will you agree that the most likely cause was traumatic head injury?"

A third reasonable goal in taking the deposition of an opposing expert is to test cross-examination—that is, to try part or even all of an interrogation that challenges the expert in her credentials or opinion testimony. The benefit is the attorney can learn about defenses the expert may have during cross-examination and then try to avoid those defenses during trial. The detriment is the expert is alerted to that possible line of cross and will be more prepared to meet it. If, however, the attorney has weighed these possible results and determined that the line of cross is too tenuous to use without some confirmation that it will work, then he has little to lose by testing it during deposition. In addition, the purpose of the cross could be to persuade opposing counsel to settle the case by demonstrating the weakness of his expert.

Finally, in the best of all worlds, the deposition cross can lead to a motion for summary judgment, which may dispose of the case.

Occasionally, counsel will seek to punish an opposing expert during the deposition by extending its length or increasing its heat, as though the witness has committed some crime by daring to appear for the other side or daring to hold contrary opinions. The theory seems to be the witness will rethink her decision to testify because the deposition was so unpleasant and cross-examination is yet to come. A strong argument exists that deposition questioning designed with this goal in mind is improper and perhaps unethical because it is not the role of counsel to delay the proceeding, to sanction witnesses, or to take a position merely to harass, annoy, or embarrass the witness.

### 19.1.8 Expert admissions.

Using the deposition of the opposing expert to confirm known facts serves the purpose of limiting the dispute—at least the dispute between the experts—and perhaps facilitating a settlement or accelerating the end of the trial. Creating a record at the expert deposition of facts on which the expert relies as true for the purposes of her analysis makes it virtually impossible for the opposing party to contest those facts during motions practice or at trial. (Indeed, a close reading of Federal Rule of Evidence 801(d)(2), especially sections C and D, has persuaded a number of courts that a party's expert makes party admissions when she speaks at deposition. As a technical matter, facts accepted as true (and admitted as such) by the opposing expert at her deposition need not be the subject of requests for admission under Federal Rule of Civil Procedure 36 because they would already be party admissions by operation of Federal Rule of Evidence 801(d)(2).)

## 19.2 DEPOSING THE EXPERT: STRATEGIES

Open questions seeking new information remain the recommended approach for expert depositions. While experts possess some advantages over lay witnesses at trial, the trial attorney often can turn those apparent advantages to his own use. Experts often feel constrained by factors beyond the lawsuit, such as a need to maintain their mainstream position in their profession, which can be used to bring them back from extreme positions. The deposition of the opposing expert provides an opportunity to discover "reliable authorities" that may provide material to be used at trial as evidence under Federal Rule of Evidence 803(18). By making the expert think of him as an ignorant but very interested student, the attorney will encourage her to teach him what he needs to know.

### 19.2.1 Deposing experts: strategies.

The single best piece of advice on deposing the opposing expert is, "Do not assume you know any answers the expert will give." When Albert Einstein was asked, "What do you consider the most powerful force in the universe?", anyone at all familiar with Einstein and his work might reasonably have guessed that his answer would be "gravity" or "mass times the speed of light squared"—or, if one were of a particularly philosophical bent, "the human mind." All are consistent with general knowledge about Einstein, and yet all would be incorrect assumptions. Einstein's actual answer: "Compound interest." The interesting thing about this Einsteinian answer is it tells more than just what Einstein saw as a potent force—it tells about Einstein himself, about his sense of humor, his perspective on himself, his work in relation to common people and their problems, and his ability to differentiate between the abstractions of a relativistic universe and the unavoidable financial realities of everyday life. By asking Professor Einstein at deposition, "What do you consider the most powerful force in the universe?" instead of, "Is it your opinion that gravity is the most powerful force in the universe?", the attorney creates an opportunity to see into Einstein's mind. "The human mind is dark to those of us who attempt to look into it and to most of us who attempt to look out from it."[3] How presumptuous of attorneys to believe they can accurately predict the answers to complex questions as analyzed by experts with opposing viewpoints, when those who study the human mind suggest people cannot even understand their own motivations.

### 19.2.1 Expert's advantages.

As the attorney approaches the opposing expert for her deposition, he should recognize that, as an expert, she has some substantial advantages that she brings to the process—advantages the attorney can sometimes diminish or turn to his advantage at deposition and trial.

---

3.   Carl Gustav Jung.

**Expert's Advantages**

◆ They are experts.
◆ They are not intimidated by the process.
◆ They can hide behind their expertise.
◆ Trial work is more lucrative than office or classroom work.
◆ They are more highly educated than lawyers.
◆ They like to teach.

One of the expert's primary advantages is she has superior knowledge in her field—superior to the lawyer, superior to her own counsel, and superior to everyone involved in the case. If the direct and cross-examination at trial had as its purpose to allow the jury to decide whether the lawyer or the opposing expert were the better geologist, endocrinologist, or mathematician, there would be little contest (and little purpose to holding the trial at all). But that is not the purpose of the trial or of the expert's testimony at the trial. Instead, she is there to offer her specialized assistance to the trier of fact, who will attempt to resolve a dispute that touches upon some small portion of her field of expertise. And in that small portion, for a very short time while the attorney and expert face one another, he may be equally expert. The attorney can improve his chances of holding his own by carefully choosing the areas of confrontation on cross-examination. The lawyer has no obligation to examine the expert on every facet of her knowledge or even in any facets that support her opinions in the case. As the attorney working in his own arena, he is entitled to ask questions limited to those areas in which the expert is factually ignorant, mistaken, or poorly prepared. If the attorney has been able to identify such areas through deposition and other discovery, he has negated the expert's advantage of superior knowledge in her field.

A second advantage possessed by the expert is that she is not intimidated by the discovery and trial process. Either she has gone through it before and understands that it is normally not fatal, or she has discussed the process with the counsel presenting her, and because she is educated and intelligent, she recognizes her limited exposure to inconvenience, embarrassment, or ridicule. While the lay witness approaches cross-examination with some trepidation (except for business people with the phrase "assistant to" in their titles, who seem to believe they are the embodiment of all business acumen), the expert generally looks forward to the challenge, relishes the intellectual exchange, and often prefers the excitement of the courtroom to the perceived drudgery of the classroom, laboratory, or doctor's office. (There are some experts who are wary of the process because they have learned how public the deposition can be. They have learned that what they say in one case can come back to haunt them in another. These experts are not intimidated by the deposition process, but they can become overly cautious and overly concerned about choosing the right words, with the result that they can appear hesitant and evasive.)

The fact that many experts are not intimidated by the deposition or trial process, however, is not an unmitigated advantage to them. That same fear or concern in lay witnesses serves to make those witnesses more cautious about allowing the deposing attorney to develop a rapport or to encourage them to speak freely. "Unintimidated" experts, on the other hand, may lose sight of the deposing attorney's goal, which is to find means to diminish the expert's credibility or to challenge the bases for the expert's opinions. Because they think they understand the process, because they think they cannot be seriously challenged, because they think they are safe within their own field, experts at deposition may be more willing to provide explanations and lengthy answers, to volunteer information, and to educate their ignorant but interested student. Therefore, if the deposing attorney can remember to smile, nod, lean forward, maintain eye contact, and ask open questions in his genuine search for illumination from the expert, the expert may allow her teaching instincts and her passion for her subject to outweigh the caution that her counsel has been advising for the previous three months.

Another advantage possessed by an expert when she appears in the legal field is that her compensation for preparation and expert testimony is normally much greater than anything she can earn back in the classroom, laboratory, or doctor's office. Sometimes in deposing a lay witness, the attorney can look across the table and, by a raised eyebrow or tilted chin, communicate that he is willing to stay at the deposition table for the next four days if she is not more forthcoming in her answers to his questions. With an expert, however, such a message is met with only a smile as she rapidly calculates how many payments on her BMW those four additional days of testimony represent. The deposing attorney can turn this to his advantage because the willingness of the expert to stay in the deposition longer results in the expert being willing to provide more complete answers and explanations. The expert's counsel cannot successfully shut off the flow of information by reminding the expert that volunteered facts or opinions extend the deposition, because extending the deposition may seem like a fine idea to the expert. There is also a certain athletic quality to depositions where the lawyer should have an advantage: stamina. This is the ability to listen and to do the hard work of "corralling" the expert about her opinion. Although the expert may be willing to stay, she may not be as able to go the distance as well as the deposing attorney.

Experts may also derive some comfort from their belief that if they encounter a question they do not want to answer, they can hide behind their expertise by using jargon, by insisting upon hyper-technical definition of terms, or by discussing the premises and conditions they claim to see as being built into the question to a point where the examiner has forgotten what the question was and has literally lost his ability to determine whether it was ever answered at all. For example, when asked whether the assumed shape of the curve showing the receipt of profits for a project was more an ascending ramp than a descending ramp, an econometrician might answer:

> Well, counsel, that question presumes more information than is readily available on the few facts you seem to be implying, and without engaging in substantial efforts at crafting a regression equation that produced a large enough $R^2$ to give us some comfort, an acceptable degree of confidence, perhaps at the 95 percent level, we will be unsure whether we are dealing adequately with problems of heteroskedasticity or multicolinearity.

This use of jargon to avoid answering the question can be dealt with and turned into some advantage for the lawyer. The expert, in using such jargon, is counting on the lawyer's unwillingness to show his ignorance by asking for explanations. She presumes (with some good reason for many trial attorneys) his ego will keep him from admitting that he is unable to determine whether she has answered his question and he will therefore go blindly forward. Because the attorney is already in the role of the interested but admittedly ignorant student, he should feel no shame in admitting his ignorance, and when faced with jargon and other expert-speak, he should say, "I'm sorry. I don't understand that last answer. Can you help me? What do you mean by regression analysis? What do you mean by $R^2$? What do you mean by large enough $R^2$? What do you mean by heteroskedasticity? Why should we be concerned about that in your analysis?" The attorney should continue with this line of questioning until he has called upon the expert to define all of the terms and has demonstrated that he has the patience and intent to cure his apparent ignorance with detailed questions. Whether the expert has been intentionally trying to dissemble by hiding behind the jargon of her expertise or has merely forgotten that English is the language in which she is normally expected to converse, the lesson will eventually become clear to her: this is the attorney's arena, she will answer the questions, and neither the attorney's ignorance nor his desire to get on with life will prevent him from slicing through her attempts at obfuscation.

In a survey conducted a few years ago, psychological researchers attempted to identify the greatest fear of American adults—a fear that caused them to wake up from nightmares in a cold sweat. The researchers anticipated (a mistake had they been dealing with experts) that they would learn adult Americans feared most the death of a loved one—spouse or child, their own death, or destruction of their home or possessions. Instead, they found the single greatest fear of American adults was public speaking. The normal American may worry for days about her need to make a presentation to a committee at work, the parent-teacher association, or the library board. (Trial lawyers, of course, relish the opportunity to speak in public and abuse it as often as possible; therefore, counsel's own experience as a trial attorney should not be taken as indicative in any way of the experience or concerns of human beings.)

Expert witnesses, like trial lawyers, have largely overcome the fear of public speaking. They have put themselves in a position in their professions that requires them to make public presentations—not only in the trial courtroom but more routinely in the classroom or before professional organizations. While some may still get the sweaty palms and a racing pulse adrenalin can produce, many of the experts the attorney encounters in the courtroom are as comfortable as he at presenting their viewpoints from the stand. In sum, they like to teach.

The fact that experts like to teach may give them an advantage at trial, but if the attorney can successfully encourage them to teach at the deposition with him in the role as student, the experts will ultimately give more information than their counsel would prefer. Giving the expert a whiteboard to use to explain her analysis at deposition may also encourage her to drop into a teaching role. Instead of remembering that the lawyer is seeking material to use to diminish their credibility and undermine their opinions, they may come to think it is their responsibility and obligation to teach him—to repeat, to simplify, to analogize, and to instruct until they are confident the attorney understands even the most esoteric and sophisticated aspects of their methodology and conclusions. As a result, their advantage has been turned to the lawyer's advantage.

### 19.2.3 Expert vulnerabilities.

> **Expert's Vulnerabilities**
>
> ◆ It is the lawyer's arena.
> ◆ They cannot resist teaching.
> ◆ You know how to use FRE 803(18).
> ◆ Their time is finite and the universe is infinite.
> ◆ They must rely on assumptions.
> ◆ They are concerned about consistency.
> ◆ They worry about facts they do not know.

Experts have other vulnerabilities, which should be exploited at deposition. An important one is that their time to devote to this particular engagement is finite, while the universe of information is infinite. Therefore, experts must always admit there is more that could have been done and more that could be known. While they may claim it is only a remote possibility that their opinion would be changed if they knew those unknown facts or had done those undone tasks, the attorney may be able to present a sufficient number of such facts and tasks to make it appear to the jury as if the experts have left their job unfinished. As an example, at deposition of a damages expert in a wrongful death action, the attorney asks the expert to identify all the people to whom she has talked in gathering information to use in calculating the future income stream, which is then reduced to present value. She answers she has talked to the decedent's superiors at work, others in the same field of work, professors who were familiar with the decedent's potential, and other experts who studied the decedent's field of employment to determine the likelihood of its economic growth. The attorney asks if there were any others to whom she spoke, and in various forms he asks again and again. She finally states clearly and without condition that she has identified everyone to whom she spoke, but she has not identified the decedent's husband. With this deposition foundation, the attorney is prepared for cross-examination at trial, which makes this apparently undone task seem significant and inexcusable:

> Q. Professor Delaney, I understand from your direct examination that you spent approximately 217 hours working for plaintiff's counsel in this matter.
>
> A. Yes, I believe that's correct.
>
> Q. And of those 217 hours, I imagine you spent, what, perhaps twenty-four hours—that is, three work days—talking with Sheila Foley's husband? That would be three days out of about twenty-six?

A.  No, I didn't. I …

Q.  Well, is it fair to say you spent at least one day talking with Carl Foley?

A.  Well, no, what I'm trying to say is …

Q.  Well, if not one day of conversation, then I presume you had some substantial correspondence with Mr. Foley. Letters back and forth, asking him for information, is that right?

A.  No, I talked to Sheila Foley's bosses and co-workers and professors. I talked to people in her computer science field . . .

Q.  So, Professor Delaney, the simple fact is in all of those hours—those 217 hours—that you spent trying to figure out how much money the plaintiff should get from the hospital, you never even spent five minutes talking to her husband about her plans to work or have a family or make other decisions about her life? Is that correct?

A.  I never talked to him.

Q.  Well, Professor Delaney, who decided you wouldn't talk to Sheila Foley's husband? You or the attorneys you were working with?

Another problem for experts that makes them vulnerable to cross-examination is some information, necessary for their work in the case, is simply not knowable. As an example, Professor Delaney in the wrongful death case is attempting to calculate the present value of the future income stream. Part of that calculation involves future interest rates, future inflation rates, and future discount rates. While these can be estimated, they cannot be known. A typical approach for an expert in such a position is to look at those same values for a similar past period; if she is projecting income for a twenty-year period in the future, she may take the average inflation rate (or discount rate or interest rate) for the immediate past twenty years. But this is not the same as knowing. The average is almost certain to be incorrect when compared to the actuality (twenty years from now), and any reasonable expert will always admit this. Nevertheless, they have little choice but to assume the past average (or some other proxy) will be a sufficiently close approximation to the future actual rate that the figures generated will be reasonably close to accurate. There is no other way to do the calculation.

In such a situation, the expert cannot logically be faulted for relying on assumptions; indeed the attorney's own expert may have to rely on assumptions, albeit different and (from the attorney's perspective) more reasonable assumptions. Of course, the attorney may have already made the decision that he is not going to present an expert—this is normally more an option for a defendant's counsel than for a plaintiff's counsel—because he does not want to lend credence to the "pseudoscience" being hawked by the plaintiff. For example, presenting his own expert to challenge plaintiff's expert witness who seeks to testify as to the emotional distress damages the plaintiff suffered in a sexual discrimination case may lend too much weight to those damages.

In challenging an expert, the attorney must remember there are many ways to diminish the opposing expert's testimony without putting his own expert on the stand. Therefore, if the lawyer is concerned with giving credence to the science represented by the opposing expert by presenting an expert in that questionable field himself, he may instead consider challenging the accuracy of the facts the opposing expert is relying upon; the reasonableness of alternative assumptions she could have made; the sources of data she did not consult; the learned treatises that do not support her conclusions; her sketchy record of publications; and the dependence of her conclusion on the honesty and truthfulness of those who have reported the facts to her. In other words, the psychologist testifying in the case alleging sexual harassment depends to an extraordinary extent upon the truthfulness of statements made by the claimed victim as that victim purports to describe her experiences; the child abuse expert must rely on the truthfulness and memory of young children as they are encouraged to describe unpleasant experiences; the damages expert testifying for the plaintiff in a patent infringement case must accept as accurate the plaintiff's statements regarding the success with which he would have marketed the product had the infringement not occurred.

In the *Texaco-Pennzoil* case, the defendant wanted to avoid a damages presentation of its own because it did not want to give credence to the plaintiff's liability case, and when the jury found it liable, it left them with no alternative to the plaintiff's gargantuan damage figure. However, this problem can be ameliorated in several ways: by presenting alternatives through cross-examination of the opposing expert; by identifying other assumptions and introducing through that opposing expert recalculations based on those other assumptions; by identifying information the expert did not take into consideration and then asking the expert to agree that such information might well reduce her damage calculations; by pointing out to that expert instances in which a conclusion crucially depended upon the truthfulness of a single witness; or by other circumstances which put the expert's figures in doubt, thereby providing the jury with an alternative figure or an indication of the direction of appropriate change.

One tie-in between expert testimony and the overall theme of the case is whether the expert has made an unreasonable assumption. The unreasonableness of that assumption can affect not only the credibility of the expert on the damages calculations, but also the overall credibility of the opponent's case. The trial lawyer can eventually argue if the expert is wrong about damages or if her assumptions are fanciful, what else is she making up to support the story she is telling?

Unlike lay witnesses, experts bear the burden of belonging to a profession; they feel themselves to be part of a larger whole, and while they may wish to stand out as superior when compared to their colleagues, they have no desire to stand out because they are outliers—that is, because they are espousing such extreme positions that few, if any, of their colleagues agree with them. Thus, as much as they are able while fulfilling the terms of their engagement (which require them to support their principal's case), they will try to remain consistent with the mainstream beliefs and approaches in their field. For example, the lawyer may be more apt to get an agreement that the texts and treatises his expert relies on are authoritative (for purposes of Federal Rule of Evidence 803(18)) if he asks about them in general before he has highlighted to the expert her disagreement with those sources. In fact, if the expert believes the attorney is examining her credentials by asking about her familiarity with authoritative texts, she may be more willing to demonstrate she has a broad knowledge of authoritative literature in the field—much more willing than she would have been if the lawyer had foreshadowed his intention of reviewing that literature to determine whether she was being consistent with it.

A further aspect of the expert's desire to appear consistent is her constant concern that she not say anything in the case which contradicts something she has said in another case or in some of her own publications. As a result, while the attorney is focusing on three pages of transcript and four pages of two articles that the attorney has identified as possibly useful on cross-examination, she is worrying about all twenty-three of her articles and the four cases in which she has given both deposition and trial testimony, and she is wondering whether she should have her graduate student assistant review them all again or perhaps cancel her vacation and review them herself.

## 19.2.4 *Daubert* and deposition strategy.

In situations where the opposing expert's report fails to contain the facts or data sufficient to support the opinion under *Daubert* that the opinion must be the product of a reliable methodology, and relevant to the issues in the case, the deposing lawyer is presented with some strategic choices. One choice is to "sandbag" the expert and not depose at all, waiting to challenge the expert at the time the expert's opinion is offered. This approach is tempting where the deposing lawyer will not be presenting expert opinion of his own, so the opposing expert will not be tipped off to the potential *Daubert* challenges that exist in her opinion. After all, it is the duty of the expert to put into the report the information she relies on in reaching her opinion, and it is her duty to supplement her report, if necessary, before trial.

However, the downside of this approach is that most courts want evidentiary issues handled pre-trial and to learn ahead of time if there are *Daubert* challenges in the works. It is also in the court's discretion to let the expert supplement her report if the court believes the interests of justice are served by it.[4] In the end then, the court may grant leave to supplement and the sandbagging attempt will fail.

A second approach could be to bring a motion *in limine* or a summary judgment motion, again arguing under *Daubert* that the expert's opinion is insufficient. Of course, under this approach the expert is put on notice and any further testing or supplementing that might be done, will be done, and affidavits of those results will be produced.

The best approach is to depose the expert and try to both expose insufficiencies and learn whether the expert has any answers to these insufficiencies. The strategy here is to discover what might be done to test the data, or improve the sufficiency of the data, or develop a known or knowable error rate, or to determine if the methodology used was peer-reviewed. If this work has been done, or peer review occurred, but has not been provided, you discover why it has not been done, or whether the results from the missing tests showed insufficiency of the data, or opinion, or who did the peer review. This last approach is particularly effective when your expert has done the missing tests or analysis, or has a methodology that has been peer-reviewed. (Her failure to provide that information earlier may also preclude some or all of her testimony.)

The last approach is based on the belief that it is better to know whether the expert will be able eventually to provide sufficient sup-

---

4.   Fed.R.Evid. 102.

port, than not to know what the expert's answer will be. It favors discovery over sandbagging, in order better to get at whether the opposing expert will be able to withstand a *Daubert* challenge.

## 19.3 DEPOSING AND DEFENDING THE EXPERT: TACTICS

The seven most useful answers are still pertinent, and the expert must be cautioned to tell the truth—briefly, unless *Daubert* requires otherwise.

In taking the opposing expert's deposition—especially today when the time available for experts' depositions is limited by rule, court order, expense, or all three—the opinions and bases should be extracted as early in the deposition as possible. The expert should be asked to describe her methodology and bases in detail and articulate fully all the indicia of reliability the questioner deems pertinent. The funnel technique, which moves from wide-open questions seeking new information to confirmation of known information and to testing of one's theories, is especially valuable with experts. Opposing experts may be encouraged to lecture about their opinions and methods if the deposing attorney assumes the role of an ignorant but interested student.

### 19.3.1 Deposing experts: tactics.

Many attorneys start the deposition of the opposing expert with a detailed examination of the expert's background.[5] Other attorneys spend a great deal of time taking the expert through a chronological recitation of how they were hired, what they were shown, what they were asked to do, and what they did before reaching their opinion. There are several disadvantages with both of these approaches. In these days of limited time for depositions and increasing expense, especially for expert depositions, the judgment should be made to postpone those areas that are less likely to be informative, are less likely to lead to material for cross-examination, and have a greater tendency to antagonize the expert and keep the expert from becoming the teacher. Additionally (especially with respect to the credentials), this material is easily checked by graduate student assistants outside of the cumbersome and expensive deposition or discovery process. Finally, in her

---

5. Some attorneys call this a *curriculum vitae* even when they are referring to it in front of the jury. Casual empiricism suggests many jurors no longer speak Latin; some attorneys avoid the problem with Latin by referring to this as a resume; indeed, French is not Latin. "List of credentials" may derive from Latin (or French or Greek) but it is currently English and, therefore, to be preferred.

preparation by opposing counsel, the expert was told, "They'll probably spend the first hour or so, maybe two, asking about your resume, when we first contacted you, and what we told you. That's fine; it gets us almost all the way to lunch before we have to deal with any hard stuff." If the attorney behaves as predicted, he increases the expert's confidence in both herself and her counsel.

Choose another topic, an important topic—one that the expert is most concerned about and one that must concern the attorney also. Ask the most important question first. In other words, ask the expert for her opinions. Her opinions are what distinguish her from the opposing expert. Her opinions are information the attorney absolutely must know in order to prepare for trial. Her opinions are something she would much rather talk about after she has settled into the process and has become accustomed to the lawyer's techniques and tempo. Her opinions are not what she wants to talk about immediately. So ask for her opinions first.

Begin the opposing expert's deposition by asking her for all of her opinions. Ask her to list them all before going back to ask for any individual opinion to be explained or for the bases for the opinion. The learning theorists say this provides the glass into which the expert will pour her opinion, or the framework in which the expert will organize her presentation to the attorney. Such a preview of the structure of the deposition provides comfort on a number of levels. It provides comfort to the attorney because he can keep track of where he is, so he can proceed in terms of importance by covering those things that are most important to him before getting to things that are of lesser importance. It provides comfort to the expert because it allows her to time the information she gives and to organize it to teach efficiently the lawyer what she knows and how she arrived at her opinions. This statement of opinions at the outset essentially becomes her teaching notes, so she can proceed in an organized fashion if counsel impresses her as a student whom she wants to educate. Of equal importance, however, is the fact the attorney must learn the expert's opinions at the deposition, even if he learns nothing else; he could forego learning about aspects of her credentials or publications, her familiarity with his expert, or the details of her initial engagement if time requires that he leave some questions unasked. Of course, the attorney may go in armed with the expert report, which in theory contains the expert's opinions and identifies information being utilized. The danger of leaving the deposition with opinions undisclosed has therefore been somewhat reduced. Nevertheless, it is dangerous to rely on the opposing counsel and his expert to present a report with an adequate and informative statement of her opinions; because the lawyer chooses the order of examination at the deposition, he should ask the expert for her opinions first and check to insure that those opinions are no more and no less than the opinions disclosed in the expert report.

### 19.3.2 Key questions to ask experts.

Therefore, here is question number one at the expert deposition:

1.   "What opinions have you reached in this matter?" After obtaining the expert's statement of each of her opinions and taking the normal steps to satisfy himself that the expert's knowledge of those opinions has been exhausted ("Are those all your opinions? You stated four opinions. Are there any more?" "Is there anything that would help you recall whether there are other opinions?" "Did you make any notes on your opinions?"), the attorney should go back to the first (or most important, or most interesting) opinion, restate it for the expert, ask her to agree that it is her opinion, and then ask for the bases for that opinion. In questioning about the bases, the next five questions are recommended. (The first four are useful in having any witness describe any process.) Indeed, they are the same four or five questions counsel would use on direct examination to have an expert describe how she came to her opinions.

2.   What did you do?

3.   Why did you do that?

4.   How did you do that?

5.   What result did you get?

6.   What significance does that result have to your conclusion?

Ask these same five questions to obtain the basis for each opinion. Ask the expert whether she has any additional bases. Are these all the bases? Did she make any notes on her bases? These questions make certain that the lawyer has exhausted the expert's knowledge on relevant points.

There are many checklists on the market which claim to anticipate and to cure all problems that might be encountered in expert depositions. Some are interesting. Nevertheless, there is no real substitute for careful preparation, thoughtful questioning, attentive listening, and intensive follow-up. If the lawyer reads his questions in order to insure coverage while deposing an expert witness, the danger is he will become wedded to that list and not respond to the cues, the body language, the voice tone, and the pauses that signal the need for follow-up not contained in his notes. When used properly, reasonable checklists can stimulate counsel's memory or imagination, but he must always be aware of the danger that they will become a crutch, keeping him from creative leaps and useful insights. If the deposition on oral examination could be reduced to a checklist, it would be called "deposition on written interrogatories."

Nevertheless, in the spirit of offering a quick and pithy checklist to provide for those in need, take the six questions above ("What are your opinions?" and the five follow-up questions) and these four following questions. Together they comprise a reasonably effective ten-question deposition:[6]

7. What are the reliable authorities in this field?

8. What assumptions did you make in your work?

9. What tasks did you not do?

10. Is this your current and accurate list of credentials?

One caveat: the attorney may be tempted by an ambush strategy to look at an expert's report for things she has left out—a key area of necessary qualifications, the absence of evidence that she can meet the *Daubert* standard, or no mention of requisite legal standard. The attorney may think it is better to choose not to depose on these areas at the deposition and to bring these omissions up at a pretrial hearing. (Some courts will require the lawyer to bring up *Daubert* objections pretrial in order to preserve them for appeal.) Counsel may decide to surprise his opponent with his *Daubert* challenge, rather then put him on notice of the witness's failing in time for the expert to supplement her report for trial. Counsel may think that at the pretrial it will be too late for the plaintiff to rebut the challenge and that the witness may be barred from testifying, which may allow counsel to succeed on a motion to dismiss.

Note, however, the parties are allowed to supplement testimony at Federal Rule of Evidence 104 conferences with affidavit testimony—just as one can in a summary judgment motion. In addition, today most judges will not take the time to hold a hearing. They will

---

6. These ten questions are not intended to present the be-all and end-all of thorough deposition questioning of an opposing expert. They are not intended to capture all the nuances of subtle and sophisticated questioning of an expert, which may reveal hidden biases, untold assumptions, or imperfect calculations. They are intended to illustrate the main areas which must be covered in any expert deposition (with questions 1 through 9) or which can be covered (with question 10).

instead order the parties to fully disclose the experts and present the depositions as their basis for opposing or supporting expert opinions. In other words, if you have support for your expert, you should present that support during the expert's deposition. (You should prepare a direct examination, complete with things considered, reliability of methodology, consistency of application, and sufficiency of data.) In opposing, you should prepare a cross that demonstrates unreliability of methodology (for example, lack of peer review, lack of known error rate, lack of consistency in application, or insufficient data). If the court allows the party to supplement the expert's testimony with additional affidavits, then it is probably a better strategy to ask the witness about gaps in her opinion before she has a chance to talk with her counsel. In other words, trial by ambush often does not work. It is better if the lawyer tests his theories in the deposition so he is not surprised by the response when it is too late to rebut. If, however, no such supplementation will be allowed, then counsel's silence on such *Daubert* points at the deposition may be appropriate.

In other words, where the court will treat the deposition as the basis for the *Daubert* ruling, the deposition should be conducted as though it were a deposition to preserve the expert's testimony for trial. The proponents of the expert's testimony have an affirmative burden to put on sufficient evidence to establish the reliability of their expert case. If they do not do so, counsel might choose not to ask questions on those essential points, saving them for a motion for preclusion, dismissal, or summary judgment.[7]

Here is another list of useful questions:

---

7.  See *Celotex v. Catrett*, 477 U.S. 317 (1986).

> ## Expert Depositions
> ## (All Things Considered)
>
> ◆  Who in the field agrees with you?
> ◆  Who in the field disagrees with you?
> ◆  What did you review and choose not to rely on?
> ◆  Who selected the documents you reviewed?
> ◆  Did you ask for anything you did not receive?
> ◆  Peer reviewed publication
> ◆  Error rate
> ◆  Acceptance in the field (*Frye*)
> ◆  Testability
> ◆  Relevance (fit)
> ◆  Reliability (scientific foundation)
> ◆  Foundation for learned treatises
> ◆  Prior testimony (and rejections)
> ◆  Sources of income, percentages

### 19.3.3 Federal Rule of Evidence 803(18): learned treatises as non-hearsay.

Federal Rule of Evidence 803(18) is, on its face, merely another exception to the rule excluding hearsay statements. In practice, however, it has become a powerful tool for cross-examining and impeaching expert witnesses. Rule 803(18) permits the introduction of relevant material from written sources which have been demonstrated as being reliable, either by the testimony of the proponent's expert, testimony of the opposing expert, or through judicial notice. The deposition provides an excellent opportunity to find out whether the opposing expert will concede the existence of reliable sources in the field, which can be obtained and reviewed for use on cross-examination. The beauty of this approach to cross-examination is that the author of the materials, although functioning as a source of expert information in the case, is never hired, paid, deposed, or cross-examined. Indeed, she may not even earn a royalty on her book because the book itself does not come into evidence, but is merely read in pertinent part (and then can be returned to the library).

At the deposition, ask the expert what sources she consults when she has a question in her field and wants a second opinion; ask about materials she directs students to if she is a teacher; ask about publications by colleagues in her company or college department—especially if she considers them useful. Her counsel may have warned her about the phrase "reliable authority," so she may shy away from providing useful answers to questions that use that language, but other language such as "useful," "well researched," or "important" will be sufficient at trial. Putting the language aside, if the expert admits to using a publication in her own work, she can hardly argue at trial that the work was not a "reliable authority." A question which is always useful at expert or lay depositions may be particularly appropriate in the learned treatise context: "How would you find out?" Ask where the expert would look for other approaches, where she checks her approach, where she looks for additional issues or to find more sources of help. If she needed help in understanding, where would she go? Did she cite sources in her last article because she thought their science was sound? Such a foundation should logically be sufficient under Rule 803(18).

Then, on cross at trial, her attention can be called to a portion of a text that favors questioning counsel, reminding the expert that at deposition she considered the writing to be sound or authoritative. When read on the record, the material comes in as substantive evidence, whether she agrees or not.

The *Daubert* decision and its progeny have changed expert deposition practice substantially. In supporting expert testimony, the attorney must demonstrate reliability of the methodology; in challenging expert testimony, the attorney has new authority to question the methodology. All of this adds new importance to the question of why an expert did a particular study or took particular steps because that "why" provides the connection (or exposes the lack of connection) between what the expert did and the results and their utility. In examining the reliability of methodology, counsel is looking for the reasonable causal nexus between what was done and the conclusion reached. When the logic of that connection is lacking (as when the astrologer opines the angle between Saturn and Jupiter makes Sagittarians prone to impulsiveness in matters of love), the court is likely to find that the reliability of the methodology has not been shown. Where an analysis of the logic is beyond the capability of a non-expert court (as where the attorney is dealing with questions of subatomic physics), counsel may profitably utilize proxies for an understanding of the causal relationships. For example, *Daubert* suggests that the lawyers and trial courts look at whether an approach has been subjected to peer review through publication. Peers will understand the process and point out errors when they read about it. Attorneys should look at whether there is a known or knowable error rate; they can argue that it is too high even without knowing what causes the errors.

The point here is the deposition is the opportunity to gather information for *Daubert* challenges or to prepare counsel's own expert to defend the reliability of her methodology.

### 19.3.4 Expert witnesses: preparation.

Just as he does with lay witnesses, the attorney must prepare his own expert witness for her deposition. Although most expert witnesses have had substantial public speaking experience—in the classroom, at professional meetings, or even in the courtroom—they still may suffer from some anxiety at the thought of giving a deposition in front of lawyers in a very formal and artificial environment. Therefore, as with lay witnesses, some preparation time should be spent in reducing the witness's anxiety about the process so the witness is able to perform to her potential. In order to reduce the witness's anxieties, it is appropriate to simplify the witness's task: to educate her that the only task she has at the deposition is to tell the truth briefly. "Telling the truth briefly" means providing accurate answers to questions after they are understood (and clarified if necessary) and stating those accurate answers in as short a way as possible without unnecessary adverbs, adjectives, parentheticals, footnotes, asides, qualifications, and other unrequested information.

Many expert witnesses are at first frustrated by the attorney's direction that they abstain from volunteering additional information. Counsel will hear statements like, "Why can't I just tell them what I know? Won't that shorten the whole process?" Or, "I know where they're going. Why don't I just tell our side of this case?" In fact, the more volunteered information the expert includes, the longer the deposition will be.

In persuading expert witnesses that volunteering will not shorten their deposition experience, the attorney might keep in mind the story of Sir Richard Francis Burton and John Hanning Speke, two noted explorers from the United Kingdom (Burton was Welsh, Speke was English) who are credited with exploration of the Nile to its source at Lake Victoria. (Richard Francis Burton gained considerable fame for the discovery of the source of the Nile as Lake Tanganyika, although subsequent disclosures reveal he may have turned back before the source was found and left John Hanning Speke to continue the trip up the White Nile to its eventual source in Lake Victoria. Speke, in fact, was seriously wounded by natives during these trips, apparently being shot with arrows in both arms and legs and pierced through his body with a spear. Nevertheless, he continued.) Each time the Burton-Speke party reached a fork in the river in their travels, they had to establish a base camp and send part of their party to explore what seemed the less likely branch of the river. When that less likely branch was found to end in a backwater (so that it obviously was not the source of the Nile), that portion of the party returned to the base camp, and, they all packed up and continued their exploration on the other branch of the river.

This is exactly how attorneys have learned to ask questions. Every time the witness uses an adjective or adverb or supplies additional unrequested information, the attorney feels compelled to inquire about those forks in the testimony. For example, if the question is, "What color is your car?", the witness should answer, "Green." If instead the witness, expert or lay, responds, "I have a green Buick," then the attorney is faced with a fork: should he ask about why the color green was chosen, why a Buick was chosen, or does he already know enough to recognize the Buick does not lead him into any relevant waters? The attorney should find a way to use the Burton-Speke story or his own examples to persuade the expert witness that she does not want to assist in turning her deposition into the exploration of the Nile River. Counsel does not want to spend weeks and months at this deposition—he wants to spend hours, or perhaps a day. In the diagrams on the accompanying page, note the similarity between a map of the Nile and a "map" of a typically volunteered answer to the question, "What color is your car?" The attorney might think about using those diagrams to make that point with his witness.

At this point in the litigation, the attorney has already gone over with the expert where she fits into the case and how she supports his theories in the case. For plaintiffs in particular, she may have a task of showing certain essential elements in the case through her testimony. For example, a causation witness must testify at the deposition that she believes to a reasonable degree of certainty in her field that there is a causal relationship between the plaintiff's injury and the alleged conduct of the defendant. The attorney should be careful in his "do not volunteer" instructions to his expert because he does not want to create hesitancy on her part to testifying fully and completely about her opinions on the causation elements or the elements upon which he has the affirmative burden of proof. One way to test this distinction between volunteering unnecessary facts and volunteering essential facts is to use role-playing. By role-playing, the attorney can review with the witness and teach her how she is to make the distinction between inappropriate volunteering and contributing those essential elements she needs to contribute.

Role-playing takes a fair amount of time. It involves the analysis of where the questions are likely to come from the opposing counsel and asking the follow-up questions the opposing counsel is likely to ask once the answers are given. In the role-playing, the attorney should fully explore the answers his expert is giving to questions that touch on the essential elements of the case, and he should display a skeptical attitude toward the answers the witness gives so the rehearsal can truly prepare the expert for the skepticism of the opposing counsel. The practice sessions can show the expert the dangers of unnecessary volunteering and encourage the expert to be as forceful and direct as possible in those areas where her testimony is crucial to the case.

### Map of the Nile

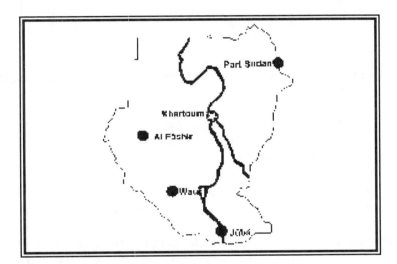

## Car-toum

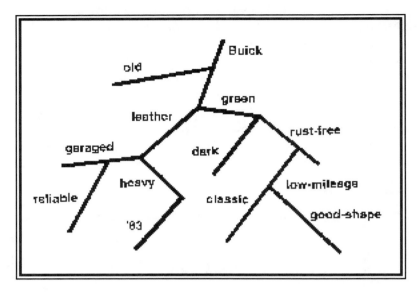

In the role-playing, one of the attorney's jobs is to diagnose what type of expert witness he has. Is she a "master of the universe" type, where she comes off in an arrogant way, an over-confident way, and a way that shows she has lost her objectivity as she becomes involved in the case? Or, on the other hand, is she overly hesitant, too concerned with making a mistake, and worried she may have said things in earlier testimony that will be used against her either in this case or in her professional arena? As the attorney gauges where this expert falls in the spectrum between the "master of the universe" and the "nervous" witness, his job is to bring her to the middle—confident where she needs to be confident and careful where she needs to be careful.

In role-playing with the witness, counsel should be aware it can be confusing to the witness to have the attorney, whom she has come to rely upon as her guide through this process, adopt a cross-examination mode—more strident tone of voice, more piercing eye contact, more insistent demeanor—as he assumes the role of opposing counsel at deposition. If he has adequate support, the attorney should consider asking one of his colleagues to assume the role of opposing counsel and to do the deposition examination while the attorney sits right alongside the witness as he will at the deposition, providing physical and moral support. Indeed, counsel should sit on the same side of the witness and keep the same side at the deposition so she becomes accustomed to having him there as her support. That way at the deposition, where the room and some of the people will be different, at least the important things—the attorney's physical and supportive relationship to her—will be the same. If the attorney must conduct the role-playing deposition himself, he should not do it from his chair alongside the witness—that is, the chair for her supporter instead, he should leave that chair, sit down across the table where the opposing counsel will be, and conduct the cross-examination from there. As soon as he has finished the moot examination, the attorney should make it clear that he is leaving the adopted role of the opposing counsel, and he is once again her supporter. Counsel should come back to his chair on her side of the table, turn partially to face her in this more friendly position, and remind her that he is in his normal role as her counsel.

As the attorney prepares the expert witness to be examined at deposition, he should also review important documents, but here "important" has a slightly different meaning. The expert has some responsibility to explain to the opposition the interpretation and significance of the various documents she has considered as part of her analysis. Although she may consider many of those documents much less important than the core she intends to use in her trial testimony, nevertheless, she must be able to demonstrate a familiarity and comfort with them as opposing counsel asks her to explain them. Therefore, the attorney will have to spend more time on documents with the expert than he did with lay witnesses. The attorney should have the expert explain the documents to him until he fully understands them. Then he should have her explain them again. The expert should make notations—even if they are decipherable only by her—on her copies of the documents if she feels making such notations will make her more comfortable and less likely to forget the relationship between various figures, entries, numbers, formulas, or other documentary content. Although the attorney should recognize such notations may be discovered at the deposition as opposing counsel sees the expert referring to them, the presence of such notes is not improper, and the expert should have little concern about using them. Understand, however, that these are minimal notes, not major dissertations or caveats written in margins or along the bottom of several succeeding pages.

If the expert is asked at deposition if she reviewed documents in preparing for the deposition, her answer will obviously be yes. Almost invariably, the opposing counsel will ask for identification of the documents reviewed. If counsel knows those documents have already been turned over to opposing counsel as part of the voluntary disclosure of expert materials, or as attachments to the expert report, or in the remainder of documentary discovery, there seems little harm in allowing the expert to identify the documents she reviewed. It is going to come out in any event, and there is no need to tie up any expert in some procedural battle between the attorney and opposing counsel. If he still has the possibility of protecting attorney work product even though it has been revealed to the expert and is therefore "considered" by her, then he must make his objections at the deposition and direct the witness not to answer the question, or the attorney work product immunity from production will be lost.

The introduction of the word "considered" to the expert discovery vocabulary in Rule 26(a)(2)(B) has created a significant distinction between the law relating to lay witness preparation and the law relating to expert witness preparation. With respect to the lay witness, documents that were reviewed but did not refresh the witness's recollection—either because they were not effective in refreshing recollection or because the witness's recollection was already sound and did not need recollection—are not subject to production simply because they were reviewed. They may be subject to production because they were called for under requests for documents or subpoenaed or for other reasons, but their review in preparation for the deposition does not in and of itself make them produceable. However, that is no longer the case with expert witnesses. By reviewing the document in preparation for deposition, the expert puts that document in the category of all the other documents she has "considered," and considered material must be produced, subject only to the exceptions in jurisdictions that still permit some protection of materials which were considered but are also attorney work product.

During the role-playing with the witness when the attorney or a colleague has been questioning her as though he were opposing counsel at the deposition, the attorney is trying to provide her with an opportunity to answer questions in a deposition context. Therefore, counsel probably used open questions—questions beginning with who, what, where, when, why, how, tell us, describe, or explain. By asking these questions of the opposing expert at a deposition, the attorney causes the expert to craft an answer and to provide content to it. This is good practice for the expert and is an appropriate way to proceed in role-playing. As has been mentioned, this is also the attorney's opportunity to talk to the witness about the need for her to explain each of her opinions fully so it will be understandable to the judge if this record is used as support in dispositive motions.

Nevertheless, because of the way most attorneys ask questions at deposition, the attorney and the expert can expect the overwhelming majority of questions asked will be closed: did you, do you, have you, were you, was there, and the like. The expert needs guidance on how to answer these closed questions. While the attorney's advice to the expert has been to state her opinions fully and completely, it may not be appropriate to attempt those full and complete explanations in response to questions that call simply for yes or no, or for some small bit of information like the color of her car or the name of her graduate student assistant. When faced with those closed or small questions, the expert must be authorized to give specific and equally narrow answers, so despite her desire to be heard and understood on her core issues, she accepts as proper the one- or two-word answers that dispose of the questions. Therefore, counsel should review with the expert the same "seven answers to most deposition questions" that he has provided to lay witnesses.

---

**The Seven Answers to Most Deposition Questions**

✦ Yes.
✦ No.
✦ Green.
✦ I don't know.
✦ I don't remember.
✦ I don't understand the question.
✦ I need a break.

---

The first and second answers to most deposition questions for expert or lay witnesses will be "yes" and "no." If the attorney has framed the question so it is properly answered with a yes or no answer, the expert is entitled to answer it "yes" or "no," and she has no responsibility to create a better question in her head than the one asked and to provide that better answer. Indeed, an attempt to improve upon the questioning attorney's performance will only lead to a longer deposition.

The third best answer to most deposition questions is "green": "What color is your car?" "Green." The witness should not answer, "My car is a green Buick." The questioner did not ask what kind of car the witness had, but on learning that it is a Buick, the questioner may feel compelled to ask both about the decision to buy a green car and the decision to buy a Buick. By referring back to the Nile diagram of the answer, "I have an old green Buick," the attorney can see that single question can present so many forks that the question, which could have been answered with the word green, is now taking up fifteen minutes or half an hour of deposition time.

The fourth answer to most deposition questions is, "I don't know." This answer is particularly hard for experts to give in deposition simply because they are experts, and as experts, they believe they are under some obligation to know everything that touches on the subject matter of their expertise. After all, they are thinking no self-respecting expert is ignorant, and the answer "I don't know" discloses ignorance. The expert must be assured in preparation that she is not obligated to know everything; in fact, there are things not related to her analysis that she legitimately does not know; there are matters she did not investigate and therefore does not know; and there may be other testimony or information in the case she has not yet reviewed and therefore does not know. The best answer in such circumstances is "I don't know." For proof, simply consider the alternative. If the expert professes knowledge when she has none, nothing but trouble is ahead of her. Therefore, she must be authorized to state, "I don't know" when that is the most accurate answer.

A closely related answer at deposition is, "I don't remember." This answer is distinguished from "I don't know" because it suggests the witness once had the information being sought but can no longer remember. If that is true, this is the best answer for the witness, lay or expert. If the expert says that she does remember some information, which she does not, she will not be able intelligently to deal with the follow-up questions that are sure to come. The way to avoid those embarrassing follow-up questions is to admit without embarrassment, "I don't remember."

No witness, lay or expert, is obligated to answer a question she does not understand. Most attorneys carefully instruct witnesses on this precise point as they approach the deposition. However, it is often the case that they do not tell the witness what to do when the witness does not understand the question. Tell the expert witness she is not obligated to answer any question she does not understand, and if she is asked a question she does not understand, she should say, "I'm sorry. I don't understand your question." Counsel should also tell her to resist what for an expert is an understandable temptation—suggesting ways in which the question could be fixed so she could understand and answer it. The likelihood is if she attempts such repairs, she will simply create more forks in the river—forks the questioner would never discover for himself, which he will feel compelled to explore, and which will further extend the deposition.

The seventh best answer to most deposition questions is simply, "I need a break." If the expert witness for some reason believes that she cannot continue the deposition or if she is not comfortable without taking a break—a break to talk to her attorney, a break to call the office, a break to check on matters at home, a break to use the facilities, a break merely to walk up and down the hall, or a break to stretch and to reflect—then she should say, "I need to take a break." She should say it on the record, either to opposing counsel or in an aside to her attorney. In either event, the result should be the same. The attorney should state, "We're taking a break," and he should stand and take the witness out of the room for a break. Almost inevitably, opposing counsel will object, especially if the break occurs while a question is pending. It is much better deposition practice for the question to be answered before a break is taken. In an aside with the witness, the attorney might inquire if she feels she must take the break before answering the question because there is something about the answer that concerns her—for example, the possibility of a privilege being involved. However, if the witness insists that she have a break before she provides an answer, then the attorney has little choice other than to take that break. He must be available to provide counsel to the witness for matters of privilege or confidentiality, personal or professional, and his relationship with her depends upon her continued confidence in his ability to protect her interests and meet her concerns.

In one sense, there is an eighth answer available at deposition to expert witnesses. An expert may be frustrated by what may fairly be characterized as trick questions, such as questions that ask whether she considered factors that are completely irrelevant to any legitimate analysis. For example, an expert in diamond appraisal may be asked whether she considered prior ownership in assessing the value, or whether she spoke with the woman who was wearing the diamond when it was last photographed; or whether she had ever considered whether there was any relationship between the two words, "carat" and "carrot." Instead of growing increasingly upset with such questions, she should be prepared to come back to her "core" positions, if they are at all responsive. She might say: "Those matters need not be considered, because my opinion depends upon the factors I have mentioned already, including cut, clarity, color, and carats; the demand in the market for diamonds of this particular quality and size; and the availability of such diamonds within a reasonable distance from the location of the purchaser. These items are so important, so overwhelmingly important, that other matters are either relatively trivial or, like the ones you mention, completely irrelevant from a gemologist's point of view. Cut, clarity, color, and carats; demand; and availability: that's what you need, and that's all you need."

Thus, instead of trying to defend whether the suggested additional factors can ever play a role and sometimes must be considered, she emphasizes her core positions and brings the discussion back to a focus with which she is comfortable. In a car accident case, a reconstruction expert, when asked whether he considered the location where the hubcap was found, in a field off the road, might say, "The debris field was wide; nevertheless, the locations of the cars' frames and engines, the heaviest parts, in relation to the skid marks, provided us with sufficient and persuasive data from which to reconstruct the movement of the cars before and after the impact. The location of the hubcap alone could not alter the conclusions we drew from the much more important information about the location of the tons of components we considered, all of which showed that your client's car crossed the center line and then struck the plaintiff's car." Thus, instead of debating whether this or that small piece of evidence, perhaps aberrational, refuted her conclusions, the expert returns the focus to the mass of much more persuasive evidence that gives support to her opinions.

In preparation, the attorney should press the expert to identify the "four pillars" that support her opinions (or the three or five). So long as those pillars remain intact on deposition and cross-examination, she need not worry greatly about bits and pieces of less important evidence, and she should not risk her credibility by trying to argue that, yes, she implicitly considered this, and yes, she implicitly considered that. She should instead consider whether challenges in questions go to her core concepts, the pillars, or whether they are an attempt to get her to make some minor difference seem like it is a major theoretical or methodological dispute. It is when the expert tries to explain everything—the location of every hubcap and license plate screw, the behavior of every diamond-buyer in the market—that she risks overreaching and inconsistencies. Her theme might well be summed up by having her practice saying, "I don't know, and it really doesn't matter, why the hubcap wound up in the middle of the field; but I have spent 300 hours determining why the cars wound up trying to occupy the very same spot on US-91 at 3 p.m. on September 30, and the answer is that your client crossed the center line."

### 19.3.5 Conclusion.

Witness preparation of an expert can no longer be conducted by the "seat of the pants." If an expert is being deposed to rebuff a *Daubert* challenge, the seven "best answers" do not apply. But if the expert is a "master-of-the-universe" type and an egoist, likely to get herself into trouble by her arrogance and verbosity, then she needs "preparation" that involves some drilling to help her keep her answers short. Tailor your preparation advice to the case, the purpose of the deposition, and the personality of the deponent.

APPENDIX A

FEDERAL RULES OF CIVIL PROCEDURE

As amended to December 1, 2005

## V. DEPOSITIONS AND DISCOVERY

**Rule 26.  General Provisions Governing Discovery;
Duty of Disclosure**

**(a) Required Disclosures; Methods to Discover Additional Matter.**

**(1) Initial Disclosures.** Except in categories of proceedings specified in Rule 26(a)(1)(E), or to the extent otherwise stipulated or directed by order, a party must, without awaiting a discovery request, provide to other parties:

**(A)** the name and, if known, the address and telephone number of each individual likely to have discoverable information that the disclosing party may use to support its claims or defenses, unless solely for impeachment, identifying the subjects of the information;

**(B)** a copy of, or a description by category and location of, all documents, data compilations, and tangible things that are in the possession, custody, or control of the party and that the disclosing party may use to support its claims or defenses, unless solely for impeachment;

**(C)** a computation of any category of damages claimed by the disclosing party, making available for inspection and copying as under Rule 34 the documents or other evidentiary material, not privileged or protected from disclosure, on which such computation is based, including materials bearing on the nature and extent of injuries suffered; and

**(D)** for inspection and copying as under Rule 34 any insurance agreement under which any person carrying on an insurance business may be liable to satisfy part or all of a judgment which may be entered in the action or to indemnify or reimburse for payments made to satisfy the judgment.

**(E)** The following categories of proceedings are exempt from initial disclosure under Rule 26(a)(1);

**(i)** an action for review on an administrative record;

**(ii)** a petition for habeas corpus or other proceeding to challenge a criminal conviction or sentence;

**(iii)** an action brought without counsel by a person in custody of the United States, a state, or a state subdivision;

**(iv)** an action to enforce or quash an administrative summons or subpoena;

**(v)** an action by the United States to recover benefit payments;

**(vi)** an action by the United States to collect on a student loan guaranteed by the United States;

**(vii)** a proceeding ancillary to proceedings in other courts; and

(**viii**) an action to enforce an arbitration award.

These disclosures must be made at or within 14 days after the Rule 26(f) conference unless a different time is set by stipulation or court order, or unless a party objects during the conference that initial disclosures are not appropriate in the circumstances of the action and states the objection in the Rule 26(f) discovery plan. In ruling on the objection, the court must determine what disclosures—if any—are to be made, and set the time for disclosure. Any party first served or otherwise joined after the Rule 26(f) conference must make these disclosures within 30 days after being served or joined unless a different time is set by stipulation or court order. A party must make its initial disclosures based on the information then reasonably available to it and is not excused from making its disclosures because it has not fully completed its investigation of the case or because it challenges the sufficiency of another party's disclosures or because another party has not made its disclosures.

**(2) Disclosure of Expert Testimony.**

**(A)** In addition to the disclosures required by paragraph (1), a party shall disclose to other parties the identity of any person who may be used at trial to present evidence under Rules 702, 703, or 705 of the Federal Rules of Evidence.

**(B)** Except as otherwise stipulated or directed by the court, this disclosure shall, with respect to a witness who is retained or specially employed to provide expert testimony in the case or whose duties as an employee of the party regularly involve giving expert testimony, be accompanied by a written report prepared and signed by the witness. The report shall contain a complete statement of all opinions to be expressed and the basis and reasons therefor; the data or other information considered by the witness in forming the opinions; any exhibits to be used as a summary of or support for the opinions; the qualifications of the witness, including a list of all publications authored by the witness within the preceding ten years; the compensation to be paid for the study and testimony; and a listing of any other cases in which the witness has testified as an expert at trial or by deposition within the preceding four years.

**(C)** These disclosures shall be made at the times and in the sequence directed by the court. In the absence of other directions from the court or stipulation by the parties, the disclosures shall be made at least 90 days before the trial date or the date the case is to be ready for trial or, if the evidence is intended solely to contradict or rebut evidence on the same subject matter identified by another party under paragraph (2)(B), within 30 days after the disclosure made by the other party. The parties shall supplement these disclosures when required under subdivision (e)(1).

**(3) Pretrial Disclosures.** In addition to the disclosures required by Rule 26(a)(1) and (2), a party must provide to other parties and promptly file with the court the following information regarding the evidence that it may present at trial other than solely for impeachment:

**(A)** the name and, if not previously provided, the address and telephone number of each witness, separately identifying those whom the party expects to present and those whom the party may call if the need arises;

(B) the designation of those witnesses whose testimony is expected to be presented by means of a deposition and, if not taken stenographically, a transcript of the pertinent portions of the deposition testimony; and

(C) an appropriate identification of each document or other exhibit, including summaries of other evidence, separately identifying those which the party expects to offer and those which the party may offer if the need arises.

Unless otherwise directed by the court, these disclosures must be made at least 30 days before trial. Within 14 days thereafter, unless a different time is specified by the court, a party may serve and promptly file a list disclosing (i) any objections to the use under Rule 32(a) of a deposition designated by another party under Rule 26(a)(3)(B), and (ii) any objection, together with the grounds therefor, that may be made to the admissibility of materials identified under Rule 26(a)(3)(C). Objections not so disclosed, other than objections under Rules 402 and 403 of the Federal Rules of Evidence, are waived unless excused by the court for good cause.

(4) **Form of Disclosures.** Unless the court orders otherwise, all disclosures under Rules 26(a)(1) through (3) must be made in writing, signed, and served.

(5) **Methods to Discover Additional Matter.** Parties may obtain discovery by one or more of the following methods: depositions upon oral examination or written questions; written interrogatories; production of documents or things or permission to enter upon land or other property under Rule 34 or 45(a)(1)(C), for inspection and other purposes; physical and mental examinations; and requests for admission.

**(b) Discovery Scope and Limits.** Unless otherwise limited by order of the court in accordance with these rules, the scope of discovery is as follows:

(1) **In General.** Parties may obtain discovery regarding any matter, not privileged, that is relevant to the claim or defense of any party, including the existence, description, nature, custody, condition, and location of any books, documents, or other tangible things and the identity and location of persons having knowledge of any discoverable matter. For good cause, the court may order discovery of any matter relevant to the subject matter involved in the action.

Relevant information need not be admissible at the trial if the discovery appears reasonably calculated to lead to the discovery of admissible evidence. All discovery is subject to the limitations imposed by Rule 26(b)(2)(i), (ii), and (iii).

**(2) Limitations.** By order, the court may alter the limits in these rules on the number of depositions and interrogatories or the length of depositions under Rule 30. By order or local rule, the court may also limit the number of requests under Rule 36. The frequency or extent of use of the discovery methods otherwise permitted under these rules and by any local rule shall be limited by the court if it determines that: (i) the discovery sought is unreasonably cumulative or duplicative, or is obtainable from some other source that is more convenient, less burdensome, or less expensive; (ii) the party seeking discovery has had ample opportunity by discovery in the action to obtain the information sought; or (iii) the burden or expense of the proposed discovery outweighs its likely benefit, taking into account the needs of the case, the amount in controversy, the parties' resources, the importance of the issues at stake in the litigation, and the importance of the proposed discovery in resolving the issues. The court may act upon its own initiative after reasonable notice or pursuant to a motion under Rule 26(c).

**(3) Trial Preparation: Materials.** Subject to the provisions of subdivision (b)(4) of this rule, a party may obtain discovery of documents and tangible things otherwise discoverable under subdivision (b)(1) of this rule and prepared in anticipation of litigation or for trial by or for another party or by or for that other party's representative (including the other party's attorney, consultant, surety, indemnitor, insurer, or agent) only upon a showing that the party seeking discovery has substantial need of the materials in the preparation of the party's case and that the party is unable without undue hardship to obtain the substantial equivalent of the materials by other means. In ordering discovery of such materials when the required showing has been made, the court shall protect against disclosure of the mental impressions, conclusions, opinions, or legal theories of an attorney or other representative of a party concerning the litigation.

A party may obtain without the required showing a statement concerning the action or its subject matter previously made by that party. Upon request, a person not a party may obtain without the required showing a statement concerning the action or its subject matter previously made by that person. If the request is refused, the person may move for a court order. The provisions of Rule 37(a)(4) apply to the award of expenses incurred in relation to the motion. For purposes of this paragraph, a statement previously made is (A) a written statement signed or otherwise adopted or approved by the person making it, or (B) a stenographic, mechanical, electrical, or other recording, or a transcription thereof, which is a substantially verbatim recital of an oral statement by the person making it and contemporaneously recorded.

### (4) Trial Preparation: Experts.

(A) A party may depose any person who has been identified as an expert whose opinions may be presented at trial. If a report from the expert is required under subdivision (a)(2)(B), the deposition shall not be conducted until after the report is provided.

(B) A party may, through interrogatories or by deposition, discover facts known or opinions held by an expert who has been retained or specially employed by another party in anticipation of litigation or preparation for trial and who is not expected to be called as a witness at trial only as provided in Rule 35(b) or upon a showing of exceptional circumstances under which it is impracticable for the party seeking discovery to obtain facts or opinions on the same subject by other means.

(C) Unless manifest injustice would result, (i) the court shall require that the party seeking discovery pay the expert a reasonable fee for time spent in responding to discovery under this subdivision; and (ii) with respect to discovery obtained under subdivision (b)(4)(B) of this rule the court shall require the party seeking discovery to pay the other party a fair portion of the fees and expenses reasonably incurred by the latter party in obtaining facts and opinions from the expert.

### (5) Claims of Privilege or Protection of Trial Preparation Materials.
When a party withholds information otherwise discoverable under these rules by claiming that it is privileged or subject to protection as trial preparation material, the party shall make the claim expressly and shall describe the nature of the documents, communications, or things not produced or disclosed in a manner that, without revealing information itself privileged or protected, will enable other parties to assess the applicability of the privilege or protection.

### (c) Protective Orders.
Upon motion by a party or by the person from whom discovery is sought, accompanied by a certification that the movant has in good faith conferred or attempted to confer

with other affected parties in an effort to resolve the dispute without court action, and for good cause shown, the court in which the action is pending or alternatively, on matters relating to a deposition, the court in the district where the deposition is to be taken may make any order which justice requires to protect a party or person from annoyance, embarrassment, oppression, or undue burden or expense, including one or more of the following:

**(1)** that the disclosure or discovery not be had;

**(2)** that the disclosure or discovery may be had only on specified terms and conditions, including a designation of the time or place;

**(3)** that the discovery may be had only by a method of discovery other than that selected by the party seeking discovery;

**(4)** that certain matters not be inquired into, or that the scope of the disclosure or discovery be limited to certain matters;

**(5)** that discovery be conducted with no one present except persons designated by the court;

**(6)** that a deposition, after being sealed, be opened only by order of the court;

**(7)** that a trade secret or other confidential research, development, or commercial information not be revealed or be revealed only in a designated way; and

**(8)** that the parties simultaneously file specified documents or information enclosed in sealed envelopes to be opened as directed by the court.

If the motion for a protective order is denied in whole or in part, the court may, on such terms and conditions as are just, order that any party or other person provide or permit discovery. The provisions of Rule 37(a)(4) apply to the award of expenses incurred in relation to the motion

**(d) Timing and Sequence of Discovery.** Except in categories of proceedings exempted from initial disclosure under Rule 26(a)(1)(E), or when authorized under these rules or by order or agreement of the parties, a party may not seek discovery from any source before the parties have conferred as required by Rule 26(f). Unless the court upon motion, for the convenience of parties and witnesses and in the interests of justice, orders otherwise, methods of discovery may be used in any sequence, and the fact that a party is conducting discovery, whether by deposition or otherwise, does not operate to delay any other party's discovery.

**(e) Supplementation of Disclosures and Responses.** A party who has made a disclosure under subdivision (a) or responded to a request for discovery with a disclosure or response is under a duty to supplement or correct the disclosure or response to include information thereafter acquired if ordered by the court or in the following circumstances:

   **(1)** A party is under a duty to supplement at appropriate intervals its disclosures under subdivision (a) if the party learns that in some material respect the information disclosed is incomplete or incorrect and if the additional or corrective information has not otherwise been made known to the other parties during the discovery process or in writing. With respect to testimony of an expert from whom a report is required under subdivision (a)(2)(B) the duty extends both to information contained in the report and to information provided through a deposition of the expert, and any additions or other changes to this information shall be disclosed by the time the party's disclosures under Rule 26(a)(3) are due.

   **(2)** A party is under a duty seasonably to amend a prior response to an interrogatory, request for production, or request for admission if the party learns that the response is in some material respect incomplete or incorrect and if the additional or corrective information has not otherwise been made known to the other parties during the discovery process or in writing.

**(f) Conference of Parties; Planning for Discovery.** Except in categories of proceedings exempted from initial disclosure under Rule 26(a)(1)(E) or when otherwise ordered, the parties must, as soon as practicable and in any event at least 21 days before a scheduling conference is held or a scheduling order is due under Rule 16(b), confer to consider the nature and basis of their claims and defenses and the possibilities for a prompt settlement or resolution of the case, to make or arrange for the disclosures required by Rule 26(a)(1), and to develop a proposed discovery plan that indicates the parties' views and proposals concerning:

   **(1)** what changes should be made in the timing, form, or requirement for disclosures under Rule 26(a), including a statement as to when disclosures under Rule 26(a)(1) were made or will be made;

**(2)** the subjects on which discovery may be needed, when discovery should be completed, and whether discovery should be conducted in phases or be limited to or focused upon particular issues;

**(3)** what changes should be made in the limitations on discovery imposed under these rules or by local rule, and what other limitations should be imposed; and

**(4)** any other orders that should be entered by the court under Rule 26(c) or under Rule 16(b) and (c).

The attorneys of record and all unrepresented parties that have appeared in the case are jointly responsible for arranging the conference, for attempting in good faith to agree on the proposed discovery plan, and for submitting to the court within 14 days after the conference a written report outlining the plan. A court may order that the parties or attorneys attend the conference in person. If necessary to comply with its expedited schedule for Rule 16(b) conferences, a court may by local rule (i) require that the conference between the parties occur fewer than 21 days before the scheduling conference is held or a scheduling order is due under Rule 16(b), and (ii) require that the written report outlining the discovery plan be filed fewer than 14 days after the conference between the parties, or excuse the parties from submitting a written report and permit them to report orally on their discovery plan at the Rule 16(b) conference.

**(g) Signing of Disclosures, Discovery Requests, Responses, and Objections.**

**(1)** Every disclosure made pursuant to subdivision (a)(1) or subdivision (a)(3) shall be signed by at least one attorney of record in the attorney's individual name, whose address shall be stated. An unrepresented party shall sign the disclosure and state the party's address. The signature of the attorney or party constitutes a certification that to the best of the signer's knowledge, information, and belief, formed after a reasonable inquiry, the disclosure is complete and correct as of the time it is made.

**(2)** Every discovery request, response, or objection made by a party represented by an attorney shall be signed by at least one attorney of record in the attorney's individual name, whose address shall be stated. An unrepresented party shall sign the request, response, or objection and state the party's address. The signature of the attorney or party constitutes a certification that to the best of the signer's knowledge, information, and belief, formed after a reasonable inquiry, the request, response, or objection is:

      **(A)** consistent with these rules and warranted by existing law or a good faith argument for the extension, modification, or reversal of existing law;

      **(B)** not interposed for any improper purpose, such as to harass or to cause unnecessary delay or needless increase in the cost of litigation; and

      **(C)** not unreasonable or unduly burdensome or expensive, given the needs of the case, the discovery already had in the case, the amount in controversy, and the importance of the issues at stake in the litigation.

If a request, response, or objection is not signed, it shall be stricken unless it is signed promptly after the omission is called to the attention of the party making the request, response, or objection, and a party shall not be obligated to take any action with respect to it until it is signed.

      **(3)** If without substantial justification a certification is made in violation of the rule, the court, upon motion or upon its own initiative, shall impose upon the person who made the certification, the party on whose behalf the disclosure, request, response, or objection is made, or both, an appropriate sanction, which may include an order to pay the amount of the reasonable expenses incurred because of the violation, including a reasonable attorney's fee.

## Rule 28. Persons Before Whom Depositions May Be Taken

**(a) Within the United States.** Within the United States or within a territory or insular possession subject to the jurisdiction of the United States, depositions shall be taken before an officer authorized to administer oaths by the laws of the United States or of the place where the examination is held, or before a person appointed by the court in which the action is pending. A person so appointed has power to administer oaths and take testimony. The term officer as used in Rules 30, 31 and 32 includes a person appointed by the court or designated by the parties under Rule 29.

**(b) In Foreign Countries.** Depositions may be taken in a foreign country (1) pursuant to any applicable treaty or convention, or (2) pursuant to a letter of request (whether or not captioned a letter rogatory), or (3) on notice before a person authorized to administer oaths in the place where the examination is held, either by the law thereof or by the law of the United States, or (4) before a person commissioned by the court, and a person so commissioned shall have the power by virtue of the commission to administer any necessary oath and take testimony. A commission or a letter of request shall be issued on application and notice and on terms that are just and appropriate. It is not requisite to the issuance of a commission or a letter of request that the taking of the deposition in any other manner is impracticable or inconvenient; and both a commission and a letter of request may be issued in proper cases. A notice or commission may designate the person before whom the deposition is to be taken either by name or descriptive title. A letter of request may be addressed "To the Appropriate Authority in [here name the country]." When a letter of request or any other device is used pursuant to any applicable treaty or convention, it shall be captioned in the form prescribed by that treaty or convention. Evidence obtained in response to a letter of request need not be excluded merely because it is not a verbatim transcript, because the testimony was not taken under oath, or because of any similar departure from the requirements for depositions taken within the United States under these rules.

**(c) Disqualification for Interest.** No deposition shall be taken before a person who is a relative or employee or attorney or counsel of any of the parties, or is a relative or employee of such attorney or counsel, or is financially interested in the action.

## Rule 29. Stipulations Regarding Discovery Procedure

Unless otherwise directed by the court, the parties may by written stipulation (1) provide that depositions may be taken before any person, at any time or place, upon any notice, and in any manner and when so taken may be used like other depositions, and (2) modify other procedures governing or limitations placed upon discovery, except that stipulations extending the time provided in Rules 33, 34, and 36 for responses to discovery may, if they would interfere with any time set for completion of discovery, for hearing of a motion, or for trial, be made only with the approval of the court.

### Rule 30.  Depositions Upon Oral Examination

#### (a) When Depositions May Be Taken; When Leave Required.

**(1)** A party may take the testimony of any person, including a party, by deposition upon oral examination without leave of court except as provided in paragraph (2). The attendance of witnesses may be compelled by subpoena as provided in Rule 45.

**(2)** A party must obtain leave of court, which shall be granted to the extent consistent with the principles stated in Rule 26(b)(2), if the person to be examined is confined in prison or if, without the written stipulation of the parties.

**(A)** a proposed deposition would result in more than ten depositions being taken under this rule or Rule 31 by the plaintiffs, or by the defendants, or by third-party defendants;

**(B)** the person to be examined already has been deposed in the case; or

**(C)** a party seeks to take a deposition before the time specified in Rule 26(d) unless the notice contains a certification, with supporting facts, that the person to be examined is expected to leave the United States and be unavailable for examination in this country unless deposed before that time.

#### (b) Notice of Examination: General Requirements; Method of Recording; Production of Documents and Things; Deposition of Organization; Deposition by Telephone.

**(1)** A party desiring to take the deposition of any person upon oral examination shall give reasonable notice in writing to every other party to the action. The notice shall state the time and place for taking the deposition and the name and address of each person to be examined, if known, and, if the name is not known, a general description sufficient to identify the person or the particular class or group to which the person belongs. If a subpoena duces tecum is to be served on the person to be examined, the designation of the materials to be produced as set forth in the subpoena shall be attached to, or included in, the notice.

**(2)** The party taking the deposition shall state in the notice the method by which the testimony shall be recorded. Unless the court orders otherwise, it may be recorded by sound, sound-and-visual, or stenographic means, and the party taking the deposition shall bear the cost of the recording. Any party may arrange for a transcription to be made from the recording of a deposition taken by nonstenographic means.

**(3)** With prior notice to the deponent and other parties, any party may designate another method to record the deponent's testimony in addition to the method specified by the person taking the deposition. The additional record or transcript shall be made at that party's expense unless the court otherwise orders.

**(4)** Unless otherwise agreed by the parties, a deposition shall be conducted before an officer appointed or designated under Rule 28 and shall begin with a statement on the record by the officer that includes (A) the officer's name and business address; (B) the date, time, and place of the deposition; (C) the name of the deponent; (D) the administration of the oath or affirmation to the deponent; and (E) an identification of all persons present. If the deposition is recorded other than stenographically, the officer shall repeat items (A) through (C) at the beginning of each unit of recorded tape or other recording medium. The appearance or demeanor of deponents or attorneys shall not be distorted through camera or sound-recording techniques. At the end of the deposition, the officer shall state on the record that the deposition is complete and shall set forth any stipulations made by counsel concerning the custody of the transcript or recording and the exhibits, or concerning other pertinent matters.

**(5)** The notice to a party deponent may be accompanied by a request made in compliance with Rule 34 for the production of documents and tangible things at the taking of the deposition. The procedure of Rule 34 shall apply to the request.

**(6)** A party may in the party's notice and in a subpoena name as the deponent a public or private corporation or a partnership or association or governmental agency and describe with reasonable particularity the matters on which examination is requested. In that event, the organization so named shall designate one or more officers, directors, or managing agents, or other persons who consent to testify on its behalf, and may set forth, for each person designated, the matters on which the person will testify. A subpoena shall advise a non-party organization of its duty to make such a designation. The persons so designated shall testify as to matters known or reasonably available to the organization. This subdivision (b)(6) does not preclude taking a deposition by any other procedure authorized in these rules.

**(7)** The parties may stipulate in writing or the court may upon motion order that a deposition be taken by telephone or other remote electronic means. For the purposes of this rule and Rules 28(a), 37(a)(1), and 37(b)(1), a deposition taken by such means is taken in the district and at the place where the deponent is to answer questions.

**(c) Examination and Cross-Examination; Record of Examination; Oath; Objections.** Examination and cross-examination of witnesses may proceed as permitted at the trial under the provisions of the Federal Rules of Evidence except Rules 103 and 615. The officer before whom the deposition is to be taken shall put the witness on oath or affirmation and shall personally, or by someone acting under the officer's direction and in the officer's presence, record the testimony of the witness. The testimony shall be taken stenographically or recorded by any other method authorized by subdivision (b)(2) of this rule. All objections made at the time of the examination to the qualifications of the officer taking the deposition, to the manner of taking it, to the evidence presented, to the conduct of any party, or to any other aspect of the proceedings shall be noted by the officer upon the record of the deposition; but the examination shall proceed, with the testimony being taken subject to the objections. In lieu of participating in the oral examination, parties may serve written questions in a sealed envelope on the party taking the deposition and the party taking the deposition shall transmit them to the officer, who shall propound them to the witness and record the answers verbatim.

**(d) Schedule and Duration; Motion to Terminate or Limit Examination.**

**(1)** Any objection during a deposition must be stated concisely and in a non-argumentative and non-suggestive manner. A person may instruct a deponent not to answer only when necessary to preserve a privilege, to enforce a limitation directed by the court, or to present a motion under Rule 30(d)(4).

**(2)** Unless otherwise authorized by the court or stipulated by the parties, a deposition is limited to one day of seven hours. The court must allow additional time consistent with Rule 26(b)(2) if needed for a fair examination of the deponent or if the deponent or another person, or other circumstance, impedes or delays the examination.

**(3)** If the court finds that any impediment, delay, or other conduct has frustrated the fair examination of the deponent, it may impose upon the persons responsible an appropriate sanction, including the reasonable costs and attorney's fees incurred by any parties as a result thereof.

**(4)** At any time during a deposition, on motion of a party or of the deponent and upon a showing that the examination is being conducted in bad faith or in such manner as unreasonably to annoy, embarrass, or oppress the deponent or party, the court in which the action is pending or the court in the district where the deposition is being taken may order the officer conducting the examination to cease forthwith from taking the deposition, or may limit the scope and manner of the taking of the deposition as provided in Rule 26(c). If the order made terminates the examination, it may be resumed thereafter only upon the order of the court in which the action is pending. Upon demand of the objecting party or deponent, the taking of the deposition must be suspended for the time necessary to make a motion for an order. The provisions of Rule 37(a)(4) apply to the award of expenses incurred in relation to the motion.

**(e) Review by Witness; Changes; Signing.** If requested by the deponent or a party before completion of the deposition, the deponent shall have 30 days after being notified by the officer that the transcript or recording is available in which to review the transcript or recording and, if there are changes in form or substance, to sign a statement reciting such changes and the reasons given by the deponent for making them. The officer shall indicate in the certificate prescribed by subdivision (f)(1) whether any review was requested and, if so, shall append any changes made by the deponent during the period allowed.

**(f) Certification and Delivery by Officer; Exhibits; Copies.**

**(1)** The officer must certify that the witness was duly sworn by the officer and that the deposition is a true record of the testimony given by the witness. This certificate must be in writing and accompany the record of the deposition. Unless otherwise ordered by the court, the officer must securely seal the deposition in an envelope or package indorsed with the title of the action and marked "Deposition of [here insert name of witness]" and must promptly send it to the attorney who arranged for the transcript or recording, who must store it under conditions that will protect it against loss, destruction, tampering, or deterioration. Documents and things produced for inspection during the examination of the witness must, upon the request of a party, be marked for identification and annexed to the deposition, and may be inspected and copied by any party, except that if the person producing the materials desires to retain them the person may (A) offer copies to be marked for identification and annexed to the deposition and to serve thereafter as originals if the person affords to all parties fair opportunity to verify the copies by comparison with the originals, or (B) offer the originals to be marked for identification, after giving to each party an opportunity to inspect and copy them, in which event the materials may then be used in the same manner as if annexed to the deposition. Any party may move for an order that the original be annexed to and returned with the deposition to the court, pending final disposition of the case.

**(2)** Unless otherwise ordered by the court or agreed by the parties, the officer shall retain stenographic notes of any deposition taken stenographically or a copy of the recording of any deposition taken by another method. Upon payment of reasonable charges therefor, the officer shall furnish a copy of the transcript or other recording of the deposition to any party or to the deponent.

**(3)** The party taking the deposition shall give prompt notice of its filing to all other parties.

### (g) Failure To Attend or To Serve Subpoena; Expenses.

**(1)** If the party giving the notice of the taking of a deposition fails to attend and proceed therewith and another party attends in person or by attorney pursuant to the notice, the court may order the party giving the notice to pay to such other party the reasonable expenses incurred by that party and that party's attorney in attending, including reasonable attorney's fees.

**(2)** If the party giving the notice of the taking of a deposition of a witness fails to serve a subpoena upon the witness and the witness because of such failure does not attend, and if another party attends in person or by attorney because that party expects the deposition of that witness to be taken, the court may order the party giving the notice to pay to such other party the reasonable expenses incurred by that party and that party's attorney in attending, including reasonable attorney's fees.

### Rule 31.  Depositions Upon Written Questions

### (a) Serving Questions; Notice.

**(1)** A party may take the testimony of any person, including a party, by deposition upon written questions without leave of court except as provided in paragraph (2). The attendance of witnesses may be compelled by the use of subpoena as provided in Rule 45.

**(2)** A party must obtain leave of court, which shall be granted to the extent consistent with the principles stated in Rule 26(b)(2), if the person to be examined is confined in prison or if, without the written stipulation of the parties,

**(A)** a proposed deposition would result in more than ten depositions being taken under this rule or Rule 30 by the plaintiffs, or by the defendants, or by third-party defendants;

**(B)** the person to be examined has already been deposed in the case; or

**(C)** a party seeks to take a deposition before the time specified in Rule 26(d).

**(3)** A party desiring to take a deposition upon written questions shall serve them upon every other party with a notice stating (1) the name and address of the person who is to answer them, if known, and if the name is not known, a general description sufficient to identify the person or the particular class or group to which the person belongs, and (2) the name or descriptive title and address of the officer before whom the deposition is to be taken. A deposition upon written questions may be taken of a public or private corporation or a partnership or association or governmental agency in accordance with the provisions of Rule 30(b)(6).

**(4)** Within 14 days after the notice and written questions are served, a party may serve cross questions upon all other parties. Within 7 days after being served with cross questions, a party may serve redirect questions upon all other parties. Within 7 days after being served with redirect questions, a party may serve recross questions upon all other parties. The court may for cause shown enlarge or shorten the time.

**(b) Officer To Take Responses and Prepare Record.** A copy of the notice and copies of all questions served shall be delivered by the party taking the deposition to the officer designated in the notice, who shall proceed promptly, in the manner provided by Rule 30(c), (e), and (f), to take the testimony of the witness in response to the questions and to prepare, certify, and file or mail the deposition, attaching thereto the copy of the notice and the questions received by the officer.

**(c) Notice of Filing.** When the deposition is filed the party taking it shall promptly give notice thereof to all other parties.

## Rule 32.  Use of Depositions in Court Proceedings

**(a) Use of Depositions.** At the trial or upon the hearing of a motion or an interlocutory proceeding, any part or all of a deposition, so far as admissible under the rules of evidence applied as though the witness were then present and testifying, may be used against any party who was present or represented at the taking of the deposition or who had reasonable notice thereof, in accordance with any of the following provisions:

(1) Any deposition may be used by any party for the purpose of contradicting or impeaching the testimony of deponent as a witness, or for any other purpose permitted by the Federal Rules of Evidence.

(2) The deposition of a party or of anyone who at the time of taking the deposition was an officer, director, or managing agent, or a person designated under Rule 30(b)(6) or 31(a) to testify on behalf of a public or private corporation, partnership or association or governmental agency which is a party may be used by an adverse party for any purpose.

(3) The deposition of a witness, whether or not a party, may be used by any party for any purpose if the court finds:

(A)  that the witness is dead; or

(B)  that the witness is at a greater distance than 100 miles from the place of trial or hearing, or is out of the United States, unless it appears that the absence of the witness was procured by the party offering the deposition; or

(C)  that the witness is unable to attend or testify because of age, illness, infirmity, or imprisonment; or

(D)  that the party offering the deposition has been unable to procure the attendance of the witness by subpoena; or

(E)  upon application and notice, that such exceptional circumstances exist as to make it desirable, in the interest of justice and with due regard to the importance of presenting the testimony of witnesses orally in open court, to allow the deposition to be used.

A deposition taken without leave of court pursuant to a notice under Rule 30(a)(2)(C) shall not be used against a party who demonstrates that, when served with the notice, it was unable through the exercise of diligence to obtain counsel to represent it at the taking of the deposition; nor shall a deposition be used against a party who, having received less than 11 days' notice of a deposition, has promptly upon receiving such notice filed a motion for a protective order under Rule 26(c)(2) requesting that the deposition not be held or be held at a different time or place and such motion is pending at the time the deposition is held.

**(4)** If only part of a deposition is offered in evidence by a party, an adverse party may require the offeror to introduce any other part which ought in fairness to be considered with the part introduced, and any party may introduce any other parts.

Substitution of parties pursuant to Rule 25 does not affect the right to use depositions previously taken; and, when an action has been brought in any court of the United States or of any State and another action involving the same subject matter is afterward brought between the same parties or their representatives or successors in interest, all depositions lawfully taken and duly filed in the former action may be used in the latter as if originally taken therefor. A deposition previously taken may also be used as permitted by the Federal Rules of Evidence.

**(b) Objections to Admissibility.** Subject to the provisions of Rule 28(b) and subdivision (d)(3) of this rule, objection may be made at the trial or hearing to receiving in evidence any deposition or part thereof for any reason which would require the exclusion of the evidence if the witness were then present and testifying.

**(c) Form of Presentation.** Except as otherwise directed by the court, a party offering deposition testimony pursuant to this rule may offer it in stenographic or nonstenographic form, but, if in nonstenographic form, the party shall also provide the court with a transcript of the portions so offered. On request of any party in a case tried before a jury, deposition testimony offered other than for impeachment purposes shall be presented in nonstenographic form, if available, unless the court for good cause orders otherwise.

**(d) Effect of Errors and Irregularities in Depositions.**

**(1) As to Notice.** All errors and irregularities in the notice for taking a deposition are waived unless written objection is promptly served upon the party giving the notice.

**(2) As to Disqualification of Officer.** Objection to taking a deposition because of disqualification of the officer before whom it is to be taken is waived unless made before the taking of the deposition begins or as soon thereafter as the disqualification becomes known or could be discovered with reasonable diligence.

**(3) As to Taking of Deposition.**

**(A)** Objections to the competency of a witness or to the competency, relevancy, or materiality of testimony are not waived by failure to make them before or during the taking of the deposition, unless the ground of the objection is one which might have been obviated or removed if presented at that time.

**(B)** Errors and irregularities occurring at the oral examination in the manner of taking the deposition, in the form of the questions or answers, in the oath or affirmation, or in the conduct of parties, and errors of any kind which might be obviated, removed, or cured if promptly presented, are waived unless reasonable objection thereto is made at the taking of the deposition.

**(C)** Objections to the form of written questions submitted under Rule 31 are waived unless served in writing upon the party propounding them within the time allowed for serving the succeeding cross or other questions and within 5 days after service of the last questions authorized.

**(4) As to Completion and Return of Deposition.** Errors and irregularities in the manner in which the testimony is transcribed or the deposition is prepared, signed, certified, sealed, indorsed, transmitted, filed, or otherwise dealt with by the officer under Rules 30 and 31 are waived unless a motion to suppress the deposition or some part thereof is made with reasonable promptness after such defect is, or with due diligence might have been, ascertained.

## Rule 33. Interrogatories to Parties

**(a) Availability.** Without leave of court or written stipulation, any party may serve upon any other party written interrogatories, not exceeding 25 in number including all discrete subparts, to be answered by the party served or, if the party served is a public or private corporation or a partnership or association or governmental agency, by any officer or agent, who shall furnish such information as is available to the party. Leave to serve additional interrogatories shall be granted to the extent consistent with the principles of Rule

26(b)(2). Without leave of court or written stipulation, interrogatories may not be served before the time specified in Rule 26(d).

**(b) Answers and Objections.**

**(1)** Each interrogatory shall be answered separately and fully in writing under oath, unless it is objected to, in which event the objecting party shall state the reasons for objection and shall answer to the extent the interrogatory is not objectionable.

**(2)** The answers are to be signed by the person making them, and the objections signed by the attorney making them.

**(3)** The party upon whom the interrogatories have been served shall serve a copy of the answers, and objections if any, within 30 days after the service of the interrogatories. A shorter or longer time may be directed by the court or, in the absence of such an order, agreed to in writing by the parties subject to Rule 29.

**(4)** All grounds for an objection to an interrogatory shall be stated with specificity. Any ground not stated in a timely objection is waived unless the party's failure to object is excused by the court for good cause shown.

**(5)** The party submitting the interrogatories may move for an order under Rule 37(a) with respect to any objection to or other failure to answer an interrogatory.

**(c) Scope; Use at Trial.** Interrogatories may relate to any matters which can be inquired into under Rule 26(b)(1), and the answers may be used to the extent permitted by the rules of evidence.

An interrogatory otherwise proper is not necessarily objectionable merely because an answer to the interrogatory involves an opinion or contention that relates to fact or the application of law to fact, but the court may order that such an interrogatory need not be answered until after designated discovery has been completed or until a pre-trial conference or other later time.

**(d) Option to Produce Business Records.** Where the answer to an interrogatory may be derived or ascertained from the business records of the party upon whom the interrogatory has been served or from an examination, audit or inspection of such business records, including a compilation, abstract or summary thereof, and the burden of deriving or ascertaining the answer is substantially the same for the party serving the interrogatory as for the party served, it is a sufficient answer to such interrogatory to specify the records from which the answer may be derived or ascertained and to afford to the party serving the interrogatory reasonable opportunity to examine, audit or inspect such records and to make copies, compilations, abstracts or summaries. A specification shall be in sufficient detail to permit the interrogating party to locate and to identify, as readily as can the party served, the records from which the answer may be ascertained.

## Rule 34. Production of Documents and Things and Entry Upon Land for Inspection and Other Purposes

**(a) Scope.** Any party may serve on any other party a request (1) to produce and permit the party making the request, or someone acting on the requestor's behalf, to inspect and copy, any designated documents (including writings, drawings, graphs, charts, photographs, phonorecords, and other data compilations from which information can be obtained, translated, if necessary, by the respondent through detection devices into reasonably usable form), or to inspect and copy, test, or sample any tangible things which constitute or contain matters within the scope of Rule 26(b) and which are in the possession, custody or control of the party upon whom the request is served; or (2) to permit entry upon designated land or other property in the possession or control of the party upon whom the request is served for the purpose of inspection and measuring, surveying, photographing, testing, or sampling the property or any designated object or operation thereon, within the scope of Rule 26(b).

**(b) Procedure.** The request shall set forth, either by individual item or by category, the items to be inspected, and describe each with reasonable particularity. The request shall specify a reasonable time, place, and manner of making the inspection and performing the related acts. Without leave of court or written stipulation, a request may not be served before the time specified in Rule 26(d).

The party upon whom the request is served shall serve a written response within 30 days after the service of the request. A shorter or longer time may be directed by the court or, in the absence of such an order, agreed to in writing by the parties, subject to Rule 29. The response shall state, with respect to each item or category, that inspection and related activities will be permitted as requested, unless the request is objected to, in which event the reasons for the objection shall be stated. If objection is made to part of an item or category, the part shall be specified and inspection permitted of the remaining parts. The party submitting the request may move for an order under Rule 37(a) with respect to any objection to or other failure to respond to the request or any part thereof, or any failure to permit inspection as requested.

A party who produces documents for inspection shall produce them as they are kept in the usual course of business or shall organize and label them to correspond with the categories in the request.

**(c) Persons Not Parties.** A person not a party to the action may be compelled to produce documents and things or to submit to an inspection as provided in Rule 45.

## Rule 35. Physical and Mental Examinations of Persons

**(a) Order for Examination.** When the mental or physical condition (including the blood group) of a party, or of a person in the custody or under the legal control of a party, is in controversy, the court in which the action is pending may order the party to submit to a physical or mental examination by a suitably licensed or certified examiner or to produce for examination the person in the party's custody or legal control. The order may be made only on motion for good cause shown and upon notice to the person to be examined and to all parties and shall specify the time, place, manner, conditions, and scope of the examination and the person or persons by whom it is to be made.

**(b) Report of Examiner.**

**(1)** If requested by the party against whom an order is made under Rule 35(a) or the person examined, the party causing the examination to be made shall deliver to the requesting party a copy of the detailed written report of the examiner setting out the examiner's findings, including results of all tests made, diagnoses and conclusions, together with like reports of all earlier examinations of the same condition. After delivery the party causing the examination shall be entitled upon request to receive from the party against whom the order is made a like report of any examination, previously or thereafter made, of the same condition, unless, in the case of a report of examination of a person not a party, the party shows that the party is unable to obtain it. The court on motion may make an order against a party requiring delivery of a report on such terms as are just, and if an examiner fails or refuses to make a report the court may exclude the examiner's testimony if offered at trial.

**(2)** By requesting and obtaining a report of the examination so ordered or by taking the deposition of the examiner, the party examined waives any privilege the party may have in that action or any other involving the same controversy, regarding the testimony of every other person who has examined or may thereafter examine the party in respect of the same mental or physical condition.

**(3)** This subdivision applies to examinations made by agreement of the parties, unless the agreement expressly provides otherwise. This subdivision does not preclude discovery of a report of an examiner or the taking of a deposition of the examiner in accordance with the provisions of any other rule.

## Rule 36.  Requests for Admission

**(a) Request for Admission.** A party may serve upon any other party a written request for the admission, for purposes of the pending action only, of the truth of any matters within the scope of Rule 26(b)(1) set forth in the request that relate to statements or opinions of fact or of the application of law to fact, including the genuineness of any documents described in the request. Copies of documents shall be served with the request unless they have been or are otherwise furnished or made available for inspection and copying. Without leave of court or written stipulation, requests for admission may not be served before the time specified in Rule 26(d).

Each matter of which an admission is requested shall be separately set forth. The matter is admitted unless, within 30 days after service of the request, or within such shorter or longer time as the court may allow or as the parties may agree to in writing, subject to Rule 29, the party to whom the request is directed serves upon the party requesting the admission a written answer or objection addressed to the matter, signed by the party or by the party's attorney. If objection is made, the reasons therefor shall be stated. The answer shall specifically deny the matter or set forth in detail the reasons why the answering party cannot truthfully admit or deny the matter. A denial shall fairly meet the substance of the requested admission, and when good faith requires that a party qualify an answer or deny only a part of the matter of which an admission is requested, the party shall specify so much of it as is true and qualify or deny the remainder. An answering party may not give lack of information or knowledge as a reason for failure to admit or deny unless the party states that the party has made reasonable inquiry and that the information known or readily obtainable by the party is insufficient to enable the party to admit or deny. A party who considers that a matter of which an admission has been requested presents a genuine issue for trial may not, on that ground alone, object to the request; the party may, subject to the provisions of Rule 37(c), deny the matter or set forth reasons why the party cannot admit or deny it.

The party who has requested the admissions may move to determine the sufficiency of the answers or objections. Unless the court determines that an objection is justified, it shall order that an answer be served. If the court determines that an answer does not comply with the requirements of this rule, it may order either that the matter is admitted or that an amended answer be served. The court may, in lieu of these orders, determine that final disposition of the request be made at a pre-trial conference or at a designated time prior to trial. The provisions of Rule 37(a)(4) apply to the award of expenses incurred in relation to the motion.

**(b) Effect of Admission.** Any matter admitted under this rule is conclusively established unless the court on motion permits withdrawal or amendment of the admission. Subject to the provision of Rule 16 governing amendment of a pre-trial order, the court may permit withdrawal or amendment when the presentation of the merits of the action will be subserved thereby and the party who obtained the admission fails to satisfy the court that withdrawal or amendment will prejudice that party in maintaining the action or defense on the merits. Any admission made by a party under this rule is for the purpose of the pending action only and is not an admission for any other purpose nor may it be used against the party in any other proceeding.

## Rule 37. Failure to Make Disclosure or Cooperate in Discovery; Sanctions

**(a) Motion For Order Compelling Disclosure or Discovery.** A party, upon reasonable notice to other parties and all persons affected thereby, may apply for an order compelling disclosure or discovery as follows:

**(1) Appropriate Court.** An application for an order to a party shall be made to the court in which the action is pending. An application for an order to a person who is not a party shall be made to the court in the district where the discovery is being, or is to be, taken.

**(2) Motion.**

**(A)** If a party fails to make a disclosure required by Rule 26(a), any other party may move to compel disclosure and for appropriate sanctions. The motion must include a certification that the movant has in good faith conferred or attempted to confer with the party not making the disclosure in an effort to secure the disclosure without court action.

**(B)** If a deponent fails to answer a question propounded or submitted under Rules 30 or 31, or a corporation or other entity fails to make a designation under Rule 30(b)(6) or 31(a), or a party fails to answer an interrogatory submitted under Rule 33, or if a party, in response to a request for inspection submitted under Rule 34, fails to respond that inspection will be permitted as requested or fails to permit inspection as requested, the discovering party may move for an order compelling an answer, or a designation, or an order compelling inspection in accordance with the request. The motion must include a certification that the movant has in good faith conferred or attempted to confer with the person or party failing to make the discovery in an effort to secure the information or material without court action. When taking a deposition on oral examination, the proponent of the question may complete or adjourn the examination before applying for an order.

**(3) Evasive or Incomplete Disclosure, Answer, or Response.** For purposes of this subdivision an evasive or incomplete disclosure, answer, or response is to be treated as a failure to disclose, answer, or respond.

**(4) Expenses and Sanctions.**

**(A)** If the motion is granted or if the disclosure or requested discovery is provided after the motion was filed, the court shall, after affording an opportunity to be heard, require the party or deponent whose conduct necessitated the motion or the party or attorney advising such conduct or both of them to pay to the moving party the reasonable expenses incurred in making the motion, including attorney's fees, unless the court finds that the motion was filed without the movant's first making a good faith effort to obtain the disclosure of discovery without court action, or that the opposing party's nondisclosure, response, or objection was substantially justified, or that other circumstances make an award of expenses unjust.

**(B)** If the motion is denied, the court may enter any protective order authorized under Rule 26(c) and shall, after affording an opportunity to be heard, require the moving party or the attorney filing the motion or both of them to pay to the party or deponent who opposed the motion the reasonable expenses incurred in opposing the motion, including attorney's fees, unless the court finds that the making of the motion was substantially justified or that other circumstances make an award of expenses unjust.

**(C)** If the motion is granted in part and denied in part, the court may enter any protective order authorized under Rule 26(c) and may, after affording an opportunity to be heard, apportion the reasonable expenses incurred in relation to the motion among the parties and persons in a just manner.

**(b) Failure to Comply With Order.**

**(1) Sanctions by Court in District Where Deposition Is Taken.** If a deponent fails to be sworn or to answer a question after being directed to do so by the court in the district in which the deposition is being taken, the failure may be considered a contempt of that court.

**(2) Sanctions by Court in Which Action Is Pending.** If a party or an officer, director, or managing agent of a party or a person designated under Rule 30(b)(6) or 31(a) to testify on behalf of a party fails to obey an order to provide or permit discovery, including an order made under subdivision (a) of this rule or Rule 35, or if a party fails to obey an order entered under Rule 26(f), the court in which the action is pending may make such orders in regard to the failure as are just, and among others the following:

**(A)** An order that the matters regarding which the order was made or any other designated facts shall be taken to be established for the purposes of the action in accordance with the claim of the party obtaining the order;

**(B)** An order refusing to allow the disobedient party to support or oppose designated claims or defenses, or prohibiting that party from introducing designated matters in evidence;

**(C)** An order striking out pleadings or parts thereof, or staying further proceedings until the order is obeyed, or dismissing the action or proceeding or any part thereof, or rendering a judgment by default against the disobedient party;

**(D)** In lieu of any of the foregoing orders or in addition thereto, an order treating as a contempt of court the failure to obey any orders except an order to submit to a physical or mental examination;

**(E)** Where a party has failed to comply with an order under Rule 35(a) requiring that party to produce another for examination, such orders as are listed in paragraphs (A), (B), and (C) of this subdivision, unless the party failing to comply shows that that party is unable to produce such person for examination.

In lieu of any of the foregoing orders or in addition thereto, the court shall require the party failing to obey the order or the attorney advising that party or both to pay the reasonable expenses, including attorney's fees, caused by the failure, unless the court finds that the failure was substantially justified or that other circumstances make an award of expenses unjust.

**(c) Failure to Disclose; False or Misleading Disclosure; Refusal to Admit.**

**(1)** A party that without substantial justification fails to disclose information required by Rule 26(a) or 26(e)(1), or to amend a prior response to discovery as required by Rule 26(e)(2), is not, unless such failure is harmless, permitted to use as evidence at a trial, at a hearing, or on a motion any witness or information not so disclosed. In addition to or in lieu of this sanction, the court, on motion and after affording an opportunity to be heard, may impose other appropriate sanctions. In addition to requiring payment of reasonable expenses, including attorney's fees, caused by the failure, these sanctions may include any of the actions authorized under Rule 37(b)(2)(A), (B), and (C) and may include informing the jury of the failure to make the disclosure.

**(2)** If a party fails to admit the genuineness of any document or the truth of any matter as requested under Rule 36, and if the party requesting the admissions thereafter proves the genuineness of the document or the truth of the matter, the requesting party may apply to the court for an order requiring the other party to pay the reasonable expenses incurred in making that proof, including reasonable attorney's fees. The court shall make the order unless it finds that (A) the request was held objectionable pursuant to Rule 36(a), or (B) the admission sought was of no substantial importance, or (C) the party failing to admit had reasonable ground to believe that the party might prevail on the matter, or (D) there was other good reason for the failure to admit.

**(d) Failure of Party to Attend at Own Deposition or Serve Answers to Interrogatories or Respond to Request for Inspection.** If a party or an officer, director, or managing agent of a party or a person designated under Rule 30(b)(6) or 31(a) to testify on behalf of a party fails (1) to appear before the officer who is to take the deposition, after being served with a proper notice, or (2) to serve answers or objections to interrogatories submitted under Rule 33, after proper service of the interrogatories, or (3) to serve a written response to a request for inspection submitted under Rule 34, after proper service of the request, the court in which the action is pending on motion may make such orders in regard to the failure as are just, and among others it may take any action authorized under subparagraphs (A), (B), and (C) of subdivision (b)(2) of this rule. Any motion specifying a failure under clause (2) or (3) of this subdivision shall include a certification that the movant has in good faith conferred or attempted to confer with the party failing to answer or respond in an effort to obtain such answer or response without court action. In lieu of any order or in addition thereto, the court shall require the party failing to act or the attorney advising that party or both to pay the reasonable expenses, including attorney's fees, caused by the failure unless the court finds that the failure was substantially justified or that other circumstances make an award of expenses unjust.

The failure to act described in this subdivision may not be excused on the ground that the discovery sought is objectionable unless the party failing to act has a pending motion for a protective order as provided by Rule 26(c).

**[(e) Subpoena of Person in Foreign Country.]** (Abrogated Apr. 29, 1980, eff. Aug. 1, 1980)

**[(f) Expenses Against United States.]** (Repealed Oct. 21, 1980, eff. Oct. 1, 1981)

**(g) Failure to Participate in the Framing of a Discovery Plan.** If a party or a party's attorney fails to participate in good faith in the development and submission of a proposed discovery plan as required by Rule 26(f), the court may, after opportunity for hearing, require such party or attorney to pay to any other party the reasonable expenses, including attorney's fees, caused by the failure.

## Form 35. Report of Parties' Planning Meeting

[Caption and Names of Parties]

**1.** Pursuant to Fed.R.Civ.P. 26(f), a meeting was held on (date) at (place) and was attended by:

(name) for plaintiff(s)

(name) for defendant(s) (party name)

(name) for defendant(s) (party name)

**2.** Pre-Discovery Disclosures. The parties [have exchanged] [will exchange by (date)] the information required by [Fed.R.Civ.P. 26(a)(1)] [local rule _____].

**3.** Discovery Plan. The parties jointly propose to the court the following discovery plan: [Use separate paragraphs or subparagraphs as necessary if parties disagree.]

Discovery will be needed on the following subjects: (brief description of subjects on which discovery will be needed)

All discovery commenced in time to be completed by (date). [Discovery on (issue for early discovery) to be completed by (date).]

Maximum of _____ interrogatories by each party to any other party. [Responses due ____ days after service.]

Maximum of ____ depositions by plaintiff(s) and _____ by defendant(s).

Each deposition [other than of _____ ] limited to maximum of ____ hours unless extended by agreement of parties.

Reports from retained experts under Rule 26(a)(2) due:

from plaintiff(s) by (date)

from defendant(s) by (date)

Supplementations under Rule 26(e) due (times(s) or interval(s).)

**4.** Other items. [Use separate paragraphs or subparagraphs as necessary if parties disagree.]

The parties [request] [do not request] a conference with the court before entry of the scheduling order.

The parties request a pretrial conference in (month and year).

Plaintiff(s) should be allowed until (date) to join additional parties and until (date) to amend the pleadings.

Defendant(s) should be allowed until (date) to join additional parties and until (date) to amend the pleadings.

All potentially dispositive motions should be filed by (date).

Settlement [is likely] [is unlikely] [cannot be evaluated prior to (date)] [may be enhanced by use of the following alternative dispute resolution procedure: [_____].

Final lists of witnesses and exhibits under Rule 26(a)(3) should be due

> from plaintiff(s) by )date)

> from defendant(s) by (date)

> Parties should have ____ days after service of final lists of witnesses and exhibits to list objections under Rule 26(a)(3).

> The case should be ready for trial by (date) [and at this time is expected to take approximately (length of time)].

> [Other matters.]


Date: _____

# APPENDIX B

## The *Daubert* Deposition Dance: Retracing the Intricacies of the Expert's Steps

By David M. Malone and Ryan M. Malone

After the decision in *Daubert v. Merrill Dow*,[1] there was some question about whether the gatekeeping responsibilities of the federal trial courts extended to all expert testimony, or merely to "scientific" expert testimony. Even among circuits that believed that only scientific testimony was covered, there was confusion as to what was scientific testimony and what was "technical or other specialized" testimony. The *Kumho Tire*[2] case resolved that confusion, by clearly stating that the methodologies underlying all expert testimony must be evaluated for reliability.

This decision therefore clarified the occasions for application of the *Daubert* approach, although it compounded any remaining problems by increasing the number of cases covered. Chief among those remaining problems is the need for trial practitioners and trial courts to develop a coherent body of analytic tools by which methodological reliability can be measured with some confidence by lawyers and judges without formal training in the specialized fields. For example, how does the trial judge assess the reliability of methodologies employed by the astrophysicist, since it is unlikely that the trial judge coincidentally has been trained in astrophysics.[3]

Although the Supreme Court in *Daubert* and again in *Kumho Tire* emphasized that the four criteria—publication in a peer-reviewed journal; known or knowable error rate; general acceptance in the relevant scientific community; and testability or replicability (including the concept of "falsifiability"[4])—were not exclusive (indeed, none of the four is even required), there seems to be some belief among attorneys and judges that we must measure reliability by those criteria alone. In an earlier article,[5] the authors suggested a number of additional, objective criteria that could be utilized in conducting this analysis, beyond those four mentioned in *Daubert*. Abstract criteria, whether four or fourteen, are not easily applied in discovery depositions, however, and we must recognize that it is in deposition that the foundation for challenge to an expert's methodology is uncovered. We therefore thought it might be useful to examine some specific questions that an attorney can ask at deposition to explore these various concepts of reliability, with follow-up and rationale explained as we go along.

**1. Publication in a peer-reviewed journal:** This criterion of reliability actually has two prongs to it: an article describing the methodology must have been published, which subjects it to scrutiny by whatever readership the journal has; and the article must have been reviewed, pre-publication, by "peers" in the particular field of knowledge, who ostensibly would scrutinize it for errors and challenge any unsupported conclusions. It is objective because it does not require the application of judgment to determine whether it has been satisfied; only examination of the literature. Deposition questions that examine whether this criterion has been satisfied are rather easy to create, but the exercise is useful:

   a.  Where has this methodology been published?

   b.  Who published it?

   c.  What is the process for pre-publication review?

   d.  What are the credentials of the reviewers (sometimes called "referees")?

   e.  What criticisms or suggestions did the reviewers make?

   f.  What changes were made as a result of those suggestions?

   g.  What other changes were made?

   h.  What comments were received post-publication?

   i.  What is known of the credentials of those persons providing comments?

   j.  What changes in methodology were made as a result of those comments?

   k.  Have you, or has anyone else, published additional articles on this methodology?

**2. Known or knowable error rate:** This criterion requests the expert to provide information about the likelihood that the methodology will produce incorrect results. It does not establish a threshold of correctness for admissibility, but it is difficult to believe that a court would admit an expert's opinions after hearing *in limine* testimony that a methodology may produce wrong results half the time. In the world of commercial litigation, economists and financial analysts may be the experts most susceptible to challenge based on a failure to satisfy this criterion; in truth, are they able even to assess their error rates when they conclude that a particular market structure is more competitive than another?

a.  Identify studies that have calculated error rates for this methodology.

b.  Describe how you yourself would determine the error rate.

c.  What mechanisms are available for reducing or eliminating errors?

d.  Is there a particular aspect of the methodology (*e.g.*, data collection, data input, interpretation of results) that is more likely to produce errors?

e.  How would someone employing this methodology know that an error had occurred?

f.  What types of errors can occur?

g.  What effect would those errors have on the utility or correctness of your opinion?

**3. General acceptance in the relevant scientific community:** This is the (previously) well-established *Frye*[6] test. The weakness of this test was not that it asked an irrelevant question—the question is indeed relevant—but rather that it depended upon the expert for an opinion on the reliability of the methodology, rather than seeking objective information. As a sole criterion, however, it also assumes that the court could identify the relevant scientific community. Today, with specialists within specialties within sub-areas within practice areas within medical board areas, as an example, the nests of Russian dolls prevent any court from knowing, on its own, whether this is a "relevant scientific community" or a sub-specialty that should be evaluated according to standards from a larger group, or merely a fringe group of radicals. Furthermore, while mechanical engineering methodology may quite reasonably be scrutinized by application of the standards of mechanical engineering, as it was in *Kumho Tire*, we are not so confident that aromatherapist methodology should be evaluated only by application of the standards of aromatherapists. There is a skepticism here that we recognize and believe to be appropriate, even while we understand that we must be able to distinguish it from mere bias or prejudice.

a. What evidence is there that practitioners in your field generally accept this approach?

b. How do you define your field?

c. What other approaches are utilized in that field?

d. What approach is utilized most often?

e. What are the advantages and disadvantages of the main methodologies?

f. Why did you choose to use this methodology?

g. When was this methodology developed?

h. What effect did introduction of this methodology have on the acceptance of other methodologies?

**4. Testability or replicability:** It is not sufficient for a researcher to state that she has discovered a relationship between certain effects and a purported cause. She must specify that relationship in a sufficiently specific way that other researchers can examine it for themselves. If their examinations corroborate her results, then the hypothesis may become accepted. Without such corroboration, however, her hypothesis stands as no better than conjecture. For example, several years ago at the National Heart, Lung and Blood Institute, a researcher noted a statistically significant correlation between people who ate sandwiches for lunch and people who developed serious heart disease. The researcher spelled out his methodology in sufficient detail that other researchers could review his approaches and data; they discovered that sandwiches and heart disease were not directly related to each other, but each was instead related to hurried meal times, a characteristic of "Type A" personalities at high risk for heart disease because of multiple stress factors. The original researcher's problem of multicollinearity would not have been observed if the original hypothesis had not been stated with sufficient specificity to permit test and replication.

a. Step by step, how have you conducted your tests or examinations?

b. Identify all of your data sources.

c. Provide all of your laboratory or session notes.

d.  Beginning with a particular item of raw (empirical) data, show us how it is treated or manipulated by the methodology.

e.  What tests did you do yourself to confirm that the methodology produced parallel results for parallel inputs? (If your methodology is addition and you input [2, 2] and get 4, then when you input [4, 4] you should get 8.)

f.  What tests did you do to confirm that disparate inputs would yield disparate results? (If the factor of few firms in an industry is said to lead to high profits, then we should not observe industries with many firms also enjoying high profits. For a simpler analogy, if a friend says that a black box will light a red light when salted pretzels are inserted, it is not a sufficient test to insert salted pretzels and watch for the light; we must also insert unsalted pretzels and stale GummiBear candies and watch for the light. Otherwise, we might merely have a machine [methodology] that turns on a light when anything is inserted.)

**5. Development and use of the methodology in non-litigation contexts:** The Ninth Circuit, on remand in the *Daubert* matter, grafted an additional criterion onto the four suggested by the Supreme Court: Was the methodology developed for non-litigation purposes?[7] Questioning on this criterion should be reasonably straightforward, because it asks the expert for historical facts, not scientific opinions or relationships. If the methodology was developed solely (or, logically, primarily) for the purpose of supporting a particular side in litigation, we are more skeptical about its objectivity.

a.  When was this methodology developed?

b.  Who was the developer?

c.  What was the original purpose of its development?

d.  Are you using any modifications that were developed for litigation?

e.  Why were modifications made to the original methodology?

f.  Is the methodology still being used for its original purpose?

g.  Has it been partially or largely supplanted?

h.  What methodologies have supplanted it? Why?

**6. Sufficiency to explain the salient facts:** The Supreme Court in Kumho Tire expressed skepticism that a practitioner of a legitimate methodology ("visual and tactile tire failure analysis") could not evaluate whether an apparently salient fact was present (whether the tire had traveled 50,000 miles or more).[8] This does involve the a priori belief on the part of the Court that this factor is significant; nevertheless, the expert should at least have been able to provide a reasonable explanation for his inability to determine this fact.

    a.  Describe all of the categories of information that were available to you for this analysis (or that are generated by the event being analyzed: profits, margins, gross sales revenue, industry concentration, firm rank, unit sales, advertising-to-sales ratios, advertising expenditure ramps, etc.).

    b.  Rank those categories of data from most to least significant, and explain the ranking.

    c.  Show us where each of those categories was used.

    d.  Tell us why some categories of data were not used.

    e.  Tell us how you adjusted for your inability to obtain some data (*e.g.*, tire travel miles).

    f.  Have you considered different data in other cases? Why?

    g.  Do other researchers consider other data or rank the data differently in importance?

    h.  Have you ever reached conclusions without data from each category?

**7. Quantitative sufficiency of the data employed:** In an industrial conveyor belt failure case,[9] the court was concerned that the mechanical engineer was relying on a very small sample to provide data points for his analysis: a few bolts from a very large conveyor assembly. While testimony from someone trained in statistical methods might satisfy the court that the data were sufficient for conclusions at a reasonable level of certainty, the mechanical engineer could not provide that foundation, and the court was uncomfortable with the minimal basis.

    a.  What were your sources of data?

    b.  How much data was available from each source?

    c.  Was there richer data available elsewhere?

    d. Was a statistical analysis performed to determine the adequacy of the data for the purpose of drawing conclusions?

    e. At what confidence level did the data allow you to draw your conclusions?

    f. At what confidence level do you typically operate in non-litigation activities in your profession?

    g. In your last published article, what confidence level did you employ?

    h. In the last article that you read or refereed, what confidence level was employed?

    i. If the data points were increased by a factor of 2, how would the confidence level have been affected? If the points were increased tenfold?

    j. If one-third of the data you used were determined to be unreliable, would your conclusions still be sound, at the same level of confidence?

**8. Qualitative sufficiency of the data employed:** In some cases, we can imagine that the data are quantitatively sufficient (we have enough data points to satisfy the statisticians among us), but we are troubled by the quality of the data or its sources. For example, in child abuse cases, experts sometimes are willing to testify based in part upon their experiences with descriptions of abuse and its sequela from numerous children. The sample may be sufficient in size; even the simple hearsay nature of the bases may be so commonly encountered that it does not disqualify the testimony; but the impressionable nature of the sources—children interviewed under unknown and perhaps uncontrolled circumstances, having been subjected to unrevealed pressures or influences—renders them suspect and may impel a court to exclude the expert testimony.

    a. What were the sources of your data?

    b. Who collected the data?

    c. Who supplied the data to the persons collecting it?

    d. What prior experience have you had with this methodology for data collection?

    e. What tests did you conduct to determine that your data were accurate?

f. What motivations were provided to the sources to encourage accurate reporting?

g. Were there any penalties for inaccurate reporting by the sources to your collectors?

h. What were the sources told about the purposes of the data collection?

i. What were the collectors told about the purposes?

j. What were the criteria for including and excluding sources of data?

**9. Consistency with general methodology:** Methodologies should be reliable regardless of the context-based biases or prejudices of the persons employing them. For example, the methodology the expert uses to determine the quality of structural steel should be the same, whether that examination is being done as quality control for an industry member, as consultant to a plaintiff in a contract suit, or as consultant to a defendant in a products liability suit. Of course, the general approach should be identified first at deposition, before questioning about specifics; otherwise, the description of what is generally done will be adjusted to match what the witness already said was done in this case. In *Kumho Tire* itself, the Court was interested in the fact that the expert said that his approach involved analysis of four "visual and tactile" aspects of the failed tire and, if any two were present, concluding that the failure was the result of owner abuse rather than manufacturing defect. The expert then found two factors to be present (apparently one just a little bit), but he nevertheless concluded that the failure resulted from defect. This departure from his general methodology may have been fatal to his opinion.[10]

a. Tell me the steps in using this analysis in your everyday, non-litigation work.

b. What are the uses of such analysis?

c. What data do you obtain; from what sources?

d. Who assists you? Why? How?

e. When have you used this analysis before?

f. Did you follow the general methodology you have just described?

g. In this litigation, what steps do you perform in this analysis?

h. Who assisted you? Why? How?

i. Was it necessary to depart from the general approach in any way? Why?

j. What precautions did you take to insure that those departures would not inappropriately affect the results of the analysis?

k. What authority did you have for believing those precautions were sufficient?

l. What other steps did you take that were different from your general approach or methodology?

**10. Existence of a body of literature on the particular methodology:** If there is no body of literature on the methodology that the expert is recommending, and the explanation for such absence is not apparent or the expert cannot or does not explain the absence of such literature, then the court is justified in exercising skepticism about the reliability of the methodology. (Of course, other factors would be affected also, such as "general acceptance in the relevant scientific community;" how would such acceptance be evidenced if there is no literature?) Of course, if the field of expertise would not be expected to generate such a body of literature ("the adequacy of methods for cleaning tomato sauce spills in supermarket aisles"), the court might well ignore this factor. A faulty syllogism could lead people to believe that, because there is a body of literature on an approach, it represents a reliable methodology; it may merely mean that there are lots of unreliable adherents who write lots of unreliable stuff.[11] The field of astrology, as an example, has generated thousands of books and articles over centuries (or millennia, if Druidic runes qualify).

a. How does one learn about this methodology?

b. How do you keep up with changes and improvements in the methodology?

c. What are the principal journals or publications in this field?

d. Who contributes to them?

e. Who referees or edits them for methodological correctness?

f. Do noted scientists contribute or subscribe? (*E.g.*, do astronomers subscribe or contribute to the "Astrologers' Journal"?)

g. Do contributors or editors appear in journals of related and accepted fields? (*E.g.*, do astrologers get published in the "American Journal of Astronomy"?

h.  How long have the main journals in the field been published?

**11. Logical derivation of the methodology:** Experience suggests that the scientific progress is, indeed, progressive; that is, new developments build in some recognizable and articulable way on past, related explorations: blood-letting did not lead immediately to heart transplantations; green Post-It™ notes followed yellow Post-It notes; and the methods for putting a human on the moon depended upon the development of methods for putting a human in Earth orbit. As a general, a priori principle that makes us comfortable, few steps are skipped. When steps are skipped in such normally evolutionary change, so that it becomes revolutionary, we look for explanations, and we expect the proponent of the new theory to provide those explanations.

a.  Describe the derivation of the methodology that you used.

b.  What prior methodology is this one most closely related to?

c.  Describe the similarities between them. Describe the differences.

d.  What problems or factors led to the change from the old to the new methodology?

e.  Who were the foremost proponents of the prior methodology?

f.  Who initiated, sponsored, or championed the change to the new methodology?

g.  What role did you have in this change?

h.  In what circumstances would the two methodologies yield different results?

i.  What specific differences in the methodologies lead to those different results?

j.  Why is the new methodology superior?

**Conclusion.**

The Supreme Court in *Kumho Tire* emphasized that it would be fruitless to attempt to list all criteria for assessing reliability of experts' methodologies, because they are as numerous as the fields of human knowledge.[12] The purpose of this article is obviously not to disagree with the Court on this point, but rather to suggest ways of thinking about reliability, approaches to assessing methodologies, that can be used across fields of expertise, and that do not depend on requiring the lawyers or the judges to develop competence in the field being assessed. As we consider these legal questions (both the question of how to determine reliability and the questions being suggested here as part of a solution), we are in fact considering questions of much broader application to the human condition: How do we learn? How do we know when we know? How can we learn what someone else actually knows? If we were concerned only with the question—trivial in this context—of determining the credibility of an expert, traditional tools are available: cross-examination, impeachment, learned treatises, omissions, and so forth. Instead, in considering *Daubert-Kumho Tire* issues, we must concern ourselves with the possibility of truth-telling witnesses, armed with patently impressive credentials, whose science may represent the future, but whose testimony should not be presented in court.

### Endnotes

1. *See Daubert v. Merrill Dow Pharmaceuticals, Inc.,* 509 U.S. 579 (1993).

2. *See Kumho Tire Co. v. Carmichael,* 526 U.S. 137 (1999).

3. Some suggest that the court could overcome this problem by obtaining its own expert (at the parties' expense, of course). This is not a solution, however, because the question of the reliability of expert methodologies would then legitimately be directed toward the court's expert and her methodologies. Pundits might suggest that another court-retained expert could be consulted, and then another, until we complete some regression back to a Prime Expert.

4. A premise is "falsifiable" if it can be proven wrong, usually through direct experience. For instance, the premise "all ravens are black" is falsifiable, since it can be proven wrong by the discovery of a white raven. On the other hand, the premise "everything in the universe doubles in size for a second, and then it halves in size the next second" is not falsifiable, since it is impossible to disprove through direct experience. (If everything is alternating in doubling and halving in size, it remains relatively the same size, and therefore the difference is impossible to measure.) Scientific premises are tentative and falsifiable, while some other premises are not. It is common for creationists to point out that evolutionary biologists often contradict parts of evolutionary theory. However, the testing of evolutionary theory by its subscribers, which the creationists see as a weakness of that theory, is actually proof positive that the theory is scientific. *See, e.g., Robert T. Pinnock, Tower of Babel: The Evidence Against the New Creationists,* xvi (MIT Press 2000): "Science imposes severe constraints upon itself to ensure that its conclusions are intersubjectively testable, constraints that require that it not appeal to supernatural hypotheses or allow the citation of special (private) revelations as evidence. The new creationists, including Johnson and philosophers such as Alvin Plantinga, reject these constraints and share the view that supernatural explanations should be admitted into science."

5. *See* David M. Malone & Ryan M. Malone, *The Zodiac Expert: Reliability After Kumho,* 22 *The Trial Lawyer Magazine* 265 (Fall 1999).

6. *See Frye v. United States,* 293 F. 1013 (D.C. Cir. 1923).

7. *See Daubert v. Merrill Dow Pharmaceuticals, Inc.,* 43 F.3d 1311 (9th Cir. 1995).

8. *See Kumho Tire*, 526 U.S. at 254.

9. *Watkins v. Telsmith*, 121 F.3d 984 (5th Cir. 1997).

10. *See Kumho Tire*, 526 U.S. at 254–55.

11. In order to be certain that we can identify faulty syllogisms, let us look at a correct syllogism and a faulty syllogism:

Correct syllogism A:

(1) All frogs are green; (2) Clyde is a frog; therefore (3) Clyde is green.

Correct syllogism B:

(1) All frogs are green; (2) Clyde is not green; therefore (3) Clyde is not a frog.

Incorrect syllogism C:

(1) All frogs are green; (2) Clyde is green; therefore (3) Clyde is a frog. This is incorrect because Clyde could be something else that is green but not a frog, such as a pet lime.

Now, applying this syllogistic template to the *Daubert* methodology questions:

Correct syllogism D:

(1) Reliable methodologies are likely to generate relatively substantial literature; (2) this is a reliable methodology; therefore (3) it is likely to generate (or to have generated) a relatively substantial body of literature.

Correct syllogism E:

(1) Reliable methodologies are likely to generate relatively substantial literature; (2) this methodology has not generated relatively substantial literature; therefore (3) this is not a reliable methodology (or, even more correctly, this is not likely to be a reliable methodology).

Incorrect syllogism F:

(1) Reliable methodologies are likely to generate relatively substantial literature; (2) this methodology has generated a relatively substantial body of literature; (3) therefore this is a reliable methodology.

12. *See Kumho Tire*, 526 U.S. at 251.

# Index